COMMUNICATION
IN SMALL GROUP
DISCUSSIONS

COMMUNICATION IN SMALL GROUP DISCUSSIONS

AN INTEGRATED APPROACH SECOND EDITION

JOHN F. CRAGAN

Illinois State University

DAVID W. WRIGHT

Illinois State University

WEST PUBLISHING COMPANY

St. Paul   New York   Los Angeles   San Francisco

Copyediting by John Mandeville
Composition by Compositors Typesetters
Page makeup by Carlisle Graphics
Art for chapter openers by Sandra Kapitan

Copyright © 1980 by West Publishing Company.
Copyright © 1986 by WEST PUBLISHING COMPANY
                    50 West Kellogg Boulevard
                    P.O. Box 64526
                    St. Paul, MN 55164-1003

Library of Congress Cataloging-in-Publication Data

Cragan, John F.
    Communication in small group discussions.

    Includes index.
    1. Communication in small groups.   2. Discussion.
I. Wright, David W.   II. Title.
HM133.C73   1986   302.3'46   85-32306
ISBN 0-314-93169-4

This edition of the book is dedicated to our children,
Katie and Keary Cragan,
and Karin, Lisa, and Doug Wright.

CONTENTS

PREFACE

In the fifteen years we have been teaching small group communication and discussion classes, we have endeavored to evolve a course that teaches practical communication skills that can be used in everyday work groups. Understandably, small group communication research on discussion serves as the primary data base for this book; however, research findings from other social sciences are also used. In this second edition, we have made a concerted effort to include the latest research findings on small group communication. Although the new findings are sprinkled throughout the book, they serve primarily as the foundation for four new chapters.

Our book is organized into three basic sections. Part One, Theoretical Considerations of Small Group Communication, integrates important small group communication theories through the use of a model that depicts the essential elements of small group interaction in a coherent whole. This model forms the basis of an entirely new chapter on communication theory that lessens the tensions between small group theory and discussion methods. Part Two, Small Group Discussion Principles and Practices, describes how small groups function using discussion methods. In this new edition, we have added two new chapters to this section: Preparing to Discuss, and Understanding and Managing Conflict Communication in Groups. The latter chapter incorporates our integrated model of small group communication to provide fresh insights into conflict resolution in groups. In Part Three, Applications to Settings and Situations, we apply the theory and practice of small group discussion to work groups as they exist in business and industry, with special attention to new research findings on quality circles and organizational cultures. We have added a new chapter on Studying and Evaluating Small Group Communication, in the belief that students need basic research skills in order to study small group communication more thoroughly.

Our experience has led us to conclude that a "learning by doing" or practical approach is the best way for you to learn basic small group discussion skills. New case studies depicting classroom and real-life groups were selected because they amplify the important aspects of small group communication. The case studies afford you the opportunity to critique work groups on the basis of the discussion principles introduced in the chapters. In addition, throughout each chapter we have provided numerous examples of groups we have observed firsthand, so that you can compare your experience in small group communication with ours.

It was not possible to do this book by ourselves. We are indebted to many people. First, we would like to thank our professors for the training they provided us in small group discussion. They are Ernest G. Bormann, University of Minnesota, and Raymond S. Ross, Wayne State University. We have also been influenced by many of our colleagues and are grateful for their insights. A number of small group communication professors have given generously of their time and talent to provide us with helpful critiques in the writing of both the first and second editions of this book. The reviewers for the first edition were Gene Eakins, G. Evans, Hazel Heiman, Raymond Ross, Donald Shields, Jimmie Trent, and Gordan Zimmerman. The reviewers for this second edition were Brenda Burchett, Rebecca Cline, Hazel Heiman, Kathy Kellermann, Jolene Koester, Gail Mason, Joseph Mele, Eileen Berlin Ray, Jo Sprague, and Lyla Tomsheck. Our students at Illinois State University are a constant source of stimulation, and they affirm our approach to the teaching of small group discussion that this book represents. We thank them for their help. Elizabeth Asprooth Cragan and Barbara Weller Wright have provided supportive criticism and help in the production of the manuscript. We deeply appreciate their assistance.

J. F. C.

D. W. W.

COMMUNICATION IN SMALL GROUP DISCUSSIONS

ONE

THEORETICAL CONSIDERATIONS OF SMALL GROUP COMMUNICATION

While strangers politely disagree about ideas, highly cohesive groups rant and rave about their differences.

CHAPTER OBJECTIVES

In order to be a more effective discussant, when you read this chapter you should focus on a definition of small group discussion and the key concepts of group discussion.

YOU NEED TO KNOW:

1. The American rationale for the study of small group discussion.
2. The characteristics of a small group.
3. The concepts that interact to form a good discussion group.
4. The concepts for measuring a good group.

INTRODUCTION TO SMALL GROUP COMMUNICATION

CHAPTER OUTLINE

WHY STUDY SMALL GROUP DISCUSSION?

We study small group discussion because it is central to our everyday lives. Most of our working lives we will participate in face-to-face discussions and will be expected to work effectively and efficiently toward common group goals. We have all experienced problems with group interaction and know that a relationship between two people is difficult to maintain. However, a relationship among three or more people is even more complex; thus, it requires our concerted efforts to study and comprehend the dynamics of small group discussion.

LIVING AND WORKING IN GROUPS

At the university we often systematically study aspects of human existence both because they are there and because we have an innate urge to observe and comprehend our surroundings. The study of small group discussion brings with it a natural curiosity to understand small group processes. At the same time there is a clear expectation that the study of the communication behavior of small groups will lead to pragmatic advice on how we might improve our small group experiences. Our experiences in small groups readily spawn many important questions about small group discussion that we attempt to answer. The following three hypothetical scenarios are typical of the kinds of situations that raise important questions about communication in our small group worlds.

The Corporation Scenario. Life in a business corporation sometimes seems like one long conference. You are "meetinged" and "bunch-for-lunched" to death. If it were not for the executive washroom and the solitude that comes from the fact that you are on one side of your office door and all those competitive groups on the other, you would probably go mad. However, your company has adopted a new policy. They took your office door away and made it possible for anyone to call a meeting for any reason, bringing together people from all levels of management. They call the new policy "The Open Door Policy for Better Communication." What behavior would you predict from the new policy? What is the difference between one-time meetings and ongoing work groups? What is the protocol for calling a meeting? How important is an agenda? What are the leader functions for one-time meetings? If you are the appointed leader of a meeting and your boss is one of the participants, what do you do? If your subordinate can call you to a meeting, what role should you play in the group? When is a meeting needed and when is it a waste of time? These are the kinds of day-to-day questions that need practical answers. One of the "whys" of studying small group communication is to get some answers to these questions.

The Firehouse Scenario. The firefighter's professional existence is almost entirely one of group participation. Engine companies and rescue squads are highly efficient small groups that not only work together but in many cities live together. A firehouse may contain three different work groups: a rescue squad, a pumper truck team, and a ladder truck group. There is generally one captain per shift in charge of the firehouse, with a lieutenant in charge of each company. Now, as any firefighter will tell you, rivalries can develop among the three work groups. In fact, the ladder company usually feels "oppressed" by the rescue squad. Members of the rescue squad have had two hundred hours of emergency medical training and make more runs per day than the ladder company. They get into the newspapers more often and into television programs about their work. In short, the rescue squad has much to be proud of and is not shy about flaunting it in the firehouse. In fact, the rescue squad can become so cohesive that the other firefighters in the house cannot stand them. Furthermore, a captain may begin to worry, not only about the morale of the ladder company, but also about whether he or she is losing control of the rescue squad, which may have become such an efficient work group that its members act as though they do not need to take orders from the captain. What does the captain do? His or her leadership is in question, the ladder company is demoralized, and the rescue squad is out of control. One answer is to break up the old groups by transferring key troublemakers to other shifts, or even to a different firehouse someplace else in town. This solution might solve the captain's problem of control over his or her work force, but the solution might produce other problems. One reason the members of the rescue squad are so arrogant is that they are good. They make five or six runs a day during which they calmly make crisis decisions about life and death, usually with beneficial results. In fact, they routinely save human lives and are proud of what they do. If the captain breaks up the rescue squad, a new work group will have to be formed. Some of our small group research indicates that this takes time and that the new work group might never become as efficient as the old one, thus resulting in loss of productivity. Yet productivity for a rescue squad is the saving of lives! Will the captain kill some unknown child if he or she breaks up a cohesive work group for the greater good of the fire department's organizational structure?

The firehouse scenario generates several questions about small groups. How does a group become a group? How long does it take to form a group? Why do some collections of people not become a group? Can a group become too cohesive? What is the relationship between group cohesion and group productivity? Is small group rivalry in large organizations inevitable? Can group conflict be managed? These are the sorts of questions to which our firehouse captain would like some answers; our knowledge of small group discussion can provide some of them.

The College Dorm Scenario.   Life in a college dorm is like being in a pressure cooker. All of the pluralistic elements of our society are put under one small roof and the rigors of academic excellence provide the pressure. If you are one of the students who agreed to be a dorm director, area manager, resident adviser, or floor supervisor, good luck! Take Carl's situation, for instance. He is one of those black, beautiful, and talented guys who was sailing along with an A average. However, he could not find a job over the summer and, against his better judgment, agreed to manage part of a large coed dorm in trade for room and board. On Carl's first day on the job the dorm director informed him and the other management assistant that they would have to go through three days of sensitivity training since there were "black-white" misunderstandings last year. Carl is the black half of the black-white management assistant staff this year. The first week into the fall semester, Carl agreed to let the black students on his floor hold a "culture" session twice a week in the lounge. At the semester break, the black students asked to be housed in rooms close together, and the white students objected. Now, every night there is a war of stereos in which musical selection reflects the two sides of the struggle.

What can the study of small group communication do to help Carl with his job? Are "culture" sessions a form of consciousness-raising? If so, what can Carl expect the outcome to be? What is sensitivity training? Is it helpful? When is it detrimental? How does Carl try to eliminate group conflict? What kind of group meeting could Carl call? What are the dynamics of pluralistic group formation?

We do not mean to overstate the usefulness of small group communication research. We also do not want to mislead you. Scientific research requires measured, conservative conclusions based squarely upon the compiled data, whereas real-life problems often demand instantaneous leaps into the unknown if solutions are to be found. Academic research will always fall short of the expectations that real life places on it. However, much useful advice can be provided about small group discussions, and we have tried to include it all in this book.

AN AMERICAN RATIONALE FOR THE STUDY OF SMALL GROUP DISCUSSION

Speech communication as a discipline, and small group discussion as a teachable subject, flourish only within a democratic setting. It is natural that free speech, public discussion, and active participation in political groups are prerequisites for a study of small group communication. This section sketches out an American rationale for building small group discussion theories by considering cultural setting and academic traditions.

Cultural Setting.   America's democratic tradition has made public discussion of affairs of state a moral obligation. Apathy is discouraged in our culture, which means that we have a great many politically concerned citizens who are actively involved in small groups. Moreover, there is a general belief that these groups should focus on rational, group decision making and avoid emotional, undisciplined group activity.

Our towns and neighborhoods are beehives of small group discussions about such issues as the fast-food store that might endanger our children with its increased traffic flow, broken sewer mains, faulty dorm showers, overpriced off-campus housing, pollution, nuclear energy, and other public issues that directly affect our lives. The first American reaction to these sorts of political issues is to call a meeting, and we sometimes forget that in many countries it is against the law to do so. We not only take public discussion as a right but, after 200 years, have developed certain expectations and protocols with regard to how these meetings are to be conducted and what kind of communication is generally considered acceptable and effective. Many of the method theories we discuss in this book have evolved out of this two-century-old American tradition of group political activity.

Our right of free association encourages us to form small group discussions about political affairs; however, our democratic form of government does not fully explain our enthusiasm for social grouping. Our country is made up of an almost infinite number of social groups. We belong to fraternities and sororities, the Moose and the Elks, flower clubs and ski clubs, bowling leagues and bridge groups. It might surprise you to find how many social groups you have become involved in since you left high school. During high school, of course, you were intensely involved in group activity, both formal and informal. Finally, you belong to a family which is your primary or lifelong group. However, this group may not have many formal meetings, as one member or another is always "on the go" to one organizational group meeting or another.

The socialization process that takes place in these groups produces a societal norm of team play in which we work for the good of the group—often at the expense of our own personal needs. Traditionally, the most popular sports activities have been the team sports of football, baseball, and basketball. However, the increased demand for more and more team play since World War II finally produced a watershed when, in the 1970s, we began to renew the emphasis on the individual and the notion that the love of self may preclude sacrifice for the group. The failures in Vietnam, the dissolution of many social movements, and the excesses of organized team sports has tempered somewhat our social group impulses. We see this in the increase in individualized sports such as jogging and swimming, yet the American culture continues to be noticeably group oriented. Many of the process theories of small group discussion that we present in this book were created from the close observation of the many American social groups.

The lessons we learn in social and play groups during high-school and college days prepare us for the small group communication demands of our professional careers. The amount of time we spend in meetings, both in our jobs and avocations, is great.

One of the recurring questions on the evaluation forms of private organizations and government agencies is one that relates to the employee's ability to be a "team player." The bureaucracy in which you will probably find yourself when you leave college will want you to do two things: (1) communicate effectively, and (2) accomplish your task objectives within a work group. Your abilities to organize, lead, and participate in small group discussions will be the major determinants of your future professional success.

Since the early 1950s, private industry has expended a lot of time and energy on the training of its employees in group discussion skills. In fact, in the 1980s this training in group skills received renewed interest with the development of Theory Z management and the adoption of quality circles (QCs) by over 2,000 American organizations. Theory Z management places a great deal of emphasis on group decision making, and quality circles are special types of problem-solving groups which focus on problems of quality and productivity in the work place. Some of the most popular books being read by Americans in the 1980s examine new ways for leading and managing work groups within an organizational setting (Ouchi 1981; Peters and Waterman 1982). When you graduate from college and begin your career in the 1990s, you will find an

American work environment that is built around team performance, and your employer will hire you with the expectation that you are knowledgeable about the subject matter upon which this book focuses.

Academic Tradition. Donald K. Smith (1954), in his chapter "Origin and Development of Departments of Speech," which is included in Karl Wallace's classic, *A History of Speech Education in America,* identifies subject matter as one reason for separating the field of speech from departments of English. Our ancient rhetorical tradition and the contributions of science to the study of speech behavior formed the new subject matter of speech departments. While the ancient subject of rhetoric is seen as the basis of modern day courses in persuasion and debate, rhetoric's counterpart, dialectic, an open inquiry in search of truth, is the foundation of small group discussion courses. By the late 1930s, speech departments throughout the country were offering courses in discussion. In a democracy, particularly one which contains an extensive mass media, public discussion was used as often, and was as important to national affairs, as speechmaking and political debating. Furthermore, as corporations turned more and more to group decision making there was more need to teach the communication skills that are necessary for business meetings and conferences.

During the 1940s and 1950s, speech, sociology, and psychology departments became intensely interested in the dynamics of work groups. Speech scholars tried to determine both the leadership style that worked best in leading small group discussions and how leaderless groups evolved and related to work environments. In fact, during those years, corporations and the government were asking academic scholars to determine under what conditions groups outperformed individuals. Atomic warfare had become a reality, and it was important to know who made riskier decisions—individuals acting alone or small groups.

In the 1960s, psychology developed a renewed interest in group therapy. The possibility of a small encounter group assisting in the healing of its members exploded into the human potential movement of the sixties. This led to the development of sensitivity training and some of today's popularized, packaged group experiences such as Synanon and EST. Sociologists broadened their study beyond the family and street gangs to a close examination of the social movements. Two of the more important group processes to evolve during the 1960s were consciousness-raising groups and prayer groups.

In 1970, the Speech Association of America formally became the Speech Communication Association. This name change reflected, in part, changes that occurred in the 1960s in the teaching of discussion in speech departments. Ernest G. Bormann (1970), argued that speech communication departments ought to teach the theories and practices associated with human work groups, with particular emphasis on the traditional, decision-making discussion group. Since 1970, speech communication departments have taught courses in discussion that generally follow Bormann's advice. Speech communication researchers during the seventies have made noticeable contributions to the content of these courses. Of the last two hundred pieces of research on small group communication produced by speech communication scholars, the majority focused on the specific communication behaviors that occur during small group discussions. Research in psychology, sociology, and speech communication over the last forty years has added greatly to our understanding of small group discussions. You as a college student need to be aware of these ideas if you are going to compete successfully within modern organizations. Based upon the research findings in speech communication, this book presents skills that you will need in order to communicate effectively in small group discussions.

A DEFINITION OF A SMALL GROUP DISCUSSION

Central to an understanding of small group discussion is the knowledge of what constitutes a small group. We define a small group as *a few people engaged in communication interaction over time, generally in face-to-face settings, who have common goals and norms and have developed a communication pattern for meeting their goals in an interdependent fashion.* This definition is based upon the research done by scholars in many disciplines. In order to understand how we arrived at this definition, it is necessary to take each of the key concepts and examine why it is a necessary part of a definition of a small group. Our definition reveals that there are nine characteristics of a small group. If you walked down the street in the presence of other people, there would be four immediate indications that would help you decide if a small group were present. They are: communication, space, time, and size. Moreover, if you observed a small collection of people systematically you would discover that there were five more characteristics that would tell you that a small group is present: interdependence, norms, structured communication patterns, group goals, and perception.

DIRECTLY OBSERVABLE CHARACTERISTICS OF A SMALL GROUP DISCUSSION

1. *Communication.* Verbal and nonverbal communication is such a fundamental behavior of a small group that we often overlook it (Fisher 1974). Yet the fact of talking and gesturing among a collection of people cues us to the presence of a group. The mere presence of several people standing at a bus stop would not alert us to the existence of a small group, but active communication among several people might.

2. *Space.* The fact that some people are standing in close proximity to one another is probably the first visual impulse we receive that points to the presence of a group (Campbell 1958). The idea that face-to-face communication must occur for a collection of people to become a small group is common to almost all definitions of small groups. Robert Bales (1950, 33), a famous small group theorist, defined a small group in part as "any number of persons engaged in interaction with one another in a single face-to-face meeting or several of such meetings."

3. *Time.* It seems that a collection of people have to communicate with one another for some period of time before they become a group. How long, we do not know; but the relationship between time and small group development is a major part of many small group theories.

4.   *Size.* Obviously, a definition of a *small* group must contain the characteristic of size. However, small group scholars have not been able to agree on the exact parameters. Some believe two is the minimum number of people (Shaw 1976, 11), while others argue that three is the smallest unit (Bormann 1975). Scholars also differ on when a small group is no longer small; Shaw says twenty (1976, 11), while Bormann indicates thirteen (1975, 3). Caplow (1959) seems to support Bormann in regard to the minimum number, inasmuch as interaction patterns of triads appear to be fundamentally different from dyads. In other words, the communication behavior of three people talking to each other is different from two-person communication. However, the upper limit of a small group may be more arbitrary in that the fixing of an exact number is dependent upon the kind of group that is formed. Research into the communication patterns in small groups may eventually resolve this problem, but for the present all we can say is that a small group can range in size from three to about twenty members.

A few people, lots of talk, limited space, and time taken together appear to be the directly observable characteristics of a small group. There are also some indirectly observable characteristics—behavior that the researcher cannot see—that are usually included in most definitions of small groups. For example, a human attitude cannot be seen directly and has to be determined by a paper-and-pencil test. As people talk face-to-face, certain things begin to happen that are highly process oriented and hard to see with the naked eye; however, they are fundamental to the evolution of a small group. There are five indirectly observable characteristics.

INDIRECTLY OBSERVABLE CHARACTERISTICS OF A SMALL GROUP DISCUSSION

1.   *Interdependence.* Kurt Lewin (1951, 146), pioneer in small group research, isolated interdependence as a key characteristic of small groups. From primitive hunting parties to NBA basketball teams, the element of interdependence seems to be present. How collections of people come to recognize their common need for each other is not clear, but the fact that interdependence must be present for small groups to exist is widely accepted by scholars.

2.   *Norms.* In the process of becoming, a small group will create a miniature culture. Certain behaviors, attitudes, and values become common to the members of a small group. Dress and language usage are two obvious variables that are subject to the norming process. A prayer group might "dress up" for a meeting, while a women's consciousness-raising group might "dress down." Some firefighter work groups prohibit swearing in the firehouse if outsiders are present, and medical teams usually act seriously in the presence of outsiders; nevertheless, their language is sometimes punctuated by expletives or humor when only insiders are present. The sharing of common traits also occurs in matters of belief and value structures that relate to a small group's goals.

3.   *Structured patterns.* We do not have a predictable communication pattern that is true of all small groups. However, almost all small group theorists maintain that as a collection of people becomes a group it does so in stages. In the work group the stages tend to involve a division-of-labor process through which members take on their various roles. Once the group is formed, however, members tend to remain in those same roles. In encounter groups the structure may not be roles but a recurring pattern of behavior that is peculiar to the group. Most small group theorists contend that groups go through predictable patterns of communication as they seek to achieve their goals.

4.   *Goals.* A similarity between interdependence and goals exists, but the concepts are not isomorphic. For example, five men could have the goal of fathering a child but not be interdependent. Yet the same five men could have the common goal of a five-dollar raise and, if they were the members of a bargaining team for their union, would have interdependence. Small groups are held together by their need to cooperate in the achievement of a group goal. If the goal can be achieved independently of group action, or only through competition among the group members, then the small group "glue" called cohesion may lose its adhesive power.

5.   *Perception.* The last way to tell a small group from a collection of people is to see if there is a perceived boundary line that separates the insiders from the outsiders. In short, do the people think of themselves as members of the group, and do they perceive other people as not being members of that group? If people perceive themselves as members of a group then they probably are (Cartwright and Zander 1968).

The preceding nine characteristics of a small group cannot be formed into a coherent concept that would be acceptable to all small group scholars, but they do, in an eclectic fashion, constitute a semantically valid statement of what a small group is.

KEY CONCEPTS OF GROUP DISCUSSION

In Chapter 2 we outline the major small group theories that are used to explain human behavior in small work groups. Unfortunately, we do not have one large general theory that can explain the communication behaviors that occur in all human groups. However, we do believe that there are a number of key concepts that come from different theories, that when mixed together, produce a rather rough and unscientific explanation of human groups, in particular the task group. In fact, Part Two of this book is an elaboration of the eight key concepts that we think blend together to form a practical description of discussion groups. The metaphor of concocting a cooking recipe will be used in our framing of the eight key group discussion concepts.

GROUP CONCEPT RECIPE

A good discussion group of five to seven people contains the four following ingredients:

generous amounts of *communication interaction,*
at least one helping *role* per person, and

equal proportions of *conflict* and *norming* behavior.

Mix and stir until sufficiently *cohesive.*

Apply three taste tests to the batter:

is the group *productive?*

are group decisions frequently *consensual?*

are group members *satisfied?*

The culinary art of preparing a cohesive discussion group that is productive, consensual in its decision-making procedures, and happy in its work, starts in a well-lit, comfortable room. At a round table, sit five to seven reasonably prepared people of sufficiently diverse backgrounds who discuss the task at hand. Allow enough patterns to develop. Reinforce positive role taking on the part of group members. At first be cautious about adding large doses of conflict, but if the group norms too quickly use generous amounts of conflict to thin the batter. When the separate group members begin to think collectively and make continual references to "us, we, they" and "the group," the mixture is becoming cohesive. Soon after signs of cohesion occur, taste testing can begin. Has the group reached consensus on some issues? Is some of the work getting done? Is the work being done efficiently? Are the members reasonably satisfied with each other and do they regularly attend each discussion meeting? Cooking up a successful discussion group is more of an art form than a science. Experienced group discussants continually taste the batter in order to help ensure successful group outcomes. (See Figure 1.1.)

DISCUSSION CONCEPTS

Communication Interaction. Fundamental to the study of small group discussion is group talk. For decades communication scholars have been observing discussion groups and recording who talks to whom, how frequently, and what they say to each other. After observing thousands of groups, it became clear that similar communication patterns developed in groups of five to seven people and that the communication interaction of successful groups is different from that of unsuccessful ones.

A communication interaction is hard to recognize. It could be just one person saying, "What is the purpose of this meeting?" Or a stimulus and response between two group members such as: "What is the agenda today?" "What do you mean, what is the agenda, didn't you read your mail?" And perhaps we should include the statement: "Why are you picking on David, none of us got the memo!" As you see, it is difficult to assess the beginning and end of communication interaction. In the example above, we could call this communication exchange conflict. Or if we added loud, boisterous laughter to the dialogue, we could call it tension releasing. But what really happened was that David was only joking about an incident that occurred several weeks ago, and so we would call this a group fantasy. In Chapters 2 and 3 we describe and label the communication interaction patterns of both prescriptive and natural discussion groups. In this chapter we want you to learn how communication interaction is central to our understanding of small group behavior.

FIGURE 1.1
GROUP CONCEPT RECIPE

The communication act of asking a question was one of the first interactions we discovered and labeled as being important to the progress of discussion. In fact, the frequency of questions has become the sign of a successful group, and if most of the question-asking was done by one person he or she was probably the task leader of the discussion. With each discovery we tended to look at the *frequency* of the communication interaction, the *distribution* of the communication interaction among participants, and the *content* or overall group meaning of the communication interaction.

Communication interaction is a key discussion concept because it is the building block we use in our attempts to generate a theory of small group communication. Prescriptive group patterns dictate communication interactions because past research has shown them to be successful. Our study of natural group processes indicates that there are successful and unsuccessful patterns of interaction. In fact, communication interaction is such a pervasive concept that you will find it is at the heart of the other seven concepts.

Roles.   In order to determine the roles that are played in a small group, researchers have looked at the frequency and distribution of communication behavior. When we found large chunks of one kind of communication coming from one person, we called this a role and labeled this role in a way that best characterized the type of communication being performed. Researchers discovered they had a role called tension releaser when they found a concentration of communication behavior that produced laughter in the group and thus broke tension. Researchers found concentrations of behavior that were basically information providing and labeled that role as information provider. In 1952 the National Training Laboratory in Group Development (NTL) in Bethel, Maine, generated a list of 24 roles that are played in group discussions in which the name of each role characterized the type of communication taking place; e.g., synthesizer, opinion giver, etc. (Potter and Andersen 1976).

Our study of natural groups has led speech communication scholars to conclude that people in groups share roles and that there seems to be a cluster of roles that are essential to a group's success. While scholars may disagree about a minimum list, we venture to say that at least five roles are required for a good discussion to take place. These include the roles of task leader, social-emotional leader (often referred to as lieutenant), tension releaser, information provider, and central negative. Leadership roles are of such importance that we devote Chapter 5 to a full treatment of them, including a description of the relationships among the task leader, the social-emotional leader, and the central negative.

Speech communication scholars have determined that there are sixteen leadership functions that need to be performed for a good discussion to take place (Wright 1975). It is our belief that it takes a minimum of the five roles that are listed in the preceding paragraph in order for the sixteen functions to be accomplished. For example, a person who plays the role of information provider performs the leadership function of contributing ideas, while the social-emotional leader engages in the communication interaction of resolving conflict. These necessary communication behaviors for leading group discussions are covered in Chapter 5.

A small discussion group necessarily involves itself simultaneously in a process of the development of communication interaction and the determination of group role specialization. It is necessary to understand the differences among flesh and blood people, the discussion roles these people play, and the communication patterns that constitute the essence of roles in a discussion.

Figure 1.2 depicts a five-person discussion group whose members share roles and communication leadership functions. Mary is the task leader and performs the most communication leadership functions, in particular, procedural functions that must be performed in the group. John plays the role of social-emotional leader and shares the role of information provider with Pam and Sally. John handles many of the leadership functions that deal with the social-emotional needs of the group. Sally plays the role of tension releaser,

FIGURE 1.2
DISTINGUISHING AMONG PEOPLE, ROLES, AND COMMUNICATION BEHAVIORS IN DISCUSSION

PEOPLE	Mary	Tom	John	Pam	Sally
ROLES	Task Leader	Central Negative	Social-Emotional Leader Information Provider	Information Provider Tension Releaser	Tension Releaser Information Provider
LEADERSHIP COMMUNICATION BEHAVIORS	Goal setting Agenda making Seeking ideas Seeking idea evaluation Summarizing Regulating participation	Instigating conflict Evaluating ideas	Contributing ideas Summarizing Climate making Resolving conflict Instigating group self-analysis	Contributing ideas Climate making	Contributing ideas Climate making

in addition to sharing the role of information provider, and also initiates much of the dialogue that relates to the social-emotional area of the group. Tom plays the role of central negative and, as such, objects to Mary's leadership. In the process, however, Tom generates many helpful leadership communication patterns that facilitate criticism of the task. Chapter 6 provides a detailed explanation of the ten most frequently played roles and thirty communication behaviors that occur in groups.

Distinguishing among people, roles, and communication interaction is important for your understanding of discussion groups for several reasons. Certain basic roles must be played for a group to function effectively. People will play different roles in different groups, and will share roles within the same group. In our work with business corporations we often hear people who are playing the role of task leader complain about the person who is playing the role of central negative. It is as if, in the preceding example, the task leader had suspected Tom had some character flaw when, in reality, he was a fine person who was playing the role of the central negative for the group's benefit. Sometimes we find people who are caught in a "role rut." By that we mean they tend to play the same role in every discussion group. The tension-releasing role is so much fun that some people like to play it all the time, when in some cases the group really needs the person to perform another role.

Group roles are in one context merely the concentration of certain kinds of communication behavior. Communication functions signal the presence of a given role, while, conversely, the role is a given set of communication functions. However, since roles and communication functions are not synonymous concepts, it is important to recognize that there are distinctions as well as a high degree of correlation between them. We should also remember that people and roles are separate entities.

Norming.   Group norms are shared values, beliefs, behaviors, and procedures in regard to the group's purpose that are generally agreed to subconsciously by the group. The more the group's norms are manifestly obvious to people outside the group, the more likely it is that the group is cohesive. If groups—for example, teenage groups, sports groups, or groups that face danger together—agree to wear clothing unique to the group, then they are publicly declaring they are a cohesive group. However, while the development of a dress code is one of the most obvious norming behaviors, it is not the most important aspect of group norming.

Norming occurs in three areas of group life: *social, procedural,* and *task.* When a group is first formed, the members bring with them their behaviors, beliefs, and values acquired from their participation in other groups. These past experiences create expectations on the way a discussion should take place. Table 1.1 lists the typical do's and don'ts of a discussion group's first meeting in an American culture.

A quick examination of the table indicates that no group in the United States would ever develop this set of group norms. And yet, most Americans

TABLE 1.1
EXPECTED NORMS FOR A DISCUSSION GROUP'S FIRST MEETING

Social	Procedural	Task
Do	Do	Do
—serve refreshments	—introduce people	—criticize ideas, not people
—dress casually	—plan to participate	—support the best idea
—use first names	—establish goals	—commit yourself to group
—discuss uncontroversial	—build an agenda	solutions
subjects	—hold a routine meeting	—share in the workload
—tell humorous jokes	one hour in length	—say so if you disagree
—tell political jokes (they	—have someone in charge	—ask questions about group ideas
will be tolerated)	—sit face-to-face	
—tell trend or one-line		
jokes		
—tell cultural truisms		
Don't	Don't	Don't
—smoke (perhaps)	—leave the meeting without	—push your idea on the group
—swear	cause	—support ideas just because of
—arrive late	—monopolize conversation	people who presented them
—be absent without	—stand up and speak in the	—be verbally violent if you
apology	meeting (generally)	disagree with ideas
—tell sexist, racist,	—demand to lead	—consider your ideas as the
ethnic, ageist, or	—refuse to speak when	only ones of merit
religious jokes	addressed	

when they first form a discussion group stay fairly close to this prescribed list. When a meeting is called we expect to have refreshments, be on a first name basis with other members, and engage in light social conversation. We do not expect a lot of profanity or crude jokes that might offend somebody. We expect that the meeting will establish a purpose and an agenda, and that we will talk about the agenda in a face-to-face context for about an hour. We do not expect people to abruptly leave the meeting, monopolize the conversation, or refuse to speak. We expect a free-flowing exchange of ideas with a lot of questioning and sharing of the work load on the group's behalf. We don't expect to be verbally assailed for the ideas we express, nor do we expect others to support ideas solely on the basis of who said them.

Table 1.1 represents our *expectations* for group norms. This protocol list never survives the first meeting intact, nor should it. Once the group has established a history—after two or three meetings—the real norms will begin to emerge. For example, the group may maintain rules against sexist, racist or ethnic jokes, but if all the members are of the same religion they may tell religious jokes. There are many stories circulating within the Catholic church that indicate that the best jokes about the pope are told by cardinals, in Latin. Likewise, the best rabbi jokes are told on the steps of a synagogue. While strangers politely disagree about ideas, highly cohesive groups rant and rave about their differences. While formal, prescriptive group meetings mandate an agenda procedure, a discussion group whose members have worked together a long time will develop its own unique way of covering agenda. There is an important distinction between what is at first expected and the eventual acceptance of group norms. The journey from expected to accepted is often a stormy and dangerous period in the group's life. For example, if one group member is a chain smoker, and another group member is bothered by tobacco smoke, there may be a protracted struggle as the group tries to establish the social norm of smoking or nonsmoking. However, the norming behavior that finally occurs with respect to the task dimension of the group is really more important. The group must eventually develop the custom of openly criticizing ideas without offending group members.

Conflict. In this book group conflict is identified as flowing from problem solving, role formation, personality differences, and clashes about professional group identity. Conflict is a most dynamic variable and is probably almost as pervasive as interaction itself. Consequently, we devote the entirety of Chapter 8 to analysis of group conflict and ways it can be managed.

At each point where conflict occurs, regardless of level, the obstacle must be resolved or minimized so that the group may proceed to work on its group goals. A major characteristic that helps identify the level of conflict is whether the intention was to instigate or resolve conflict. For example, there is purposefulness in a devil's advocate engaging in task conflict; however, social-emotional obstacles which appear in the form of interpersonal conflict may be more difficult to pinpoint as to formal intentionality.

Imagine, for instance, that a number of group members have engaged in positive head-nodding behavior throughout the majority of a discussion on the topic of abortion. Perhaps the norms and standards of the group are such that the mother's condition is always the top priority. A group member, in the role of devil's advocate, could suggest that the condition of the fetus should be given top priority in any abortion decision. This instigation of task conflict could aid the group in reevaluating its position on the mother's condition and whether it should always have top priority in the discussion of abortion. This might start the group thinking and working hard again on criteria for abortion decisions. On the other hand, it is possible that the individual was just being argumentative and was not a devil's advocate as he or she was initially perceived. In this particular example, the intent would be hard to identify. However, as with all groups, one should try to distinguish the major kinds of conflict.

Conflict is a two-edged sword. Used one way it is the necessary instrument for the critical evaluation of ideas and the formulation of group roles. When conflict is used inappropriately or too frequently at the ideational level the group's work does not get done. When conflict is not resolved at the social-emotional level, role formation does not take place as it should, work is not done efficiently, and participation is unpleasant for group members. Thus, in our cooking recipe for a good group, conflict is the counterpart of norming in that it thins the batter. Too much thinning and the mixture will not jell, too little and the stuff will not pour.

Cohesion.   This small group discussion variable can be defined as the extent to which the members are attracted towards the group and its membership. Cohesiveness focuses on commitment to work collectively toward group goals. Cohesion increases as communication interaction facilitates role taking, and as the group stabilizes its norms; moreover, it continues to increase as the quality of the group's productivity increases and the group reaches more and more consensual decisions.

Thus, cohesiveness is the bridge between the four ingredient variables—that is, communication interaction, roles, norms, and conflict—and the three tasting or output variables of productivity, consensus, and membership satisfaction. Cohesiveness is a measure of how successfully the four ingredient variables have blended, but it is also an ingredient itself in that it positively influences the three output variables.

It is easier to give an example of a cohesive group than to say exactly what it is. So far we have only been able to approach an understanding of it metaphorically. For example, if group members were particles and the group were a magnetic field, cohesion would be the magnetic force that held the particles together, and that force would be in constant flux. Once the group is formed, successful productivity, consensual agreement, and membership satisfaction are the biggest determinants in the increases and decreases of cohesiveness.

Hall (1953), in his study of aircraft commanders and bomber crews, defined cohesion as "the average resultant force to remain in the group." In other words, there must be more forces on the average to persuade the members to remain in the group rather than leave or disband it. In essence, a small group must have cohesion in order to have "groupness." Individual differences may abound in a particularly small group discussion, and yet members must desire to work together to the extent that the common good of the group is served. One can see that this "togetherness" and "willingness to belong" element of small group communication is crucial to the very existence of a small group; for all practical purposes, if cohesion isn't present, then neither is our concept of a small group.

Some groups have a long history of success which often exceeds the life span of the original members. Groups that have developed a strong tradition of group success are attractive groups for us to join. The social, procedural, and task dimensions of these groups have been established and traditionalized, and each member is asked to conform to the group's tradition. Since it is such an attractive group to be a part of, new members readily adopt their assigned roles. We all can name these long-standing groups. In sports it is teams like Notre Dame in football and UCLA in basketball. On campus it might be the leading fraternity or sorority. In public services it might be a given police district or firehouse. In corporations certain departments develop long-standing reputations. In these situations, it is relatively easy to maintain cohesion. The real problem is—how do you get cohesion when you haven't got any? Consciousness-raising talk, which we discuss in the next chapter, is one of the major ways to increase cohesion.

Most of the work groups we belong to do not have glorious traditions that compel us to do our best. Thus, we have to build cohesion by first becoming a group; i.e., producing the proper blend of the four cooking ingredients, and then beginning to celebrate the first signs of successful productivity. In other words, we build our own group tradition that is a source of our pride. Before we know it, people will be wanting to join our group because they heard it was a great team to be on. Why is it a good team? Because the members are satisfied, we share in decision making, and we do good work.

Productivity. Many times after people have worked very hard to form a cohesive task group, particularly a discussion group that can be counted on to formulate clear policies, they become cynical and frustrated with what appears to be a lot of wasted effort. In any organization you can hear daily ventilations of the problem of getting work done in groups. We continually ask ourselves if group work is superior to individual work. In periods of depression we say things like "A camel is a horse that has been built by a committee." "If you want to kill or delay an idea, appoint a task force to study it." We all feel that we waste a lot of time attending group meetings.

The frustrations in participating in group discussions and committee meetings are further compounded by mismanagement. Even when groups are formed for the right reasons, the meetings are not well run. We have all been called to meetings that were not well planned. We have all sat through rambling monologues that extended even beyond the already generous amount of time allotted for the group meeting. Our own past experience tells us that group discussions are overused and misused. However, there is a firm research base to support the contention that in a number of different settings and over a range of different types of problems, groups outperform individuals.

Marvin E. Shaw (1976, 71–81) provides a succinct summary of hypotheses gleaned from the small group research, identifying differences between individual and group productivity. One of the more important hypotheses that Shaw proposes is the following: "Groups usually produce more and better solutions to problems than do individuals working alone." The essence of this hypothesis is twofold. First, groups have a tendency to produce more ideas in general and more discussion solutions in particular. This is especially true when we look at the number of ideas that can be produced in a brainstorming session. We can take five individuals and have them brainstorm individually and collectively; almost without exception the collective group will produce more ideas. A second aspect of the Shaw hypothesis focuses on the belief that groups produce better solutions to problems than individual group members working alone. Other things being equal, this is a valid assumption. With a larger number of ideas produced, we hope to be able to include a larger number of proposals of high quality. The tendency to produce quality decisions is heightened if the decisions have been processed by individuals working in a group.

Sometimes we use groups to solve problems and make decisions when one superior member of the group might have made a better decision on his or her own. We will often opt for a group decision knowing full well that it will take twice as long to arrive at it than if we made the decision on our own. The reason for doing this is not necessarily because we think the decision will be better, but because some decisions *ought* to be group decisions. As Americans, we have strong commitments to democratic ideals. Every organization has a collection of decisions that must be reached through group processes.

At our university we have a parking problem. We tend to think it is worse than at most places, but it may be that all colleges and universities have parking problems "worse than anybody else's." We are convinced that either one of us, or any other professor taken at random, could make better decisions about how to handle parking tickets than does our parking committee. We venture to say that every faculty member and student on campus believes he or she could do the same. We use a parking committee, not because it makes better decisions, and certainly not because it makes faster decisions, but because we are committed to the organizational principle that says disputes involving competing interests should be resolved through a group process. Although it is tempting to suspend this ideal in the case of parking, we would become hysterical if the principle were to be suspended regarding the curriculum of the university. We would feel fundamentally disenfranchised if professors and students did not participate in the design of the curriculum, and there we have the nub and rub of it. The college curriculum committee does not necessarily make faster or better decisions, but we feel unalterably committed to the principle that this committee's work should reflect a group decision. And so, in all organizations, in varying degrees, we find a collection of policies that must be decided upon by a group. So the question is not really whether a group decision is better than an individual decision, but how to get the best group decision.

Even if we lived in a totalitarian society and philosophically were committed to autocratic management, we would find that as primates we like to do our work in the presence of other primates. Indeed there is research to support the conclusion that we do better work in nominal groups than we do by ourselves because the presence of other people motivates us to work harder (Shaw 1976, 78). However, there are some problems that, if solved in a group, would produce not only a poor product but also considerable conflict among the members. Try solving the following problem reaching a consensual group decision: "On one side of a river are three wives and three husbands. All of the men but none of the women can row. Get them all across the river by means of a boat carrying only three at one time. No man will allow his wife to be in the presence of another man unless he is also there" (Shaw 1976, 62). Aside from the obvious sexism in the example, you will find that this type of problem produces frustrating conflict in face-to-face discussion. Furthermore, if your group is competing against other groups for the right answer with a time deadline, anarchy will occur until a logician dictator takes over and solves the problem. It is therefore not surprising that we are often members of groups that are presented with problems that one or two members solve by themselves, even though credit goes to the group as a whole. How groups handle uneven participation, but equal reward, takes us back to the concept of cohesion and forward to the concept of member satisfaction. We would hazard an experienced-based hypothesis that the more cohesive a group is and the greater the membership satisfaction, the more the group can tolerate uneven work but equal reward. And the more a group can tolerate a product that is unequally produced, the more successful the group will be, simply because groups often are forced to solve problems that do not keep to the ideal of equal participation in the solving of them.

Consensus.   Consensus, or unanimous agreement on a decision by group members, is a key small-group-discussion outcome variable. In fact, this output variable of consensus has long been regarded by speech discussion scholars as a fundamental concept. (Baird 1937, 357–59; McBurney and Hance 1950, 14; Keltner 1957, 192; Gulley 1968, 240.) When complete agreement is achieved by a group, the benefits the group receives in terms of increased cohesion and commitment to the agreed-upon course of action make this kind of group outcome superior to compromise or majority vote.

If a group commits itself to a consensual decision, the journey will be longer and harder, and the discussion will have more conflict, than if a decision by majority vote could prevail. However, the communication patterns that are needed for consensus encourage active participation on the part of all group members and require a fair weighing of the major issues. This not only produces a more enthusiastic group but increases the possibility of a better decision.

A compromise or majority vote decision is not the same as a consensual decision. It is important for a group to be able to say they all agreed on one course of action. If the agreement is not consensual, then there were members who were unable to state they were for the course of action. If the group establishes a history of having the same members in the role of the minority, the group's cohesion, and ultimately its performance, will suffer. If a group decision then requires group collective action, the "no" votes during the discussion may turn to negative behavior in carrying out the group's policy. So in the long run it may be worth the extra time and effort to find a policy that everyone can agree to, so that no member will drag his or her feet.

Since consensual agreement is such a valuable output of group discussion, inexperienced discussion leaders sometimes try to force consensus when it is really not there. This apparent consensus can be much worse than compromise or a majority vote decision in that members feel herded and browbeaten into agreement. In this situation the leader might say, "We are all in agreement on Sally's solution, aren't we?" when in fact the group members may not yet have achieved consensus on all aspects of the problem. If a discussion leader is to err, it should be in the direction of seeking out points of disagreement when in fact none remain.

In the day-to-day work of a discussion group, time does not allow consensual agreement on all, and in some work environments not even on most, group decisions. This does not mean that a group should not strive for consensus. When a group reaches consensus, the members should celebrate that moment and make it a vivid part of their group history.

Member Satisfaction.   Within our work environment we are often assigned to groups. In our communities we volunteer to be part of civic and social-service groups. In the work environment we say we tolerate groups because we have to work in them, although if that were the case how do we explain the social-service groups we eagerly join? The answer is that groups fulfill needs that vary from individual to individual; that is, we enjoy being a part of some groups. Thus, membership satisfaction is an important test of a good group.

Membership satisfaction is an important discussion-group outcome variable. We know this, not only because we like to go to certain group meetings just for the personal satisfaction it brings us, but also because we find some status in being associated with a group effort. We would not feel the intensity of this variable of member satisfaction unless we were also satisfied to some extent with the group product. Although membership satisfaction is the most interpersonally oriented discussion-group outcome, it is also related to group composition factors and productivity.

In the course of your academic career, you will probably be a part of some loosely formed study group that has as its purpose the intellectual advancement of its members. Sometimes these groups are formed for only one semester for one course, while others last for several semesters and range over many areas of intellectual interest. If you stop to analyze what attracts you to this kind of group, you might notice that you enjoy the intellectual stimulus of other students. If your group develops some history, you may discover that you derive member satisfaction from the better grades that have been proved to be one of the results of interaction. If your group begins to celebrate its proven track record and develops enough pride to name itself and prescribe some regular rituals, you will soon feel a third kind of member satisfaction that derives from the status of belonging to a known intellectual group on campus. Thus, member satisfaction occurs at three levels: (1) the enjoyment of interaction with fellow members; (2) the quality of product produced; and (3) the pride of group membership.

EXPECTATIONS IN THE STUDY OF SMALL GROUP DISCUSSION

1.   *To know what a small group is.* In this chapter, we presented nine characteristics of a small group. To know a small group when we see one and to understand the communication interactions that occur is a complex undertaking. We hope that this book is a reasonable statement of what a small group is, particularly as it involves face-to-face discussions.

2.   *To grasp the basic small group concepts.* When you take a course in astronomy, you are taught concepts such as planet, comet, gravitational pull, and entropy. You are introduced to these concepts in order that you will be able to discuss our solar system coherently. In this chapter we explain eight group concepts: roles, communication interaction, consensus, and others, so that we can explain the workings of a small group discussion using a common conceptual vocabulary. Many of the chapters focus entirely on one of the eight small group concepts; for example, Chapter 8 focuses entirely on conflict communication.

3.   *To acquire a theoretical understanding of small group communication.* A reasonable expectation to have after completing a study of small group discussion is a working theory frame, or lens, that will provide you with a useful explanation of small group behavior you observe every day. In Chapter 2 we discuss three generic types of small group communication and present them in a coherent frame that should allow you to understand and explain most communication behavior you see in small group discussions. However, the remaining chapters will help clarify and focus your theoretical lens so that you will automatically process what is going on in a small group discussion.

4.   *To learn to select the appropriate discussion technique.* Different group problems require different group strategies to solve them. Decisions need to be made about the format of the discussion, the agenda system that will be used, and the selection of the correct one-time meeting techniques. The six discussion formats, the six problem-solving agenda systems, and the seven discussion techniques that you can use to make meetings more effective are described in Chapter 3. In Chapter 4 we explain how to prepare for group discussions.

5.   *To learn how to lead small group discussions.* When you graduate from college, chances are you will find yourself leading a small work group in which you will conduct many face-to-face discussions. One of your expectations from your study of small group discussion is a practical knowledge of how to effectively lead groups. Chapter 5, which is devoted to an examination of the leadership role in group discussions, examines such things as the four leadership styles of a formal leader—telling, selling, delegating, and participating—and sixteen leadership communication behaviors of a discussion group in reaching its goals. Practicing these communication behaviors should improve your ability to lead small group discussions.

6.   *To learn how to be an effective participant in small groups.* So much attention is given to the leadership role in small groups that we often overlook the necessity of other group roles to the success of the group. The ten roles active in discussion groups, and the descriptions of leadership and followership communication behaviors that each tends to perform, are outlined in Chapter 6. This chapter explains a set of performance standards that each person has an obligation to meet.

7.   *To learn the management of interpersonal communication in the small group.* Some people do not like to work in small groups because of the interpersonal dimension of groups. They have difficulty making personal self-disclosures and developing trust and empathy with other group members. Chapter 7 indicates how interpersonal communication in groups can be better managed.

8.   *To learn the management of conflict communication in the small group.* There is ideational, role, personal, and professional conflict in small groups. In Chapter 8 we suggest a number of ways for managing group conflict.

9.   *To apply discussion principles and practices.* Often the theory and practices learned at the university do not transfer well to the work environment. Chapter 9 suggests how discussion principles and practices can be applied directly to routine day-to-day meetings and conferences.

10. *To understand intergroup communication in organizations.* Just as individuals in groups develop role conflicts, so do work groups in organizations. Communication behaviors that might work in a small group discussion might have a negative impact on parallel work groups in an organization. The fact that small discussion groups do not work in a vacuum but are part of an ongoing integrative whole makes them even harder to understand and to lead effectively. Chapter 10 makes recommendations on how you can effectively lead your group within an organization.

SUMMARY

The introductory chapter highlights several of the important considerations we make in studying small group discussion. In part these considerations are based on cultural setting and certain academic traditions. The major expectations of what we can derive from our study of discussion serve as learning guidelines for the remaining chapters in the book.

A definition of small group discussion was posited, based in large measure on nine directly and indirectly observable characteristics of a small group. A small group is *a few people engaged in communication interaction over time, generally in face-to-face settings, who have common goals and norms and have developed a communication pattern for meeting their goals in an interdependent fashion.*

Eight group discussion concepts are believed to be necessary for a good group to accomplish its goals. Four of these key concepts—communication interaction, role, conflict, and norming behavior—are required for the achievement of an appropriate group blend, or cohesion. Three concepts are classified as group outcomes: productivity, consensus, and member satisfaction.

Communication interaction was the first discussion concept presented in the chapter. The frequency, distribution, and content of communication are believed to be crucial to the group process. Group *roles* occur when certain concentrations of group talk are attributed to specific members; at least five roles were identified as being vital for good group discussions. The third key concept, *norming,* was discussed. Norms are values, beliefs, behaviors, and procedures shared by the group members that work towards a group's cohesiveness. *Conflict* was identified as flowing from disruptions in problem-solving and role formation, personality differences, and clashes about professional identity.

Cohesion was defined as the amount of attraction the members feel toward the group and its membership. This key discussion variable was viewed as the bridge concept between the four ingredient variables listed in the preceding paragraph and the following three output variables.

The first output variable, *productivity,* deals with the group task outcomes accomplished through group work. *Consensus* was defined as unanimous agreement on a decision by group members. *Member satisfaction,* the last important group outcome variable discussed, emphasized that group members must be satisfied with both task productivity and the interpersonal relations of the group. To varying degrees the above eight key discussion concepts are emphasized in the basic kinds of groups covered in this chapter. The relative importance of each concept will vary in respect to the group situation and the discussion group pattern employed.

REFERENCES

Baird, A. C. *Public Discussion and Debate.* Boston: Ginn and Co., 1937.

Bales, R. F. *Interaction Process Analysis.* Reading, Mass.: Addison-Wesley, 1950.

Barnlund, D. C., and Haiman, F. S. *The Dynamics of Discussion.* Boston: Houghton Mifflin Company, 1960.

Bormann, E. G. *Discussion and Group Methods.* 1st and 2nd editions. New York: Harper and Row, 1969 and 1975.

_____ . "Pedagogic Space: A Strategy for Teaching Discussion." *The Speech Teacher* 19 (1970): 272–77.

Campbell, D. T. "Common Fate, Similarity, and Other Indices of the Status of Aggregates of Persons as Social Entities." *Behavioral Science* 3 (1958): 14–25.

Caplow, T. "Further Development of a Theory of Coalitions in the Triad." *American Journal of Sociology* 64 (1959): 488–93.

Cartwright, D., and Zander, A., eds. *Group Dynamics: Research and Theory.* 3rd edition. New York: Harper and Row, 1968.

Donohue, W. A.; Cushman, D. P.; and Nofsinger, R. E., Jr. "Creating and Confronting Social Order: A Comparison of Rules Perspectives," *Western Journal of Speech Communication,* 44 (Winter 1980): 5–19.

Fisher, B. A. *Small Group Decision Making: Communication and the Group Process.* New York: McGraw-Hill, 1974.

Gouran, D. S. "Variables Related to Consensus in Group Discussions of Questions of Policy." Ph.D. Dissertation, University of Iowa, 1968.

Gouran, D. S., and Fisher, B. A. "The Functions of Human Communication in the Formation, Maintenance and Performance of Small Groups." In *Handbook of Rhetorical and Communication Theory,* edited by Arnold, C. C., and Bowers, J. W. Boston: Allyn and Bacon, 1984.

Gulley, H. E. *Discussion, Conference, and Group Process.* 2nd edition. New York: Holt, Rinehart and Winston, Inc., 1968.

Hall, R. L. "Social Influence on the Role Behavior of a Designated Leader: A Study of Aircraft Commanders and Bomber Crews." *Dissertation Abstracts* 13 (1953): 1285.

Keltner, J. W. *Group Discussion Processes.* New York: Longmans, Green, 1957.

Lewin, K. *Field Theory in Social Science.* New York: Harper and Row, 1951.

McBurney, J. H., and Hance, K. C. *Discussion in Human Affairs.* New York: Harper and Row, 1950.

McGrath, J. E. *Groups: Interaction and Performance.* Englewood Cliffs, N.J.: Prentice-Hall, 1984.

Ouchi, W. G. *Theory Z.* Reading, Mass: Addison-Wesley, 1981.

Peters, T. J., and Waterman, R. H., Jr. *In Search of Excellence.* New York: Harper and Row, 1982. Reprinted by Warner Books, 1984.

Potter, D., and Andersen, M. D. *Discussion in Small Groups: A Guide to Effective Practice.* 3rd edition. Belmont, Calif.: Wadsworth, 1976.

Shaw, M. E. *Group Dynamics: The Psychology of Small Group Behavior.* 2nd edition. New York: McGraw-Hill, 1976.

Smith, D. K. "Origin and Development of Departments of Speech." In *A History of Speech Education in America,* edited by Karl R. Wallace. New York: Appleton-Century-Crofts, 1954.

Wright, D. W. *Small Group Communication: An Introduction.* Dubuque, Iowa: Kendall/Hunt, 1975.

. . . if you can recognize the type of talk occurring in the group, you can become a more effective participant in small group discussions.

CHAPTER OBJECTIVES

In order to be a more effective discussant, when you read this chapter you should focus on the theoretical explanations of small group discussion.

YOU NEED TO KNOW:

1. The general types of small group discussion theories.
2. The generic types of small group communication.
3. The types of group talk that form a general explanation of small group communication.
4. The benchmarks to understanding small group discussion.

SMALL GROUP
COMMUNICATION
THEORIES

CHAPTER OUTLINE

In the last forty-five years, scholarly thought on small group communication has naturally produced honest but sometimes intense differences of opinion about what a small group is and what discussion practices should be taught to undergraduate students. We do not have space in this book to get deeply involved in these theoretical controversies. However, in the final chapter we will discuss directions that small group communication research is taking. For now, let us begin with a very simple system for classifying small group communication theories. The different types of small groups that people find themselves in fall into the two general categories of *prescriptive* and *descriptive* groups. The prescriptive category contains the group patterns that list the rational steps that group members *ought* to follow in reaching some predetermined goal. The descriptive category houses the natural group processes that small group researchers have discovered to exist in organized societies. The first set of theories we will label method theories and the other process theories.

For nearly half a century, a dichotomy has existed between discussion methods and small group communication processes. Both strains of research have been valuable in developing useful advice that will help you become a more successful group participant. Rioch argued in 1951 that most psychotherapy consists of theories of method, inasmuch as it prescribes procedures that a clinician should follow in providing help to a person in need of emotional support. An examination of play-acting theories will also reveal that they include hints to actors on how roles should be played—for example, the Stanislavski method. This has led to the common epithet, "method actors." Any human activity, whether it is hitting a baseball or playing a violin, soon develops a collection of suggestions on how to perfect its necessary skills. When this is done in a systematic way it provides a rich description of the procedures one should follow in perfecting some activity.

Our culture is inundated with method theories, and our bookshelves are full of how-to-do-it books. An Irish playwright once argued that you could tell the nature of a country by envisioning what kind of elephant book its writers would produce. He argued that the English would write an elephant book entitled *The Hunt,* or *How I Killed the Elephant.* The French would write a very thin book entitled *The Loves of an Elephant.* The Germans would laboriously write a two-volume set concerning the left ear of the elephant. And Americans would unquestionably write a book called *How to Build a Bigger and Better Elephant.* So it would not be surprising if you subtitled this book: *How-to-do-it Advice.* Some of this advice has been very prescriptive and systematic over the years.

The second type of theories we will discuss is the type known as process theories. These theories do not initially contain any how-to-do-it advice. They describe how members of small work groups communicate with each other, not how they ought to communicate. For example, we might go out into our society and observe a baseball game, and through some systematic procedure develop a scientific explanation of what happened out on the baseball diamond. This kind of theory is different from a method theory in that it does not prescribe how to play the game but merely describes how it is actually played. However, close observation of well-played games soon produces a list of suggestions to assist the rookie ballplayer in playing the game better.

Thus, both sets of theories (method and process) eventually mesh into a set of guidelines on how to be a better participant when attending meetings and being involved with problem solving in your work group. In this chapter we will focus on descriptive process theories, explaining three types of generic group communication processes: task, encounter, and consciousness-raising. In Chapter 3 we will discuss prescriptive method theories, focusing on three discussion patterns that are a part of meetings: formats, problem-solving agenda systems, and one-time meeting techniques. By the time you finish the first section of the book, we hope you will be able to understand these two sets of group theories not only individually, but as they uniquely and continually become intertwined with each other. (See Figure 2.1.)

NATURAL GROUP COMMUNICATION PROCESSES

Through many years of research, we have discovered that there are three distinct group processes of communication. They are *task, encounter,* and *consciousness-raising* groups. The purpose of the task group is to do work; however, communication scholars have observed that there are predictable group processes that a group must go through in order to get the job done. The purpose of the encounter group process is to enhance self-understanding and growth, and heighten trust and empathy among group members. The purpose of consciousness raising (CR) is to create, heighten, and sustain a person's group identity.

In this chapter we will systematically describe each of these generic group types so that you can distinguish one group process from another. We believe that these are naturally occurring group processes that you have participated in dozens of times (e.g., "CR sessions," "encounter sessions," and "task group sessions"). Our reason for describing these three generic processes in detail is quite straightforward. It has been our experience that if you can recognize the type of "talk" occurring in the group, you can become a more effective

FIGURE 2.1
SMALL GROUP COMMUNICATION THEORIES

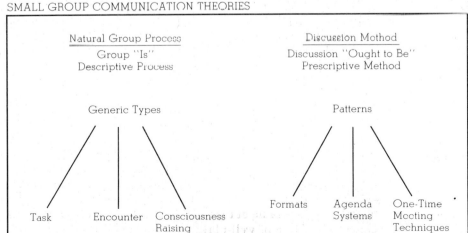

participant in small group discussions. After describing each generic type individually, we then provide you with an integrated model of small group communication which will allow you to classify the major forms of group talk in such a way that you can be a more informed and productive group member. In fact, our model integrates the three generic types of groups in such a way that you will be able to classify and explain all communication that occurs in a typical problem-solving discussion.

TASK GROUP PROCESS

Speech communication scholars have worked on building communication explanations of group processes since the 1930s. Historically, our discipline has used discussion and pragmatic procedures for reaching group decisions. However, in the 1960s the field of speech began to expand its view to include task groups, of which the decision-making group was one. This evolutionary process arose primarily out of a need to provide richer explanations of the communication processes that occur in groups. (Bormann 1970; Cragan and Wright 1980.)

After some 30 years of study in decision-making groups, we have discovered that there are two dimensions of a work group: the *task* dimension and the *social* dimension. These dimensions emphasize problem-solving talk and role talk, respectively. Later in this chapter we will present our model of a work group which integrates what we regard as the four different kinds of communication talk that occurs in groups: problem-solving talk, role talk, CR talk, and encounter talk. Presently, we want to explain in detail the task and social dimensions of a work group.

In 1939, McBurney and Hance, two scholars working on small group discussion, published one of the first and certainly one of the most influential books in the field. Their approach to the teaching of discussion was constructed directly upon John Dewey's theories about human thought processes. In 1910, Dewey published his famous work *How We Think* in which he explained the process of human thought as a careful, step-by-step consideration of a problem. He labeled this process, "reflective thinking." Dewey identified five distinct steps to this process of reflective thought:

1. a felt difficulty;
2. its location and definition;
3. suggestion and possible solution;
4. development by reasoning of the bearings of the suggestion; and
5. further observation and experiment leading to its acceptance or rejection, that is, the conclusion of belief or disbelief.

McBurney and Hance (1939) adapted Dewey's five steps—which describe how an individual analyzes a problem—to group discussion. This adaptation to group analysis of problems and solutions is evident in their first steps:

1. definition and delineation of the problem;
2. analysis of the problem;
3. the suggestion of solutions;

4. reasoned development of the proposed solutions; and
5. further verification.

McBurney and Hance's adaptation of John Dewey's process of reflective thinking was only one example of its use by numerous small-group-discussion theorists. In Chapter 3 we will discuss in detail the many useful patterns and agenda systems that have been developed over the years in a continuing effort to help groups think and work together.

Kurt Lewin (1951), is generally regarded as the father of group dynamics. In the 1930s, scholars from a number of disciplines began to see that small groups had a special identity and that the understanding of them could be an important goal of research. Lewin provided the first coherent explanation of groups in what we have come to call field theory. His notion of a field is essentially the space that individuals share within a group. One of Lewin's basic concepts of field theory is "life-space," that is, the concept that each individual possesses a life-space within the field or group. In this theoretical explanation of a group, individual group members share some of their life-space with each other; that is, they are interdependent. The notion of a group as a field and the interdependence of the various life-spaces within the group, provide a foundation for understanding the group concept of cohesion. Lewin regarded group cohesion as the "stuff" which holds the group members together in a common life-space.

Robert Bales (1950, 1970) is an influential scholar working on the development of small group communication theories. The work he has done at Harvard in describing the task and social dimensions of groups, the stages the group goes through in its development, and the major roles that are played by members in small groups, forms the basis of most modern attempts to describe how a small group works. Bales's work has been emphasized by speech communication scholars because he studies communication acts among group members in his efforts to explain the complex interactions of a discussion group.

In 1950 Bales developed an instrument for coding communication acts in a task group that has had a major impact on how small group theorists conceive of task group communication. Bales built a descriptive model of a task group based on the data he compiled with this coding instrument, which he called a system of Interaction Process Analysis (IPA). The instrument sorted all human behavior into the two major categories of social-emotional and task. Almost all subsequent attempts at describing the pattern of communication in task groups have sorted out these two separate but interacting clusters of communicative behavior. An adaptation of Bales's IPA can be found in Table 2.1. After many years of observing discussion groups in numerous organizational settings, Bales determined that communication acts could be divided into two basic dimensions: task and social. The social dimension consists of two major categories, positive reactions and negative reactions, each broken into three subcategories. Bales found in a typical adult task group that twenty-five percent of the communication could be classified as positive social-emotional reactions; whereas twelve percent of the communication acts could be classified as negative social-emotional reactions. Thus, a "good" group would maintain approximately a two to one ratio between positive and negative comments.

TABLE 2.1
ADAPTATION OF BALES'S INTERACTION PROCESS ANALYSIS*

Major Categories	Subcategories	Percentage of Communication Acts
SOCIAL	*Shows solidarity*, raises others' status, gives help, rewards.	
Positive Reactions	*Shows tension release*, jokes, laughs, shows satisfaction.	25
	Shows agreement, shows passive acceptance, understands, concurs, complies.	
	Disagrees, shows passive rejection, formality, withholds help.	
Negative Reactions	*Shows tension*, asks for help, withdraws out of field.	12
	Shows antagonism, deflates others' status, defends or asserts self.	
TASK	*Gives suggestion*, direction, implying autonomy for other.	
Answers	*Gives opinion*, evaluation, analysis, expresses feeling, wish.	56
	Gives information, orientation, repeats, clarifies, confirms.	
	Asks for information, orientation, repetition, confirmation.	
Questions	*Asks for opinion*, evaluation, analysis, expression of feeling.	7
	Asks for suggestion, direction, possible ways of action.	

*Reprinted from *Interaction Process Analysis* by R. F. Bales, by permission of The University of Chicago Press. © 1976 by The University of Chicago. Reprinted also by permission of author.

The task dimension also consists of two major categories: answers and questions. The three subcategories of each of these include reciprocal pairs in the areas of information, opinions, and suggestions. Bales found in a typical adult task group that 56 percent of the communication acts could be classified as answers; whereas 7 percent could be called questions. Therefore, a task group maintains about a two to one ratio between the task and social dimensions; however, an eight to one ratio between answers and questions may be too great. Bales argued that a group attempts to maintain equilibrium through three stages on the way to solving a problem. The first stage, which he called orientation, is that in which the members arrive at a common definition of the problem. The second phase—evaluation—is the stage in which the group works out a common standard for assessing the problem; and the third phase—control—deals with the members' struggles for status as the group attempts to accomplish its task.

For the last twenty years, Ernest G. Bormann and his graduate students at the University of Minnesota have been systematically studying the communication behavior of small groups, particularly task-oriented groups. The body of research that has evolved has come to be known as the Minnesota Studies in Small Group Communication. The research findings from Minnesota were first reported in 1969 in Bormann's book, *Discussion and Group Methods*. An update of the Minnesota research is contained in the second edition (Bormann 1975).

After a number of years of teaching and research using Dewey's approach to group discussion, Bormann became dissatisfied with the rationalistic assumptions that are implicit in the step-by-step thought-pattern models that Dewey's reflective-thinking procedure inspired. Bormann and his students set up leaderless group discussions (LGD) and began to study them scientifically in order to determine how small groups form and make decisions, with special emphasis on the communication behaviors that are associated with each development. Their research efforts produced one of the richest and most widely used explanations of how people communicate in groups in making decisions.

The genesis of Bormann's theory is Bales's equilibrium theory of groups. Bormann felt that Bales's use of both task and social dimensions and the constant tug and pull between them was a useful place to begin, but he also felt that it was important to be able to describe the interplay of these two dimensions over time. After ten years of scientifically observing zero-history, or test-tube, groups discuss and complete tasks, Bormann set forth what we will call a role-emergence theory of small groups. He found that two kinds of group tension existed: *primary* and *secondary*. Primary tension is the formal uneasiness that every group member feels when a meeting is called. Secondary tension, a more serious kind, occurs later in the discussion and deals primarily with role struggles, especially struggles for leadership. Bormann and his students found that group members "try on" various group roles and that the group, through a series of rewarding and punishing communication acts, fits people into certain roles. The Minnesota studies also discovered that this role emergence followed noticeable patterns.

We have all experienced the phenomenon that Bormann has labeled primary tension. When a group of people first come into a room and sit down for a meeting, there is a lot of social tension. There are long periods of silence, people struggle to find light topics to discuss, everyone is very careful not to offend anyone else. This is especially true if the group is meeting for the first time. The research at the University of Minnesota indicates that primary tension is broken when somebody finds a common base for humor. This person will many times emerge in the role of tension releaser. Most groups can break primary tension but secondary tension seems to be a more consistent and serious problem. If primary tension is marked by silence, secondary tension is marked by loudness. Verbal and nonverbal signs of disagreement can often lead to open antagonism and hostility. Bormann's research indicates that there is no set formula that groups can use for resolving secondary tension, that each group must develop its own scheme for handling these disagreements and personality conflicts. A good deal of this secondary tension is often caused by a struggle for leadership. A discussion of the role of leader and other group roles is presented in Chapters 5 and 6.

Groups develop different tolerance levels for handling social conflicts. Some groups can accomplish work amid a great deal of bickering, while other groups must resolve all elements of secondary tension before they can go about their task. Thus, each group will establish a base line for social conflict such that when it is exceeded work will stop, and the group will focus on the elimination of social tension. In their observation of leaderless zero-history groups, Bormann (1975, 176–95) and his students did not find a lock-step or sequential development of a social dimension in work groups. Instead they observed that groups went through primary tension each time they met and suffered secondary tension at irregular intervals throughout the group's history. They found that successful groups developed ways of handling this tension, and that when the leadership role was resolved, the more severe aspects of secondary social tension disappeared.

In keeping with Bormann's belief that lock-stepped rational models such as Dewey's did not reflect ways in which groups made decisions, Fisher (1970) studied both LGD test-tube groups in the lab and real decision-making groups in corporations and churches in order to see if there is a natural pattern that groups follow in reaching a decision. By observing the communication patterns of a number of decision-making groups, Fisher determined that groups go through four basic stages in arriving at a decision. He labeled them orientation, conflict, emergence, and reinforcement. Typical communicative behavior during the orientation stage includes showing agreement, being tentative with assertions, and seeking to clarify points of information. During this stage, group members tend to be ambiguous about the proposal. During the conflict phase, on the other hand, members express disagreement, substantiate their beliefs on a given proposal, and generally align themselves on the favorable or unfavorable side.

The third phase, emergence, sees a reduction in the polarization and in the strength of disagreement; in essence, people who opposed the original proposal now become more ambiguous toward it. The final phase, reinforcement, emphasizes consensus by group members on the proposal at hand and, in fact, produces a tension-releasing phase in which members celebrate their agreement in cheerful verbal interaction (Fisher, 1970 140–45). Subsequently, speech communication scholars including Gouran and Baird (1972), Putnam (1979), Poole (1981, 1983), and Hirokawa (1983) have described the rich and complex communication process by which groups discuss and solve problems.

Although it is true that each task group tends to develop its own unique way or pattern for reaching group decisions, research in small group communication does allow us to describe a likely process by which the task and social dimensions of a group occur during the decision-making process.

Stage One: Orientation (Task); Primary Tension (Social). It seems clear that all human groups in all cultures, when they first get together, experience initial periods of awkwardness. You certainly can remember times in which you were one of the first persons to show up at a meeting and you carried on a rather nervous conversation with a few other people, but usually the conversation was marked by a long period of silence. Even when your task group formally turned attention to the purpose of the meeting, conversation was awkward. Bormann's research indicates that this is when somebody can release the tension through a humorous comment. The humor that seems to work best is that which relates to the common predicament that all members find themselves in. Once the initial tension is broken, a group tends to devote a lot of energy to orienting themselves to the task. It is at this time that many questions about the purpose of the group, the agenda for the particular meeting, and so forth are asked. In fact, Bales's research suggests that asking a lot of questions to help the group get oriented correctly is very important. He found that successful groups asked more questions than groups who weren't successful. Not all groups complete the orientation stage the first time they attempt it. In fact, they may have to return to this stage several times before completing their task. Also, some groups appear to do an inadequate job as a group, in part, because they did not properly or thoroughly orient themselves to their work.

Stage Two: Conflict (Task); Secondary Tension (Social).   Stage Two of a task group is the most complex and difficult portion of a problem-solving group's existence. At the task level, group members are suggesting ideas about the problem and these ideas are being accepted or rejected by the group. Simultaneously, there is a form of a hidden agenda which is secondary tension at the social level. As the Minnesota research indicates, members are trying out for leadership roles in the group, not by simply saying, "I want to lead," but by demonstrating knowledge of the topic, social maturity, and self-confidence in the way they suggest ideas and evaluate ideas of others. In Chapter 8, we go into much greater detail about the kind of conflict that is occurring in Stage Two, but now it is important to note that the group can become so fearful of Stage Two ideational conflict and Stage Two role conflict that the group will take flight. Poole's (1983, 330) research indicates that these "breakpoints" frequently occur as groups go through a decision-making process. He identified three types of breakpoints: (1) *normal breakpoints*—times when the group will stop work (scheduled 9:15 A.M. coffee break) or times when the group switches from one topic to another; (2) *delays*—instances when the group continues to resummarize its analysis of the part of a problem it has already completed, causing a delay in moving to discussion of the next major part of the problem; and (3) *disruptions*—occasions in the process of trying to move on to solutions, when the group may abandon its original orientation to the problem and try to create a new structure. Many times, these types of breakpoints that Poole describes at the task level may signal that the group is experiencing a secondary tension episode in which the leadership situation is unstable.

In addition to the three breakpoints that can occur in the task dimension of the group, groups will also experience two break moments that can occur throughout a group's discussion, but frequently occur because of the tension of ideational conflict and role formation. One is an *encounter moment* when a group member will start discussing his or her personal agenda; another is a *CR moment* when the group members will discuss their professional identity. We will discuss these later in the chapter. Our point here is that, generally, the more ideational conflict a group can tolerate without taking flight, the better the group decision will be.

Stage Three: Emergence (Task); Recurring Primary and Secondary Tension (Social).   Even though it would seem rational and orderly that a group would discuss the nature and causes of a problem before they would entertain possible solutions to a problem, not all discussion groups proceed in this manner. Sometimes a group member will prepare in advance of a group meeting his or her solution, and introduce and argue for it early in the discussion—long before the group has had a chance to discuss the parameters of the problem. In situations like this, decision-making groups tend to do a lot of bouncing back and forth between Stages Two and Three. They may experience several bouts of secondary tension, and there will be delays and disruptions. Hirokawa (1983) discovered that groups that start with the problem (Stage Two) and then proceed to solutions are more successful, on average, than groups that start with possible solutions and work their way back. So it would seem that, where possible, groups should try to get through Stage Two before going to Stage Three. In Chapters 6 and 8, we make specific recommendations on how to improve group decision making.

Stage Four: Reinforcement (Task). Once a group decision appears to be emerging, there seems to be very little social tension. The group compliments itself on what a fine solution it settled on and generally spends some time assessing the impact of its solution. Groups will generally spend a good deal of time working for consensus and group member commitment. Oftentimes, a group decision will emerge by a bare majority, and then in Stage Four the group will attempt to convince everybody to get behind the solution and be a good team player in supporting it.

In doing research on the task and social dimensions of work groups, it became apparent to small group scholars that not all group communication could be accounted for by looking at problem-solving talk and role talk. As we indicated earlier, the two additional types of talk are person-to-person talk and professional-to-professional talk. We discovered that the hidden agenda of a task group contains not only role struggles but also interpersonal tension among group members. Moreover, these feelings sometimes surface when the group is not working on its task. Thus, some researchers started creating groups whose sole task was to discuss members' feelings toward other members. From this research, we found a second generic type of group called the encounter group, and we were also able to understand more of the hidden agenda of task groups.

ENCOUNTER GROUP PROCESS

In our study of small discussion groups, we have long been aware of the interpersonal dimension and the effects that interpersonal relations have on the productivity of the group. Moreno (1934), was one of the first scholars to explain the interpersonal conflicts that occur in small groups. His attraction-repulsion theory stated simply that we tend to like some group members more than others; that, in fact, some members tend to be "stars" in that they are liked by most in the group while others became "isolates" in that hardly anyone likes them.

By the 1940s, we began to realize that the interpersonal or social dimension of groups was far more complex than simply liking-disliking. Moreover, there seemed to be a hidden agenda during group discussions that needed to be uncovered and explained. At the National Training Laboratories in Group Development (NTL) at Bethel, Maine, in the summers of the late

1940s and early 1950s, researchers began to uncover this hidden agenda, at first quite by accident. They discovered that when you took away the task assignment of the discussion group, the group soon developed a new task and started to discuss how the members themselves related to each other. These early training groups, or "t" groups, later evolved into sensitivity, therapy, and general encounter groups which dealt exclusively with self-development.

Gerald Phillips (1966), in *Communication and the Small Group,* explained the importance of understanding the hidden agenda of interpersonal needs that each person brings to the group if we are to have successful communication and accomplish group goals. William C. Schutz (1966), postulated that there are three basic interpersonal needs that each person expects his or her group to satisfy. These are inclusion, control, and affection. In general, inclusion deals with the feeling of being "in" or "out" of the group; control deals with "top" or "bottom," i.e., status in the group; and affection deals with "close" or "far," i.e., "cold" or "warm." Schutz feels that people need others to whom they can give, and from whom they can receive, these three fundamental interpersonal needs. Thus, he called his theory Fundamental Interpersonal Relations Orientation (FIRO). We will explain this theory in relation to group communication behavior in greater detail in Chapter 7.

By the 1960s, the focus of encounter groups had shifted from learning about people in groups to learning about one's self, with the encounter group as the basic means of self-discovery. Carl Rogers and other clinical psychologists began holding group therapy sessions for "normals." In the 1960s, college students were deeply interested in self-growth, and encounter groups were one of the chief means by which they accomplished their personal goals. By the 1970s, it had also been discovered that encounter groups not only had the potential to produce self-growth, but also self-destruction. Lieberman, Yalom, and Miles (1973, 264), in *Encounter Groups: First Facts,* document some of the psychic damage that can occur as the result of encounter group sessions. They point out that several different leadership styles in encounter groups lead to substantial harm to group members. The leadership of encounter groups is best left to trained clinical psychologists: the use of this group process as a parlor game can definitely be harmful to some participants.

After studying the communication of encounter groups, we have been able to describe its stages of development and have some understanding of why this group process has such an impact on its participants. A typical encounter group has as its goal the personal growth of its individual members. People join encounter groups to learn about themselves and how they are perceived by others. When an encounter group is formed, it has no formal agenda or structure. We have discovered that when a group of people are put together with no agenda a rather predictable pattern tends to occur.

Bennis and Shepherd (1956) described encounter groups in terms of the two major phases of dependence and interdependence, with three subphases in each major phase. The choice of goal and the dependence of the members on their trainer mark the first subphase of an encounter group. As an encounter group moves to the second subphase, the group members are in conflict with one another over the trainer. Bennis and Shepherd found that encounter group members deal first with the problem of authority and then with the problem of intimacy. During this conflict, group members divide into three categories: members who look to the trainer for leadership; members who are really dependent on the leader but who solve this problem by attacking him or her; and members who are independent and are not threatened by a leaderless group that has no agenda. Task groups and consciousness-raising groups do not exhibit the three-way conflict behavior that is so typical of encounter groups. Encounter groups move from dependence to independence to interdependence and in the process strip away the role facades of group members, thus revealing their increasingly "naked" selves.

The task group in its pure form requires the taking on of roles for the successful completion of work. The pure CR group focuses on a new sociopolitical identity or a professional identity, with the effect of fusing self with group identities. A pure encounter group has the people themselves as the agenda, and the group process focuses on the individual's feelings and beliefs, with the end product being self-growth. Although these three generic types of groups do exist in their pure form, most of your experience in groups is probably of the hybrid variety.

Many business retreat seminars and religious retreats, which are held away from normal sites, form groups which blend these processes of CR and encounter. If a group at one of these retreats focuses on "what it's like to be a manager at Xerox," the communication process will more than likely produce a consciousness-raising group. However, if the topic a group focuses on is personal values that are stressed in the work environment, the group communication could produce an encounter group. Likewise, at a religious retreat, if the topic is "What is it like to be a Christian?" it will be CR; however, if this kind of group focuses its members' religious values on a topic such as abortion, it would be encounter. The biggest single indication that you are in an encounter group is self-disclosure about you and your values, as well as feelings about others in the group. When you moved into a dorm as a freshman or into off-campus housing, you may have found yourself talking all night long with several of your roommates about your personal beliefs. In these discussions you may have disclosed many things about yourself. Also, as you continued to live together, you may have become more and more open about what habits and values are irksome to you.

Many of the self-help groups that have become popular over the last thirty years are hybrid encounter-CR groups (e.g., Parents Without Partners, Alcoholics Anonymous, and Weight Watchers). The self-help groups definitely have a "we-they" syndrome, characteristic of CR, in which the villain is alcohol or fatty foods as well as the people in society who tempt the group members to sin. These groups work very hard on creating a new identity of the sober alcoholic or the successful single parent. However, these groups also have intense encounter moments, in which there is clear indication that members will disclose personal feelings and beliefs to the group.

Everyday work groups in organizations also have encounter moments. These are times in the group discussion when the conversation breaks from the task at hand and centers on the personal feelings or beliefs of an individual member or the group as a whole. Small group researchers have identified this phenomenon as the hidden agenda that periodically surfaces when group members discuss personal issues. The management of this agenda is so important that a group role called the social-emotional leader exists in all successful task groups. We will discuss this role in detail in Chapter 6. It appears that the amount of personal disclosure, or encounter moments, or indeed full-scale encounter group sessions, appear to vary from occupation to occupation and even from work group to work group.

Army combat teams, firefighting teams, police units, and medical emergency work groups who face danger together and are highly interdependent on each other for their survival need to self-disclose. Usually these groups demand high levels of personal disclosure on the part of the membership. The group members generally argue that they need intimate knowledge of each other so that they can trust each other in emergency situations. It is common for members of these types of groups to report that their work-group colleagues know them better than their own families do. Joseph Wambaugh's book, *The Choir Boys,* certainly demonstrates this reality for police officers.

Many work groups can find themselves involved in full-blown encounter group sessions that spontaneously occur because of the availability of "down time." *When a work group is kept together but does not have work to do, it will make itself the agenda.* The group will either talk about itself in terms of its professional identity, and thus generate a CR session; or it will focus on the team members as individuals in terms of their values and feelings, thus becoming an encounter group. The Japanese work groups, for example, have a much higher expectation than American work groups that members will play together as well as work together. Japanese workers and families may actually take vacations together, whereas a group in an American company may find involvement at the personal level in cocktail parties, golf outings, or after-work social hours. However, if any collection of five or six people leave their work environments for a common vacation (i.e., sharing food and housing), encounter group sessions are almost inevitable. Two movies that vividly depict this phenomenon are *Four Seasons* and *The Breakfast Club;* but if you have ever taken a group vacation over spring break, you no doubt have experienced the self-disclosure that occurs and the social conflict that tends to arise, which are the anticipated communication behaviors of encounter-group sessions.

Although you may not participate in a clinical encounter group run by qualified trainers, it is apparent that in the course of working in groups within organizations you will be involved in spontaneous encounter group sessions. While these sessions may not go through all the stages that a formal encounter group does, which has personal growth as its expressed agenda, we believe it is important for you to recognize the communication patterns that are unique to encounter groups. This will help you to better understand *encounter moments* that occur in your everyday work group.

While Bennis and Shepherd sketched out the macrocommunication patterns of encounter groups, Edward Mabry identified microverbal exchanges that characterize stages of an encounter group. He found and labeled three stages of interaction in encounter groups—boundary-seeking, ambivalence, and actualization (Mabry 1975, 305) after observing the following nine kinds of communication behavior: antagonistic, assertive-supportive, dominant-assertive, aggressive-assertive, assertive, reactive to group laughter, task-determinative, reactive to tension, and supportive (Mabry 1975, 303).

Stage One: Boundary Seeking.   This first stage is dominated by antagonism, task-determining activity, and assertiveness, and, as Bennis and Shepherd have pointed out, most of this is directed at the trainer or is part of the dialogue about the trainer's role. Mabry labeled this stage boundary-seeking since the group has not yet resolved questions regarding its structure, functions, and overall direction. When twelve people sit in a circle and look at each other uncomfortably for several minutes, some member soon begins to break the tension with humor. However, before long somebody becomes irritated. He or she is angry because the trained leader (who has been through this before), refuses to give directions and set an agenda, thereby allowing the emergence of a new leader. When the trainer does not take charge, some of the members form a coalition and attack the trainer for his or her lack of leadership. Another coalition soon forms and defends the trainer's right not to lead. Rebellion reigns supreme until the group members discover that they are free to form their own structure and have their own unique experience.

Stage Two: Ambivalence.   Mabry's Stage Two is dominated by types of communication behavior that fit into the categories of aggressive-assertive and supportive. These findings are consistent with the rhetorical descriptions that Bennis and Shepherd provide of the authority dependence that an encounter group goes through and the brief enchantment that follows when the group's dependence on the trainer has ended. Once the group members realize that they are on their own, they immediately become infatuated with each other and go on a "false honeymoon." They believe that they have now resolved their conflicts and put away their "false faces." They take turns pointing out how phony they were when the group began and how honest and open they are with each other now. The false honeymoon is short-lived.

Stage Three: Actualization.   The decline in supportiveness accurately parallels the beginning of verbal conflict that Bennis and Shepherd found as characteristic of what they described as disenchantment-flight. Mabry's study also found that toward the end of the encounter group, reactions to group laughter increased. The group begins by an intense search for the true identity of each individual group member. As intimate disclosures on the part of some members occur and others refuse to be equally open, the group again breaks into two coalitions in which one side pushes for even more interpersonal disclosure and the other opposes it. This is the period in the life of an encounter group when many people experience self-growth; however, this is also the period in which emotions are rubbed raw, in some cases producing emotional damage to individuals. It is during this period that the skills of a trainer are needed, preferably of one who is a licensed clinical psychologist or psychiatrist. This emotional intensity finally produces catharsis and the group generally finds itself feeling very close and interdependent. In fact, it was this euphoric afterglow that produced a significant number of encounter group junkies during the late 1960s and early 1970s. These people went from one group experience to the next, and some of them began to call themselves "trainers" and started their own groups. When properly supervised, the encounter-group communication process can produce what Bennis and

Shepherd call "valid communication," which can and does lead to personal growth.

Mabry's description of the communication interaction that occurs throughout an encounter group provides evidence to support the idea that the encounter-group process first described by Bennis and Shepherd is a fundamentally different small group process than the communication behavior that occurs in pure CR groups and task groups.

Bales's research at Harvard and Bormann's research at Minnesota have clearly demonstrated that not all important group communication can be explained by problem-solving talk, role talk, or person-to-person talk. There exists a fourth kind of group talk which relates to the group members' common symbolic identity (Bales 1970; Bormann 1975). The communication that tends to generate this group feeling of oneness Bales and Bormann have called "group fantasies." Bales (1970, 152) describes the effect of a group fantasy as "stimulating in each of its members a feeling he has entered a new realm of reality—a world of heroes, villains, saints, and enemies—a drama. . . . The culture of a group is a fantasy established in the past, which is acted upon in the present." When group members focus exclusively on their common identity, we get a third generic type of small group which has come to be called the "consciousness-raising" group.

CONSCIOUSNESS-RAISING GROUP PROCESS

In the early 1960s, feminist groups discovered a group process that was extremely powerful in galvanizing a group of women together in a sisterhood that had a common symbolic wholeness. The women who attended these group meetings had their consciousness raised about their socialized identity as women. They began to see the American society as male-dominated and oppressive toward women. As women's liberation organizations began to form in the late 1960s, these group consciousness-raising sessions became central to the internal development of the women's liberation movement (Morgan 1970).

Other radical revolutionary groups that formed in the 1960s began to adopt the women's technique of holding consciousness-raising sessions. They also reported that the CR process was effective, not only in creating new political values and revolutionary commitment, but also in the actualization of those value structures in society. By the late 1970s, political and religious groups on both the left and the right had adopted the use of CR sessions as an integral part of producing converts to their political causes.

In the late 1960s, a President's council was formed to study the problem of student unrest. In their report to the President, the council members expressed their concern about the processes that had produced the fanatical commitment to causes that was demonstrated by revolutionary acts committed against the government. (Report of the President's Council on Student Unrest). In the 1970s, our country was again shocked by the fanatical commitment of people to a cause. This time the organizations or groups were religious cults such as the Moonies and the Hare Krishnas. The world was shocked in 1978 when over nine hundred members of Reverend Jim Jones's

People's Temple committed mass suicide. Jones had made extensive use of CR sessions in the running of his People's Temple, and once again there was a public cry to understand this process.

In 1970, James Chesebro, John Cragan, and Patricia McCullough conducted a field study in Minneapolis, Minnesota, of gay radical revolutionary groups in an attempt to characterize the consciousness-raising group process. They defined consciousness raising as: "A personal, face-to-face interaction which appears to create new psychological orientations for those involved in the process" (Chesebro, Cragan, and McCullough 1973, 136). These speech communication scholars found that a small group consciousness-raising session was quite different from a task group or an encounter group. They found that if like people gather together for the purpose of discussing a common social, political, or religious value structure, certain predictable communication patterns occur.

For the last fifteen years, communication researchers have been studying CR groups in an attempt to understand the role of CR processes in "ordinary" work groups that exist in business organizations. We are not alone in our interest in CR. In the 1960s CR was the tool of political revolutionary groups. In the 1970s CR was used systematically by many religious groups. In the 1980s major American corporations are using this process as a means for creating, heightening, and sustaining an employee's identity with his or her work group and company. Some of the more visible corporations are Amway, Mary Kay Cosmetics, and Williams Insurance Company. However, the popularity of Japanese management theory (Theory Z) and the success Japanese workers have sustained in the areas of productivity and quality control have caused many more American companies to adopt the use of formal or informal CR to build esprit de corp in work groups. A best selling book of the 1980s, *In Search of Excellence* (Peters and Waterman 1982), punctuates the importance of building effective work teams.

A major way in which team pride is built is through the small group communication process of consciousness raising. In addition, companies periodically bring small work groups together for a companywide "rally." Not only will we describe the stages of CR in work groups but also the techniques that are used at rallies to make everybody feel they are part of a larger "we." This is true whether we're talking about Hitler's rallies in Nazi Germany, the national Democratic and Republican conventions held every four years in the United States, religious rallies held by Billy Graham or other ministers, or corporate rallies held by Amway or Mary Kay Cosmetics.

Stage One: Self-Realization of a New Identity. For consciousness-raising to occur, it is necessary for everybody in the group to possess the crucial characteristic that forms the basis for the discussion. A women's group must have only women in the group, while a men's group must have only men in it. Likewise, CR sessions on Christianity must contain only Christians, CR sessions on gay liberation must contain only gays, and so on. This CR process could also begin if a group consisted of students meeting to talk about university life, or firefighters discussing their identity as public employees. Thus, the first stage of consciousness raising begins with the group members establishing their credentials. This is often done through storytelling. A member will relate a personal story about oppression she has experienced because she is a woman, or because she is gay, or whatever. This story will stimulate other members to tell their stories. The stories heighten the excitement of the group, and there is much laughter and conversation as they establish that they are all of like mind. The personal stories generally depict the oppressor in dramatic fashion. For women's groups the oppressor would be a male chauvinist, for gays an ugly straight. For college students in an all-night CR session in a dorm, it may be the incompetent professor. The stories also portray the group members as distinct minorities dominated by a powerful oppressor, and the group members need to raise their consciousness about this societal evil so that they and their comrades can be liberated.

Organizations that are using CR sessions as a formal part of their management strategies will train team leaders in the techniques of CR. For example, if an Amway group is meeting, the trainer may encourage each member to tell stories about what he or she plans to do after having successfully sold Amway products. An organization that sells retirement homes in the Sun Belt of the United States might invite a married group of people in their fifties to dinner and after dinner encourage a discussion about the kind of retirement life they envision. If you have ever participated in a religious retreat, you will remember that you were broken up into small groups and your group leader began the discussion by encouraging people to share religious experiences. This technique will almost always produce Stage One of consciousness raising in which the group members realize they have a common group identity.

CR sessions can also start spontaneously without any group member intentionally trying to start one. A group of workers may be having lunch in the company cafeteria when one of the people at the table describes how tense it was going through a job performance interview with the supervisor. This story might spark a half-hour discussion in which group members contribute their experiences with job performance situations. Members usually find these to be very enjoyable discussions which are punctuated with humor and laughter. If a group of college students having lunch together discover they all received a Catholic education, having been taught by nuns and priests, they may spend the entire lunch hour taking turns telling humorous stories about the "theys": nuns and priests. A group of insurance salespeople attending an insurance convention may find that a lot of their conversation is the telling of stories in which they are the heroes, wrestling with the "theys." Nobody planned these discussions; they just got started. In fact, all professional conventions tend to produce a large number of CR sessions simply because all who attend the convention are part of the same profession (e.g., physicians, professors, etc.). Today in American corporation life, over 2,000 companies have formally instituted management structures which encourage CR sessions. These are companies that have adopted some form of quality circle program— a topic we will discuss later in the book. However, in most American companies, CR occurs among workers on a "hit or miss" basis. Most spontaneous CR sessions never get past Stage One or Two (Bolkum 1981). If the CR session gets past Stage One, you will know that very quickly because the type of communication of the discussion will change dramatically.

Stage Two: Group Identity through Polarization.   The laughter and storytelling of Stage One disappears and the group intensely discusses the nature of "the enemy." Rhetorically, this stage of the CR session is characterized by a "we-they" dichotomy. In a gay-liberation CR session the "we" would refer to liberated gays and the "they" to the oppressive "straight-dominated" society. This stage in a CR session often focuses in great detail on the nature of oppression and the specific identity of the oppressors. Thus, women's groups contain detailed discussions of the specific behaviors that constitute male chauvinism, while a college student group might discuss the lecturing and grading policies of the professor. As people continue to hold CR sessions, the polarization between the "we" and the "they" becomes greater.

In work groups within organizations, three types of "theys" can emerge in Stage Two of CR discussions. There are the *upward they,* the *lateral they,* and the *downward they.* The *upward they* is the boss—sometimes an immediate supervisor or sometimes the entire upper management of an organization. Many times when groups are doing a lot of CR, these discussions at Stage Two will contain rich, vivid descriptions of the "they." The supervisor might be called the "red pheasant" because of the way red pheasants look walking down the rows of a cornfield. When this label was first created, it may have been the result of workers imitating the pheasantlike walk of the boss, to the amusement of the group. While initially this may be a description by the "we" workers of the "they" boss, eventually the supervisor and workers can resolve the we-they polarization and all share in the joke. The boss may even take to wearing a T-shirt which designates him- or herself as the "red pheasant"! However, if there is a lot of conflict between the work group and the supervisor, the CR sessions may generate vicious descriptions that are kept secret from the boss. In working with groups in business and industry, we have run into descriptions of superiors such as "Attila the Hun," "The Ice Queen," "The Mumbler," and "Rose the Nose." Vicious descriptions can highlight some perceived power misuse on the part of the superior. The work group then has some fun with a person's behavioral mannerism, and the description is born and sustained.

All organizations have acquired nicknames, usually humorous, for the building that houses the upper management of the company. This is especially true if the home office is located in a town and regional offices are located throughout the country. In this type of situation, both workers and first-line supervisors can become a "we" versus the "they" at the top. At our university the central administration building is called Hovey Hall, but many professors when evaluating administrators' decision making refer to it as "Hovey Heaven." In part it is called "Hovey Heaven" because the rank and file believe this is what you do with incompetent professors—promote them to "Hovey Heaven." It is also called "Hovey Heaven" because central administrators tend to hover around decisions instead of making them. One Fortune 500 pharmaceutical company has a central administration building that has a reflecting pool in front of it and an escalator that works only when a person walks onto it. When sales personnel get together and become involved in a CR session, they refer to the home office as "the Taj Mahal," and have great fun describing the senior administrators floating around on their magic carpets. Another major American firm refers to its main office as "the Puzzle Palace."

Other names for home offices of American corporations that we have heard of are "the Head Shed," "the Square Donut," "Disney World East," "the Glass House," and "the Mindbenders Dungeon." These descriptions have the same commonality that the nicknames for supervisors have. The label weaves together some characteristic of the home office building and some frustrating characteristic of the decision making done by the administrators housed in the building.

When consciousness-raising groups are engaged in *lateral we-they* polarization discussions, they are generally talking about competing group situations. On campus this might be those students who live on the floor above you or in the dorm across the quad. It could be one sorority talking about another sorority. Sometimes it's students from one college describing students from a competing college. In the U.S. armed forces, it might be the "jarheads" versus the "swabbies" versus the "wingnuts," or "lifers" versus enlisted. In typical American business organizations, these we-they discussions will be about competing work groups such as sales, accounting, and marketing. These discussions generally revolve around the competency of the other group, the importance to the overall mission of the organization, and whether the group is receiving its fair share of financial rewards and promotions vis-à-vis the other group. As a student on campus you are often asked, "What is your major?" It soon becomes apparent that there is a stereotype of who belongs to each group, and competing groups have derogatory one-liners about your major. When you are in an organization, the question becomes "What department are you working in?" You will discover, if you haven't already, it is the same game as "What's your major?" Competing work groups have developed stereotypic descriptions that, in a derogatory way, describe that group's role in regard to the organization's mission.

The third type of we-they polarization that occurs in CR sessions is the *downward they,* characterized by a "bite-the-hand-that-feeds-you" dialogue. We have often observed that at the same time students are studying for finals and engaging in heavy CR sessions in which the professor (the *upward they*) is vilified, faculty are sitting in groups and consciousness raising about students (the *downward they*). The professors' conversations will mirror the students, in that they are describing ill-trained students who have trouble walking and thinking at the same time. Usually a *downward they* Stage Two conversation will stop if one professor reminds the others that they are being paid to teach students and that, if they are competent professionals, they should improve the students' performance.

We believe that *downward they* CR discussions occur in all organizations. Physicians will have derogatory discussions among themselves about their patients. As one surgical nurse once said to us, "if you only knew what we said about your body after you had been anesthetized!" Army units or police officers often have CR sessions in which civilians are the object of ridicule. Data processors regularly "rag" about the stupidity of "N-users." We often feel guilty when we realize we wouldn't have a work group, if it weren't for the *downward theys.* That's why we label this kind of CR talk as "biting the hand that feeds you."

It appears that new work groups and new members in work groups want and enjoy spending time on Stages One and Two. It also appears to be true that the more consciousness raising a group does, the wider the symbolic gap between the "we" and the "they" becomes, and the more difficult it will be for the "we" and the "they" to work in concert together. Established work groups, which have stable membership and have done similar kinds of work for a number of years, spend less time in Stages One and Two. They have developed very efficient nicknames for their "theys" and do not appear to need to constantly rehash them. Instead, most of their CR talk occurs in Stages Three and Four (DeVuono 1982).

Stage Three: Establishment of New Values for the Group.   We have discovered that Stage Three of a political activist group is dominated by a dialogue which is essentially a constant comparison and contrast of the oppressor's established value structure with the new values the CR group hopes to promulgate. Gay groups might reject "straight" society's value structure and argue instead that the quality of the relationship is more important. Women's groups might compare their belief in equal pay for equal work with the societal practice in which men receive more money than women in the same job classification. A CR group will often transport itself into the future and vividly describe what the new society would look like if its values were accepted. A Christian CR group might envision a world free of sin and discuss that utopia with great excitement, while a black CR group might see a country free of racism.

Work groups, particularly work groups that work under tremendous deadline pressure or face mutual danger, will frequently engage in intense Stage Three talk. These conversations invariably produce consensus on the part of the group members as to the unique abilities that allow their group to be successful. These Stage Three CR sessions generally produce nicknames and slogans for the group. In an American organization, this generally leads to the making of T-shirts and bumper stickers that display the name, logo, and slogan of the group. Police SWAT units; hospital emergency, surgical, and intensive-care units; fire department teams (ladder companies, rescue squads, etc.); television news teams; data processing system-design units; and the sales teams of almost any corporation are likely groups who will engage in heavy CR sessions after their crisis-oriented work is completed. CR communication is so dramatic and intense that it is a major feature of novels and movies (e.g., Dolly Parton, Jane Fonda, and Lily Tomlin in the movie *Nine to Five;* Joseph Wambaugh's novel *Choir Boys;* Dennis Smith's novel *Engine Number Six*).

It is difficult to predict when a group is formed what attributes are unique to it that will make the "we" better than the "they." Ideally, trained small group discussants should focus on the job-related skills that the individuals possess and on good teamwork, which can account for their high productivity. However, since CR group communication is spontaneous, and generally engaged in by people who are not familiar with small group theory, the qualities that the group settles on are unique and may have no relationship to their work behavior. The group may decide it is good because it is all white or black, all male or female, all Italian or Irish, all Catholic or Jewish, etc. When this occurs in an American work group, problems generally arise.

An example of how extreme a group can become occurred in a midwestern fire department we were studying. The city had a large Swedish-American population, so it was not surprising that by pure chance an engine company of five firefighters who were assigned to the same firehouse were all of Swedish descent: Johnson, Peterson, Olson, Larson, and Anderson. In Stage One CR discussions they began to share common stories of being raised in a Swedish-American family. In Stage Two conversation, they talked about competing *lateral-they* fire teams not being as good as they were. By the time they got to Stage Three talk they became convinced that it was their common Swedish heritage that enabled them to be so good at putting out fires. This led them to name themselves the "Oly Brigade." They made up T-shirts for themselves, they cooked Swedish meals at the firehouse, and their menus were written in the Swedish language. They even developed a team cheer that was completely in Swedish. Finally, they moved to Stage Four consciousness raising and went public. At the next fire, they wore their special T-shirts, had blue and yellow ribbons streaming from the back of the truck, and arrived at the scene of the fire singing their Swedish cheer, much to the chagrin of the other fire teams and fire chief of the city. The "Oly Brigade" was an excellent fire team. They did good work, but they attributed their work success to the fact they were Swedish, and their rivalry with other groups had become too competitive. Thus, the group was disbanded by order of the fire chief.

It appears that a continuing problem with CR discussions involving emergency work groups is that they raise their consciousness too high and become elitist. They become increasingly difficult to manage, demanding special privileges because they are known for their good work, and they cause morale problems among work groups who are not as intense. Yet the potential benefits in terms of productivity output that come from consciousness raising are such that many American and Japanese organizations have made CR sessions a normal part of the work place for even nonemergency and nonsales work groups. Quality circle programs are knowingly, or unknowingly, encouraging CR sessions to occur among their problem-solving groups (quality circles).

Stage Four: Acting Out New Consciousness.   Chesebro, Cragan, and McCullough, in their study of radical gay groups, found that the final stage of consciousness raising dealt with how gays might relate to other oppressed people who were seeking a cultural revolution. More generally, many times the last stage of a CR session might deal with specific action a group might take to further its own cause. When a professor finds six students knocking on his or her door with specific demands about how a course should be changed, chances are the students participated in a CR session the night before which led them to confront the professor. Much of the zealot behavior we see flowing from organized groups of people may be traced directly to their participation in consciousness-raising sessions that have helped build their new social identity.

Some organized groups of people combine CR sessions with complete social isolation and continuous fear of punishment. This combination tends to produce bizarre behavior in which people are transported into a sociopolitical identity that is far removed from society's norms, and in which they become capable of behavior that the rest of us would not contemplate. The SLA's transformation of Patty Hearst into "Tanya," and the documented techniques used by the Moonies and Jim Jones, vividly demonstrate the ability of CR sessions, when used in combination with other techniques, to produce significant changes in the sociopolitical identities of the people who participate in them.

It seems clear from our observation of American corporations, that CR communication is a regular and integral part of all work group communication. It directly affects the group member's sense of identification and pride. Stage Four CR talk is easy to spot because it is filled with suggestions on how the group can advance or sustain its identity. Sometimes this conversation becomes a formal planning session for the group and begins to transform itself into a task group.

In weekly sales meetings the salespeople are clearly in Stage Four CR when they repeat slogans that are directed toward the goal of selling more products. This is the "rah-rah" part of the conversation right before they go out the door to sell. This is the same type of communication that occurs at the end of a high-school pep rally (dancing around the fire, etc.). National real estate franchises in the United States frequently engage in Stage Four CR at the end of weekly meetings. At Toyota and other Japanese companies, the work groups in their manufacturing plants participate in Stage Four CR each morning before they begin their workday. All organizations periodically bring together the organization's work groups, who have been consciousness raising on their own, to a company rally—for the purpose of reinforcing that they are all part of the large "we" of an organization. This has the effect of reducing all three types of we-they conflict: upward, lateral, and downward. When the small group CR sessions are synchronized with the large group rally, dramatic short-term effects can be created in terms of raising the consciousness of all organizational members. Thus, it is important to know how the communication process of a rally works in coordination with the small group process of consciousness raising. This rally process is described in Chapter 10. But in this chapter, we want to stitch together the three generic types of groups—task, encounter, and CR—into one integrated model which depicts communication in everyday work groups.

AN INTEGRATED APPROACH TO SMALL GROUP COMMUNICATION: A MODEL

After many years of observing everyday problem-solving groups in organizations, we are now convinced that the three generic types of group processes (task, encounter, and CR) fuse together in a rather complex, but understandable, way. At a very practical level, we believe that there are four different types of group talk that constitute all the essential communication that you need to comprehend in order to be an effective small group member. Figure 2.2 displays our integrated model of small group communication.

Quadrant 1 is problem-solving talk. Here we have the orientation, conflict, emergence, and reinforcement stages that Fisher has found. When problem-solving talk is processed effectively, the amount of understanding and agreement in the group increases, and this directly affects the group outputs we described in Chapter 1 (productivity, membership satisfaction, and consensus). Quadrant 2 is role-formation talk. This type of talk forms our five major roles, and once the group is formed, this is our role-to-role communi-

FIGURE 2.2
AN INTEGRATED MODEL OF SMALL GROUP
COMMUNICATION: FIELD OF COMMUNICATION INTERACTION

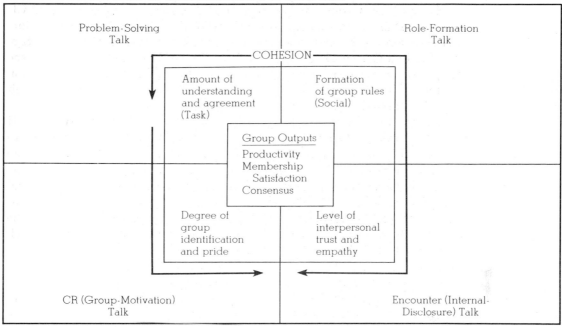

cation—such as lieutenant-to-leader talk. And, of course, when group roles are developed and properly played, group outputs are positively affected. Quadrant 3 depicts encounter talk. These are the interpersonal disclosures that are necessary to increase empathy and trust among group members. While this level varies from one group to another depending on their type of work, when it is at its proper level, productivity, membership satisfaction, and consensus are increased. Quadrant 4 is CR talk. This, of course, affects the degree of group identification and pride, which in turn affects group outputs. When a group has sufficient understanding and agreement, role formation, interpersonal trust and empathy, and group identification and pride, we have a cohesive work group that has high levels of productivity, membership satisfaction, and consensus.

The perfect group is easier to describe than to create. When a person is actually participating in a real group, it is extremely difficult to observe the development of various communication stages in the group. There are, however, some rough benchmarks to help determine what is going on at any given time. These benchmarks are designed to help you assess the four types of talk that occur in groups and help you determine if the correct amounts of each are occurring in your various work groups.

Benchmark One: Amount of Understanding and Agreement.   Both Bales and Fisher have found the first stage of a task group to be orientation. The communication during this stage should contain a lot of questions so that the group will understand the nature of the task. There also should be tacit agreement that everybody accepts the general goals of the group. If a group does not have genuine agreement initially, disagreement and conflict over goals will arise in later discussions, and the group will have to return to its orientation stage. What this means is that the group experienced a "pseudo-orientation" phase. Many of the members probably held back their feelings at the beginning of the discussion because they felt socially awkward. The difficulty with interpreting the second stage of a task group—labeled ideational conflict by Fisher and evaluation by Bales—is determining whether the misunderstandings and disagreements are really about the task, or whether they are the manifestation of the role struggle for leadership that Bormann called secondary tension. As indicated above, Bales provides some suggested ratios between positive and negative actions, and between the task and social dimensions. Therefore, if group members constantly agree to everything, the group will experience a "pseudo-orientation" phase and ideational disagreements will need to occur if it is ever to get into the second stage of its development.

Task group communication is very complex. Problem-solving talk and role-formation talk are occurring simultaneously, while CR talk and encounter talk tend to stand out from the task-related discussion. In fact, we have argued that work groups have natural breakpoints in their discussion: sometimes encounter moments; at other times, CR moments; and at still other times, group flight. For example, a group could be deeply involved in the conflict stage of problem-solving talk when the rash of ideas becomes so intense that the group spontaneously breaks from the task discussion. One of the group members begins a "CR moment" by ventilating about the supervisor who had given them this task. For the next few moments, the group is in Stage Two polarization as its members villify their supervisor in a classic upward-they moment. After this ventilation, the group may then return to the ideational conflict with renewed zest to fight it through. So secondary tension in the social dimension and conflict in the task dimension can often produce CR moments. But it is also possible that the stress of problem solving can produce an encounter moment—such as a situation where a group member discloses how frustrated his or her spouse is about the amount of time being devoted to this research project. Such a disclosure might cause the group to break from their task to spend time in interpersonal discussion about themselves. Finally, the pressure of group problem-solving work may cause a group to take flight to a topic that has nothing to do with any one of the four dimensions of group talk: it is not encounter, CR, role, or problem-solving communication; instead, it is procrastinating chit-chat about such general topics as weather or sports, allowing the group to take a "break" in place.

Sometimes groups are so afraid of interpersonal conflict, either for fear of losing their jobs or because they can't stand to see people argue, that they will agree to almost any suggestion. Eventually time will run out on this group in that their productivity will be quite poor. Thus, while understanding and agreement are the necessary objectives of a task group, if there is too much of it something is probably wrong. For any task group to produce a worthwhile product, a certain amount of disagreement or ideational conflict must occur. This is especially true of newly formed work groups.

Benchmark Two: Formation of Group Roles.   As we just pointed out in discussing group understanding and agreement, disagreements about how to solve the group's task occur almost simultaneously with role struggles in the development of a group. Bormann states that there are a number of different ways in which role formation may take place in the development of a task group, but that central to all group scenarios is the notion that people compete for roles and that our society has attached more status to some roles than others. It stands to reason then that the most coveted role, namely that of leader, is the one we compete for the most. In fact, some companies give monetary and promotional rewards to the person who emerges as leader, and this of course heightens the competition.

There is much that can be done to reduce the tension that accompanies role formation. Mature, experienced small group discussants recognize that the best group product will be produced if each group member will attempt to determine what is the best role for him or her to play in terms of the group's needs rather than his or her own. We all need to recognize that our social-cultural blinders tend to produce certain stereotypes of certain group roles. We also know that if we act on the basis of these stereotypes we will have problems. For example, we may give nonverbal cues to a woman in the group to take notes, and make the athlete the task leader, and the heavy-set Latino the tension releaser. In order to get by these problems, one must listen carefully and attentively to each group member in order to determine what members should play what roles for the group's success. As a general rule, the more culturally and racially pluralistic the group membership is, the greater the struggle in role formation. However, once the pluralistic group solves its role problems, it will generally be above average in its productivity. On the other hand, if one does not perceive that the group members are playing various roles, the chances are great that competition for role formation has not yet occurred; and if it has not, the group will not have become a group in fact, and the subsequent group productivity will be low.

Benchmark Three: Level of Interpersonal Trust and Empathy. A work group must by definition divide up the workload, some of which often gets done outside the group's scheduled meeting time. Oftentimes, interpersonal mistrust sets in when some members feel they are doing more work than others and are being used by the "lazy" members of the group. Brief interpersonal conflicts may occur at meetings; for example: "Did you get your bibliography done?" "No, I didn't get to the library yet." When this kind of interpersonal conflict occurs in a group, sometimes a mini-encounter session will take place at lunch, or in the evening at one of the member's homes. Group members will accuse each other of wearing false faces, and unimportant behaviors that occurred weeks ago during a regular meeting are brought up as clear communication signposts to show that the member does not care about the group. When a group struggles through this phase and reaches a resolution, members generally develop a great deal of empathy for each other's situation and the group renews its energy and improves its effectiveness.

Occasionally a work group will perform quite well in its day-to-day group functioning. The group's productivity will be high and the role struggles will have been resolved. Then, in a moment of jubilation, the task leader of the group will suggest that the work group go socialize together for a weekend. The group members suddenly discover that while they can work together, they can't play together. Interpersonal conflicts that were controlled in task situations become unmanageable in a social setting, and the ensuing encounter session results in the conclusion that the group cannot work together anymore as a work group. The level of self-disclosure that it takes for a work group to perform its task is not nearly as high as the self-disclosure that occurs in an encounter group session. Therefore, work groups must carefully consider whether they should meet at irregular times, particularly in social settings. All work and no play might be just the way it should stay.

Benchmark Four: Degree of Group Identification and Group Pride. Just as people learn to take pride in their accomplishments, so do groups. Work groups that are full of pride are easy to identify because the members will generally exhibit symbols and other behaviors that let everyone know their group exists. As a group competes with other groups, it finds itself holding mini-CR sessions. The reinforcement stage of a task group will contain many consciousness-raising moments. However, CR sessions, like encounter groups, usually occur outside the work schedule.

After work, group members may sit around in a social setting and begin to discuss how much better they are than the other work groups and what are the qualities of their group that make them superior. Or they may decide that they are oppressed by another arrogant work group. In either case, the group will produce a polarization between "we" and "they," the oppressed group also moving through the traditional CR stages which can lead to confrontation between it and other work groups in the company. There is a perceivable level of group pride present in most groups which is continually changing; yet long-standing work groups may develop a somewhat stable, even traditional, level of group pride so that each new member has his or her pride raised until he or she strongly identifies with the group.

Consciousness-raising sessions are not always beneficial for work groups. Some work groups keep pumping up their level of pride to the point where they become uncontrollable by any outside force. When this happens, the organization usually disbands the group. Some of the specialized police and fire units in large cities experienced the negative effects of too much consciousness-raising, and their supervisors were forced to disband them.

Another situation where CR sessions are harmful to a group is when one faction of a work group engages in CR in which the other members of the group are the "they" or "the enemy" of Stage Two. This can occur when a scheduled meeting is held and only part of the group shows up, or when one segment of the work group regularly socializes together. So CR sessions are a mixed blessing for work groups. CR is a powerful means for raising group pride and increasing a member's sense of group identity. Nonetheless, not only can CR sessions make a group so arrogant that no other groups will work with it or alongside it, but they can also intensify the polarization between factions within the group itself.

SUMMARY

This chapter presented a discussion of the basic natural group processes that are included in small group communication. An initial discussion on how small group communication theories differ focused on what a group "is" and what a discussion "ought to be." After comparing the descriptive processes of groups versus prescriptive methods of discussion, this chapter concentrated on three generic types: task, encounter, and consciousness-raising (CR) group processes.

The major purpose of a task group is to do work. The two fundamental dimensions of a work group are the *task* dimension and the *social* dimension. Although it's true that each task group tends to develop its own unique way or pattern for reaching group decisions, research in small group communication does allow us to describe a likely process by which the task and social dimensions of a group occur during the decision-making process. These stages include: (1) orientation (task); primary tension (social); (2) conflict (task); secondary tension (social); (3) emergence (task); recurring primary and secondary tension (social); and (4) reinforcement (task).

Encounter group processes provide individuals and groups with an opportunity to look at themselves and allow for self-growth. Task groups can find themselves having "encounter moments" or becoming an encounter group for a period of time. Encounter-group process stages include: (1) boundary seeking; (2) ambivalence; and (3) actualization. Another major group process one sees develop in work groups is consciousness raising (CR). Team pride and group identity are fostered through the CR process. The stages of consciousness-raising are as follows: (1) self-realization of a new identity; (2) group identity through polarization; (3) establishment of new values for the group; and (4) acting out new consciousness.

These three natural group processes provide us with four basic influences (task, social, encounter, and CR) that are fundamental to the four kinds of talk (problem-solving, role, CR, and encounter) that occupy the four quadrants, or windows, of our small group communication model. This integrated model of communication shows the interrelated elements that work toward the realization of the three major group outcomes of productivity, consensus, and member satisfaction. These outcomes are realized, to no small extent, by the achievement of four benchmarks: (1) amount of understanding and agreement, (2) formation of group roles, (3) level of interpersonal trust and empathy, and (4) degree of group identification and group pride.

REFERENCES

Bailey, K. "A Descriptive Analysis of the Group Communication Interaction of Television News Teams." Unpublished master's thesis, Illinois State University, 1985.

Bales, R. F. *Interaction Process Analysis.* Reading, Mass.: Addison-Wesley, 1950.

Bales, R. F. *Personality and Interpersonal Behavior.* New York: Holt, Rinehart and Winston, 1970.

Bennis, W. G., and Shepherd, H. A. "A Theory of Group Development." *Human Relations* 9 (1956): 415–37.

Bolkum, A. T. "A Descriptive Analysis of Communication Behavior Occurring in Consciousness Creating Groups." Unpublished master's thesis, Illinois State University, 1981.

Bormann, E. G. "Symbolic Convergence: Organizational Communication and Culture." In *Communication and Organizations: An Interpretive Approach,* edited by Putnam, L. L., and Paranowsky, M. E. Beverly Hills, Calif.: Sage, 1983.

_____ . "Symbolic Covergence Theory of Communication: Applications and Implications for Teachers and Consultants." *Journal of Applied Communication Research* 10 (1982): 50–61.

_____ . *Discussion and Group Methods.* 2nd edition. New York: Harper and Row, 1975.

_____ . "Pedagogic Space: A Strategy for Teaching Discussion." *The Speech Teacher* 19 (1970): 272–77.

Bormann, E. G., and Bormann, N. C. *Effective Small Group Communication.* Minneapolis: Burgess, 1976.

Bosmajian, H. *Silent Messages: Readings in Nonverbal Communication.* Glenview, Ill.: Scott, Foresman and Company, 1971.

Chesebro, J. W.; Cragan, J. F.; and McCullough, P. "The Small Group Technique of the Radical Revolutionary: A Synthetic Study of Consciousness-Raising." *Speech Monographs* 40 (1973): 136–46.

Cragan, J. F., and Shields, D. C. *Applied Communication Research: A Dramatistic Approach.* Prospect Heights, Ill.: Waveland, 1981.

Cragan, J. F., and Wright, D. W. "Small Group Communication Research of the 1970s: A Synthesis and Critique." *Central States Speech Journal* 31 (1980): 197–213.

DeVuono, J. "A Descriptive Analysis of Consciousness-Raising Occurring in Everyday Task Groups." Unpublished master's thesis, Illinois State University, 1982.

Dewey, J. *How We Think.* Boston: D.C. Heath, 1910.

Fisher, B. A. "Decision Emergence: Phases in Group Decision-Making." *Speech Monographs* 37 (1970): 53–66.

Gouran, D. S., and Baird, J. E., Jr. "An Analysis of Distributional and Sequential Structure in Problem-Solving and Informal Group Discussions." *Speech Monographs* 39 (1972): 16–22.

Hirokawa, R. Y. "Group Communication and Problem-Solving Effectiveness: An Investigation of Group Phases." *Human Communication Research* 9 (1983): 291–305.

Lewin, K. *Field Theory in Social Science.* Edited by O. Cartwright. New York: Harper and Row, 1951.

Lieberman, M. A.; Yalom, J. D.; and Miles, M. B. *Encounter Groups: First Facts.* New York: Basic Books, 1973.

Mabry, E. A. "Sequential Structure of Interaction in Encounter Groups." *Human Communication Research* 1 (1975): 302–7.

McBurney, J. H., and Hance, K. G. *The Principles and Methods of Discussion.* New York: Harper and Brothers, 1939.

McGrath, J. *Groups: Interaction and Performance.* Englewood Cliffs, N.J.: Prentice-Hall, 1984.

Moreno, J. L. *Who Shall Survive? A New Approach to the Problem of Human Interrelations.* Washington, D.C.: Nervous and Mental Disease Publishing Company, 1934.

Morgan, R. *Sisterhood Is Powerful.* New York: Random House, 1970.

Peters, T. J., and Waterman, R. H., Jr. *In Search of Excellence.* New York: Harper and Row, 1982. Reprinted by Warner Books, 1984.

Phillips, G. M. *Communication and the Small Group.* Indianapolis: Bobbs-Merrill, 1966.

Poole, M. S. "Decision Development in Small Groups I: A Comparison of Two Models." *Communication Monographs* 48 (1981): 1–24.

———. "Decision Development in Small Groups II: A Multiple Sequence Model of Group Decision Development." *Communication Monographs* 50 (1983): 321–41.

Putnam, L. "Preference for Procedural Order in Task-Oriented Small Groups." *Communication Monographs* 46 (1979): 193–218.

Rogers, C. R. *Carl Rogers on Encounter Groups.* New York: Harper and Row, 1970.

Schutz, W. C. *The Interpersonal Underworld.* Palo Alto, Calif.: Science and Behavior Books, 1966.

Shepherd, C. R. *Small Groups: Some Sociological Perspectives.* Scranton, Penn.: Chandler, 1964.

CASE
STUDY

CASE BACKGROUND

Harry Gordon, Sue Brodeski, Felicia Jones, Donna Doyle, Bill Braksick, Angela Juarez, and Juan DeCardona were members of a sophomore speech communication discussion class. Their professor had arbitrarily assigned them to one discussion group. Their assignment was to present a forty-five-minute panel discussion before the class. They were allowed three weeks to select the topic and prepare for the classroom presentation. They were given four class periods in which to prepare; however, they were urged to meet outside of class as well. Their topic was limited to some relevant campus issue. The professor indicated they would receive a group grade based on the quality of their panel discussion. This grade would account for fifteen percent of their course grade. Each member was to keep a diary of the group interaction and turn it in one period after the panel discussion. There was no grade attached to the diary assignment; however, credit was given for turning it in. The instructor required the group to come up with a name and slogan for itself.

CASE LOG

Meeting One: In Classroom

After the seven members of the group had moved their chairs into a circle, Harry broke what seemed like a long silence with a suggestion that they move around the circle with each person introducing him- or herself, stating his or her major and year in school. Harry indicated he was a senior business administration major. Sue stated she was also a senior, majoring in speech communication; Juan was a second semester freshman who had not yet declared his major and Bill was a corrections major. After instructions, Harry immediately suggested that the group select the topic.

(Long Silence)

FELICIA: Before we go about the task of selecting a topic, perhaps we should just name ourselves.

(Silence)

JUAN: Let's call ourselves the "chain gang," since the professor forced us to name ourselves.

(Laughter)

DONNA: That's a good idea! Maybe our group slogan should be "With ball and chain the seven links will be as strong as its weakest link thinks!"

(More Laughter)

ANGELA: Yeah, we're chained together in Room 223 for the rest of the semester! The Twilight Zone!

(At this point in time, Juan jumped up and started walking around the room with an imaginary ball and chain. Group continued to laugh at Juan's miming behavior).

FELICIA: OK, it's agreed then. We'll be the Chain Gang!

HARRY: I don't care what we call ourselves. What's important is our discussion topic and doing a good job with it. With fifteen percent of my grade riding on this, I can't afford a ''C'' in my senior year!

SUE: This group can't be all fun and games with me either! I have to keep my 3.5 average to get my internship, spring semester. But, since I have my own ''ball and chain'' that I've been married to for ten years, I can identify with the group name!

(Uneasy group laughter)

ANGELA: We like the name too, as Donna, Felicia, and I are roommates in Waterson Towers. But I can't imagine living with them for ten years!

JUAN: Do you have any children, Sue?

SUE: I'm chained to two of them, too. I've been a mother and wife for the last ten years, but rarely Sue!

(Uneasy silence following Sue's remarks. Felicia finally suggested that they exchange names and phone numbers, and schedules. To their dismay, the group found that the only available time to meet was in the evening.)

Meeting Two: In Classroom

Sue was absent for this meeting.

JUAN: Our chain gang has a missing link!

ANGELA: Maybe one of her kids is sick. It must be difficult coming back to college in your thirties!

HARRY: Well, are we ready to select a topic for our discussion?

BILL: What about the new basketball arena? I think everyone would be interested in that!

JUAN: Well, you're interested in that because you're on the basketball team!

BILL: I thought it was a good idea because I have information on this topic. But, you can do what you want!

FELICIA: That's a good one, Bill! Why doesn't everyone else contribute an idea for a topic?

HARRY: I transferred in from a community college and there is no organization to help J.C. transfers! We should have a discussion on that!

ANGELA: I'd like us to discuss the process for bringing entertainment to campus. It seems directed more towards the "townies"! What students want to see Tony Bennett or Liberace?

(Laughter)

JUAN: Or what about the "townies'" attitudes towards college students' drinking?

BILL: Yeah, we're the only university that doesn't allow tailgating parties!

(The next ten to fifteen minutes of the meeting were spent discussing townspeople's attitudes towards college students).

FELICIA: We've gotten off the topic, I think! Perhaps we should have our next meeting outside of class. Where, my dorm room?

(Everyone agreed to meet at 7:00 that night.)

Meeting Three: In Dorm Room

By 7:30 P.M., Bill, Harry, and Juan had not arrived.

SUE: Here are the *women* waiting for the *men* again! Men haven't changed! They were threatened by female leadership fifteen years ago and they still can't handle it!

(Laughter)

DONNA: Maybe Bill didn't show up because Juan trashed his idea about the basketball arena.

FELICIA: Speak of the devil, here comes Bill now!

BILL: Sorry I'm late, but Coach kept us late at practice. Where are we?

FELICIA: We're still trying to select a topic! Has anyone got any suggestions?

(After lengthy discussion, the five group members who were present tentatively agreed on "Town-Gown Relations.")

Meeting Four: In Class

Sue was the only group member not present for this meeting. The group stumbled through long periods of silence, with Juan making several futile attempts to get the group to laugh. Finally, Felicia bluntly asked why Harry and Juan missed the last meeting. Juan said that he had simply lost the phone number and dorm room; and Harry said that an old friend from high school unexpectedly dropped in. There was a long silence, but the three female roommates indicated nonverbally that they didn't believe either excuse. Harry broke the silence by asking where Sue was. Felicia responded that Sue had come to the meeting in the dorm room and that she had agreed the discussion should be town-gown problems.

HARRY: I wish I had had an opportunity to object to the topic. I commute to town and this topic is not of interest to me!

ANGELA: We'd have been more than willing to listen to your ideas at the last meeting, but I don't think we have time to go back and pick a topic. Let's go back and make this one work!

FELICIA: I agree. Let's spend this class period working out the major issues of the town-gown topic. First, why don't we each list three major problem areas we see between the town and the university. That should get us started!

(The group spent the rest of the period boiling down their problem lists to five main issues, with everyone but Harry agreeing to research one of the five topics. Harry agreed to interview some townspeople for their side of the story.)

Meetings Five and Six: In Classroom

These two meetings were very productive ones for the group. They effectively sorted out everyone's responsibilities and everyone came with his or her library research done. The only problem was that the missing link continued to be missing. Felicia assured the group that there must be some good reason for Sue's continued absence. The group agreed to hold one marathon work session the night before the presentation, and Felicia said she would call Sue to make sure she was there.

Meeting Seven: In Dorm Room

Everyone but Sue arrived on time for the meeting. As time passed, the discussion began to focus more and more on Sue's absence.

FELICIA: I've called Sue's house several times, but no one answers! I don't know what to think. She seemed so reliable when she came into the group.

HARRY: Let's just write her out of the discussion, and she can get an "F" for the project!

BILL: Maybe part of our assignment is to try and solve this kind of problem! Let's call the professor and see what he wants us to do about Sue.

JUAN: We could just dress up a doll, sit it in a chair, and call it "Sue!"

(Laughter)

FELICIA: We agreed that she would be the moderator. I'll try to get ahold of her from now until the presentation time. If I can't reach her, I'll do her job too!

DONNA: That's a good idea, Felicia. Who knows what might have happened with a husband and two kids to worry about! Let's give her the benefit of the doubt.

HARRY: Just as long as it doesn't affect my grade, I can live with it.

(The rest of the meeting was spent on finalizing the discussion.)

Formal Presentation

Sue met Felicia, Donna, and Angela in the hallway before class. She explained in an emotional voice that she had left her husband and that the last two weeks she had been out of town with her children at her mother's house. Felicia accepted her excuse. The group frantically explained to Sue her role as moderator. The professor and the rest of the class agreed that the "Chain Gang" had presented a very thoughtful and stimulating discussion. The professor gave the group a grade of "A" for their panel discussion.

CASE QUESTIONS

1. Can you identify moments in the group's history when members engaged in CR talk? Encounter talk? Role Talk? Problem-solving talk?
2. Can you identify major group roles in the discussion meetings and who predominantly played them?
3. Should Sue receive the same grade as the other group members?
4. How did CR talk and encounter talk affect the productivity of the group?

Whatever the type and nature of each [discussion] format, each of them is concerned to varying degrees with where you sit, when you talk, and how long you talk.

CHAPTER OBJECTIVES

In order to be a more effective discussant, when you read this chapter you should focus on the following group discussion ideas and communication skills.

YOU NEED TO KNOW:

1. The major objectives of the various discussion formats.
2. The steps and the unique features of each of the problem-solving agenda systems.
3. The steps and unique features of specific discussion techniques.

DISCUSSION PROBLEM-SOLVING METHODS

CHAPTER OUTLINE

PRESCRIPTIVE DISCUSSION GROUP PATTERNS

The different types of small groups that people find themselves in fall into the two general categories of *prescriptive* and *descriptive* groups. The prescriptive category contains the group patterns that list the rational steps that group members *ought* to follow in reaching some predetermined goal. The descriptive category houses the natural group processes that small group researchers have discovered to exist in organized societies.

There are many systematic procedures that have been recommended as ways for groups to accomplish their ends. In this chapter we intend to describe what kinds of group procedures fall into the prescriptive category. One way to classify discussion is by its format. The six most common formats are (1) round table discussion, (2) symposium, (3) panel discussion, (4) forum types, (5) colloquy, and (6) parliamentary procedure. The round table discussion format is the most common, since its face-to-face interaction pattern facilitates problem solving. A symposium serves an informational function in that it consists of a series of short speeches on a controversial topic in which pro and con positions or various aspects of the topic are presented; or both types of speeches may be included. A panel discussion is a format in which group members interact in a face-to-face context both among themselves and with an audience on a controversial discussion question. Forum types include such subformats as debate forums and lecture forums, in which audiences are given an opportunity to ask the discussion participants questions at the end of the formal presentations. Colloquies usually take the form of an intentional provocation of panel participants by one or more members of an audience. Parliamentary procedure is a formal meeting technique that is utilized to help meetings run smoothly and in an orderly fashion.

Another way in which some group procedures fall into the prescriptive category comes under the heading of problem solving agenda systems. Agenda systems that are used routinely include the following: (1) Dewey's reflective thinking pattern; (2) the Ross Four-Step Agenda System; (3) the "Wright 494" Agenda System; (5) the Brilhart-Jochem Ideation-Criteria Schema; (5) Maier's Decision-Making Formula; and (6) the group's own idiosyncratic agenda system. Dewey's reflective thinking pattern is composed of five steps and, although it is the most widely known, is not necessarily the best discussion group pattern. The Ross Four-Step Agenda is an adaptation for discussion based on John Dewey's steps of reflective thinking. The "Wright 494" Agenda System comprises ten steps which facilitate a sense of process order and the implementation of a variety of group thought patterns into group discussion. The Brilhart-Jochem Ideation-Criteria schema emphasizes the importance of the establishment and arrangement of criteria in a basic agenda system. Maier's Decision-Making Formula emphasizes the relationship between idea getting and idea evaluation. The problem-solving agenda systems that are among the most widely used are the ones that groups create; that is, the idiosyncratic nature of the group facilitates an agenda system that is uniquely the group's own.

One further set of prescriptive discussion group patterns is labeled Specific Discussion Techniques, which includes seven forms: (1) nominal group discussion; (2) the Delphi technique; (3) brainstorming; (4) buzz groups;

(5) single question form; (6) ideal solution form; and (7) PERT. Buzz groups occur when larger groups are broken into small groups in order to facilitate participation and idea exchange. Brainstorming is a widely used ideational technique for generating new and fresh ideas. The nominal group discussion procedure emphasizes an equalness of participation and eventually determining priorities for areas of importance to a group. The Delphi technique is similar in a number of ways to the nominal group discussion procedure but varies in that members of the group are not located in the same place, and a written mode of group member participation has to be used to gather the data. PERT is a detailed planning strategy that is used by certain groups; the acronym (PERT) stands for Program Evaluation and Review Technique. The last two discussion techniques, ideal solution form and single question form, are similar in that they emphasize one specific thing that must be accomplished in the group. For example, what is the ideal solution to the problem of an impending strike? Or, what is the single question we are trying to answer in order to achieve our group's goal?

Thus, the formats, problem-solving agenda systems and specific discussion techniques briefly identified in the preceding paragraphs constitute the major prescriptive discussion group patterns. We discuss each of these in some detail during this chapter (see Table 3.1).

DISCUSSION FORMATS

Discussion formats are often passed over as trivial detail in the larger analysis of small group discussion. It is our belief, however, that decisions about the format in which a discussion will take place are major ones. The seating arrangement of a discussion, the sequencing of who speaks when, and the regulation of how long people speak will evolve out of an ongoing group that holds frequent meetings. People will develop a sense of possession over "their

TABLE 3.1
PRESCRIPTIVE DISCUSSION GROUP PATTERNS

Discussion Formats	Problem-Solving Agenda Systems	Specific Discussion Techniques
Round Table Discussion	Dewey's Reflective Thinking: McBurney & Hance	Nominal Group Discussion
Symposium	Ross Four-Step Agenda	Delphi Technique
Panel Discussion	"Wright 494" Agenda	Brainstorming
Forum Types	Brilhart-Jochem Ideation Criteria	Buzz Groups
Colloquy		Single Question
	Maier's Decision-Making Formula	Ideal Solution
Parliamentary Procedure	Group's Own Agenda	PERT

TABLE 3.2
MAJOR OBJECTIVES OF DISCUSSION FORMATS

Format	Objective
Round Table	To promote equality of participation and spontaneous conversation.
Symposium	To present different viewpoints using a series of short preplanned speeches of equal length.
Panel Discussion	To facilitate semistructured communication interaction among participants on a single topic for the benefit of an audience.
Forum Types	To stimulate audience participation on an important issue through the use of questions and answers combined with one or more of the other discussion formats.
Colloquy	To elicit unprepared responses from discussion participants through the means of prepared questions for the enlightenment of an audience.
Parliamentary Procedure	To strictly regulate participation of a large discussion body through an organized set of rules in order to facilitate orderly decision making that reflects the will of the majority.

seat." Also, the group will develop an unstated time regulation on how long a member can talk. And some people will tend to be allowed to speak longer than others. The six formats we present in this chapter are a formalization of seating arrangements, sequencing of who talks when, and the regulation of time that members are allowed to speak. These formats evolved out of speech communication literature because they were found to be useful in orchestrating the exchanges of busy people in face-to-face meetings. (See Table 3.2.)

ROUND TABLE DISCUSSION

Round table discussion has become the most customary way for private discussions to take place. This format is the least prescriptive of the six formats. The seating arrangement is designed to maximize the flow of communication among the members and also to produce a sense of equality among them. Yet, variations of the round table seating format exist which drastically change the open communication and sense of equality. For example, if a rectangular table is used and the designated leader sits at the end by him- or herself, there will be a tendency for the communication to flow between the participant and the designated leader and back to the participant. The rectangular table is often used when a designated leader has a prescribed agenda, since the rectangle-shaped table facilitates control by the designated leader. In fact, if a designated leader used a round table setting and a rigid agenda system, he or she might be resented for trying to make it appear that an open free-flowing discussion will take place when in fact it will not. You may have experienced this phenomenon when you have had an autocratic professor who put the class in a circle in order to appear more democratic. If the professor had left the class in straight rows, you would not have felt badly. It was the mixing of a democratic format with an autocratic style that caused the problem. So it is with discussion formats. The format signals the participants

FIGURE 3.1
THE SIX DISCUSSION FORMATS

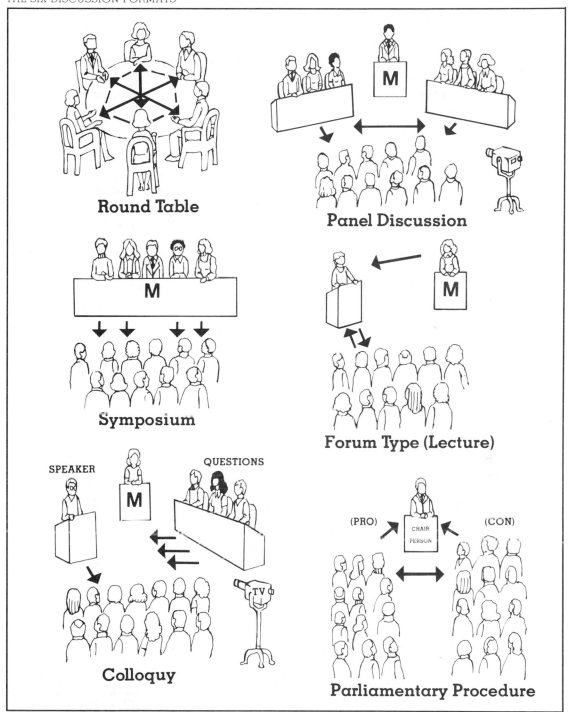

Round Table

Panel Discussion

Symposium

Forum Type (Lecture)

Colloquy

Parliamentary Procedure

to expect a certain type of discussion; that is, it tells you *where you sit, when you talk,* and *how long you talk.*

In most round table discussions there is an expectation that anyone can talk when they have something to say. The minute you make the table a rectangle, there is a tendency to seek the approval of the designated leader before speaking. Therefore, a college discussion group would feel more comfortable sitting around a round table, while a Monday morning forty-five-minute briefing by a supervisor might be more appropriate around a rectangle. If the study group finds itself around a rectangular or square table, it tends to disregard its shape and still form a circle with chairs around the table. A formal business meeting, if taking place around a round table, will reshape it to make a rectangle generally by leaving a space on each side of the designated leader. In fact, research on these seating arrangements has demonstrated that round table seating arrangements facilitate more democratic and spontaneous participation patterns, and rectangular seating arrangements promote more autocratic and stilted participation patterns (Shaw 1976).

Finally, a round table format implies unregulated and unrestrained discussion. If you were a designated leader calling a group together to discuss a topic, and you had forty-five minutes to reach a decision, you probably would not wish to seat the members around a round table unless they had had a great deal of experience working together. In our culture, it is not acceptable behavior to have everyone occupy equal space around a round table with one person tightly regulating the speaking time of each. At a rectangular table, on the other hand, we expect some regulation from the designated leader.

If one wanted to get mystical about shapes, in the world of small group discussion the circle or the round table would connote timelessness and equality of participation. When we leave the format of the circle and form any other shape, we are signalling that time is our enemy and that we must structure our interaction in order to reach group goals.

Thus, the rectangular table implies—as the remaining five formats prescribe in a formalized fashion—where people sit, when they talk, and how long they talk.

SYMPOSIUM

A symposium is a series of short speeches that present various aspects of a topic, or the pro and con positions of a controversial issue, within a prescribed discussion format. These speaking assignments are prearranged with the symposium participants and are expected to be of the same length. In essence, each speaker covers parts of a whole topic, usually in order to provide helpful information for the members of an audience to use in their future decision making.

You have probably been a member of an audience at a number of symposiums without realizing it. If you saw a sign posted on campus that stated there would be a symposium on the question of legalized abortions, you might not know whether you were going to hear a series of speeches supporting legalized abortions or opposing them. However, if the symposium announcement stated that the pros and cons of legalized abortion would be addressed, you would expect that both sides would be covered adequately. If you were the person in charge of the symposium, you might plan to have six speakers, three for and three against. Furthermore, you might expect to have two physicians, for and against, to talk about the medical ramifications; two lawyers, for and against, to deal with the legal aspects of the issue, and two members of the clergy to represent religious concerns. You would also prescribe the maximum amount of time the speakers would be allowed to speak, and the audience and other symposium participants would expect you to enforce it.

When you entered the university, your orientation probably included a series of symposiums that provided exposure to various aspects of campus life. Perhaps you went to a session that focused on social activities, and as you sat anonymously in the crowd, several speakers were paraded before you. Each speaker seemed enthusiastic about his or her topic and told you just enough to interest you, but not enough to answer your questions. By the end of the day, you were experiencing extreme mental fatigue and frustration. We don't mean to say that all college orientation symposiums are poorly done or that the symposium format inherently produces information overload. We do suggest that, more frequently than not, the symposium format is misused or abused.

Sometimes people in charge of orientation symposiums string together a series of people important in the organization more with an eye to protocol of who should be invited to speak than to what the audience needs to know. Any time the list of speakers exceeds six you have too many.

Designated leaders of symposiums often fail because they do not do enough to ensure that the speeches will be closely tied together so that, when taken as a whole, they will constitute a coherent picture for the audience. Simply bringing together for one hour, on one stage, six people whose job functions relate to the social activities on campus, will not ensure a good symposium. The designated leader should explain diplomatically to his speakers that their talks should be prepared in such a way that a common thread runs through them.

The protocol of the symposium format extends beyond the contextual dimension; there are also various expectations. The audience expects all members of the symposium to be on a platform facing them and that the moderator will rise and introduce each speaker formally. Culturally we expect symposium speakers to give their speeches standing up at a podium, while we expect panel discussants to debate sitting down.

PANEL DISCUSSION

A panel discussion is a specialized format in which group members interact among themselves and with an audience on a controversial question. The interaction may be face-to-face, through a mediator, or through a combination of face-to-face and mediated communication. Traditionally, the seating arrangement of a panel discussion had the discussants sitting on one side of a rectangular table facing the audience, with the moderator seated either among the discussants or at one end of the rectangle. As television became a widely used medium, a second format was developed in which the discussants sat at either end of the rectangle and the moderator in the center of one of the sides with the camera opposite him or her. The use of satellites to facilitate the transmission of information instantaneously around the world has also led to the development of new panel discussion formats. The network news programs regularly beam mini-panel discussions into our homes. The panel discussants may be physically in three different countries but, working from a planned agenda and with an anchor person as discussion leader, they are able to discuss controversial topics before millions of people. The award winning "MacNeil-Lehrer Report," which has been aired weeknights for years on public television, pioneered a new seating arrangement for a half-hour panel discussion. In this program the panel discussants are in two different places and the discussion is co-chaired. MacNeil and Lehrer keep tight control by using a planned agenda known by them but rarely by the participants. Through the use of rear-screen projectors the TV audience can see on their screen two discussants in face-to-face interchange with MacNeil; at the same time, two other participants on a rear screen projection interact with Lehrer. Thus the format allows the TV audience to see the spontaneous nonverbal reaction to everyone's comments and to hear the unplanned verbal interaction among participants. This format also allows tight facial close-ups of a panel discussant when he or she presents a prepared monologue that was stimulated by a prepared question. Thus the MacNeil-Lehrer Report has all the classic elements of a live panel discussion. At the same time, their use of modern media technology has enabled them to produce a format that is well suited to television discussion and vastly superior to the format of talking heads sitting in a line before a fixed camera that was common in the 1950s and 1960s. The traditional seating arrangement for panel discussions with live audiences has been adapted to fit both television and the faster pace of our lives. However, the fundamental factors that make a panel discussion what it is remain constant.

Extemporaneous speeches and panel discussions have one thing in common in that they appear to be spontaneous while in fact a lot of planning and preparation has gone into the outline of both. The panel discussion leader, or moderator, is responsible for keeping the discussants to the planned agenda. A more difficult skill for the moderator lies in planning how much prediscussion interaction is needed by its members. If the discussion is rehearsed, it generally fails, and the audience feels it has been manipulated. If no advance work is done with the members, a discussion may appear shallow and random. A good discussion is marked by a diversity of viewpoints interacting within a cooperative mode. If the discussion moderator works too closely in preparing the discussants, the panel participants may feel manipulated and fail to perform to the expectations of the moderator or the audience. Even when the moderator has done appropriate amounts of advance planning and has worked out a reasonable agenda, it is difficult to balance the time allowed for each item on the agenda against the time allotted each discussant. Most people need years of practice to become truly skilled in the role of discussion moderator. However, one principle should govern the development of a moderator, and that is that truth can emerge only in a permissive and reflective atmosphere. In short, a sense of fair play is all-important. The moderator should not rig the discussion to suit his or her bias, nor should he or she allow undue time to be spent on one item of the agenda or on one discussant of the panel.

Obviously, there is not a prescribed period that is the "right amount of time" for each discussant. A general rule of thumb is that the discussant should never speak more than one minute at a time. In a televised panel discussion, the allotted time would be less than that. As a discussant you should resist the urge to respond with your opinion on every issue, but be prepared to speak cogently on the issues that the panel and the audience expect you to speak on. The panel discussion, then, is a *coacting* situation. The discussants not only carry on a semispontaneous dialogue with each other, but they also interact with a live, radio, or TV audience. It is this instantaneous dual interaction that forms the basis of a panel discussion. One final note about the panel discussion is its relationship to the round table discussion. Often before the lights are lit for a panel discussion, the discussants have been involved in a backstage round table discussion. This advance planning will only appear manipulative if the net result of the panel discussion is a slick, biased view of the topic under discussion.

FORUM TYPES

The best known example of the forum in America is the New England town meeting. The freedom for all members of the audience to question ideas in a public place is a basic right of our governmental system, and the format of the forum aids this democratic practice of evaluating and questioning policies. As defined here, a forum is a question and answer period that arises out of another type of public discussion format; for example, a symposium. Whatever the stimulus-response nature of the forum, there is one key ingredient to it: the audience must have the opportunity and capacity to ask questions and respond to statements. What distinguishes different types of forums from each other is that each type arises from a different communication event. The five specific public discussion types include: (1) the lecture-forum; (2) the debate-forum; (3) the dialogue-forum; (4) the panel-forum; and (5) the symposium-forum.

The lecture-forum is a discussion format established mainly to facilitate the purpose of information-sharing. Lectures can be presented on television to various classrooms; however this is not a public discussion format because the audience usually does not have the opportunity to ask the television lecturer questions about the material he or she has presented. The debate-forum, on the other hand, is designed primarily to present the pros and cons of a controversial proposition, and it is hoped, provoke the audience to ask questions.

The dialogue-forum has some rather interesting features. A unique combination of the modes of advocacy and inquiry are blended into a dyadic or triadic structure to create the dialogue-forum. The very fact that an interview is being conducted as public discussion makes its format that of the dialogue-forum. The Phil Donahue show, a syndicated television program, is one example. In it, Donahue weaves together his own questions, questions from the live audience, and phoned-in questions from the TV audience to produce a generally entertaining and informative public discussion. Radio and TV programs have used variations of the Donahue format for decades as a means of stimulating public discussion of current issues.

The panel and symposium formats become forums when they add questions from the audience. Otherwise they remain as described above. The regulation of where people sit, when they talk, and how long they talk is controlled by the type of forum used. The lecture is generally a twenty to thirty minute speech. The debate gives equal time to both affirmative and negative sides—generally fifteen minutes divided between two speakers on a side. The dialogue-forum will generally begin with a brief statement by the major participant, followed by stimulus questions by the interviewer and audience.

COLLOQUY

A colloquy is a specialized discussion format which provides an opportunity for representatives from an audience to ask prepared questions of one or more experts on a topic. The colloquy is somewhat formal and the discussion is closely regulated by a moderator. The TV program "Meet the Press" is an example of a colloquy. In it, three news reporters ask the questions the larger TV audience would ask if it had the opportunity. Protocol of a colloquy generally requires that the moderator allow each questioner to ask one question at a time in serial fashion. The expert is generally allowed only to answer questions and not ask them.

The colloquy is also a favorite discussion format for politicians on the campaign trail. At college campuses the political colloquy generally presents one or two politicians on a stage with three or four student representatives who ask rather blunt, prepared questions in the presence of a large live audience. The nationally televised "debates" between Ronald Reagan and Walter Mondale in the 1984 presidential campaign were really much more in the format of a colloquy than a debate. Most of the format was dominated by carefully prepared questions from journalists, followed by Reagan's and Mondale's responses. These interactions were carefully regulated by a moderator and little "direct-clash" debate occurred between the candidates. One of our students told us after watching the so-called "debates" on television that she voted for the reporters. She felt that they had asked better questions than either candidate gave answers.

PARLIAMENTARY PROCEDURE

Parliamentary procedure is a format for strictly regulating participation of large discussion bodies in specified time periods when a number of decisions must be reached. The bylaws of a given organization combined with a strict adherence to the rules of parliamentary procedure can easily immerse a group in a bog of literally hundreds of rules that require a professionally trained parliamentarian to sort out. Because it is so complex, most formal organizations that meet regularly use a modified form of parliamentary procedure and even then tend to use it only as a last resort. The person chairing the meeting will many times say something to the following effect: "If we can't reach consensus on this policy" or "If this unruliness continues, I will enforce Robert's Rules of Order."

Parliamentary procedure is almost as old as the English culture. It dates back to those romanticized times of armed knights and lords, who were early members of Parliament. One of the rules that evolved from their meetings was that a sergeant at arms should be appointed to literally disarm the members. Thus, when arguments broke out they could not take out their swords and kill each other. The sergeant at arms was also needed to forcibly eject members of the group who did not engage in verbal argument in a civilized manner. Not only did each meeting have its police force, it had its "supreme court" in the person of the parliamentarian, who interpreted the rules and regulations and their uses.

However, when the more than three hundred rules are boiled down they are found to be designed to accomplish just a few basic objectives. The first is to nonviolently impose the will of the majority, and to even suppress the voices of the minority if the majority swells to two-thirds of the assembly. With a two-thirds vote, one can stop discussion on a topic and demand a vote, or even adjourn the meeting. The second objective of parliamentary procedure is to rigidly force the group to discuss one, and only one, problem at a time. This is called the main motion on the floor. The chair strictly regulates who will talk by formally recognizing a speaker, and if necessary by ruling a member out of order if his or her comments are not germane to the main motion.

This formal regulation of communication is one of the elements that distinguishes parliamentary procedure from other forms of deliberation. No other group format has a formal system for determining if a member's contribution is germane to the discussion.

The third objective in the use of parliamentary rules of order is to ensure that members have equal opportunity to participate. This objective also ensures that arguments for and against the main motion will be given. When rules of parliamentary procedure are strictly enforced, they produce a discussion pattern that specifies who can talk for how long and how often. They also ensure that there is a major and minor speaker for and against the main motion, that each speech is limited to ten minutes, and that after they are done, members of the group are allowed to speak only twice for a limited time of two minutes each. Finally, a limit of three hours will be placed on the whole discussion, at which time a vote will be taken. However, as we indicated previously, most groups do not contain enough vested interests to require these elaborate procedures.

Although parliamentary procedure is used less today than in the past, if it is used it is vitally important that the members know the rules so that they may protect their rights. You will undoubtedly find yourself in an organization that uses parliamentary procedure, and it is important for you to acquire a working knowledge of it at some time during your formal education.

PROBLEM-SOLVING AGENDA SYSTEMS

In Chapter 2 we indicated that two speech communication scholars had used Dewey's discussion of how a rational mind works as a springboard for devising a rational group thought pattern for problem-solving discussions. Just as the parliamentary procedure format forces a group to discuss one idea at a time, so problem-solving agenda systems dictate the manner in which we can resolve a problem and recommend a course of action. The six problem-solving agenda

TABLE 3.3
UNIQUE FEATURES OF PROBLEM-SOLVING AGENDA SYSTEMS

Agenda System	Unique Feature
Dewey: McBurney & Hance	Five-part system: 2 parts on problem and 3 parts on solution, with emphasis on testing alternative solutions.
Ross	Four-part system: 2 parts on problem and 2 parts on solution, with emphasis on criteria step for evaluating solutions.
Wright 494	Ten-part system: 3 parts on problem and 7 parts on solution, with emphasis on an exhaustive examination of solutions.
Brilhart & Jochem	Five-part system: 1 part on problem and 4 parts on solution, with emphasis on brainstorming possible solutions before developing criteria.
Maier	Two-part system: both parts on solution, with emphasis on efficiency of use.
Group's Own	Uniquely adapted to the group and its problems.

systems described in this section are not only recommended as a procedure for a group to solve a problem, they are also used successfully as an outline for conducting a panel discussion. Dewey is probably right to say that moving from a "felt difficulty" in a step-by-step sequence to the verification of the solution is an aesthetic way to bring the mind to the resolution of a problem. However, as we will discover, the problem solving agenda of the everyday, ongoing group that we describe in this section does not follow Dewey's prescriptive procedures. (See Table 3.3.)

DEWEY'S REFLECTIVE THINKING: MCBURNEY AND HANCE

In Chapter 2 we indicated that McBurney and Hance created the first prescriptive agenda system for a problem-solving group to be derived from John Dewey's five-step reflective-thinking process. The McBurney-Hance five-step problem-solving agenda system comprises the following:

1. definition and delineation of the problem;
2. analysis of the problem;
3. the suggestion of solutions;
4. reasoned development of the proposed solutions; and
5. further verification (McBurney and Hance 1939, 11–13).

McBurney and Hance break the group thought process into two parts: consideration of the problem and evaluation of the possible solutions. We still see this dichotomy today in the field of rhetoric. In the late 1960s and early 1970s, it was fashionable to say that a person was part of the problem or part of the solution. McBurney and Hance, like Dewey, devote two steps to an analysis of the problem and three steps to the solution. The two problem steps allow the group to focus on the causes of the problem in the belief that (1) once causes are explicitly stated, solutions will be manifestly obvious, and (2) through the testing of various solutions the group will arrive at the best solution.

As we said at the beginning of this section on agenda systems, this five-step procedure makes a fairly good outline for a panel discussion. However, speech communication scholars observe that everyday groups that are not aware of the McBurney and Hance agenda system generally do not follow the five-step process sequentially when presented with a problem. Yet practical experience with this agenda system and ones similar to it indicates that groups of people who have only limited work experience with each other, and who can meet only a few times, work quite well if they follow the five-step agenda system. As long as the discussion leader does not zealously force the groups through the steps, but allows for needed digressions and regressions, the system works adequately as a problem-solving agenda system.

ROSS FOUR-STEP AGENDA

As speech communication scholars taught the McBurney and Hance problem-solving agenda system to discussion students, adaptations of it began to appear. One of the more important ones was developed by Raymond Ross (1974, 323). His agenda system comprises four major steps as follows:

1. *Definition and Limitation*—a concise but qualified statement of the felt difficulty, problem, or goal.
2. *Analysis*—the determination of the type or nature of the problem and its causes.
    a. Puzzles—questions of fact
    b. Probabilities—reasonable predictions—chance
    c. Values—beliefs, attitudes
3. *Establishment of Criteria*—a group consensus on the standards to be used in judging solutions.
    a. Minimum or maximum limits, or both
    b. A rating of hierarchical importance
4. *Solutions.*
    a. Suggested solutions
    b. Evaluation in terms of the criteria
    c. Decision and suggested implementation or action.

As one can see, Ross's agenda system concentrates two steps each on the problem and solution phases. His system differs from McBurney and Hance's in two significant ways. First, the Ross agenda presents a much more systematic examination of the nature of the problem. Ross recommends that the three substeps included under the analysis stage should be taught sequentially; he argues that one should look objectively at the facts of a situation before making a value judgment about it. For example, if a group were discussing the topic of legalized abortions, Ross would recommend that the group determine how many abortions were occurring before the judging whether it was a detriment to society. The second addition that Ross makes to a problem-solving agenda system is the introduction of the criteria step. Ross (1974, 328) explains this step as follows: "*A criterion is a standard or yardstick by which we may measure or evaluate something.* In the case of group discussion, it refers to an *agreed-upon* standard." In other words, criteria are the standards by which a group evaluates its solution. Ross additionally suggests the concept of *weighting*, i.e., rating criteria according to their hierarchical importance: "Weighting may be profitably considered by a group if some of the criteria are close together in importance." The solution step in the Ross Four-Step Agenda is dependent on the criteria step being satisfied.

The utility of the Ross system is that it seeks consensus on criteria for judging potential solutions. If a problem-solving group can achieve this goal, their chances of reaching agreement on a course of action are greatly enhanced. Our observation of groups using this system is that discussion groups do not clearly establish criteria and then judge solutions against it, but that an interaction occurs between suggested solutions and the establishment of criteria to judge them by. However, the fact that the group is directed to develop criteria makes for better problem-solving discussion and probably enhances the quality of the decision reached by the group.

"WRIGHT 494" AGENDA

The ten-step "Wright 494" Agenda system is, to some extent, an accumulation of previous group thought patterns and agenda systems that were developed in the past by various speech and small group scholars. However, the "Wright 494" Agenda system is unique in many respects in that it adds several new dimensions that permit a high degree of flexibility and utility for various kinds of groups. The ten steps of the "Wright 494" Agenda system are as follows:

1. *Ventilation*—period of primary tension for the group.
2. *Clarification of Problem and Establishment of Group Goals*—definitions and limitations occur here.
3. *Analysis of the Problem*—according to the facts, probabilities, and values.
4. *Establishment of General Criteria*—basic minimum standards necessary for considering general solutions, e.g., feasibility, utility, etc.
5. *Suggestion of General Solutions*—typical ways of completing this step include "brainstorming" for solution ideas at this stage.
6. *Evaluation of Solutions According to Steps 3 and 4*—if proposed solutions do not meet general criteria disregard those solutions for remainder of this problem-solving discussion.
7. *Development of Situational Criteria*—group standards and norms appropriate to this specific problem area.
8. *Evaluation of Solutions According to Step 7 Criteria*—situational criteria play an important part in narrowing solutions in order to select best solution for this particular problem area.
9. *Selection of Solution(s)*—the best solution(s) for this specific problem area.
10. *Implementation of Solution(s)*—how will solution(s) best be adapted and actually put into practice? (Wright 1975, 34.)

As one can easily see, this agenda system is much more solution-oriented than the two previously mentioned in that seven of the ten steps (numbers 4 through 10) deal with the solution in some way. The first step—ventilation—is appropriate for problem-solving groups, especially if the group has not met before. The second and third steps—problem-oriented—are very similar to the first two steps of the Ross Four-Step Agenda System discussed previously. And although steps 4, 5, and 6 appear fairly traditional, their relationship to the two unique steps which immediately follow them offers a satisfactory way for groups to suggest and evaluate solutions. This would be especially appropriate for ongoing groups.

Perhaps a detailed example would be helpful in outlining and emphasizing the solution steps of the "Wright 494" Agenda System. Imagine that a town council were to consider designating "jogging routes" throughout the city. Some general criteria (step 4) might already be established: streets must be wide enough to accommodate joggers, and so on. Several jogging routes are suggested (step 5). The town council then evaluates the solutions—the proposed jogging routes—according to the general criteria. For example, Vernon Avenue is wide enough for joggers, but it also happens to be one of the most heavily traveled streets in the city. In other words, the solution might meet the general criteria, but it will not solve the specific problem, i.e., the fact that Vernon Avenue has a great deal of automobile traffic. The town council now moves to step 7 and develops situational criteria that are most appropriate for the specific problem area. In our "jogging route" example, council members suggest the following situational criteria:

a. jogging routes should offer scenic beauty with trees and greenery;
b. routes should favor pleasure-oriented users over business users;
c. trails should not be too hilly in order that families may run and jog together.

The council members then evaluate solutions according to the step 7 criteria, and come to the conclusion that Vernon Avenue definitely should not be used as a jogging route. At step 9, in which solutions are selected, the emphasis is placed on solving the specific problem in the best way. Finally, Broadway Avenue is selected as the best place in the city to locate jogging routes. This location meets both general and specific criteria.

The "Wright 494" Agenda System is a highly functional one for both one-time-meeting and ongoing discussion groups. For one-time-meeting groups, the ten steps provide the necessary structure for the achievement of a meaningful solution to a problem. Ongoing groups are able to adapt their group thinking patterns with the aid of the "Wright 494" agenda. This adaptability is the advantage of this problem-solving agenda system over a number of others.

BRILHART-JOCHEM IDEATION CRITERIA

In 1964, two speech communication scholars, John Brilhart and Lurene Jochem, reported the results of their research on the utility of a new problem-solving agenda system. Their research demonstrated that if members of a group brainstormed their possible solutions to a problem and then determined the criteria for evaluating their solutions they would generate more and better ideas than groups that used the traditional procedure such as the Ross and

Wright agenda systems which propose evaluative criteria before suggesting solutions (Brilhart and Jochem 1964).

As a result of this research, Brilhart (1974, 110–11) recommended the following five-step creative problem-solving sequence:

1. What is the nature of the problem facing us—present state, obstacles, goals?
2. What might be done to solve the problem or the first subproblem?
3. By what specific criteria shall we judge among our possible solutions?
4. What are the relative merits of our possible solutions?
5. How will we put our decision into effect?

Brilhart makes two contributions to the development process of agenda systems. The first one, mentioned above, says that the group should consider possible solutions before developing criteria to evaluate them. The second contribution is closely tied to the first. In it, Brilhart and Jochem (1964) introduce the idea of using the discussion technique of brainstorming at a new place in the problem-solving agenda system. In fact, Brilhart (1974, 111) recommends that in step 2 one should "list *all* ideas which group members suggest without evaluation." One of Brilhart's contributions to problem-solving discussions is his demonstration of the utility of integrating specific discussion techniques into problem-solving agenda systems. In the case study for this chapter we present an integrated agenda system that we use at organizational retreats.

MAIER'S DECISION-MAKING FORMULA

Norman R. F. Maier (1970, 182) has provided us with the simplest agenda system that is appropriate for us in problem-solving discussions. His agenda system is as follows: Decision Making = Idea Getting + Idea Evaluation. This simple two-step agenda system is solution-oriented in that it focuses on getting out ideas and then evaluating the solutions to problems. A primary use of this decision-making model would be when the group feels a fundamental need for an agenda system and yet has only a very short time to spend in following one.

GROUP'S OWN AGENDA

As useful as the preceding agenda systems appear to be, they are only appropriate to certain discussion situations. It is entirely possible, and very often the case, that the groups develop their own agenda systems. This should not be considered undesirable by any means, but normal group behavior that is determined by a variety of environmental and psychosocial factors particular to each group. By and large, it seems that there are two general patterns by which groups decide to select or not select a specific agenda system. First, a group may develop its own agenda system, then adopt a specific *agenda strategy* when needed. On the other hand, a group initially may select a traditional agenda system and then eventually develop its own. Often it is helpful to select or assign an agenda system that fits the particular situation.

Consider for example, a group of people who have never been together before and yet are to interact in a problem-solving panel discussion. In this case, the Ross agenda system might be helpful. On the other hand most ongoing groups develop their own agenda systems over time. And yet there might be instances where an ongoing group might need to adopt a specific agenda system to use as an agenda strategy for a specialized occasion—for example, Brilhart's step 2 for getting out ideas in a solution step.

Usually, if a group has little or no structure, it will probably adopt an agenda system to satisfy the specific task, as did the town council, for example, in our "jogging route" illustration. However, if a group has an excessive amount of structure, it may try to find the middle ground by allowing an agenda system of its own to evolve. In developing its own agenda, a group should keep in mind one additional factor: Hirokawa (1983) discovered that if decision-making groups start proposing solutions before analyzing the problem, they are not as successful as groups that follow more traditional agendas.

These general assumptions about how groups either evolve their own agenda systems or use those of others, probably reflect how most groups operate in everyday situations. Basically, the norming behavior of each group will determine how prescriptively an agenda system or systems will be utilized and whether they will be selected as strategies for decision-making.

SPECIFIC DISCUSSION TECHNIQUES

Over the years, speech communication professors have become more and more involved as consultants for private industry and government organizations. We are brought in to handle some specialized discussion problems, or in some cases to do an overall evaluation of the ongoing groups that exist within the organization. In doing this field consultation work, a number of specialized discussion techniques have evolved and are currently used by most consultants and a number of group leaders in organizations. In this section we present seven of the most popular techniques; however, communication consultants who work daily with organizations generally evolve their own adapted variations. In fact, we present in the case study for this chapter our own version of some of these specific discussion techniques.

It is important to know that these seven discussion techniques are highly prescriptive and that the rules contained in each procedure must be adhered to if you are to benefit from them. For example, brainstorming is a valuable prescriptive procedure only if the rules are religiously followed. Unfortunately, most people who are not trained in discussion methods will tell a group to "brainstorm" for ten minutes without giving them any direction and later conclude that the procedure is worthless. You may have been in a group that was told to brainstorm on some topic and found itself involved, first in a random discussion of the topic and then in telling humorous anecdotes, all the time moving away from the task of the group. Your conclusion could well have been that brainstorming was a useless technique. So let us repeat: these procedures only work if you follow their rules. All seven of these techniques are designed to dramatically increase the productivity of a group. (See Table 3.4.)

TABLE 3.4
UNIQUE FEATURES OF DISCUSSION TECHNIQUES

Technique	Unique Feature
Nominal Group	Four-step process that separates idea generation from idea evaluation, with emphasis on guaranteeing equal participation among all group members.
Delphi	At least a four-step process that allows a large collection of people to reach group decisions without face-to-face meetings.
Brainstorming	Four-step process containing four specific rules that separates idea generation from idea evaluation, with emphasis on spontaneous group creativity.
Buzz Groups	Three-step procedure that allows large assemblies of people to quickly generate ideas on a topic.
Single Question	Five-step process that produces an in-depth answer to a specific question.
Ideal Solution	Four-step analysis of a solution where the group has previously agreed on the nature of the problem.
PERT	Eight-step process for implementing group decisions that require complex coordination and careful planning on the part of different groups in attempting to meet a common goal.

NOMINAL GROUP DISCUSSION

We have all been part of a social group that could be said to be a group in name only. By that we mean the group had very little interaction, did not work as a unit, and had very little rapport among its members. In short, there was no group cohesion. Thus, to say a collection of people is nominally a group could be a derogatory statement. However, nominal group discussion (NGD) should not have any of these negative connotations attached to it. It is simply a specialized discussion technique that is designed to ensure equal contributions and participation by all the members in order to achieve some common goal.

The procedure evolved from two rationales. First, research at universities repeatedly found that people produced more and better ideas working in the presence of others than if they worked separately on the same task. Thus, if we put six people in a face-to-face setting and have them silently work on the same problem we will get more and better work from them than if they worked on the same problem in the privacy of their offices. The second rationale that produced the widespread use of the NGD procedure involved the uneven participation patterns that usually occur in round table discussions and some brainstorming sessions. There was obviously a need to find a way to ensure that each member of the group would contribute his or her best ideas, and to ensure that this would be done in a relatively short period of time.

Delbecq, Van de Ven, and Gustafson in *Group Techniques for Program Planning: A Guide to Nominal Group and Delphi Processes* (1975), provide the most comprehensive treatment of the nominal group technique. Huseman (1977), a speech communication scholar, has presented a much more abridged and concise treatment of the nominal group procedure for use in group discussions. While the NGD procedure could contain as many as six steps, the four steps that are most commonly used are the following:

1. silent generation of ideas;
2. round-robin recording;
3. serial discussion; and
4. preliminary vote. (Delbecq, Van de Ven, and Gustafson 1975, 71)

Imagine that you are the chairperson for the committee in charge of identifying events for Black History Week on campus. Your committee has met several times and generally kicked around some notions about what speakers and musical groups should comprise the program. However, you are a busy group and have to determine at the next two-hour meeting the events that will occur during Black History Week. One of the things you might do to meet your goal is to use a modified form of the NGD. You could seat the even members of your group in a semicircle and seat yourself facing them with a large flipboard with an easel standing next to your chair. You should tell the group that you are going to use a procedure to help in the decision-making that will require you to be very autocratic and rigid in your regulation of the meeting. You should also say that you intend to suspend debate and evaluation of ideas in order to get everyone's viewpoint. You would now be ready to begin the first step of our four step NGD procedure.

Step 1. Silent Listing of Ideas.   This step requires that the members sit quietly in a face-to-face setting and spend twenty minutes writing down every good idea they have. In this case, participants would be asked to make two lists: one of possible speakers and another of musical groups that could be included on the program for Black History Week. It is important that you provide a model of the behavior you want to take place, therefore, you should work to produce the best list that you can in twenty minutes. Use polite but firm verbal and nonverbal cues that eliminate humorous exchanges of conversation among the members.

Step 2. Creation of Master Idea List.   When the twenty minutes are up, or it is clear that everyone has exhausted his or her repertoire of ideas, you should begin the round-robin process of putting each idea on the master flipboard next to you. You ask the first person to state one, and only one, idea, and you record it on the flip chart. Do not allow discussion about the merits of the idea. Move clockwise to the next member and retrieve one suggestion from his or her list. Continue to move from member to member, remembering to include yourself until everyone's list is exhausted. Sometimes it is helpful to record how often each idea comes up.

Step 3. Clarification of Ideas.   This step allows the group a controlled opportunity to clarify the meaning of phrases that appear on the master chart list. Sometimes there are only a few ideas that are not clear to all group members, sometimes there are a lot. If you are leading the nominal group, it is important you limit the discussion to clarification of ideas and leave evaluation until later. Delbecq, Van de Ven, and Gustafson recommend that you move in serial fashion to each member and achieve clarification of his or her ideas in this way. However, many times this is too elaborate a procedure and you need only to seek clarification of a few phrases.

Step 4. Straw Vote for Testing Acceptance of Ideas.   Step 4 is a secret vote that asks each member to rank each idea on the chart in terms of its acceptableness. You should hand out standard-looking pieces of paper on which each member records his or her vote. Collect the votes, randomize the ballots for anonymity, and then record the votes on the master list. This should give you some idea of consensus. For instance, I. Reed, an author, may have emerged as the top-ranked speaker, and Quincy Jones may be the landslide choice for the Saturday night dance. On the other hand, there might be quite a diversity of opinion as to who should be brought to campus; but at least you will now have those differences on the table and should be in a good position to proceed in a round-table discussion to reach consensus on a decision.

DELPHI TECHNIQUE

The Delphi technique is a method for generating group interaction on a discussion topic with the potential for reaching a decision without the group ever meeting face-to-face. This procedure is not frequently used, but when it is it requires that the group members be highly motivated, adept at writing out their comments, and have sufficient time to participate in this rather lengthy process. One way to conceptualize the Delphi technique is to think of it as a nominal group discussion that is carried on via the mails and allows a large number of people to participate.

The name "Delphi technique" stems from the story of the oracles at Delphi who foretold the future for the Greeks. The Delphi model, designed by Dalkey (1967) and his colleagues, forecasts technological innovations for the Rand Corporation. The technique consists of a series of probes, the first of which is a questionnaire that asks the participants, much like the first step in the NGD procedure, to list all the issues that might fall under a broad discussion question. After responses to the first probe have been classified into major headings, subsequent probes requesting the same participants to rank or rate the ideas are used until the discussion group starts to arrive at agreement, or until sufficient information has been gathered, or until a satisfactory combination of agreement and information gathering has occurred.

Delbecq, Van de Ven, and Gustafson (1975), describe a full-blown Delphi technique which comprises ten major steps and takes at least a month and a half to complete. An abbreviated version of the technique involves four steps. They include:

Step 1.   Collection of participants' ideas.
Step 2.   Synthesis of list of ideas by each participant.
Step 3.   Integration of synthesized lists by one person.
Step 4.   Ranking in order or rating of the ideas on the integrated list by the participants. Step 4 is repeated until agreement occurs.

Professional organizations, for example the American Medical Association, often have memberships spread around the world whose job commitments only allow them to get together once a year at a convention. The leadership of such professional organizations often finds itself in need of participatory discussion and consent on broad policy issues. However, time and distance prohibit frequent meetings. An example of this kind of organization is the International Communication Association (ICA). In 1978, the ICA leadership sponsored a Delphi probe to seek members' opinions and ideas about the future goals and roles of the International Communication Association as a world organization. If you had been coordinating this or a similar project, you would probably have employed the following four-step procedure:

Step 1. *Participants' Ideas Are Collected.* This step requires that a questionnaire be mailed asking each participant to respond to two or three broad discussion questions. For example, if a mailing went out to college student-government leaders, they might be asked to identify their major responsibilities and forecast the major concerns of college students for the next five years. They would be asked to type out their responses and return them in one or two days to a central location point.

Step 2. *List of Ideas is Synthesized.* Step 2 of the Delphi method requires that the people running the probe produce a master list of all the ideas they have received in the mail, and send them out again to the participants requesting that they classify them in terms of their importance. Participants could also be encouraged to make brief comments on any item that seemed especially important to them.

Step 3. *An Integrated Master List is Prepared.* This step requires a lot of work from the designated leader of the Delphi. If you were the student government leader responsible for this probe, you would probably have several hundred thick, completed questionnaires on your desk which expressed each participant's opinion about what are the important and unimportant ideas. It would now be your task to order all these opinions into some manageable questionnaire. The student leaders around the country must trust that you will leave in the major and controversial issues, throwing out only the tangential ones, and that you will not bias the questionnaire in the direction of your favored conclusions.

Step 4. *Participants Vote on the Issues.* This step requires that each participant "vote" on the acceptableness of each idea contained in the streamlined questionnaire. This voting is generally done in the form of some rating or ranking procedure. For example, if one of the forecasted problems is that within the next five years there will be a demand for quiet study-hour periods in the dorms, the participant might be asked to rank that problem among a list of twenty-five in order of importance, or to rate it on a scale of 1 to 7. Once all the questionnaires are returned, the results can be quantified, summarized, and mailed back to the participants. In addition, the results might be published in a student-government magazine or presented in a talk at a national meeting of student-government associations.

Sometimes the Delphi technique is used in combination with other group procedures to determine group consensus. For example, the leadership of an organization might engage in nominal grouping about a broad discussion topic and afterwards use a modified Delphi technique as a means of validating or quantifying the results of the initial NGD session. The Delphi technique can also be used as a preconvention method for large organizations, the membership being probed via Delphi to determine not only consensus but also disagreement, in order that the convention programs can focus on similarities and differences at the conference itself.

BRAINSTORMING

Alex Osborn (1959) popularized the "brainstorming" technique in his now-famous book, *Applied Imagination*. As a co-owner of an advertising agency, he was intensely interested in creative answers to the marketing problems of his clients' products. Over the years of conducting group sessions with his coworkers in attempts to come up with new ideas or ads, he discovered that the spontaneous group creativity that created some of the famous TV commercials can be systematically and predictably produced if four rules are religiously followed. They are: (1) all evaluation and criticism of ideas is forbidden; (2) wild and crazy ideas are encouraged; (3) quantity, not quality, of ideas is the goal; (4) and new combinations of ideas are sought. However, we recommend that the following four-step procedure be used in addition to Osborn's four rules when a group is brainstorming some aspect of a discussion question.

Step 1.   *Conduct a warm-up session.*
Step 2.   *Employ Osborn brainstorming procedure.*
Step 3.   *Eliminate duplication of ideas.*
Step 4.   *Clarify, order, and evaluate ideas.*

A social chairperson of any organization is constantly beset with the need to come up with themes for annual events. A fraternity's spring formal is a perpetual problem for a fraternity's social chairman. If you were assigned the task of generating potential ideas for a theme for the annual formal dance, you might do well to gather some members of the fraternity into a discussion group and follow the four steps of brainstorming.

Step 1. *Conducting a warm-up session.* Even though most people are familiar with the technique of brainstorming, they often forget the importance of following Osborn's rules. It is especially important to remind the group not to evaluate any idea prematurely. A brief warm-up session, practicing on some nonsense issue, often helps to get the group into the wild, freewheeling mood that is needed if spontaneous group creativity is to occur. For example, you might ask members to shout out the many uses of a ball-point pen or a concave navel. Answers such as that the pen could be used as an earplug while skin diving, or that your navel could be used to hold salt while eating radishes in bed would not be groaned at or disallowed. It is this sort of silliness that will suddenly spring a truly creative idea that will solve the group's problem.

Step 2. *Brainstorming.* This step is the actual brainstorming session which should not last more than thirty minutes. It often helps if a person from outside the group records the ideas on a large flipboard as they spring forth in rapid succession. Sometimes it helps to have the designated leader write the ideas on the flipboard while a disinterested person takes more copious notes at the side of the group. It is important that the leader encourage "hitchhiking" on ideas; i.e., one idea may spring two or three more. He or she should also be enthusiastic, to keep the group excited about their task. Finally, the leader should jump in with the rest of the group in order to generate as many ideas as possible in a thirty-minute period.

Step 3. *Eliminating Duplicated Ideas.* Once the brainstorming session is completed, the leader takes the group through the flipboard and eliminates all duplications. The group still does not evaluate the quality of ideas but simply condenses the number of words used to describe them.

Step 4. *Clarifying, Ordering, and Evaluating.* In this final step the group categorizes the large volume of ideas into some sensible outline. In the process of doing this, most of the vague ideas will be clarified or discarded. Once the ideas are on a flipboard in front of the group in clear outline form, evaluation of them can begin. How the evaluation of ideas is handled depends upon group processes other than brainstorming. The brainstorming technique does not provide for a specific method for determining good ideas from bad ones. It was Osborn's belief that the group would consensually recognize the good ideas as they emerged, and in fact, many times this is the case. However, brainstorming works best when all members freely contribute ideas. In fact, research done recently by Jablin (Jablin, Seibold, and Sorenson 1977; Jablin 1981) indicates that levels of communication apprehension that might exist among group members negatively affects the productivity of a brainstorming session.

BUZZ GROUPS

J, Donald Phillips (1948), created a prescriptive group technique called "Phillips 66" or "Buzz." The procedure is designed to maximize the input of all the members of a large assembled group by breaking them down into groups of six and having them "buzz" for about six minutes on some very specific issue such as, "What topics should we be concerned with at our next meeting?" An appointed leader of each buzz group reports their findings to the large group. If the questions that the buzz groups deal with are well thought out, then a master list can be made by combining the useful ideas of each group. If the Phillips 66 buzz group technique is well managed, it increases group effectiveness.

The two keys to this procedure for the buzz group are careful management and structuring. In order for these requirements to be met, the following three steps should be adhered to whenever possible:

Step 1. *Identify the Question.* For this technique to work, the question asked of the assembly must be a meaningful one that requires the participation of everybody. If the question is ambiguous or trite, the various buzz groups will treat it flippantly, and in terms of the answers to the question and the general morale of the assembly the entire effort will be wasted.

Step 2. *Assign Duties of Designated Leaders.* In advance of the meeting it is important that the leaders of each buzz group be assigned and that they be properly located throughout the hall with the necessary materials. They will each need a table for six or sometimes for as many as eight or nine, a flipboard, writing materials, and instructions on how to run the meeting. The instructions to the designated leader should inform him or her of the following items: first, he or she should adapt the "telling" style, which we will describe in Chapter 5; second, the leader should be responsible for compiling the list of suggestions; and third, he or she should prepare the buzz group's list in written form for presentation to the assembly. Sometimes the designated leaders are requested to make an oral presentation in the form of a short report to the assembly.

Step 3. *Actualize the Assembly's Ideas.* After the designated leaders have made their reports and a composite list has been compiled, it is important that the program chairperson of the assembly take some action based on the collective opinions and suggestions of the group.

An example of how the results of a buzz group discussion can be used is in combination with a keynote speaker at a convention. Frequently, an organization will invite a national figure to keynote their convention and to speak about the issues central to the interests of the membership. In this situation, the chairperson will ask the keynote speaker in advance to make a twenty-minute opening presentation, after which the buzz technique is used to solicit specific questions that the audience wants answered. The Phillips 66 method will facilitate the identification of the five most important questions that were generated in the buzz groups. The speaker, sensitive to the group's needs and interests, spends approximately five minutes answering each of the five questions. This technique has provided a valuable feedback vehicle for the speaker and has generated interaction among the assembly's participants.

SINGLE QUESTION FORM

Carl E. Larson (1969) reported this discussion technique in a research study that he conducted on forms of analysis and their effectiveness in small-group problem solving. A major feature of this discussion technique is that it is especially appropriate for use in one-time meeting groups in educational settings. Larson advocates the following five steps be followed in the single question form:

Step 1. What is the single question, the answer to which is all the group needs to know to accomplish its purpose?

Step 2. What subquestions must be answered before we can answer the single question we have formulated?

Step 3. Do we have sufficient information to answer confidently the subquestions? If yes, answer them. If no, continue below.

Step 4. What are the most reasonable answers to the subquestions?

Step 5. Assuming that our answers to the subquestions are correct, what is the best solution to the problem? (Larson 1969, 453)

This technique is a useful procedure in a one-time meeting when a tentative decision is needed to meet some pressing deadline. For example, assume you are the chairperson of the Student Entertainment Committee (SEC), and the student body president suddenly wants to know how many concerts the SEC will sponsor next year. If you have time for only one meeting of the SEC, you might well use the single question technique, as follows:

Step 1. *What is the single question?* The answer might be, how many groups can we bring in for the $80,000 allocated to the SEC.

Step 2. *What subquestions must be answered?* What groups do we want? How much is the fee for each group? What is the rental on the auditorium? How much money will we make from each concert?

Step 3. *Do we have sufficient information?* The answer is no, so we must proceed to Step 4.

Step 4. *What are the most reasonable answers to the subquestions?* The answer to question one is that we could not agree on what groups to bring in; however, we did agree on three categories of groups we would like: rock, country, and soul. We estimate their fees at about $20,000 per group. The rental on the auditorium is approximately $5,000 per concert. We estimate $10,000 revenue from each concert.

Step 5. *What is the best solution to the problem?* The SEC concludes that the student association can plan on five musical concerts for the next year.

The single question form, as discussed in the preceding paragraphs, has no doubt been used in your classroom and extracurricular groups.

IDEAL SOLUTION FORM

Another discussion technique, the ideal solution form, was used by Carl Larson in his 1969 study on small group forms of analysis. Larson lists the following essential steps in this discussion pattern.

Step 1. Are we all agreed on the nature of the problem?
Step 2. What would be the ideal solution from the point of view of all duties involved in the problem?
Step 3. What conditions within the problem could be changed so that the ideal solution might be achieved?
Step 4. Of the solutions available to us, which one best approximates the ideal solution? (Larson 1969, 453)

The above technique is a good one for determining the best among several alternatives. The ideal solution form can be used, as is the single question form, as a one-time meeting technique. The ideal solution technique works well when there are vested interests in the group. For example, in our community a group made up of city officials, home owners, and builders sat down to solve a common problem using the ideal solution technique.

Step 1. *What is the problem?* Everyone at the meeting agreed that basements were being flooded by sanitary sewer back-ups.

Step 2. *What is the best answer for each party?* The home owners felt the builders should pay for the "illegal hookups" of the sanitary sewers. The builders felt the city was responsible, and the city felt the home owners were responsible.

Step 3. *What change is needed?* Some party has to accept responsibility for the problem.

Step 4. *What is the best solution given the circumstances?* The city agreed to accept some responsibility and to approach the Environmental Protection Agency for funds. The city manager agreed to contact the appropriate state agency to begin the solution phase of the problem.

With the ideal solution form, the above group was able to address solution alternatives in a constructive way, even though each party had strong feelings about each of the alternatives and had met in a less than friendly atmosphere to try to select the best solution.

PERT

PERT, or program evaluation and review technique, is a systematic technique for implementing group decisions that require complex coordination and careful planning on the part of different groups in attempting to meet a common goal. The United States Navy in 1958 developed PERT, a quasi-mathematical procedure, in an attempt to meet their goal of the Polaris missile system (Phillips 1966, 88–89). Since PERT was first used by the United States government, it has been widely adopted both by government and private organizations.

PERT is an elaborate planning system generally containing eight steps that cryptically display each event that must take place in order for the project to be completed. These eight steps are:

Step 1. *State final event or goal of project.* Here the group clearly defines the event that must take place; such as the event of putting a man on the moon.

Step 2. *List events that must happen before the final event can occur.* A group generally brainstorms a list of all these events without regard to their chronology.

Step 3. *Assess the order of the events.* The group takes the brainstormed list and places it in chronological order, noting especially those events that must happen simultaneously.

Step 4. *Make a diagram that connects all events in chronological order.* Sometimes groups develop elaborate wall charts so that they can trace the progress of their project.

Step 5. *State specific activities that occur between events.* The group often identifies strategies and action plans in order to move to and through events. If a goal were to build a car, the group would list the activities that would have to occur between completed drawings and completed die castings of each part.

Step 6. *Specify time needed.* The group needs to develop a time line for the whole project and estimate the time for completing each event in the PERT chart.

Step 7. *Are the deadlines feasible?* After the project has been estimated in terms of time, the group must compare its expected deadlines with the actual time allocations. If you were working on such a project and had allowed yourself more time to complete the project than your superiors had allowed, you would need to rethink the project and find a quicker way to do it.

Step 8. *Determine critical path.* In the PERT chart there will be certain events that will be more crucial and more difficult to accomplish than others. In this step the group determines what those steps are and makes certain that enough resources have been allocated for their accomplishment (Phillips 1966, 89–104).

Most decision-making groups do not need PERT to implement their decisions; however, most groups are guilty of not following through with the implementations of decisions *as a group.* Too often the follow-up is left to one or two people in the group who soon begin to feel overworked. At the same time the group loses control as the members who do all the work put into effect the group's decisions according to their own, rather than the group's interpretation. PERT, or a modified version of it, forces the group to systematically and in participatory fashion plan the necessary follow-through that is needed to accomplish the decisions of the group.

SUMMARY

This chapter has focused attention on the prescriptive group patterns that can be applied to discussion situations in both ongoing and one-time meeting groups. A total of nineteen different patterns were described, and the time and place at which each would be useful was explained. The prescriptive discussion-group patterns were classified according to the following major headings: *formats, problem-solving agenda systems,* and *specific discussion techniques.*

The section on discussion formats addressed such issues as the seating arrangement of a discussion and the participation patterns of various types of discussion. Six major discussion formats were examined: the round table discussion, the symposium, the panel discussion, forum types, colloquy, and parliamentary procedure. The round table discussion was developed as a private discussion format, whereas the remaining five were designed to serve as formats for public discussion. Whatever the type and nature of each format, each of them is concerned to varying degrees with *where you sit, when you talk,* and *how long you talk.*

Problem-solving agenda systems constituted the second set of prescriptive discussion-group patterns. The agenda systems discussed in this chapter included: the five-step agenda system based on Dewey's steps of reflective thinking, the Ross Four-Step Agenda, the "Wright 494" Agenda, the Brilhart-Jochem Ideation-Criteria schema, Maier's Decision-Making Formula, and the group's own agenda. An illustration of the use of each of these methods was given. Some agenda systems were viewed as more problem oriented and others more solution oriented. The discussion of each of these highlighted the analysis, criteria, and solutions phases of the problem-solving sequences.

Specific discussion techniques was the third major type of prescriptive discussion patterns covered in the chapter. The following seven specific techniques were identified and explained: nominal group discussion (NGD), Delphi technique, brainstorming, buzz groups, single question form, ideal solution form, and PERT. The majority of these were described in terms of their utility in one-time meeting groups. In addition, some of the techniques, for example brainstorming, were discussed in light of the ways in which they could be used within problem-solving agenda systems. The extent to which the prescribed discussion techniques and problem-solving agenda systems work effectively in group discussions is largely determined by the kind of group that uses them. A knowledge, then, of the three major classes of prescriptive discussion patterns presented in this chapter is vital to our understanding of what makes good group discussions work.

REFERENCES

Brilhart, J. K. *Effective Group Discussion.* 2nd edition. Dubuque, Iowa: Wm. C. Brown Company, 1974.

Brilhart, J. K., and Jochem, L. M. "Effects of Different Patterns on Outcomes of Problem-Solving Discussion." *Journal of Applied Psychology* 48 (1964): 175–79.

Dalkey, N. D. *Delphi.* Chicago: Rand Corporation, 1967.

Delbecq, A. L.; Van de Ven, A. H.; and Gustafson, D. H. *Group Techniques for Program Planning: A Guide to Nominal Group and Delphi Processes.* Glenview, Ill.: Scott, Foresman and Company, 1975.

Dewey, J. *How We Think.* Boston: D. C. Heath, 1910.

Hirokawa, R. Y. "Group Communication and Problem-Solving Effectiveness: An Investigation of Group Phases." *Human Communication Research* 9 (1983): 291–305.

Huseman, R. C. "The Role of the Nominal Group in Small Group Communication." In *Readings in Interpersonal and Organizational Communication,* edited by Huseman, R. C.; Logue, C. M.; and Freshley, D. L. 3rd edition. Boston: Holbrook Press, 1977, 493–507.

Jablin, F. M. "Cultivating Imagination: Factors That Enhance and Inhibit Creativity in Brainstorming Groups." *Human Communication Research* 7 (1981): 245–58.

Jablin, F. M.; Seibold, D. R.; and Sorenson, R. L. "Potential Inhibitory Effects of Group Participation on Brainstorming Performance." *Central States Speech Journal* 28 (1977): 113–21.

Larson, C. E. "Forms of Analysis and Small Group Problem Solving." *Speech Monographs* 36 (1969): 452–55.

Maier, N. R. F. *Problem Solving and Creativity in Individuals and Groups.* Belmont, Calif.: Brooks/Cole, 1970.

McBurney, J. H., and Hance, K. G. *The Principles and Methods of Discussion.* New York: Harper and Brothers, 1939.

Osborn, A. F. *Applied Imagination.* New York: Scribner's, 1959.

Phillips, G. M. *Communication and the Small Group.* Indianapolis: Bobbs-Merrill, 1966.

Phillips, J. D. "Report on Discussion 66." *Adult Education Journal* 7 (1948): 181–82.

Ross, R. S. *Speech Communication: Fundamentals and Practice.* 3rd edition. New York: McGraw-Hill, 1974.

Shaw, M. E. *Group Dynamics: The Psychology of Small Group Behavior.* 2nd edition. New York: McGraw-Hill, 1976.

Wright, D. W. *Small Group Communication: An Introduction.* Dubuque, Iowa: Kendall/Hunt, 1975.

CASE
STUDY

THE PARKING COMMITTEE

CASE BACKGROUND

A "blue ribbon" committee was appointed by the president of the university to explore the perennial problems of parking on campus. There were nine members on the committee:

Charles Borris, Vice-President of Administration Service, Chairperson of Committee

Paul Ruzzo, President of the Civil Service Council

Arlene Turner, Assistant to the University Engineer

Bill Robertson, Professor and Chairperson of Political Science

Roberta Jones, Assistant Professor of Special Education

Barbe Johnson, Graduate Student and Teaching Assistant in the Department of Communication

Melinda Hubbert, Student Government Representative

Mike Winchell, Vice-President of Student Government Association

This committee has had three previous meetings. During these meetings a great deal of ventilation has taken place in that everyone got an opportunity to vividly describe their best examples of the parking problem. The problem seemed to extend beyond parking regulations into the operations of the parking department itself. Faculty and students depicted the parking department as a place populated by insensitive administrators who enforced parking regulations like "fanatical fascists." In equally stereotypic fashion, the administrators and staff on the committee continually described faculty and students as "lawbreakers who constantly try to circumvent campus regulations."

At the close of the most recent meeting, Charles Borris had strongly urged members to "bury the hatchet" and come to the next meeting with positive suggestions on how to solve the parking problem.

CASE LOG

Charles Borris opened the meeting by reminding committee members that they were to come prepared to present reasonable solutions. Arlene passed out a typed sheet of paper that contained her four suggestions. The rest of the group seemed somewhat surprised by this behavior and Mike and Melinda were openly upset.

MELINDA: We were not told to write out our suggestions to be handed out. I think it's unfair! This committee is stacked against the students!

MIKE: I agree! Why are you doing this, Dr. Borris? You're acting just like the parking department—making regulations without consulting the constituents!

CHARLES: I have no intention of co-opting any committee member's right to make suggestions, nor have I closed my mind to any suggestions! I happen to think that Arlene has some good ideas here. Let's provide her with an opportunity to at least present her ideas.

ROBERTA: Frankly, Arlene, if our committee were to recommend this idea to the president, the student newspaper would crucify us. I can just see the headlines: "Committee duped by Borris: Fines Increased from $15 to $25"!

MELINDA: I can just see the cartoon that goes with that caption—it'll show us as committee members all peeking out of Dr. Borris's pocket! (laughter)

MIKE: Yeah, we'll have a pretty "blue ribbon" tied around our collective necks with the ribbon being held by Borris's hand! (more laughter)

(While the group is in a state of laughter, Bill Robertson got up from the table and calmly wrote each person's name on the top of the chalkboard.)

PAUL: Hey, Bill, are you planning on giving a lecture on the "Fall of Greek Democracies?"

BILL: Well, Paul, as a matter of fact, in a way I am. It's clear this committee is going to fail, unless we begin to pull together. We were all in favor of forming this committee, and we all volunteered to serve on it. I believe we all truly want to find a solution to our parking problem, so let's get to work. What I propose we do is the following:

1. Go around the room and have each person list their best solution to the parking problem;
2. Give an explanation on why it would work; and
3. After all the solutions have been presented let's take a vote by secret ballot and see what solutions emerge that we have in fact agreed to.

Barbe, why don't we start with you. What is your favorite suggestion?

BARBE: The most important suggestion I have is "pay-by-the-day lots" for commuter students. Presently, you either have to pay by the hour or buy a sticker for the year! Many students commute only two or three days a week, and it would be more economical to pay only $2 a day.

BILL: Fine, Barbe. What's your idea, Paul?

PAUL: I feel that any employee of the university should not have to pay for a place to park. However, if we must charge a fee, it should be based on one's ability to pay. The civil service personnel only receive half the average salary of faculty members, and yet we still have to pay the same. That's just not fair!

BILL: Charles, why don't you give us your best suggestion next?

CHARLES: I don't care to make a suggestion at this time.

BILL: Come on, Chuck, give me one.

CHARLES: What I really think is that this is a waste of time writing ideas on the board like this. What we should be doing is writing our ideas down, like Arlene did, and bring them to the next meeting.

MELINDA: With all due respect, Dr. Borris, I think we are doing the right thing. We need to openly discuss our ideas even if there is conflict.

MIKE: Yeah. Besides, we already came prepared to this meeting. We don't need to go home and think about our ideas all over again.

CHARLES: I think we should adjourn the meeting until all of the people have written down their suggestions.

ARLENE: I can go along with the way we are doing it now, Charles. Bill, write down my idea about raising the parking fine to $25.

BILL: Now wait a minute, Chuck. You and I have served on a lot of university committees together and we've never gotten this formal before. Where does it say in the University Handbook that individuals must write out their ideas before submitting them for discussion?

CHARLES: I am just trying to provide some order and direction for this committee. I thought that was my job when the president appointed me chairperson of this committee. This meeting is getting out of control like the previous meetings have.

ROBERTA: Dr. Borris, I believe you put your finger on it. For you the meeting is "out of control" when ideas are introduced that you do not agree with. You seem unwilling to let this committee reach conclusions that run counter to your present positions.

CHARLES: Sounds like you no longer want me to serve as chairperson of this committee. You can go to the president tomorrow and ask him to remove me as chair of this committee!

PAUL: Nobody wants you to resign as chair, Charles. We just want a little more freedom to discuss our ideas.

BILL: Maybe Chuck's got a point. What do you say that we all type up our three top ideas and the rationale behind them, and have a free-flowing exchange of ideas at the next meeting.

ARLENE: I can support that.

CHARLES: Fine. Our next meeting will be at four o'clock on Wednesday. Please bring your *written* suggestions to the meeting, with copies for everyone.

CASE QUESTIONS

1. In polarized groups, what is the best way to insure equal participation in presenting suggestions?

2. Was Bill Robertson's suggestion for solving the group's conflict a good one?

3. Is it normal for a committee to create ground rules as they go, or should Dr. Borris have introduced his ideas of meeting procedure earlier?

4. Given the fact that Arlene had written out her suggestions and no one else had, how could Borris have avoided conflict in this meeting?

5. How can you allow ideational conflict without the discussion turning to procedural and interpersonal conflict?

TWO

SMALL GROUP
DISCUSSION
PRINCIPLES
AND
PRACTICES

. . . there are basic research and organizational strategies you can use to ensure that you are well-informed and able to make a positive contribution to the group.

CHAPTER OBJECTIVES

In order to be a more effective discussant, when you read this chapter you should focus on the following preparation and discussion skills.

YOU NEED TO KNOW:

1. The commitments of an ethical discussant.
2. The research and organizational strategies for good discussion.
3. How to test evidence and construct arguments in a discussion.
4. How to prepare a discussion outline.

PREPARING TO DISCUSS

CHAPTER OUTLINE

In our complex society, small groups have very short periods of time in which to meet for face-to-face discussion. In corporations, a decision-making team of four or five people may only manage one hour a week, while volunteer groups working on community issues may only be able to schedule one meeting a month. Given the complexity of group structure and the brief time that groups have for discussion, it is amazing that any work gets done. Groups that have successful discussions are groups that have done their homework! Each member has done extensive preparation on the topic for discussion so that those precious sixty minutes that the group is in face-to-face discussion will be productive.

In this chapter we detail the essential preparation skills you need in order to be an effective discussant. In addition to behaving ethically in a discussion, you need to know how to research and organize the material in order to converse intelligently on a complex topic. Also, you need to be able to analyze evidence and construct and analyze arguments that occur during the discussion.

A DISCUSSANT'S ETHICAL STANDARDS

Work groups in general, and decision-making groups in particular, have, over time, established certain unstated ethical standards that most people assume will be operative when they interact with other people in a small group. The speech communication discipline has a long tradition of teaching these ethical behaviors as a part of its teaching of discussion courses. The expected ethical behavior in a discussion includes five commitments to your fellow discussants: a commitment to do your best, a commitment to the group good, a commitment to rationality, a commitment to fair play, and a commitment to good listening.

1. *Commitment to do your best.* Each group member brings a unique personality, set of social experiences, and knowledge of the job, the discussion topic, or both to the group. Implicitly, the group expects each member to make available his or her special talents for the group's benefit. When it appears that a member is holding back some talent or knowledge, conflict generally ensues. The individual who is "sandbagging" usually feels he or she has the right not to contribute. But the group will feel that an ethic has been violated. Sometimes these conflicts develop over role selection. An individual may possess vast experience at handling interpersonal conflict but refuse to play the role of the social-emotional leader.

Other times an individual may avoid the responsibilities of task leadership because he or she does not want the extra work, but again if the group feels this person is best suited for task leader, they will feel very offended if he or she does not assume the role of leadership. In fact, some people may go through life constantly asking the question, "Why me?" It seems as though every group they join demands that they play roles they do not want to assume.

People who possess expert knowledge or skills that are in high demand often find themselves in a "role rut" in that each group they work in "forces" them to play a role that draws on their expertise. In discussions, that role is often information-provider if the person has exceptional research and synthesis skills. On basketball teams it is often the person who is forced to play the rebounder, when he or she would prefer to be a top scorer.

People who have had a lot of experience working in groups, and who are constantly forced to play roles they do not like, oftentimes hide their talents from the group. This then becomes an ethical issue: does an individual have a right to withhold knowledge and expertise from the group? The ethical standards that have emerged from group discussion say no, that a person must do his or her best.

2. *Commitment to the group good.* Of the ten most frequently played roles in group discussion that are presented in Chapter 6, the one negative role is the self-centered follower. The communication behavior that is frequently exhibited by this role is special-interest pleading. When people work in groups, there is an assumption that they are working for a common good. When a group member appears to be using the group for his or her individual ends, conflict ensues in which the self-centered follower is accused of unethical behavior.

A violation of this ethic in team sports is easy to spot. The self-centered follower is the player who sacrifices team victory in order to achieve individual honors. In group discussions the self-centered follower is not always so apparent. Sometimes it is a person who has personality conflicts with the leader and thus works against the group's goals as a means of attacking him or her. Occasionally, a person will use the group for his or her own professional advancement. This often happens in corporate settings when people must produce a group product, but are rewarded and promoted on an individual basis.

The ethical issue is, of course, must a person sacrifice his or her individual goals for the group's goals when the two are not in concert? Many small group theorists would argue that a a person has an ethical responsibility to put the group good ahead of his or her own.

3. *Commitment to rationality.* Group decisions pose threats to individual convictions. The process of reasoning out a conclusion that several people can accept requires a commitment to rational thinking. It means that each member must be willing to abandon his or her previous beliefs on an issue if sufficient arguments are marshaled in the discussion to justify a change in opinion. Later in this chapter we briefly sketch out the kinds of rational argument that are normally accepted as the means to establish a conclusion that the group can accept. You will discover that most of the rational thinking that occurs in groups has already become normative behavior. What you may have difficulty with, if you have had little experience in group discussion, is the tact that is required to persuade somebody in the group to change his or her opinion, while still maintaining his or her active cooperation in the group.

Ideally, groups should only reach conclusions that have been rationally accepted by the group's members. However, in day-to-day discussion groups this ideal is rarely achieved. Groups will develop procedures for handling beliefs that are intensely and emotionally held by the group members. Each person in the group may have the unwritten right to have the group agree with him or her, not because the member has demonstrated rational argument, but because it is a very important emotional issue for that member. Sometimes we call these issues "pet peeves." One member of a group may dramatically assert that their weekly meetings must break immediately at noon in order that they have a full lunch hour. Another member may become totally irrational about the thought of a week-end meeting; while another member will meet any place but at one certain spot. Groups will generally attempt to accommodate one or two pet peeves per member if their acquiescence does not jeopardize the major work of the group.

Finally, a commitment to rationality has its justification rooted in our intellectual search for truth. Certainly one of the most time-honored ethics of discussion is the belief that well-meaning people who have been trained in group methods can reason together and that the product of their discussion is our best facsimile of intellectual truth.

4. *Commitment to fair play.* In a court of law, the prosecuting attorney presents only those arguments that prove the guilt of a defendant with the expectation that the defense attorney will present those arguments that suggest the defendant's innocence. The judge and the jury then objectively sort out the truth of the matter. The fair play of the courtroom is not fair play in a group discussion. Group members must objectively search out all evidence and arguments that support their individual viewpoints; however, during a discussion they should not conceal arguments or evidence that might help the group.

Group discussants should not attempt to manipulate or entrap each other in their common search for truth. In a court of law, lawyers may use clever strategies that unnerve witnesses or infuriate their opposition. But in a discussion, there is no opponent; everyone should be working cooperatively for the common good. Therefore, a good discussant does not compete against the other group members.

In small groups that are composed of more than seven members, there is a tendency for cliques to form. Power struggles ensue between rival factions. These struggles can often subvert the group good. Members can get so intense about their internal structure that no work gets done. A commitment to fair play requires that power plays within the group should not jeopardize the group's goals.

5. *Commitment to good listening.* An ethical standard that all discussants should endorse is a commitment to good listening. Listening goes beyond just hearing fellow group members talk. In order for us to be able to play the role of an active listener in a discussion, we must listen attentively to what fellow group members are saying. How often we respond to member contributions shows whether we have been listening or not! Heightening our awareness of good listening and employing favorable listening habits can only help us in achieving the other previously mentioned ethical standards that discussants should continually try to attain.

DETERMINING TOPICS FOR DISCUSSION

Groups often struggle with defining their purpose, especially in identifying the goals which the group hopes to reach. Even within an organization, when a company executive has mandated that a collection of employees form a group, the group's mission is usually so vague that the members must hold several discussions in their attempts to determine what kinds of questions they need to ask in order to meet the group's goals. In Chapter 3 we list numerous one-time meeting techniques that are designed to help discussion groups efficiently formulate and organize their task.

Traditionally, groups have clarified their purpose and structured their discussions by breaking down their topic into three general question types: *questions of fact, questions of value,* and *questions of policy.* Table 4.1 depicts the major characteristics of these discussion questions.

1. *Questions of fact.* A typical topic for discussion in a city government might be: "Should the city contract with a private garbage collector to supplement city efforts?" In a meat-packing company, an executive discussion group might deal with the topic: "Should we continue to use nitrates for preserving meat products?" Both of these discussion groups have a question of policy before them; however, before they attempt to answer their respective policy questions, they will seek answers to numerous questions of fact and value.

Both groups will have a natural tendency to ask, is there a problem? This question, of course, is not solely a question of fact as there is an implicit value judgment involved. But initially they will treat the question as a question of fact, and the discussants will try to present the facts that will answer the question. The city government group might ask the question: "Is all the garbage collected weekly?" while the meat-packing group might ask: "Are any consumers being harmed by ingesting the company's meat products?" Both groups would seek expert testimony in attempting to answer their questions, but what if authorities on the subject came to conflicting conclusions regarding these questions of fact? In other words, what if some council people claimed that garbage was collected in their wards, while others claimed it was not?

TABLE 4.1
DISCUSSION QUESTIONS AND THEIR CHARACTERISTICS

Type of Discussion Question	Characteristics of the Discussion Question	Area of Emphasis in Problem Analysis	Discussion Question Potential	
			Controversial	Useful
Question of Fact	1. empirically verifiable 2. individual can usually answer question of fact by himself or herself	Fact		X
Question of Value	1. deals with unquantifiables such as "worth," "good," "benefits" 2. not empirically verifiable	Value	X	
Question of Policy	1. almost always uses "should" or equivalent word in question 2. advocates a change from the status quo	Probabilities	X	X

What if some experts claimed that nitrate in meat causes cancer, while others asserted the opposite? Caught in the swirl of conflicting testimony, the groups may seek more explicit information to help answer their questions of fact. The members of the meat-packing group might examine the original cancer studies in an effort to determine what they believe are the facts. The city discussion group might conduct its own study to determine if all the garbage is collected each week. While these two groups may think it a simple matter to answer their respective questions of fact, they will discover that most facts are hard to verify. It requires research and reasoning on the part of the discussion group, and decision-making groups will often move on to questions of value, and ultimately questions of policy, even though the members differ about what the facts are. As a general rule, the more a group can agree upon the facts of a topic, the easier it will be to reach a consensus on their ultimate question of policy.

2. *Questions of value.* Questions of value are even more difficult to answer than questions of fact, in part because it is difficult to frame the question so we can verify the answer, but mostly because of the emotions that are attached to each value. Questions of value produce the biggest breaches in a group's commitment to rationality. It is difficult for us to compromise our values, and yet compromise is required for decisions to be reached.

Many times groups attempt to answer their questions of value by establishing criteria that will allow for verifiable evidence to be used. The aborting of a human fetus has been a long-standing emotional topic in the history of western culture. A group discussing the legality of abortion might ask the value question: "Is an abortion immoral?" After much discussion the group might discover all the members believe in the sacredness of human life; and then proceed to reduce their question of value on the morality of abortion to the question of fact: "When does human life occur?" The group members would then be able to seek out expert testimony and examine scientific research reports. They may then find that some people believe that life occurs at conception (the spiritual argument); some believe that life occurs when the baby can sustain its life outside the mother (the clinical argument); and some argue that human life occurs at birth (the legal argument). The group would probably conclude that they had three value structures present in the group that were almost impossible to resolve, and that a policy decision would by definition violate somebody's value structure. Successful groups manage to reach decisions that contain explicit compromising of some member's values, while at the same time maintaining group unity.

3. *Questions of policy.* Despite the lack of clarity and agreement that exists in the group in regard to questions of fact and value, eventually the group must act. The group must decide what must be done. Answering a question of policy is ultimately a comparative process in which various alternative courses of action are compared. This process is generally quite rational and pragmatic in that the advantages and disadvantages of each proposal are examined. However, the problem in answering a question of policy lies in the difficulty of forecasting the impact of new courses of action.

After various alternatives have been set forth and examined, the group must finally recognize the "right" policy. What is the right policy is rarely verifiable because of the inherent limitations of assessing what the outcome of our action will be. This is one of the reasons why discussion theorists have clung to the process of group discussion for arriving at truth. In our legal system we do not defend any given jury's decision as being just, but we defend the legal system's "due process" as our best chance at achieving justice. Small group theorists have devised numerous systems for dealing with questions of policy.

RESEARCH AND ORGANIZATIONAL STRATEGIES FOR DISCUSSION

In some quarters group discussions have the bad reputation of being an inefficient use of valuable time. In the business world you frequently hear people complaining about the low productivity of a meeting they just attended. Some people even calculate the salaries of the seven or eight people present and estimate the amount lost to the company. This sort of criticism is often justified. Part of the reason why groups waste time relates to a lack of time spent in preparation for the meeting. We sometimes harbor the feeling that the leader is responsible for setting the agenda and therefore all we have to do is show up and see what happens. The fact of the matter is that good discussants spend as much time researching the discussion topic as the leader. When we see a good round table discussion on television that appears casual and relaxed, you can be sure that a great deal of time was spent by each panel member researching the subject. On occasion, a television discussant will have a whole research staff to support those few minutes of air time. Whether you are participating in a campus discussion, attending a corporate business meeting, or working in a public group on social policy, there are basic research and organizational strategies you can use to ensure that you are well informed and able to make a positive contribution to the group.

1. *Library research strategies.* Libraries of the future may be called informational retrieval systems; and with computer, laser-beam, and microfiche technologies, we may one day do a literature search from our home-based terminal. Even today, there are corporations that already have placed all their data on computer cards so that all information has to be retrieved at the computer terminal. However, for most of us, particularly when dealing with a political policy issue, the conventional library is still our major resource for printed material. So it is important to know how to obtain information in college and public libraries.

Four indexes form the basis for gathering materials on a given subject. They are: *The New York Times Index, The Monthly Catalog of United States Government Publications, The Reader's Guide to Periodical Literature,* and the library's card catalog of its holdings. Start with the library's card catalog and locate the four most recent books on your subject. Go to these books and look at their footnotes and bibliographies to determine what materials authors used in writing their books. Find the major works that were most often footnoted on the four books and examine their bibliographies to see where the authors got their information. This process will soon reveal to you the major works on the subject, and who most people regard as the experts on the subject.

After determining the major authors and books in your literature review, you should then go to *The Monthly Catalog of United States Government Publications*. This catalog lists research and statements that the U.S. has published. Since the U.S. government is the largest publisher in the world, there is a good chance that it has published important works on your topic. One part of the index lists the publications by subject. So if you were to study the "problem of atomic radiation" you could look under this subject heading. If the government has commissioned any studies on radiation, they will be cited in the index which will also list any Senate or House hearings that may have been held on the subject. Finally, the index lists the annual reports of each agency.

The New York Times claims it reports "all the news that's fit to print," and the newspaper is one of the best-indexed dailies in the world. Therefore, *The New York Times Index* is a quick means to survey what has been published in newspapers about your topic. Since most libraries keep *The New York Times* on microfilm, it is easy for you to gain access to the relevant articles.

The Reader's Guide to Periodical Literature lists a wide range of popular magazines and popularized "professional" journals under topic headings. In most cases, this index will quickly produce a hundred worthwhile articles for you to read on your subject. When you add this list to the newspaper articles from *The New York Times,* you will get an idea what the average well-read person knows on the subject. On the other hand, the books you have found plus the government studies should give you an idea of what expert knowledge is available on your subject. If you need to go into more depth about your topic, you need to examine the more specialized indexes in the library. If you are dealing with a legal question, there are numerous law-school indexes. The same is true for catalogued medical information. If your topic touches on the natural sciences or the social sciences, you will find that each discipline has its own set of professional journals which you may examine.

2. *Interviewing research strategies.* The nature of your discussion topic may be such that there is not a great deal of published material on it. This is especially true if you are dealing with a local issue that relates to your school or community, or if you are on a planning committee in a company or volunteer organization. In situations like this, you need to gather your own data from people who suspect have the knowledge you are seeking.

The three channels you can use are face-to-face discussion, the phone, and the mail. Some predetermined set of questions is needed that systematically gets at the information. In the face-to-face situation you may want to tape record the answers you get, or at least take notes on what your selected expert has to say. In the phone and mail approaches, you need to phrase your questions so that short, manageable answers can be provided.

Occasionally, you need to systematically gather your interview information. This is generally done in one of three ways: (a) you sample everyone, or in effect take a census; (b) you take a random sample; or (c) you take a random, stratified sample. For example, consider the problem of refuse collection in your city. If the city council wanted to know what the citizens thought about garbage collection, they could: (a) talk to or mail something to everyone in town, i.e., conduct a census; (b) they could randomly select citizens to talk to, e.g., every fifth name in the phone book; or (c) they could select a sample of the citizenry based on such demographics as age, sex, or section of the city, i.e., use a stratified sample. As long as the questions you ask seem reasonable, and the systematic way in which you gathered your information is defensible, the results of your work should be acceptable to the group.

3. *Observational research strategies.* The information you receive second-hand can be very confusing and contradictory. When this occurs there is no substitute for direct observation. If you are a member of a P.T.A. group that has received continual complaints about traffic patterns at an intersection near a school, you may determine that the printed material you got from the police department, such as traffic flow studies, and your random phone calls to parents in the school neighborhood, leave you unable to decide whether there really is a traffic problem. In this case you may wish to go see for yourself.

Systematic observation includes more than just your direct observation. Certainly walking down to the intersection and watching the traffic flow when school lets out is one way to look at things, but there are ways to make your observational patterns more reliable. One way is to provide an operational definition of "traffic flow," which might mean simply counting the number of cars that go through the intersection during a given time period and comparing this information with the number of cars flowing through another intersection that has traffic lights. A second procedure is to provide an observational definition of "dangerous." This could be done by having several people during specified periods of time record their subjective evaluation of the "dangerousness" of the intersection on several scales such as "most dangerous" to "least dangerous." If the observers all tended to evaluate the traffic situation in the same manner, you may have through your own systematic observation the data you need to form your opinion.

4. *Interpersonal research strategies.* Our technological society tends to highlight questions of fact and underemphasize questions of value in regard to many questions of policy. Many times discussants come well-prepared to discuss the facts of a problem but have not carefully thought out their position on the fundamental values of a policy change. We may think we know our value structure, but in the heat of a discussion, we may find ourselves unable to articulate it, or we may even state positions that in retrospect are not really ours. Therefore, it is important that you carefully consider in advance of a discussion what your values are on the topic. One good technique that will help you in this preparation is to make a list of what values are at stake in the discussion and then talk out to yourself the feelings you have about each one. This exercise will help you refine your thinking so that you can make a better contribution to the group. It also will help you control any excessive emotionality that may be present when you articulate your value structure on a given topic.

5. *Organizational strategies.* Occasionally discussants have overresearched and underorganized their topics. They bring voluminous materials to a discussion, but they discover that an hour-long face-to-face meeting provides little time to search through books or fumble through notes for needed material.

Therefore, experienced discussants condense their information onto notecards and may well make up visual aids that display critical charts and tables for the group to refer to during its deliberations. When public discussions are held on television, vital items of information, particularly statistical tables and charts, are prepared in advance so that they may be called forth on the television screen for the home viewer's benefit. No matter how well researched a discussion topic is, it must be organized to meet the time and situational constraints of the particular discussion situation.

REASONING SKILLS OF THE PARTICIPANT

When a group member goes off to the library to do research on a topic, he or she must determine what information should be gathered in order that the group can make a rational decision. Generally speaking, three types of evidence are gathered: facts, statistics, and opinions. If the campus parking problem is being researched, a good fact to gather may well be a written copy of the current parking policy. Since these policies are generally vague, interviews might be conducted with the parking officials to gather their opinions about the parking policy. Statistics on how many tickets are given annually, and how much money students pay in fines might also be valuable evidence. Thus, the evidence gathered for discussion can be classified into factual evidence, authority opinion, and statistics.

In the process of gathering evidence, the context in which we find it will later help us test its acceptableness. As the researcher reads the parking policies over several years and listens as experts sketch in the evolution of the policy over a period of time, he or she begins to place the parking issues into perspective. He or she might learn, for example, that the parking policies have been examined and altered in the midst of great conflict every year. Or that they are etched in stone and are handed down unchanged from year to year. He or she might find that there is systematic data on parking or that there is a dearth of statistics. Although the researcher does not write down the historical backdrop or context in which evidence is found, he or she tends to form a mental picture of what has taken place, which will form a valuable part of the discussion when the group attempts to evaluate the problem.

TESTS OF EVIDENCE

Finding and testing evidence occur simultaneously during the research process. Presumably, a discussant would only present to the group evidence he or she thought was valid. It is often embarrassing to present evidence in a discussion only to find out that other group members have dismissed the same data because of obvious deficiencies in it. Therefore, it is useful to have some general rules of thumb for assessing the acceptableness of evidence in a discussion. (See Table 4.2 on page 112.)

1. *Tests of factual evidence.* A discussion group's eyewitness observation produces what the group calls *directly observable* facts. The written parking policy is a fact that can be directly observed by the group. However, most of

the factual evidence that a group will deal with is dependent upon *authoritative reporting*. Thus, most work groups must examine the authoritativeness of the source of its facts. This means that the group must treat factual statements as though they were opinions. If the evidence passes the opinion-evidence test, the group will then regard the evidence as fact. Likewise, most of the "facts" present in a discussion are derived from statistics. Therefore, most factual evidence in discussion will have to pass the statistical tests.

If a group is dealing with a problem of unemployment in the United States, the seeking out of actual unemployed people to prove that they actually exist would probably not be a wise or feasible expense of the group's time. Yet, the group might reasonably examine the authoritativeness of agencies and people who report the number of the unemployed. And the group might examine the statistical acceptableness of their reports in attempting to determine how many people are unemployed in the United States.

2.   *Tests of opinion evidence.* In deciding whether we should accept somebody's opinion as acceptable evidence, we generally first determine if it is authoritative—that is, if the person knows what he or she is talking about. If we are dealing with medical opinions, we regard the possession of a medical degree as at least a sign that the person can be believed. On the other hand, we also accept firsthand information as authoritative; for example, you know when you have a headache! However, most discussions generate a large number of authoritative opinions which typically seem to contradict one another. When this occurs, we generally decide whom we are going to believe on the basis of *objectivity, recency, consistency,* and *sufficiency.*

In reading a magazine article, a scientific study, or just listening to someone talk, we try to determine if he or she is objective about the issue in question. If he or she seems unduly biased, we tend to dismiss his or her opinion unless the statements are in contradiction to the known bias of the speaker. In a court of law this is called reluctant testimony. If the director of student parking says the parking laws are unjust toward the students, we tend to write that statement down. Likewise, if a student receives an "F" in class but still maintains that the course and the professor are outstanding, the testimony is believable because it contradicts an expected bias.

When we have two statements by physicians that list the causes of lung cancer, and one statement is from 1933 and the other from 1985, we might accept the more recent statement, under the general belief that new knowledge has come to light since the first statement was made. If we have two statements from unbiased sources and compare them on the basis of consistency and sufficiency, we will choose the one that is logically consistent, not only with itself, but also with other assertions that we have already found to be acceptable. In addition, the statement chosen should contain sufficient information so that the group will feel confident that the source is reliable. Fragmented opinions sometimes indicate the presence of a dishonest source. For example, if a source claimed that the rain yesterday cost Jane Doe the election, that statement by itself might be regarded as internally inconsistent, or at best insufficient.

3.   *Tests of statistical evidence.* The *objectivity* of a source is very important to a group in determining whether or not the members should believe the statistics reported. For example, an organization that is already on record as opposing national medical care might claim to have shown that the average American family has $1,000 for medical care. Yet they might not report that the mode (that is, the amount most frequently found) in this study is $200 per family. So the old adage is still true, "Statistics don't lie, but people lie with statistics."

Even when a discussion group accepts that the source of a statistic is objective, members may still question the findings because of their disagreement with the operational definitions of key concepts used in the study. A study reported in a professional journal might report that twenty percent of the people experience stage fright when giving a public speech. The group members' own experience may indicate that they very rarely see people who experience stage fright—that is, who are unable to give a speech. A close examination of the study could reveal that the researcher's operational definition of stage fright arose from one item on a questionnaire that asked people if they had ever experienced stage fright when giving a speech. In almost every piece of research, there is room for argument about whether the operational definitions used in the study really capture the meaning of what is actually under investigation. So when group discussants read a statistic that thirty percent of the American people live in poverty, they should immediately ask themselves "What is the operational definition of poverty used in the study, and do I agree with it?"

Sometimes work groups by necessity get deeply involved with a topic and, as a result, must closely examine a number of statistical studies. The results of these examinations will lead the group into a consideration of the research designs of the major studies to see if they have been replicated. The controversies that surround birth control pills and their linkage to medical problems such as cancer produce highly technical public discussions that often center on the design of the research; i.e., how the experiments were set up. Discussants want to know if there were good controls; how the sample was taken; what was the size of the dose; and if it is possible to generalize from the laboratory animals used in the experiments to humans. They will also ask whether several researchers using the same procedures came up with the same

TABLE 4.2
TESTS OF EVIDENCE

Evidence Type	Questions to Test Evidence
Factual	Directly observable?
	Authoritatively reported?
	Statistically acceptable?
Opinion	Authoritative?
	Objective?
	Recent?
	Consistent?
	Sufficient?
Statistical	Acceptable operational definition?
	Well designed?
	Replications?
	Objectively reported?

findings; that is, was there replication? Lay discussion groups are very capable of delving into and competently evaluating very complex issues if they have been given sufficient time and motivation. However, superficial treatment of important problems by uninformed sources is not only boring to listen to, but dangerous in terms of the conclusions that can be reached.

TYPES OF ARGUMENT

In our commitment to rational discussion, the normative behavior for a discussant is not only to thoroughly research evidence on a topic but to marshal that evidence in some fashion so that logical arguments are built that will justify the conclusions the group reaches. There are four different types of small arguments that are most frequently performed using the facts, statistics and opinions that we gather. They are arguments from *authority assertion, sign, example,* and *cause.*

In fifth and sixth grade, most of us learned the important parts of a sentence and how they relate to each other by going to the blackboard and diagramming sentences. In 1958, Stephen Toulmin developed a system for laying out logical arguments that is very much like diagramming sentences. Toulmin (1958), a British logician, stated that a rational argument is essentially movement from acceptable data through a warrant to a claim. This definition of argument was interpreted and developed by two American speech communication scholars, Douglas Ehninger and Wayne Brockriede, and has now become a routine way for explaining rational argument to debaters and group discussants (Brockriede and Ehninger 1960).

Toulmin's system contains six components: three major parts and three minor parts. The major components are data, warrant, and claim; the three minor parts are backing, qualifier, and reservation. So an argument starts with acceptable evidence. From that evidence we make an inferential leap, i.e., warrant, to some claim or conclusion. The backing is evidence that supports the warrant and thus helps justify the acceptableness of an inferential leap. A qualifier expresses the degree of confidence or probability we attach to our claim. The reservation expresses our doubts about the acceptableness of the argument. The layout of these six components is as follows:

1. *Argument by Authority Assertion.* Probably the most common form of rational argument in discussion is argument from authority assertion. Since we live in such a complex society, we are often forced to form conclusions which are merely restatements of conclusions reached by people we regard as experts. This kind of argument lays out on the Toulmin system in the following manner.

As you can see in Figure 4.1, the acceptableness of an authority-assertion argument finally boils down to the group's belief in the credibility of Dr. Jones as an authority and, if that is not sufficient, to an examination of Dr. Jones's

FIGURE 4.1
ARGUMENT BY AUTHORITY ASSERTION

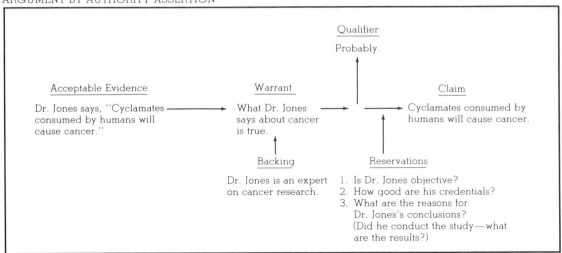

reasons for reaching these conclusions. If Dr. Jones did not rely on another authority for his or her conclusion, then he or she probably reached his or her conclusion on the basis of one or more of the following arguments; sign, example, and cause.

2. *Argument by Sign.* In our day-to-day lives, we rely upon sign argument to survive. Road signs, weather signs, and nonverbal cues from people are used almost instantaneously in drawing conclusions about danger, rain, and emotional mood respectively. Economists use economic indicators as signs that point to the health of the economy, and physicians use physiological systems as indicators of sickness or health.

Finding a reliable set of signs that always point to the same conclusion is hard to come up with on most topics. In the argument in Figure 4.2, we can see the two weaknesses in sign argument. First, the same signs may point to more than one conclusion, and sometimes things occur without the accompanying telltale signs. Thus, reaching group conclusions based solely on sign argument should be quite tentative.

3. *Argument by Example.* Group discussions are filled with arguments from example. No sooner does somebody state an opinion in a meeting than someone will ask for several examples to support it. Sometimes the examples are short "for instances" and at other times they are statistical summations of hundreds of examples. But in either case we are generally making some sort of similar comparisons, thinking that what has been true in past situations will be true in the case that the group is currently discussing.

Arguments from example can be broken down in the way that is shown in Figure 4.3. If you look closely enough, you will find that two cases are hardly ever the same. Either the people or the situation are different. However, if we get too picky, we become skeptics and a group will never reach any conclusion. That is why we have developed statistical procedures that allow us to make probability statements such as ninety-five times out of a hundred Sam will

FIGURE 4.2
ARGUMENT BY SIGN

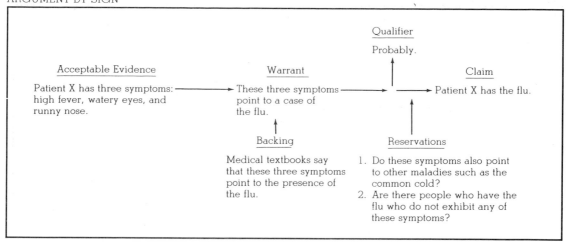

climb the stairs successfully. So carefully examine the examples in your data to see if they are similar to the ones in your claim, but don't get fanatical about it.

4. *Argument by Cause.* Ultimately, groups hope to understand the causal forces involved in a given issue because this tends to produce the best-founded conclusions. Before we knew the causes of such diseases as polio or Black Death, well-meaning groups drew all sorts of outrageous conclusions based only on arguments by authority assertion, sign, and example. Yet even when our evidence allows us to form causal arguments, there is still much room for disagreement in a discussion group. Cigarette smoking, and its cause-and-effect relationship to cancer, is a good example of a controversy that first

FIGURE 4.3
ARGUMENT BY EXAMPLE

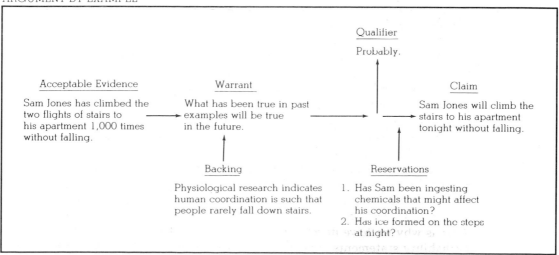

FIGURE 4.4
ARGUMENT BY CAUSE

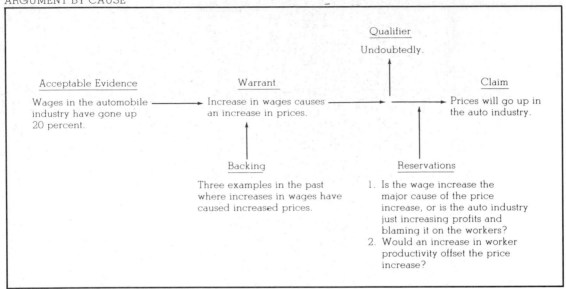

started out with the argument dependent only upon authority, sign, or example and has lasted for decades. As more and more research was done, however, the argument began to center on the issue of causality. Sustaining a causal argument is difficult—first, because most things we call effects have multiple causes. Thus, groups spend a great deal of time listing the various causes of effects and trying to determine what are the major causes. Another problem we have with causal arguments is that intervening factors may offset the normal cause-and-effect relationship. (See Figure 4.4.) Nonetheless, discussion groups should work hard to establish as many causal relationships as their evidence will allow.

PREPARING DISCUSSION OUTLINES

The best way we know how to help you prepare a discussion outline is by providing you with sample outlines developed and used by work groups in our classes. The assignment for the students was to prepare and present a forty-five-to-sixty-minute panel discussion on a question of policy using Ross's Four-Step Agenda System. The students used brainstorming techniques to help determine their topics. All of the discussants spent several hours in the library gathering evidence and developing their arguments. The outlines were developed in advance of the discussion, but the actual panel discussions featured spontaneous interaction before a live audience. In preparing your discussion outlines, you may wish to refer to the material in Chapter 3 on formats, agenda systems, and specific discussion techniques, and you might want to be able to test evidence and evaluate arguments. Below are two discussion outlines that were developed by Illinois State University students.

SAMPLE DISCUSSION OUTLINE #1

PANEL DISCUSSION AGENDA

TOPIC: Robots In Industry

DISCUSSION QUESTION: To what degree should robots be integrated into industry?

I. DEFINITIONS

    A. Robots: "A reprogrammable, multifunctional manipulator, (links and joints capable of movement), designed to move material, parts, tools, or specialized devices through variable programmed motions for the performance of a variety of tasks," according to the Robot Institute of America.

    B. Industry: A collection of firms engaged in the manufacturing and/or production-related process.

II. LIMITATIONS

    A. Robots
        1. Immobile
        2. Limited to a fixed path

    B. Industry
        1. Large, labor employment
        2. Production processes

III. ANALYSIS

    A. Facts
        1. Basic information
            (a) Description
            (b) Application
        2. Economics
            (a) Robots in industry
            (b) Labor market
            (c) Industrial use
        3. Social, psychological, unions
            (a) Displacement of workers
            (b) Workers most affected
                (1) Unskilled
                (2) Women
                (3) Old
                (4) Young
            (c) Problems of adjustment
            (d) Creation of new jobs
            (e) Job satisfaction
            (f) Inside the U.A.W., Local 974
                (1) Fears of robot implementation
                (2) Requests of U.A.W.
                (3) Advantages of robot use
                (4) No choice position
        4. Safety
            (a) OSHA regulations
            (b) Worker protection

         (c) Repetitious jobs
      5. International competition
         (a) U.S. falling behind
         (b) Improvement

   B. Probabilities
      1. Economics
         (a) Robots in industry
         (b) Worker displacement
         (c) Production capabilities
      2. Social, psychological, unions
         (a) Takeover by robots
         (b) Displacement of workers
      3. International competition
         (a) Numbers of robots
         (b) World leaders

   C. Social Values
      1. Economics
         (a) Robots in industry
         (b) Labor market
         (c) Industrial use
      2. Social, psychological, unions
         (a) Jobs
            (1) More rewarding
         (b) Technology
            (1) Easier work
            (2) Better work
            (3) Less fear
         (c) Education
            (1) Appeals for greater funding
            (2) More technological training
            (3) More courses offered
      3. International competition
         (a) Aiding other countries

IV. SOLUTION CRITERIA

   A. Cost benefits
      1. Less waste
      2. Increased production
      3. Less total wages paid out
      4. Reduced employee-benefit costs
      5. Greater world competition

   B. Health and safety
      1. Better working environment
      2. Eliminating tedious jobs
      3. Fewer on-site injuries

   C. Quality control
      1. Reduced human errors
      2. Greater accuracy
      3. Repeatability
      4. Improved inspection techniques

D. Human factors
   1. Greater job satisfaction
   2. Increase in new technological jobs
   3. Retrained displaced workers

V. POSSIBLE SOLUTIONS

A. Implemented to fullest extent
   1. Remain internationally competitive
   2. No regard to social costs

B. Robots should be used
   1. The given technology is available
   2. Protection from hazardous jobs
   3. Cost effective
   4. Improved quality
   5. Retrain workers

C. Should not be implemented
   1. Too expensive
   2. High social costs

SAMPLE DISCUSSION OUTLINE #2

THE ARAB-ISRAELI CONFLICT

I. DEFINITIONS

A. Question of policy—what should U.S./Israeli policy be towards the Palestinians to achieve peace in the Middle East?

B. Key terms
   1. Palestinians—the geographically dispersed people, some of whom previously or currently live in the area that was formerly Palestine which is now Israel. They have a group identity and regard the Palestine Liberation Organization (the PLO) as the sole legitimate representative of the Palestinian people.
   2. Zionism—Jewish nationalism and the belief in a Jewish state or homeland.
   3. Current policies
       (a) U.S.—does not recognize the PLO, but wants Israel to stop expansion of the Jewish settlements on the West Bank and to negotiate the establishment there of a Palestinian entity linked to Jordan.
       (b) Israel—does not recognize the PLO and intends to build more settlements on the West Bank with the goal of 1 million Israelis on the West Bank by 2010.
       (c) PLO—does not recognize Israel's right to exist and has as its ultimate goal a free Palestine. (Note—this platform is a moderation of its earlier goal of the destruction of Israel by force of arms).
   4. Occupied lands—areas of the Golan Heights, West Bank, and Gaza Strip that were taken in the 1967 Arab/Israeli war and contain a majority population of Palestinians who feel oppressed by the Israelis.

II. LIMITATIONS

    A. Military
        1. U.S. involvement
        2. Israeli military policy
        3. PLO

    B. Political
        1. U.S. foreign aid and policy towards Israel and PLO
        2. Israeli policy towards the Palestinians
        3. PLO policy towards Israel

    C. Social
        1. Palestinian attitudes towards Israel
        2. Israeli attitudes towards Palestinians
        3. The perception of the U.S. public in terms of Israel and the Palestinians

III. ANALYSIS

    A. Facts
        1. Military
            (a) History—when, where, and how of battles
            (b) Current military status
            (c) Current amounts of U.S. foreign aid
        2. Political
            (a) Major leaders
            (b) Palestinian nationalism
            (c) Official policies
        3. Social
            (a) Palestinians in the Israeli occupied lands

    B. PROBABILITIES
        1. Military
            (a) Arafat will reunite the military units of the Palestinians that were dispersed when Israel invaded Lebanon.
            (b) Continuation of the status quo would most likely lead to another Middle Eastern war.
        2. Political
            (a) The shift of Israeli policy towards favoring negotiation with the Palestinians will continue.
            (b) Arafat and the PLO have moderated their stance.

    C. Values
        1. Political
            (a) Israel tied to West
            (b) Palestinians to Arabs
        2. Social
            (a) Zionism
            (b) Islam

IV. CRITERIA

    A. Feasible for both parties

    B. Intermediate solutions that are fair to both parties

    C. The cessation of military action against each other

V. SOLUTIONS
   A. Suggested policies
      1. U.S. policy
         (a) Have the U.S. exert pressure on the Israelis to start direct talks between the Palestinians and the Israelis.
         (b) Have the U.S. recognize the PLO as the official political representatives of the Palestinian people.
         (c) Do not move the U.S. embassy to Jerusalem.
      2. Israeli Policy
         (a) Recognize the PLO as the official representatives of the Palestinian people, with the condition that the PLO will concede Israel's right to exist.
         (b) A willingness to moderate their stance and agree to bilaterally stop all military operations.
         (c) Treat the people in the occupied lands better, and develop immigration laws that will allow some of the refugees back into Israel.

SUMMARY

In this chapter, group expectations for participating in discussions were presented on a number of different levels. A discussant's ethical standards were found to include five commitments to fellow discussants: a commitment to do your best, a commitment to the group good, a commitment to rationality, a commitment to fair play, and a commitment to good listening. Another expectation is preparing to discuss. In order to meet this expectation, various research and organizational strategies for discussion were presented.

The reasoning skills of the participants are also found to be crucial to good participation. These include applying the tests of evidence both before the discussion in the research process and during the discussion as you work with material you have gathered. Evidence based on facts, opinions, and statistics should all be appropriately tested. In a commitment to rational discussion, the normative behavior for a discussant also includes the facility to use logical arguments in reaching group conclusions. Four common types of arguments were analyzed; these included arguments from authority assertion, sign, example, and cause.

Finally, two discussion outlines were provided as a means for organizing group members' thought patterns.

REFERENCES

Bormann, E. G. *Discussion and Group Methods.* 2nd edition. New York: Harper and Row, 1975.

Brilhart, J. K. *Effective Group Discussion.* 4th edition. Dubuque, Iowa: Wm. C. Brown, 1982.

Brock, B. L.; Chesebro, J. W.; Cragan, J. F.; and Klumpp, J. F. *Public Policy Decision-Making: Systems Analysis and Comparative Advantages Debate.* New York: Harper and Row, 1973.

Brockriede, W., and Ehninger, D. "Toulmin on Argument: An Interpretation and Application." *Quarterly Journal of Speech* 46 (1960): 44–53.

Gouran, D. S. *Making Decisions in Groups: Choices and Consequences.* Glenview, Ill.: Scott, Foresman and Company, 1982.

Gulley, H. E., and Leathers, D. G. *Communication and Group Process.* 3rd edition. New York: Holt, Rinehart and Winston, 1977.

Scheidel, T. M. and Crowell, L. *Discussing and Deciding: A Desk Book for Group Leaders and Members.* New York: Macmillan, 1979.

Toulmin, S. *The Uses of Argument.* London: Cambridge University Press, 1958.

The leader's responsibilities begin long before the group discussion begins and last long after the actual discussion is over.

CHAPTER OBJECTIVES

In order to be a more effective discussant, when you read this chapter you should focus on the following leadership ideas and communication skills.

YOU NEED TO KNOW:
1. The differences between designated and emergent leadership.
2. The bases of leadership power.
3. The sylistic approaches of designated leadership.
4. The motivational styles of designated leadership.
5. The leadership communication behaviors.
6. The responsibilities of group discussion leaders.

LEADING SMALL GROUP DISCUSSIONS

CHAPTER OUTLINE

DEFINING DISCUSSION LEADERSHIP

APPROACHES TO LEADERSHIP IN SMALL GROUP DISCUSSIONS

Designated-Leader Perspective
1. Trait approach
2. Power approach
3. Stylistic approach
4. Motivational approach

Emergent-Leader Perspective
1. Situational approach
2. Role-emergence theory
3. Functional approach

Discussion-Leader Model

NECESSARY COMMUNICATION BEHAVIORS IN LEADING GROUP DISCUSSIONS

LEADERSHIP COMMUNICATION BEHAVIORS IN THE TASK AREA
1. Contributing ideas
2. Seeking ideas
3. Evaluating ideas
4. Seeking idea evaluation
5. Visualizing abstract ideas
6. Generalizing from specific ideas

LEADERSHIP COMMUNICATION BEHAVIORS IN THE PROCEDURAL AREA
1. Goal setting
2. Agenda-making
3. Clarifying
4. Summarizing
5. Verbalizing consensus

LEADERSHIP COMMUNICATION BEHAVIORS IN THE INTERPERSONAL AREA
1. Regulating participation
2. Climate making
3. Instigating group self-analysis
4. Resolving conflict
5. Instigating conflict

RESPONSIBILITIES OF GROUP DISCUSSION LEADERS

RESPONSIBILITIES OF A DESIGNATED LEADER

RESPONSIBILITIES OF AN EMERGENT LEADER

RESPONSIBILITIES OF A SOCIAL-EMOTIONAL LEADER

GUIDELINES FOR EFFECTIVE DISCUSSION LEADERSHIP
1. Put the group goals ahead of your own.
2. Have a genuine concern for group members.
3. Set a good work pattern.
4. Communicate well and often.
5. Know when to be the leader.

SUMMARY

REFERENCES

CASE STUDY: LEADING A CORPORATE TASK FORCE

DEFINING DISCUSSION LEADERSHIP

You will spend much of your professional life leading small group discussions. It is because we all continually find ourselves in leadership positions that a great deal of research has been devoted to determining the qualities of a leader and the proper leadership behaviors. In this chapter we present seven different approaches to small group leadership showing how each approach tends to emphasize a different aspect of leading a small group. These seven approaches have been tied together in our definition of leading small group discussions.

The first distinction that needs to be made is the one between leader and leadership. We define discussion leadership as *communication which positively influences the group to move in the direction of the group's goals.* A leader of a discussion may be appointed or may emerge from group discussion. Later in this chapter we will discuss the differences between a designated and an emergent leader. Are the two terms "leadership" and "leader" synonymous? We feel the answer is no. Leadership is a much broader term. It is part of the communication process of a discussion and can be performed by any group member. Therefore, it is possible to have a person appointed as leader of a discussion group who exhibits no leadership. Conversely, a person does not have to be the "leader" to move the group toward its goals. However, most people who have emerged as leaders have previously performed leadership functions for the group.

Although most leadership behaviors can be performed by a number of individuals in the group, we generally assume that a leader possesses certain qualities or abilities to aid him or her in moving the group toward its goals. Certain situations—for example, the kind of organizational structure of which a group is a part—will cause one person to emerge as the appointed or elected leader, in preference to another with similar leadership qualities and communication abilities. Although we can be quite specific about leadership functions in a discussion, and we will be, it is very difficult in the abstract to define who a leader of a discussion is and how that person came to be leader. There are several key concepts that fit together in a rough fashion to form a composite picture of a group discussion leader. When we look for personal qualities in a leader, we tend to think in terms of maturity, fairness, fluency, and so on. We may also think of the person in terms of how authoritative he or she is, or how much power he or she possesses. We also consider whether the person has the ability to motivate group members and whether he or she would have better leadership qualities than others in a given situation. After we have detailed these seven basic approaches, we present a conceptual model of how these various concepts interact to form a definition of a discussion leader.

APPROACHES TO LEADERSHIP IN SMALL GROUP DISCUSSIONS

The seven approaches to discussion leadership are classified according to two research perspectives. The first perspective reports research that compared the formal or designated leader to nonleaders. At the same time an attempt is made to highlight the features of each approach. The second perspective views leaders as emerging from the small discussion group and describes the qualities and functions of leadership. The first research perspective focuses on trait, power, stylistic and motivational approaches. Our second leadership perspective discusses situational approach, role-emergence theory, and functional approach.

Designated-Leader Perspective. Most small work groups and most group discussions take place within formal organizational structures. The formal structure spells out designated leader roles that are typically filled through appointment rather than election. When a member of a group is appointed leader he or she may or may not have received support from other group members. In fact, the designated leader could be brought in or transferred to the group never having met the members of the work group. Sometimes a person designated discussion leader for a one-time business meeting has his or her first contact with the group when he or she phones the members to call the meeting. This is particularly true when a problem-solving discussion group is formed on a company-wide basis and people are brought together because of their given areas of specialization. While many designated leaders may have emerged from their group to become the designated leader, many researchers have found it useful to disregard how a person became a designated leader and focus instead on distinctions between people who are designated leaders and those who are not.

1. *Trait Approach.* Small group researchers have long been concerned with the task of determining the differences between leaders and nonleaders with respect to how they *look, talk, think, act,* and *feel.* For the most part, trait research has proved to be a dead end for speech communication scholars. The differences that have been found to exist between leaders and nonleaders are often trivial and almost always difficult to generalize across small group situations. However, certain characteristics have been found repeatedly by social psychologists. The ones that are most important to a student of small group discussion are those personal traits that can be improved upon such as speech fluency, cooperativeness, and knowledge of task. A supervisor would be ill advised to appoint a person as designated leader of a work group simply because he or she possesses the physical, mental, and personality qualities that we report here. However, the possession of certain attributes may influence the supervisor to appoint a person as leader.

Research demonstrates that leaders tend to look different from nonleaders. Physical appearance has proven to be a distinguishing variable over the last forty years. Designated leaders tend to be slightly taller, heavier, and physically more attractive than other group members, and seem to possess the athletic ability and stamina necessary for leadership.

Leaders tend to talk better than nonleaders. Researchers from various disciplines have discovered that fluency of speech, confidence in tone, and frequency of communication sort leaders from nonleaders.

The findings of small group researchers also support the idea that leaders tend to think better, in that they score higher on standard I.Q. tests and tend to show more mental agility in performing problem-solving tasks. While leaders tend to be brighter, they must not be too much brighter than the average members of the group, or they will tend to be rejected. This point of diminishing returns is also true of height; although leaders tend to be taller, they tend to be only slightly taller than other group members.

In addition to the preceding kinds of traits that appear to distinguish leaders from nonleaders, leaders tend to act differently from other group members. Many of these actions are in turn governed by certain personality characteristics that leaders possess. By and large, small group communication research findings seem to suggest that leaders are generally more extroverted, self-assertive, persistent, and responsible than other members of the group. In essence, the favorable personality characteristics cited in the preceding sentence will help their possessor to be a good leader. Leaders tend to be active, not passive, group members, displaying a panorama of personality characteristics that assist them in leading group discussion (Stogdill 1974).

Psychologists have demonstrated repeatedly over the last sixty years that people can be crudely classified into four emotional states that affect the type of designated leader they might become. They were originally labeled: dominance, inducement, submission, and compliance (Marston 1928). If you're a big D (dominance), you tend to be a take-charge, hard-driving, risk-taking leader. If you're a big I (inducement), your view of leadership is one of persuasion, in that you convince your subordinates to work hard, and you sell the importance of your work group within the organization. If you are a big C (compliance), you manage your work group "by the book;" you are a stickler for rules and regulations. If you are a big S (submissive), you tend to let the group have its way and you delegate a lot of leadership decisions to the group. Currently, there are numerous paper-and-pencil tests being used by management consulting companies that will profile you in terms of your emotional bases of leadership. One of the most popular instruments has been developed by a communication scholar, John Geier.

The trait approach to leadership asks us to look at a composite of desirable qualities that generally distinguish leaders from nonleaders. Our discussion to this point has focused on how leaders look, talk, feel, think, and act differently from other members of the group. For an excellent report of research findings in support of the trait approach, consult one or more of the following: McGrath and Altman 1966, Shaw 1981, and Stogdill 1974. Other important qualities of a leader, such as sex, race, and communication skills, are discussed in Chapter 7.

2. *Power Approach.* Since leadership includes influencing and controlling group members in the direction of the group's goals, scholars have focused on the concept of power as one of the means by which a leader can exert influence on the group. French and Raven (1968), reporting in Cartwright and Zander's volume, *Group Dynamics: Research and Theory,* have identified five bases of power that a designated leader may have in varying degrees: legitimate, expert, referent, reward, and coercive.

In formal organizations, legitimate power flows from the job title, and most group members will follow reasonable directives simply because they come from the formally designated group leader. In group discussions, a designated leader tends to exercise the legitimate power of calling a meeting and setting the initial agenda.

Expert power is power attributed to a person for what he or she knows. If a designated leader is knowledgeable about the work the group is doing, expert power and legitimate power will combine to exert control over a group's direction. However, expert power may be possessed by a group member who is not the designated leader. If the latter is the case, a leadership struggle may occur between the designated leader, who has legitimate power, and the group member who has expert power.

The third basis of leadership is referent power—sometimes called attraction power, or charisma. This power is generated by the desire of the group members to identify and associate with an attractive leader. A sociogram would probably reveal that most members of a group would prefer to associate with a leader who has referent power.

The fourth basis of leadership is information power. This is information about the organization that does not come primarily through the formal channels of communication. Group members who have a lot of this power know how to get things done because they have contact with organizational members outside the work group.

Reward and coercive bases of power (the fifth and sixth) are treated together because we see them as being two sides of the same coin, although many designated leaders may complain that they have too few rewards to hand out to group members and that they prefer not to use their coercive power. French and Raven argue that coercive power will be accepted by group members if it comes from a person who also has legitimate power. The person who has the most referent power, of course, may also have the most coercive power, because if he or she refuses to associate with a given member the rejection may be quite painful. The designated discussion leader frequently rewards group members by publicly complimenting them for their contributions to the discussion.

One way to analyze the ability of a designated discussion leader in terms of the influence and control that leader has over the group, is to examine the distribution of the bases of power among the group members. The more these six bases of power are concentrated in the designated discussion leader, the greater that person's ability to control and influence a discussion, or lead a work group. Conversely, the more these powers are shared equally, or occur disproportionately among group members, the less influence and control the designated leader will have.

Effective designated leaders must use leadership power that they don't personally possess but that is present in the group. For example, a designated leader may assign an inexperienced worker to a new task and, on completion of the work, ask the group member with the most expert power regarding the task to evaluate the rookie's job. If the expert gives it high praise, the rookie will feel rewarded, more so than if the appointed leader had praised the task. Thus, the designated leader used power he or she did not have for the group good.

3. *Stylistic Approach.* Under the first research perspective of comparing leaders with nonleaders, it was only natural that the type or style of leadership performed by the designated leader would be examined. A major study, often referred to in discussions of stylistic approach, is reported by White and Lippett (1968). They examined the adult designated leader in the following three contexts: autocratic, democratic, and laissez faire. In essence, the first style of leader was able to set policies, whereas the democratic type of leader facilitated group discussions about policy decisions, and the laissez faire type allowed complete freedom among the group members. This classic study found that autocratic leaders tend to give a lot of orders, have power to approve and praise people and their ideas, and in general be somewhat critical. On the other hand, the study showed that democratic leaders tend to give a fair number of suggestions, exercise self-discipline and be noncritical and matter-of-fact in their relations with the other group members. White and Lippett found that laissez faire leaders exceed the other two styles only in information giving. Two communication researchers, Sargent and Miller (1971), reported much the same kind of results in terms of the behavior of autocratic and democratic leaders, particularly in relation to task-oriented communication. Autocratic leaders tend to rush through the question and answer process, whereas democratic leaders try to encourage much more member participation and discussion.

A tendency in analyzing the styles of leadership approach is to character-ize one leader as being more leader-centered and another as being more group-centered. Typically, we think of leader-centered leaders as more autocratic than the group-centered leader who follows a more democratic, or even laissez faire style of leadership. A designated leader who follows a leader-centered approach in a discussion may do so because of time constraints and the fact that the meeting will run more efficiently if he or she controls member comments and the like. On the other hand, a group-centered leader encourages member participa-tion and interaction. Wischmeier (1955), in one of the more important studies done in the field of speech, pointed out the paradox of designated discussion leadership styles: group members perceive the leader-centered leader as doing a more effective job; however, they seem to enjoy greater individual satisfaction, and like the group better in general, under a group-centered leadership. Not surprisingly then, when one leadership style is favored over another, there will be pluses and minuses for the task and social dimensions of small groups. One communication researcher, Raymond Ross (1974), has suggested that when you visualize the styles of discussion leadership on a continuum, the individual who has been designated leader must learn to play the styles-of-leadership contin-uum like a violin. He further suggests it takes a "virtuoso" to play the styles of leadership appropriately for given group discussion situations.

Furthermore, researchers have been defining the leadership styles of designated leaders of work groups, which parallels the research done initially on leaders of discussion in the 1940s and 1950s. Douglas McGregor (1960) popularized two different views of management or leadership style. McGregor posited that some leaders reflect a Theory X style ("my way or the highway" approach). This style flows from an assumption that an organization is controlled through the exercise of authority and that subordinates must be carefully watched. McGregor's second style (Theory Y) emphasizes "people skills." This style assumes that workers enjoy work and that they will work hard if they are kept motivated by humanistic leaders. A leader using this style would be sensitive to group member needs and seek input before making decisions. A third style is called Theory Z (a team management approach). William Ouchi (1981) believes that much of Japanese management's success is due in part to the use of Theory Z. A leader using Theory Z would continually invite group members to participate in management decision making. Thus the line between the designated leader and other members would be blurred.

Today decision-making groups that focus on quality and productivity, and contain both supervisors and subordinates, are called quality circles (QC). The QC movement, which started in Japan, has now spread throughout the United States. In 1983, it was estimated that over 10,000 American companies were using QC's (Cuffe and Cragan 1983).

4. *Motivational Approach.* The motivational approach to the designated leadership is the last to be considered. Researchers who work on the motivational approach to leadership try to explain how a designated leader influences the group to get the job done. Some scholars of group leadership refer to general styles by which people motivate their work group. These motivational styles should not be confused with the stylistic approach to leadership that was discussed in the preceding section, although there are some striking similarities. The motivational styles focus on the social and task dimensions of the group and attempt to explain how much direction and control the leader needs to have to get the work done. The two theories we will discuss here are Blake and Mouton's "managerial grid" and Hersey and Blanchard's leadership theory.

Robert Blake and Jane Mouton (1964) build a two-dimensional matrix for classifying a designated leader's motivational style. One side of the matrix consists of nine cells of concern for people—that is, the social-emotional dimension—while the other side consists of nine cells of concern for production, i.e., the task dimension. Thus, Blake and Mouton's managerial grid contains eighty-one potential slots in which a given designated leader might fit. Low production but high concern for people would be rated 1/9 "country club." This kind of leader is extremely concerned with the members' happiness but not too concerned about reaching a decision in the discussion group. On the other hand, a 9/1 rating or "task master" would be just the opposite, with no concern for the feelings of the group members and highly task oriented in wanting to get the job done at all costs. The ideal leadership style, using the Blake and Mouton approach, is the 9/9 or "team player." This leader is extremely interested both in accomplishing the task and in group member satisfaction. For a number of years, managers in corporations referred to themselves as 5/5's, 2/8's, etc., although they really hoped that they approached the ideal of a 9/9 rating.

Although most scholars accept the position that a good designated group leader must be concerned with both the task and the social dimension of the group, many disagree with the notion that people have a fixed number of abilities with which to lead a group. Moreover, some researchers object to the idea that the ideal motivational leadership style is 9/9. Paul Hersey and Kenneth Blanchard (1977) argue that an effective group leader varies his or her motivational leadership style depending on the ability of the members, their maturity, and their willingness to do a given assignment. They argue that an effective leader needs a repertoire of four motivational leadership styles: *telling, selling, participating,* and *delegating.* Figure 5.1 shows our conceptualization of Hersey and Blanchard's four motivational leadership styles, which are quite different from each other in terms of the amount of control the leader exerts on the group.

The "telling" style is used by a discussion or work group leader when the group lacks the maturity to know how, when, or where to do a given task. The leader is very directive and walks the group through the work that needs to be

FIGURE 5.1
THE FOUR MOTIVATIONAL LEADERSHIP STYLES

Style	Telling	Selling	Participating	Delegating
	High task ↑ Low social ↑	High task ↑ High social ↑	Low task ↑ High social ↑	Low task ↑ Low social ↑
Maturity level of group	Low	Moderate		High
Amount of time working together	None	Little	Some	Extensive

From Paul Hersey and Kenneth H. Blanchard, *Management of Organizational Behavior: Utilizing Human Resources,* 3rd ed., © 1977, p. 170. Adapted by permission of Prentice-Hall, Inc., Englewood Cliffs, New Jersey.

done. The fact that this style is low in relationship behavior does not mean that the leader is not friendly or personable, but that his or her energy is focused on how the job should be done. When this type of leadership style is called for, it usually means that a collection of people has just formed a work group and that the designated leader has considerable knowledge and experience with the group's task. Corporations will often bring together new employees under the supervision of an experienced worker. If the company is an accounting firm, it may bring together four new accountants and have them report to a veteran C.P.A. While the new accountants are well trained and know accounting procedures, they will still need a supervisor to tell them how the company does its audit. In fact, most of the initial meetings will emphasize the handling of tasks.

The telling style is also used in emergencies. If a person has a heart attack in your class, and there is a student who has had emergency medical training or EMT, this person usually steps forth to give orders. The EMT-trained student will be so wrapped up in telling everybody how to do his or her job that little time will be left for social-emotional stroking. In any case, most of the students working on the heart attack victim will not expect to be reinforced with positive statements by the emergency group leader.

A Monday morning meeting of a divisional sales force is typical of the situations that call for the "selling" style of motivational leadership. The sales manager has probably made up the coming week's sales goals and mapped out the kind of effort it will take to accomplish them. Furthermore, he or she is directly responsible for the results and probably has a mixture of novice and experienced sales people. In this meeting the sales manager will spend considerable energy on convincing the sales force that it can meet the week's goals. This will be done by a lot of positive reinforcement, based on past successes and substantial firsthand knowledge of how a sales campaign should go. In fact, any work group that must constantly re-prove its worth on a week-to-week basis will probably have a designated leader who uses the "selling" motivational leadership style. The coaches of our high-school and college athletic teams continually employ this style in getting their teams ready for the next game. However, some of the large professional athletic teams have such a mature group that the coach can revert to a "delegating" style of leadership.

The "participating" motivational leadership style is typified by numerous small group situations. Volunteer groups and decision-making discussion groups are two excellent examples of where this motivational leadership style is often applied. A volunteer organization for the Cancer Society or Heart Association usually has a paid designated leader in charge of an all-volunteer work group. In this situation, the success of the group is dependent upon the designated leader's ability to get active participation from various volunteer members. The designated leader has little or no legitimate power and must spend a great deal of time stroking the volunteer work force. Any volunteer work group needs to be constantly told that they are nice people and that they are doing a good job! Designated leaders of decision-making groups have much in common with the paid staff leader of volunteer groups. If a group of executives is brought together to make decisions about a company policy, the designated leader for this decision-making group will probably want to adopt a "participating" style of motivational leadership, sometimes falling back to the "selling" style where consensus seems possible.

When a designated leader is placed in charge of a long-standing, effective work group, the leader may often adopt a "delegating" style of motivational leadership because the group is mature, knows its job, and is confident of its ability. Chairpersons of academic departments in colleges often adopt this style of motivational leadership in their day-to-day handling of faculty, the chairperson changing to a "selling" style of leadership when conducting monthly staff meetings.

Hersey and Blanchard stress that a designated leader must adapt to changing situations when selecting his or her appropriate leadership style—for example, if the membership or the task of a group changes. Hersey and Blanchard believe that the designated leader should adopt a leadership style according to the maturity level of the group.

Emergent-Leader Perspective. Many of the more informal discussion settings in which we find ourselves take considerably different leadership patterns from those described above. As a matter of fact, certain ongoing groups in organizational structures follow what appears to be a rather low-key, democratic work group approach. In many of these ongoing work groups, where the group has developed a definite history, leaders may be emergent rather than designated. The major approaches to the study of leadership we will consider here are the situational approach, role-emergence theory, and the functional approach to leadership. Even when there is a designated leader, a natural leader may emerge. In addition, group members can perform certain leadership functions whether there is an assigned leader or not. The emergent-leader perspective gives us another lens through which to look at leadership behaviors, regardless of where they originate, and contributes to our study of small-group-discussion leadership in general. The emergent-leader perspective has been emphasized by speech communication researchers for essentially two reasons: (1) our interest in providing communication training for discussion leaders, and (2) our general scholarly interest in describing the communication of work groups in order to understand their effectiveness.

1. *Situational Approach.* Fred Fiedler (1967) studied over 800 work groups, from B29 bomber crews to Boy Scout troops, in a twenty-year search for a theory that would predict leader effectiveness. Fiedler argues that there are four variables that interact in a work situation to determine a leader's effectiveness. They are: (1) how much power the leader has; (2) how structured the task is; (3) how well the leader is liked by the group members; and (4) whether the leader is basically a relationship-oriented or task-oriented leader. By studying these variables, Fiedler developed what he called a contingency model that can predict or improve a given leader's performance. His model indicates that task-oriented leaders function best in highly structured and highly unstructured situations; that is, in mechanical or automatic situations, or in situations of crisis. Fiedler's findings are consistent with Hersey and Blanchard's recommendation that in either of these situations the leader should adopt a "telling" style. According to Fiedler, relationship-oriented leaders perform best in middle-range structured tasks and situations where formal leadership is not well liked and the leader must depend on developing willing participation of the group members.

Fiedler's Contingency Model hinges on one key test he administers to leaders. He calls this test the Least Preferred Coworker (LPC) rating scale. Fiedler asks a subject to think of a person with whom he or she least prefers to work and then asks him or her to rate the person on a sixteen-item scale. Some of the items on the scale are efficient-inefficient, cooperative-uncooperative, friendly-unfriendly, quarrelsome-harmonious. If a leader tends to fill out this scale in a way that describes his or her least preferred coworker in terms of the worker's inability to do the job, then Fiedler classifies the leader as task oriented. Conversely if the leader scores high on the social dimensions, Fiedler describes this person as a relationship-oriented leader.

Fiedler is so convinced by his findings that he would adjust situations before he would try to train leaders. We, on the other hand, believe that a person can develop a wide range of communication competencies that will serve that person well in a number of different leadership situations. Our belief is supported by Julia T. Wood (1977), a communication researcher, who has studied the situational approach to leading group discussions.

Wood acknowledges Fiedler's attempts to match leader styles with situational requirements; however, she focuses on "adaptive behavior" and how it calls for some form of adjustment by a leader to the constraints of a situation. Wood's most important finding, in our opinion, is that adaptive behavior is engaged in by leaders of purposive discussions. This idea seems to be supported by the fact that the leaders in her study were responsive to failures in previous discussions; i.e., the leaders varied their oral behaviors in order to achieve overtly expressed discussion goals. For example, it was found that a certain type of discussion leader—Leader B—was found to adapt his or her leadership behaviors from the first meeting to the second. He or she wished to arrive at consensus in an expeditious manner in the second meeting and was much less interested in drawing out the ideas of all members than he or she had been in the first meeting. Consequently, Leader B adapted his or her leadership behaviors on the basis of the group situation, with particular emphasis on the members' expressed discussion goals.

2. *Role-Emergence Theory.* We have all observed the situation where a work group in an organization has a designated leader, but the members turn to another person as their "real" or "natural" leader. Often the formal and natural leader are one and the same person, but when this is not the case some accommodation must be worked out. For example, in the army a second lieutenant may be the formal leader of a rifle platoon, while the "lifer" sergeant is the natural leader of the group. When this situation occurred in Vietnam, the sergeant would often be the decision maker while on patrol in the field; the second lieutenant would function as leader back at the base camp.

As we indicated in Chapter 2, Ernest Bormann (1975) and his graduate students have been interested in how a natural leader emerges in a small discussion group. Their research reveals several communication processes or paths by which a leader emerges. Bormann metaphorically refers to this process as the "method of residues." Members of the group are gradually eliminated from competition until one person remains. He or she is the "residue" or candidate for leader. The Minnesota studies report that while there are many patterns of leader emergence, all the patterns go through two basic stages. The first covers a relatively brief period, generally no longer than one meeting, in which about half the group's membership is eliminated from the possibility of being the group leader. How people come to be eliminated from the leadership role is under continual, intense study, but certain communication behaviors seem to be important. The first is the total absence of communication; if a member does not take an active part, he or she will probably be eliminated during the first phase of consideration of who will be the leader. In fact, many times people intentionally remain quiet because they have no desire to become leader. Among the communicatively active participants, those members that seem irrational, uninformed, or extremely dogmatic also tend to be eliminated during the first phase of Bormann's "method of residues."

Bormann's Minnesota studies describe the second phase as a very intense struggle for leadership. Bormann uses four typical scenarios to illustrate how leaders emerge. Scenario I is a pattern of leader emergence, relatively free of conflict, in which, during the second phase, a leader candidate picks up what Bormann calls a "lieutenant." A lieutenant is a group member who will reinforce the ideas and suggestions of the leader candidate. He or she will also provide much of the emotional stroking of other group members during this emergent process. If only one leader candidate picks up a lieutenant, then that candidate will generally emerge as leader, and thus the discussion group will have formed and be ready to go to work.

The second scenario of leadership emergence found by the Minnesota studies is the pattern that boils down to two leader candidates, each of whom has a lieutenant. This scenario produces intense competition and an extended second phase simply because candidates are so well matched that either one could probably lead the group successfully. If the struggle is never resolved, the group never really becomes cohesive. There is a lot of bickering and arguing, and it is uncomfortable to be part of a meeting when this type of struggle is taking place. Since the struggle is not overt—and by that we mean the candidates are not saying "I want to be leader"—the struggle manifests itself in discussions about the problem at hand and how it best can be solved. If one candidate finally emerges, the group's problems are not over, because the second-place candidate will generally become a central negative. A central negative is an articulate, active group member who will forcibly argue against the will of the majority and particularly against suggestions that are championed by the new emergent leader. How the new leader treats the central negative is crucial to the future success of the group. Ernest and Nancy Bormann (1976), advise group leaders not to purge their central negatives, but instead give them important tasks to do since they are obviously capable and are respected by other group members.

Scenario III of the Minnesota studies illustrates how a leader is produced as a result of a crisis. Movies and television programs often use this scenario as their basic plot outline. A group of normal people are thrust into a very abnormal situation such as an earthquake, a fire, a flood, or a pestilence, along with assorted malfunctionings of air, sea, and land modes of transportation. In this sort of crisis a leader quickly emerges who is uniquely suited to deal with it. Unfortunately, this Hollywood-genre leader tends to reinforce rather unrealistic, "macho" male characterizations that distort the attributes normally required for a person to emerge as a natural leader of a typical work group in industry and government.

The fourth scenario of leader emergence reported by Bormann is essentially a diary of a group that failed. In this scenario a leader does not emerge, although there are continual struggles for leadership. The struggle is more diffused than in Scenario II in that hardly anyone can agree on a likely candidate. The reasons for this complete fragmentation are quite complex, but recent studies at Minnesota indicate that some of the problems relate to the racial and sexual composition of the group. Some white members may not accept black leadership or vice versa, and some males may not accept female leadership, or vice versa. Bormann, Pratt, and Putnam (1978) in a monograph entitled, "Power, Authority, and Sex: Male Response to Female Leadership," reported on a rich case history of a simulated corporation, made up of several work groups, that essentially failed. The failure of the entire company revolved around male-female conflicts in the struggle for various leadership roles. The study shows graphically how careful attention must be given to intervening variables such as sex and race as they relate to group formation. Thus, while the studies of leader traits, as compared to nonleader traits, prove to be a scholarly dead end, the way in which traits interplay with communication patterns may provide many useful insights into understanding how leaders emerge.

3. *Functional Approach.* Since 1960, when Barnlund and Haiman's classic small group textbook, *The Dynamics of Discussion,* entered the market, speech communication scholars have been concerned with the significant influences that can be used to move the group closer to its goal. These significant influences we identify as leadership functions. As early as 1953, Barnlund had convinced many speech scholars that certain leadership skills can be taught, and had illustrated how certain skills—that is, leadership functions—could be taught even to those group members who were not leader types.

The functions of leadership include anything that influences a group regardless of its source. In other words, a leadership function can be performed by a designated leader or by any group member. The key point is that the function moves the group toward the group goal. Of course it is possible, and frequently happens, that a leadership function moves the group away from the group goal. For example, if the leader of your discussion asks a member to summarize the main points of the solution and she responds by suggesting that the group adjourn to a local bar, the leadership function performed has been a significant influence that moves the group away from its stated goal. Regardless of who initiated this move, a designated leader or other group member, it nonetheless influenced the group either positively or negatively.

The many specific leadership functions that can be performed in a group have typically been classified into two, three, or four major headings. Goal achievement and group maintenance are two general headings for leadership functions. Three-part classification schemas include task, procedural, and social; or creative-critical, maintenance, and interpersonal. However specific functions are classified, they are significant needs that must be fulfilled or things that must be done to move the group towards its goals. The next major section of this chapter specifies in detail those leadership functions you should know how to perform, whether you are the leader or a participating member in your group discussions.

Discussion-Leader Model.   The seven leadership approaches that are described above provide valuable insights for the student of group discussion. Figure 5.2 displays our belief that parts of each approach go into the creation of an idealized discussion leader. Scholars who focused on designated formal leaders have demonstrated that certain personal traits such as extroversion and speech fluency are generally possessed by a discussion leader. It also seems clear that a leader has certain bases of power that are used to move the group toward its desired goals and that leaders have a repertoire of governing styles and motivational styles from which to select. Fiedler's research indicates that the leader's traits, power bases, and style interact in ways that determine how effective a leader of a small group will be. Wood's study suggests that a leader can learn from past mistakes and adapt his or her communication behavior in future group situations. The Minnesota studies explain the communication process that determines who will emerge as the natural work or discussion leader. Barnlund and Haiman's research identifies the specific leadership functions that must be performed in order for the group to be effective. The actual or real discussion leader of a group working with a formal organizational structure is potentially a blend of these seven leadership approaches.

NECESSARY COMMUNICATION BEHAVIORS IN LEADING GROUP DISCUSSIONS

A functional approach to leadership is basically an attempt to specify the necessary communication behaviors that are needed in order for the group to work toward its perceived goals. As we indicated earlier in this chapter, there is a difference between leader and leadership. In this section we describe three general classes of communication behaviors—task, procedural, and interper-

FIGURE 5.2
DISCUSSION LEADER MODEL

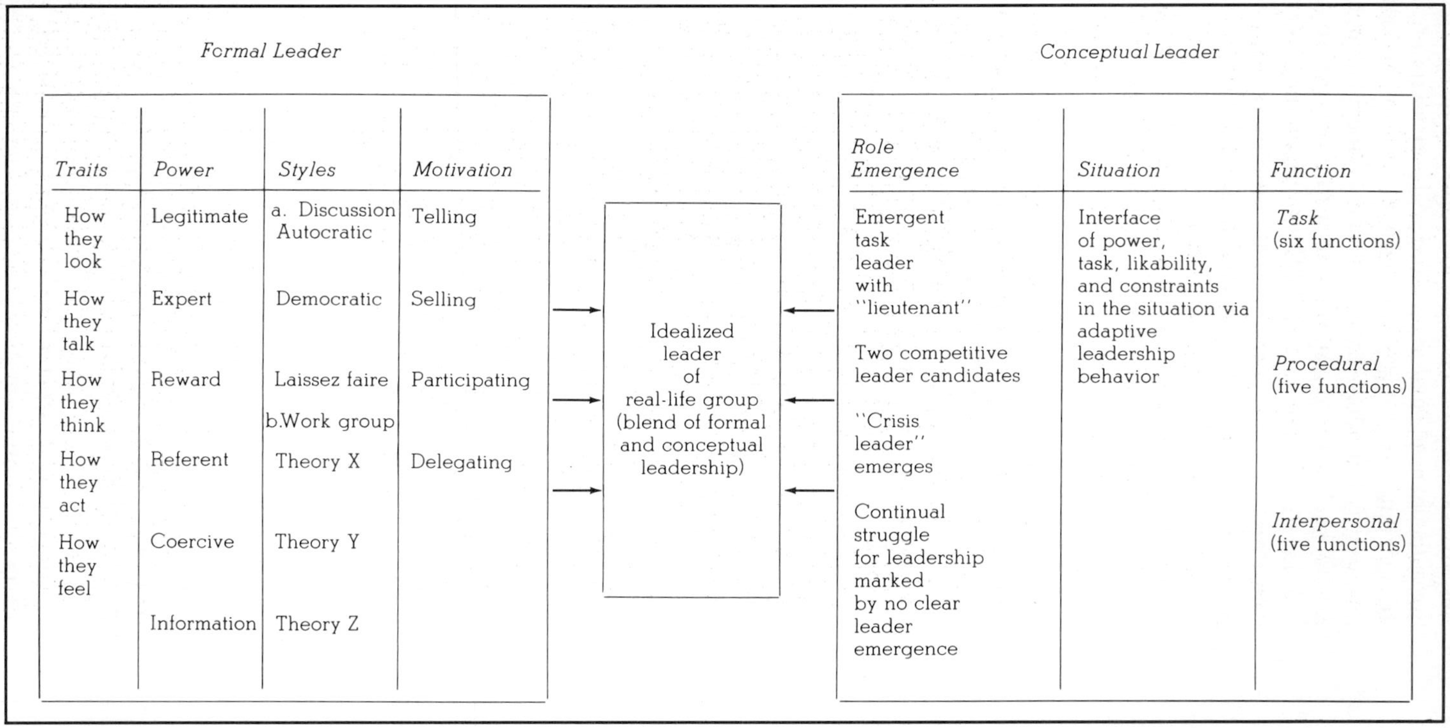

Formal Leader

Traits	Power	Styles	Motivation
How they look	Legitimate	a. Discussion Autocratic	Telling
How they talk	Expert	Democratic	Selling
How they think	Reward	Laissez faire b.Work group	Participating
How they act	Referent	Theory X	Delegating
How they feel	Coercive	Theory Y	
	Information	Theory Z	

Idealized leader of real-life group (blend of formal and conceptual leadership)

Conceptual Leader

Role Emergence	Situation	Function
Emergent task leader with "lieutenant"	Interface of power, task, likability, and constraints in the situation via adaptive leadership behavior	*Task* (six functions)
Two competitive leader candidates		*Procedural* (five functions)
"Crisis leader" emerges		
Continual struggle for leadership marked by no clear leader emergence		*Interpersonal* (five functions)

sonal—that constitute leadership of a discussion. These leadership behaviors that speech communication scholars have isolated occur in any good discussion, but the initiator of them is not necessarily the appointed or natural leader of the group. Thus, regardless of what role you may play in a small group, it is important that you understand the minimum communication leadership behaviors necessary in group discussions.

Leadership communication behaviors, when assessed in terms of who performs them, will depend on a number of the interacting phenomena we partially isolated in our preceding discussion of leadership theories. Obviously, if a designated leader uses an autocratic style, adopts a "telling" approach in terms of motivation, has considerable legitimate power, and has emerged as the leader according to Bormann's crisis scenario, then we would expect to find that most of the leadership communication performance needed to maintain the group is done by the designated leader. On the other hand, if an appointed leader adopts a laissez faire style, uses a "delegating" approach to motivation, has little referent power, and is challenged by several candidates for the emergent leadership of the discussion group, we would expect that leadership communication functions would be dispersed among the group members and that not many of the behaviors would be in evidence.

It is possible that there could be no connection between a leader's success or failure and his or her communication performance, but once a group has formed and is going about its daily tasks, we can expect that the group members will have developed some unstated agreement as to which members perform certain leadership communication functions. Our examination of student diaries reveals that most classroom discussion groups are quite aware of their particular communication pattern in terms of sharing leadership functions. These group diaries also indicate that when a strong natural leader emerges, the majority of these functions tend to be performed by that leader. It is important to remember that in government and business organizations many one-time meetings are called in which the specific group members have rarely worked together collectively. In this situation, there is the expectation that the designated leader will perform the necessary communication leadership behaviors in order to get expeditiously through the planned agenda. Thus, most formal organizations have the expectation that their administrative personnel will possess the necessary communication skills to adequately run discussions. The following sixteen communication behaviors are the leadership functions needed by groups to service their task, procedural, and interpersonal needs and move them toward the accomplishment of their perceived goals.

LEADERSHIP COMMUNICATION BEHAVIORS IN THE TASK AREA

There are a number of significant communication behaviors that have to be performed in the task area regardless of type of group.

Typical task communication behaviors are questioning, commenting, attempting answers, and the like. What is often necessary is for the task leader, or active members of the work group, to initiate leadership functions in this area in order to generate enough ideas, evaluation, and description to move the group toward task achievement. The following six communication behaviors must be performed in the task area.

1. *Contributing ideas.* This leadership communication behavior can be identified as a new or fresh idea presented for the first time in the group. Designated leaders often perform this function when they introduce an item on the planned agenda; however, good discussion groups have active members who contribute their original thoughts on the topic. Sometimes established groups will develop a custom of "brainstorming" a new topic in order to maximize the number of ideas. One of the advantages that a good group has over an individual is that active groups can outperform even the best individual in the group in terms of the total number of ideas contributed. Thus, contributing ideas is a fundamental leadership communication behavior for discussion groups.

2. *Seeking ideas.* Many times discussion groups do not develop formal procedures for generating ideas. In many groups, some members are reluctant to contribute their ideas; thus, a recurring leadership function is the seeking of ideas from group members without threatening or embarrassing them.

3. *Evaluating ideas.* One of the most difficult leadership behaviors to perform, particularly in a public discussion, is the evaluation of ideas. A group will constantly take flight when faced with the reality of having to eliminate from consideration opinions that have been expressed by group members. This is such a sensitive issue that formal procedures have been developed for separating a group member from his or her ideas. We will talk about these in Chapter 8. Groups that have a long and successful history generally develop the ability to evaluate ideas openly and freely, but even in the best groups this is done with concern for the sensitivity of the person who originated the idea.

4. *Seeking idea evaluation.* Early in a discussion group's history, before group members have developed a sense of group trust, the needed communication behavior is that of seeking idea evaluation. The first stage of brainstorming may have produced a flood of ideas, not all of which are good. If the group is to reach a good decision, it must sort the wheat from the chaff. This effort requires the active participation of all group members if each idea is to be competent evaluated. Drawing out people's evaluative opinion is even more of a delicate matter than getting their initial idea. The person who can tactfully perform this leadership function provides a valuable and necessary service for the group.

5. *Visualizing abstract ideas.* Discussion groups are prone to conversations that become abstract and full of jargon. Sometimes groups communicate only in vague, abstract terms because to equate their ideas with specific, concrete examples would point up obvious differences of opinion among group members regarding the discussion topic. However, not all abstract ambiguity in discussion is flight behavior. Some of it is the natural vagueness that is inherent in symbolic communication. When a group of executives is sitting in a board room discussing the building of a new company facility, the group must discuss their ideas in terms of specific examples. This leadership function not only clarifies points of disagreement but also promotes general understanding of what is being discussed.

6. *Generalizing from specific ideas.* The old adage that one cannot see the forest for the trees is an appropriate observation of most discussions. We have all been in discussions where we have been overwhelmed by trivia. Groups sometimes stone a given idea to death with small pebbles. This problem is at the opposite end of the communication continuum that calls for the performance of task leadership function #5. When the problem is too much specificity, the needed leadership communication is to generalize from the series of specific examples to the main idea being discussed. Basically task leadership functions #5 and #6 work in tandem to keep a balance between too much abstraction and too much specificity in the discussion of ideas.

LEADERSHIP COMMUNICATION BEHAVIORS IN THE PROCEDURAL AREA

By and large, task leadership functions are performed fairly naturally in small groups, while communication behaviors in the procedural area need to be actively fostered and nurtured throughout the course of the discussion. Many times the designated leader will perform the necessary procedural functions while in other situations a member who is experienced in group operations will emerge to perform them. The five leadership communication behaviors that follow must be performed in the procedural area.

1. *Goal setting.* The first expectation that we all have when we are brought together for a one-time meeting is that we will need to decide what the purpose of the meeting is and why we are there. Although it is the clear duty of the designated leader to state the purpose of the meeting, it is also understood in most group settings that the issue of purpose or goal of the group is open for discussion and modification. The leadership function of goal setting is also a recurring communication behavior, in that ideas are continually evaluated in terms of their ability to move the group toward its goal. This evaluation process will often reinitiate discussion of what the group's goals are. A sales group may have set its discussion goal as the establishment of sales procedures that will produce a minimum amount of productivity for a given three-month period. However, during the discussion the group may agree to the idea that a training program is needed. When the idea of a training program is measured against the group's sales goal for the next three months, the salespeople might discover that they like the potential for a long term training program, and in light of that they may wish to change their three-month sales goal. This continual evaluation of both the short-term and long-term goals of a discussion group is a procedural communication behavior inasmuch as it regulates the ongoing ideas of the group in terms of its stated purposes. This function is also procedural in the sense that it ought to be the first agenda item of a small group.

2. *Agenda making.* Agenda making is the "map-making" function in small groups which helps the group accomplish its goals in an orderly manner. In Chapter 3 we discussed different kinds of agenda systems in detail. In one-time meetings one of the clear responsibilities of the designated leader is the advance preparation of the agenda or outline for the group discussion. Some formal organizations even develop written policies regarding the advanced development and distribution of a one-time meeting agenda as a prerequisite for calling a meeting. In discussions in which there is not a designated leader, the specific agenda will emerge, and the arguments that ensue over what the agenda items should be are manifest signs of a leadership struggle. Once a leader has emerged, arguments over the agenda tend to decrease both in frequency and intensity, and the new leader, whether he or she knows it, will be responsible for agenda setting. Once the agenda has been settled and agreed to by the group members it is now incumbent upon them to follow it in order to achieve the group's goals. In essence, the goal-setting function helps the group identify *what* the group's goals are, while the agenda-making function aids the group in *how* it achieves them.

3. *Clarifying.* Group communication is messy! There are always a lot of loose, dangling ends, and when people are thinking out loud it is difficult to know if everyone knows what is being said. The clarification function is a communication behavior that produces intentional redundancy in the communication patterns in order to ensure that all group members understand what is being said. A typical example of clarifying might be the question, "What do you mean by that?" or by the statement, "Let me restate your idea in my own words to see if I understand it." Audiotapes of good group discussions are liberally sprinkled with restatement of ideas. In fact, some researchers have found that redundant group member contributions account for about 50 percent of all oral communication in small groups. This finding supports the idea that successful group discussions require a great deal of clarification of ideas in order to be effective.

4. *Summarizing.* Good speeches and good discussions have at least one thing in common: they both contain many internal summaries. A novice public speaker is often advised to tell an audience what he or she is going to say, say it, and then tell them what he or she has said. This is also good advice for a designated leader. Each point of the agenda should be introduced, accomplished, and summarized. This "adding-up" process at each stage of the agenda helps to keep in focus both the ideas under discussion and the logical progression of the discussion. Most face-to-face discussions occur without the group members' taking notes; thus, the leadership function of frequent summaries helps to imprint the topic under discussion in the minds of the discussants.

5. *Verbalizing consensus.* One of the most important outcomes of group discussions is consensus. In most formal organizations we like to be able to say that a work group has reached unanimous agreement on a course of action. We prefer to talk for another several hours about a problem rather than force a premature vote that might produce a split decision on a policy question, thus hurting the group's cohesion and seriously impairing its ability to function. It is therefore very important that verbalizing-consensus communication behavior occurs frequently in the discussion. This difficult leadership function involves finding areas of agreement at different points of the agenda and through various phases of decision making in general. An experienced designated leader will constantly look for places where he or she can get a least nonverbal agreement on an agenda item. Experienced discussion leaders will very often follow the summarizing communication behavior with the verbalizing-consensus function. These two functions working in tandem can help produce consensus in decision-making discussions. In fact, speech communication researchers have demonstrated that a form of verbalizing consensus—orientation behavior—is directly related to the chances of the group's ultimately reaching agreement. In other words, you cannot wait until the end of the meeting to seek consensus, because it is an incremental process that occurs throughout the discussion.

LEADERSHIP COMMUNICATION BEHAVIORS IN THE INTERPERSONAL AREA

There are five interpersonal leadership communication behaviors. The first three are, in fact, oriented toward meeting the social-emotional needs of the group members. However, the last two functions in this category are more "overriding" in nature; by this we mean the two conflict functions might deal with ideational obstacles as well as interpersonal ones. The five leadership functions in the interpersonal area are described in the following paragraphs.

1. *Regulating participation.* Rules in parliamentary procedure contain many explicit regulations that limit a member's speaking time. Symposium discussions also generally include speaking-time limits for the participants. We discuss these rather formalized discussion procedures in detail in Chapter 3. However, the everyday discussion that occurs in business and other work environments rarely has formal time limits. Yet there are clear expectations about the need for regulating participation. Nobody likes to attend what is supposed to be a group discussion and discover it is a monologue. Thus, it is essential that each member be given the opportunity to speak. This leadership communication function is often performed by the designated leader, but most trained discussants will impose some self-discipline and will regulate their own communication behavior so as not to either monopolize the time or withdraw from the dialogue. Experienced designated leaders will tactfully manage the time allocation of participants. The communication skill that is required to reduce one member's contributions while increasing another's takes a great deal of practice. Nonetheless, this is an interpersonal communication leadership function that must be performed in all group discussions.

2. *Climate making.* Providing and maintaining a positive group atmosphere in which each member has a sense of "psychological safety" is the essence of the climate-making function. This communication behavior might manifest itself in the following interchange. The designated leader might say, "John, you haven't said anything for awhile. What are your feelings about this issue?" If the leader's tone makes the member feel secure, John might respond by saying, "Well, Mary, I really agree with what Tom has been saying. What I believe is. . . ." Having our ideas and feelings held up for public examination is very threatening. If we do not feel the group climate is supportive and open, we will withdraw and conceal our opinions. Thus, experienced discussion leaders, as well as facilitators of encounter groups, project primarily through nonverbal cues that a safe climate exists for the exchange of ideas and feelings. This is not to say that conflict will not occur, but that the conflict will not exceed the safety barriers of good taste and the group's threshold for psychological hurt.

3. *Instigating group self-analysis.* Experienced group discussants often initiate a "discussion about the discussion" when the group becomes hung up on something. This sort of navel gazing is necessary to maintain the health of the group. Sometimes a group has normed out a level of group productivity that is not sufficiently high to attain the group's goals. When a group member becomes aware of this, he or she might jump into the middle of the conversation and initiate the group's self-analysis of its past work performance. Sometimes a group may argue over agenda and it becomes clear that a leadership struggle needs to be resolved if the group is to progress. In this situation a group member will sometimes put the "hidden agenda" on the table; that is, the leadership struggle, not the topic under discussion. These are typically emotionally charged moments in group discussions and should not be entered into flippantly. Unfortunately, some people like to play amateur psychologist and keep the group psyche forever prostrate on the counseling couch. This continual navel watching can become dysfunctional and even hazardous to the group's health. Much of the "hidden agenda" should stay hidden, as it will eventually work itself out; yet, when it does not, an experienced group leader will perform the leadership function of instigating group self-analysis.

4. *Resolving conflict.* Discussion groups that have a long history of working together usually have a group member who plays the role of peacemaker and is in fact very good at performing this leadership function of resolving conflict. Whether the fight is over ideas or personalities, the peacemaker can wade into the middle of the fracas and calm things down. Inexperienced designated leaders usually overreact to group conflict and sometimes turn a minor skirmish into a brawl. However, experienced leaders develop a sense of which conflicts need to be stopped and which ones will work themselves out. There is a fine line between a healthy exchange of ideas and an ugly scene that can mar the group's ability to work together. Until a group has developed its social and task norms—that is, until it has discovered which topics and mannerisms are taboo—members will innocently insult someone else's sacred cow. Language usage is a typical candidate. Profane, sexist, or racist language has the potential for causing the most conflict. Also, the way in which ideas are accepted and rejected in the group will produce conflict until norming occurs. Needless to say, the resolving-conflict function is vital to the group's survival, and the person who can best perform this function in the group is an essential member.

5. *Instigating conflict.* The "devil's advocate" is a role we all have played on occasion in order to instigate conflict. The leadership function of instigating conflict usually occurs on the ideational level. The function needs to be performed when group members are so afraid of offending each other that they sheepishly, and often silently, accept each other's suggestions. This meek acceptance by members of positions to which they are adverse cannot be resolved until somebody decides to play the "devil's advocate." Usually a group member will say, "Let me play the devil's advocate for a moment," or he or she might say, "Just for the sake of argument let me say...," but whatever verbal expression is used the implicit meaning is, "Let me separate the idea from the person so that the idea may be challenged." Occasionally, an experienced designated leader will react to a lethargic group by intentionally picking a fight with one or more group members. Teachers in a discussion with students over classroom material frequently perform this leadership function. This will often be done by stating an obvious falsehood in order to see if anyone will challenge it. The leadership functions of resolving and instigating conflict form a continuum of communication behaviors that experienced group leaders select from to assist them in managing the interpersonal dimension of small groups.

RESPONSIBILITIES OF GROUP DISCUSSION LEADERS

It is obvious from our previous analysis of discussion leadership that there are at least three distinct forms of leader and that the responsibility of each kind differs when considered in the context of group discussion. The three kinds of leader are the designated leader, the emergent leader, and the social-emotional leader. The Minnesota studies under Bormann's direction have labeled as "lieutenant" the social-emotional leader who often works under the emergent leader. Other scholars label this person simply "the social-emotional leader." However, the designated leader and the emergent leader may well be one and the same person in some discussions, and sometimes one person might be the designated, emergent, and social-emotional leader.

As we indicated in the preceding section, all members of a work group, particularly a discussion group, will perform various leadership communication functions in a meeting. However, there is a tendency for certain functions to be performed primarily and repeatedly by different kinds of leaders. This section describes the responsibilities that go with each leadership role in terms of the communication functions that must occur in order for a group to reach its goals.

RESPONSIBILITIES OF A DESIGNATED LEADER

The designated leader's responsibilities begin long before the group discussion begins and last long after the actual discussion is over. Experienced designated leaders recognize that their primary function is the handling of procedural issues for the group. This includes several important tasks before the meeting takes place. These tasks are concerned with three types of protocol: environmental, social, and conference.

Social protocol includes informing the participants of the time, topic, and place of the meeting, an estimation of how long the meeting will be, and if possible a published list of meeting attendees and the agenda. *Environmental protocol* deals with the provision of creature comforts to ensure that the discussants will not be distracted from their tasks. There are troublesome but important details that must be taken care of before each meeting such as seeing that the meeting room is reserved, unlocked, large enough, and generally comfortable enough for the group in terms of ventilation, temperature, and lighting. The location of rest rooms and the availability of refreshments should also be concerns of the designated leader. *Conference protocol* is concerned first and foremost with the determination of the agenda and the format of the discussion. In Chapter 3 we listed specific kinds of agenda that can be used or adapted to fit the meeting's purpose. In addition, seating arrangements, name tags, paper and pencils, multiple copies of supportive information all require advance conference planning.

During the course of the discussion, the designated leader concentrates on the procedural leadership functions. Preconference planning provides the primary agenda and some initial goal setting; however, the designated leader of a discussion is responsible for the introduction of these two items for group consideration and for continuous maintenance of the group's direction on the agreed upon goals. In addition to the five procedural functions, the designated leader tends to perform the interpersonal leadership behavior of regulating participation of group members. This may be done in part by the way in which the leader plans the format of the meeting, but he or she must also monitor and regulate member participation throughout.

After the discussion has concluded, the designated leader is in charge of the cleanup detail, although other members usually volunteer to help. The designated leader is also in charge of the follow-up details of the meeting which generally include a written report to each member. This report generally reflects those items upon which the group has achieved consensus.

RESPONSIBILITIES OF AN EMERGENT LEADER

The emergent leader of a decision-making work group has many responsibilities during a discussion. Group members expect the emergent leader to be well informed about the discussion topic at hand and to be enthusiastic about reaching the group's goals. Group members also expect the group leader to make major contributions in terms of the task leadership functions. Not only does the emergent leader have responsibilities for contributing ideas: he or she must actively draw out the ideas of others and constantly seek by continual questions the evaluation of the ideas under discussion. Also, the emergent leader tends to perform the interpersonal leadership function of instigating conflict when the group seems unusually reluctant to engage in evaluation. While the designated leader has the obligation to formally report the results of the meeting, the emergent leader has the obligation of informally promoting the decision that the group has agreed upon.

RESPONSIBILITIES OF A SOCIAL-EMOTIONAL LEADER

The social-emotional leader should be sensitive to the moods that the various members are likely to bring with them to the meeting. Have they been working long and hard all day? Have they just come off a long weekend? Does one of the group members have a pressing personal problem such as a hospitalized family member? The established social-emotional leader asks him- or herself these kinds of questions before the discussion even takes place. During the discussion, the social-emotional leader is ever mindful of the emotional fallout that occurs as a result of the clash of ideas. This observance allows the social-emotional leader to perform the communication functions of resolving conflict and climate making. Occasionally, the social-emotional leader will instigate group self-analysis if the group seems stagnated because of inter-personal sensitivities.

The social-emotional leader also performs a "lieutenant" role at the procedural level for the emergent leader. Many times this is done through the procedural functions of clarification and verbalizing consensus. The social-emotional leader has overall responsibility for the group's morale. Experienced social-emotional leaders will continually reinforce the group's sense of pride and group esteem. This is done through stories of past successes, lavish praise for the hard work of various group members, and by informally relating the group's accomplishments to people outside the work group. The social-emotional leader is the group's cheerleader and protector of the social-emotional climate of the group.

GUIDELINES FOR EFFECTIVE DISCUSSION LEADERSHIP

1. *Put the group goals ahead of your own.* Unethical people occasionally use groups for their own personal advancement in a corporation. But Abraham Lincoln's comment eventually catches up with them: "You can't fool all of the people all of the time." In the short term it is possible for a leader to "rip off" the hard work of a group and take personal credit for it, but in the long run organizations tend to isolate these kinds of people. If you ask for a group product, then you must give that group the collective credit it is due.

2. *Have a genuine concern for group members.* Leadership of a work group should include the deep-seated belief that individual group members' opinions should be respected. If you think you should lead because you know best, you have probably made a mistake either in your assessment of your capabilities or in your need to be a team player. Group success is based upon collective wisdom through participation, not on the domination of one bright person. Respect for the feelings of others is a necessary prerequisite for effective group leadership. Most people are thin-skinned; therefore, a leader must constantly be on guard to see that the collective and individual feelings of the group are not harmed. At some time or another, most experienced leaders have said, "It just isn't worth it!" By that they meant that the task goal was not worth achieving, given the interpersonal price that had to be paid. Some of our professional and collegiate athletic teams seem to set team victory as a goal without regard for the emotional casualties that occur.

3. *Set a good work pattern.* The assumption of the leadership role in a group means that you will do more work, not less. Good group leaders set the work pattern through example; you cannot reasonably expect any group member to work harder than you do. Therefore, your willingness to actively involve yourself in the group activity, particularly some of the more unattractive menial tasks, will greatly improve the group's overall productivity. If you clean off the table or make the coffee, other members will not regard these chores as a put-down when they do them.

4. *Communicate well and often.* Research from all the social-science disciplines in regard to small groups supports the necessity of the leader possessing good oral communication skills. If you plan to lead groups, practice your communication skills. Learn to give short extemporaneous presentations.

Orally prepare statements of ideas in a clear fashion for presentation to the group. Work especially hard on your interpersonal communication patterns. Try to eliminate mannerisms and behaviors that have proved to be offensive to people in your past group histories. If you have a tendency to be shy, work on assertiveness. If you have a tendency to be verbose, try to state your ideas more succinctly.

5.   *Know when to be the leader.* Some people have bad experiences in groups because they constantly refuse leadership when they should not or because they continually attempt to lead every group they belong to. A group becomes frustrated when an obviously capable person continually refuses to accept the responsibility of leadership. While certainly the person has the right to refuse, group members tend to become increasingly impatient and socially punish these group members. So occasionally you should examine your past work behavior and see if you should be the leader. Some people make leadership their only goal and forget that all members perform some leadership functions. You should be on guard and determine in which groups you should concentrate on leadership functions, even in a given communication area, and in which groups you should attempt to be the leader.

SUMMARY

Discussion leadership was defined as *communication which positively influences the group to move in the direction of the group's goals.* Seven leadership approaches were classified according to two major perspectives: those of the designated leader and the emergent leader. The designated-leader perspective examined four approaches to leadership in some detail. The trait approach focused on how leaders look, think, talk, feel, and act. The power approach emphasized six general bases of power: legitimate, expert, reward, referent, coercive, and informational. Autocratic, democratic, and laissez faire styles of leadership were the major concern of the discussion of the stylistic approach, while Theories X, Y, and Z are stylistic approaches for work group leadership. The telling, selling, participating, and delegating styles formed the basis of the motivational approach.

On the other hand, the emergent-leader perspective concentrated on more informed, ongoing group types of discussion leadership. The three approaches to discussion leadership treated here were the situational, role-emergence, and functional theories. The situational approach was identified as the one where various situational constraints came into play and determined not only who would be leader but also some of the adaptive behavior the discussion leader would have to exercise. The role-emergence theory presented four basic scenarios; several of them showed successful role-emergence patterns and another showed unsuccessful ones. The final approach considered was that of identifying leadership functions that have to be performed in the group. It was emphasized that the performance of leadership functions could be done by a designated leader and by any other member of the discussion group. In fact, the next major section of the chapter emphasized the necessary leadership communication behaviors that must be performed in the task, procedural, and interpersonal domains of the group.

Discussion leaders have certain responsibilities to the members of the group. Specific responsibilities of designated, emergent, and social-emotional leaders in a group discussion were mentioned. The chapter concluded with the presentation of five guidelines for effective discussion leadership. We feel that by following these guidelines, performing the necessary leadership communication behaviors, and having a general understanding of the nature of and the correct approach to leadership, you can only improve in applying these leadership skills to your discussion situations.

REFERENCES

Barnlund, D. C. "Experiments in Leadership Training for Decision-Making Groups." *Speech Monographs* 22 (March, 1955): 1–14.

Barnlund, D. C., and Haiman, S. *The Dynamics of Discussion.* Boston: Houghton Mifflin, 1960.

Blake, R., and Mouton, J. *The Managerial Grid.* Houston: Gulf Publishing Company, 1964.

Bormann, E. G. *Discussion and Group Methods.* 2nd edition. New York: Harper and Row, 1975.

Bormann, E. G., and Bormann, N. C. *Effective Small Group Communication.* 2nd edition. Minneapolis: Burgess, 1976.

Bormann, E. G; Pratt, J.; and Putnam, L. "Power, Authority, and Sex: Male Response to Female Leadership." *Communication Monographs* 45 (June 1978): 119–55.

Cragan, J. F.; Cuffe, M.; Pairitz, L.; and Jackson, L. H. "What Management Style Suits You?" *Fire Chief* 29 (March 1985): 25–30.

Cuffe, M., and Cragan, J. F. "The Corporate Culture Profile." *International Association of Quality Circles Annual Conference Transactions.* Memphis: International Association of Quality Circles, 1983.

Downs, C. W., and Pickett, T. "An Analysis of the Effect of Nine Leadership Group Compatibility Contingencies upon Productivity and Member Satisfaction." *Communication Monographs* 44 (1977): 220–30.

Fiedler, F. E. *A Theory of Leadership Effectiveness.* New York: McGraw-Hill, 1967.

French, J. R. P., and Raven B., "The Bases of Social Power." In *Group Dynamics: Research and Theory,* edited by Cartwright, D., and Zander, A., 259–69. 3rd edition. New York: Harper and Row, 1968.

Gulley, H. E. *Discussion, Conference, and Group Process.* 2nd edition. New York: Holt, Rinehart and Winston, 1968.

Haiman, F. S. *Group Leadership and Democratic Action.* Boston: Houghton Mifflin, 1951.

Hersey, P., and Blanchard, K. H. *Management of Organizational Behavior.* 3rd edition. Englewood Cliffs, N.J.: Prentice-Hall, 1977.

Larson, C. U. "The Verbal Response of Groups to the Absence or Presence of Leadership." *Speech Monographs* 38 (1971): 177–81.

Marston, W. M. *Emotions of Normal People.* New York: Harcourt, Brace and Company, 1928.

McGrath, J. E., and Altman, I. *Small Group Research: A Synthesis and Critique of the Field.* New York: Holt, Rinehart and Winston, 1966.

McGregor, D. *The Human Side of Enterprise.* New York: McGraw-Hill, 1960.

Ouchi, W. G. *Theory Z.* Reading, Mass.: Addison-Wesley, 1981.

Rosenfeld, L. B., and Fowler, G. D. "Personality, Sex and Leadership Style," *Communication Monographs* 43 (1976): 320–24.

Rosenfeld, L. B., and Plax, T. G. "Personality Determinants of Autocratic and Democratic Leadership." *Speech Monographs* 42 (1975): 203–8.

Ross, R. S. "Leadership in Small Groups." Lecture No. 5 in the Illinois State University Speech Communication Audio Cassette Library, Normal, Ill., 1974.

Sargent, J. F., and Miller, G. R. "Some Differences in Certain Communication Behaviors of Autocratic and Democratic Leaders." *Journal of Communication* 21 (September 1971): 233–52.

Sattler, W. M., and Miller, N., eds. *Discussion and Conference.* 2nd edition. Englewood Cliffs, N.J.: Prentice-Hall, 1968.

Shaw, M. E. *Group Dynamics: The Psychology of Small Group Behavior.* 2nd edition. New York: McGraw-Hill, 1976.

Stogdill, R. M. *Handbook of Leadership: A Survey of Theory and Research.* New York: The Free Press, 1974.

White, R. K., and Lippett, R. "Leader Behavior and Member Reaction in Three Social Climates." In *Group Dynamics: Research and Theory,* edited by Cartwright, D., and Zander, A., 318–35. 3rd edition. New York: Harper and Row, 1968.

Wischmeier, R. R. "Group and Leader-Centered Leadership: An Experimental Study." *Speech Monographs* 22 (March 1955): 43–48.

Wood, J. T. "Leading in Purposive Discussion: A Study of Adaptive Behavior." *Communication Monographs* 44 (June 1977): 152–65.

Yerby, J. "Attitude, Task and Sex Composition as Variables Affecting Female Leadership in Small Problem-Solving Groups." *Speech Monographs* 42 (1975): 160-68.

CASE
STUDY

CASE BACKGROUND

Mary Schilling is a bright, upwardly mobile executive in a midwestern corporation. She has all the formal training and skills that the company expects of her. For the last five years, she has worked hard and successfully for the company. She has received three promotions and held management responsibilities for two years. Her personal file contains glowing reports about her abilities.

Last year one of the senior vice-presidents of the company put her in charge of a special task force that was to reposition an old company product that had leveled off in sales growth. This was the sort of management opportunity Mary wanted. She knew that the clear road to top management always included success with a product through the effective use of a task force.

The senior vice-president gave Mary complete authority to bring together whatever materials and human resources were necessary to complete the task. Mary gave a lot of thought and planning to the designing of the task force and the calling of the first meeting. She selected a vice-president—Tom—who had been her supervisor when she came to work at the company. She felt sure that he would support her, and that his twenty-five years of management experience would be a valuable reservoir of expert knowledge. Mary invited two hotshot marketing experts—Jim and Bill, who were fresh from graduate school—because of their skills in quantitative research. She also included two of the company's best sales people—Carl and Vince—because they had worked firsthand with the product. Finally, she included an accountant—Sally—who had worked out the original unit cost of production. Mary was pleased that she could include another woman on the task force. She would not have done so if Sally had not been competent, but she was pleased that there was another woman on the task force.

CASELOG

Mary personally contacted her six group members by phone and secured their enthusiastic support to participate in the task force. Only Tom, the vice-president, seemed somewhat tentative. Mary reserved a meeting room, set a time for the first meeting, consulted everyone's calendar, and sent a printed agenda and the list of all the members to all of the participants. She checked the meeting room out in advance and was convinced that every premeeting detail had been taken care of. She was truly excited about the prospect of the first weekly meeting.

First Meeting

Mary was elated by the results of the first meeting. It had started with a lot of nervous conversation and she had envisioned failure. Jim and Bill, the two marketing experts, sat on one side of the table engaged in private conversation; Carl and Vince, the two salespeople, sat huddled on the other side of the table. Sally, the accountant, sat by herself and appeared to be very nervous. However, just when things looked grim, Tom came to her rescue. He told one humorous story after another and soon the group was talking and laughing boisteriously about their common problems with the company cafeteria and parking. Mary seized this relaxed atmosphere and moved right into the planned agenda.

The group worked smoothly for over an hour, reaching general agreement on the broad goals for the task force and the year-long timetable for the completion of their task. They reinforced each other's belief that they had formed a good group and that it would be fun to work together on this enjoyable task. After the meeting, Tom made a special point of complimenting Mary on what a fine job she had done and said that he was glad the company had recognized her leadership potential.

Second Meeting

Mary was not surprised that the second meeting did not run as smoothly as the first. After all, she had built in some real differences of opinion when she brought in two marketing people and two salespeople, but she had not anticipated that the two pairs would polarize so quickly or that there would be so many cheap jokes with hidden meanings traded back and forth about who knew more about the product—the sales force or marketing people. She also thought that Sally would come out of her shell, but she seemed even more withdrawn. Fortunately, Tom was there and he continued to relieve the tense moments with a wealth of jokes. Mary became more aware of her job in terms of resolving the conflicts between Jim and Bill, and Carl and Vince.

Third Meeting

This meeting Mary characterized as a disaster! The two salespeople really got into it with the marketing people on why the product was not showing growth in sales. Mary quickly stepped in to resolve the conflict but, to her surprise, was rebuffed by all four of the combative participants. Jim, Bill, Carl, and Vince seemed to challenge her leadership of the group, on the grounds that she had no expert knowledge of the product. She had not worked out in the field selling the product, nor did she possess the technical knowledge about marketing the product. Mary got a bit defensive and quickly listed several of her accomplishments in designing the product while working in Tom's division of the company. At this point, Tom stepped in and put the two young marketing hot-shots in their place. The meeting went silent. Mary was pleased that Tom had resolved the bickering but resentful that his action seemed to challenge her leadership of the task force. But Mary was most resentful of stoic Sally. How could she just sit there and not take a position? At least Mary knew where Jim and Bill stood. The agenda that Mary had set for this meeting remained unaccomplished.

Meetings 4 and 5

These meetings were marked by continual conflict between the marketing experts and the salespeople. Sally continued to remain silent. Tom became more and more involved in settling disputes between Jim and Bill, and Carl and Vince. Mary felt more and more as though she was on the outside looking in. The group simply ignored her for long periods of time. What troubled Mary the most was why Tom was challenging her leadership of the task force. She was deeply troubled and felt betrayed.

Sixth Meeting

Tom surprised Mary by approaching her right before the meeting and suggesting that he be taken off the task force. Mary gushed that that was the last thing she wanted him to do. She reassured him that the problems would work out and he finally agreed to stay in the group. During the meeting, Mary was angry with herself for talking Tom into staying. Tom continued to challenge Mary's leadership and Mary was now firmly convinced that if Tom were not on the task force she could easily manage the remaining five members—especially if she could get Sally's support. After the meeting she approached Sally and asked her directly for her open verbal support for the remaining meetings. Sally suggested they meet for dinner that evening. The results of this dinner meeting were that Sally agreed to actively support Mary's leadership of the task force. Mary then drove to Tom's house and after a long and friendly chat, they agreed that Tom should leave the group so that Mary would be the undisputed leader.

Meetings 7 and 8

These meetings were even less productive than when Tom was present. Sally was rather obvious in her sudden support of Mary. The four males had clearly closed ranks in opposition to Mary and fought her every suggestion. More and more of the workload, both in and out of the meetings, fell onto Mary's and Sally's shoulders.

Ninth Meeting

This meeting was never held. Mary had great difficulty finding a time when all members could meet. Reluctantly she went to the senior vice-president who had put her in charge of the task force and calmly explained the problems she had encountered over the last two months. Much to her surprise, the senior vice-president was well aware of the personal and productivity failures of the task force. In fact he informed Mary that a decision to reposition the old company product would be postponed for a year. Mary was asked to turn in a report of anything that was accomplished, and with Sally's assistance she prepared a short report of the task force's progress. With the completion of this report, Mary's responsibility for the task force was terminated.

CASE QUESTIONS

1.   Was the failure of this group inevitable, or was this the most success that Mary could have hoped for?

2.   Was Mary's problem in leading the group the result of latent sexism on the part of the male members?

3.   Should Mary have asked Tom to leave the group earlier, or even included him in the group in the first place?

4.   If you were writing a diary for other members of the group, what would you say about Mary's leadership in the group?

... people play different roles in different groups and can share roles in the same group ... in a sense roles are a concentration of communication behaviors.

CHAPTER OBJECTIVES

In order to be a more effective discussant, when you read this chapter you should focus on the following participation ideas and communication skills.

YOU NEED TO KNOW:

1. The most frequently played roles in group discussions.
2. The followership communication behaviors.
3. An integrated view of group roles in discussion.
4. Suggestions for effective participation in discussion.

PARTICIPATING IN SMALL GROUP DISCUSSION

CHAPTER OUTLINE

Leadership communication behaviors that are performed by many group members are a crucial dimension of a discussion. And yet there is a great deal of important communication that takes place in the course of a discussion that is more properly classified as nonleader behavior. We hesitate to call this communication "follower behavior" because the person in the role of leader may also engage in nonleader types of activities.

In Chapter 5 we defined discussion leadership as "communication which positively influences the group to move in the direction of the group's goals." Discussion participation is defined as *communication behavior that positively or negatively moves the group in the direction of the group's goals.* Our discussion participation definition includes all of the communication leadership behaviors, plus communication which supports or disrupts leadership behavior. These communication behaviors are usually performed by people playing follower types of roles. However, it is not uncommon to find a person in the role of leader who occasionally engages in disruptive communication behavior that moves the group away from its goals. For example, an emergent leader might engage in some blocking behavior in attempts to stop the central negative from playing his or her role. In Chapter 1 we pointed out the importance of separating the basic concepts of people, roles, and communication behaviors. We suggested that people play different roles in different groups and can share roles in the same group. We also explained that in a sense roles are a concentration of communication behaviors.

In this chapter we draw distinctions between people, roles, and communication behaviors. We present the ten most frequently played roles in group discussion. We add fourteen followership communication behaviors to the sixteen leadership communication behaviors to provide an integrated view of the communication that takes place in a discussion. In addition, we list participation skills that are needed for good discussions.

FREQUENTLY PLAYED ROLES IN GROUP DISCUSSIONS

In the late 1940s and early 1950s, a number of social scientists were interested in identifying different roles people play in small groups. The National Training Laboratory in Group Development came up with a list of roles. Benne and Sheats (1948) reported a similar list of twenty-five roles that people tend to play in group discussion. They utilized a three-part schema for categorizing group roles: group task roles, group building and maintenance roles, and individual roles. Examples of group task roles are information giver, energizer, and opinion seeker. Encourager, harmonizer, and compromiser are examples of group maintenance roles. The "individual" category includes such roles as blocker, playboy, and dominator.

The labeling of some phenomenon as a role or a communication behavior is often arbitrary, in that a role may be a label for a communication behavior that a person continually uses. The problem with just listing roles and not separating them from communication behavior is that we tend to label a person as a blocker, for example, when in fact blocking communication may be performed by various people playing different roles in the group. Thus, we have found it is easier to explain what is going on in a group discussion by limiting our category of group roles to the ten major ones, and by explaining the thirty communication behaviors of leadership and followership that people playing different roles will use.

1.   *Task leader.* Typically, we have come to recognize the task leader in a general sense by who he or she is and what he or she does—or has the potential to do—in the group. The task leader enjoys, for the most part, high group status. He or she is recognized as a mature person who has good problem-solving ability and has had training in leadership skills. In most instances, the task leader is as well educated as any other group member and has a firm grasp of the discussion topic. The task leader's influence generally includes expert power (McGrath and Altman 1966, 62).

While the task leader has high group status, the person playing that role also feels very responsible for the group members and the work that the group does. For when the lights are dim and the bands are gone, there is the gaunt stark reality of leadership. When a discussion goes silent all eyes turn to the task leader, whether he or she has been appointed or has emerged from the group. This silence is generally filled by procedural communication leadership behaviors initiated by the task leader. As we indicated in Chapter 5, the task leader will also perform many of the other leadership behaviors. In addition to talking more in a group, the task leader typically does more work.

Sometimes, because of the workload that the task leader has and the pressure of that role, he or she might engage in negative followership behavior. The task leader might attempt to block critical comment, or even look for sympathy from the group. When this happens in a well-established group, the members of the group—especially the social-emotional leader—will try to reassure the task leader that they understand the difficulty of the leader role and express appreciation for the person's ability to play that role.

2.   *Social-emotional leader.* A social-emotional leader is well liked by the rest of the group members. This leader may not be the most popular in the group, but certainly most members are attracted to him or her. Although a task leader may lead a group and not be personally liked, the social-emotional leader must be well thought of. Social-emotional leaders tend to have some experience with handling interpersonal problems and score high on the ability to empathize with other people. The social-emotional leader does not rival or compete with the task leader of the group and may actively support the task leader in a complementary lieutenant role.

Like the task leader, the social-emotional leader is extroverted and speaks frequently in the group. In terms of leadership communication behaviors, he or she will frequently initiate the five leadership communication behaviors in the interpersonal area. The concentration of "climate making" and "instigating group self-analysis" tends to be a major function of the social-emotional leader.

The person who predominantly plays the social-emotional leader is acutely aware of the emotional heartbeat of the group and is constantly on guard for any interpersonal damage that might take place in solving the task. While the task leader is responsible for the group's productivity, the social-emotional leader is responsible for the group's well-being and the individual members' satisfaction (Wischmeier 1955, 48). When the discussion is completed, the group members will thank the social-emotional leader for making it an enjoyable experience.

3. *Tension releaser.* The individual who plays this role not only has the ability to be funny but is also aware of the sensibilities of the group in given work environments. The ability to tell a joke is not sufficient to play the role of tension releaser. A person may tell humorous jokes in a men's locker room that turn out to be tension creating, not tension releasing, in a male-female discussion group. Tension-releasing humor for a discussion group must be funny to all the group members. Thus, the more heterogeneous the group membership, the harder it is for a person to play this role.

In addition to providing humor to break tension, the individual can resolve interpersonal conflict with well-timed humorous barbs. In a way this role mirrors that of the social-emotional leader in that the person must be sensitive to the social demands of the group. What the social-emotional leader accomplishes with empathy, the tension releaser accomplishes through the use of light humor featuring satire or sarcasm.

The tension releaser is always on call to break up debilitating interpersonal tension in the group and to smooth over those awkward moments of first meetings. The more dependent the group members are on one another and on the work the group does, the more important the role of tension releaser is. When a person tries to play this role and fails, or plays the role when it is not needed, the group members will accuse that individual of engaging in the followership communication behavior we label "playing the clown."

4. *Information provider.* The role of information provider is probably one of the most shared roles in group discussion; however, when a group tends to have one member play this role, that member has group status for his or her ability to provide accurate and concise data instantly for all major aspects of the discussion topic. The information provider has research skills that exceed the group's norms and sometimes has expert knowledge of the discussion topic. As well as providing a volume of accurate information, the information provider will frequently perform the leadership communication behavior of contributing ideas and will critically evaluate ideas that are not soundly based in the research data.

The job of the information provider is to research and prepare accurate information. When the person playing the role of information provider feels abused by the group, it is generally because the rest of the group members have thrown all the data-gathering responsibilities on him or her. That is why effective groups tend to share the information-provider role.

5. *Central negative.* The central negative in a small group is usually not pleased with what is going on. The person tends to have the same abilities as the task leader and in fact continually challenges him or her for the leadership of the group. When the task leader envisions what the criticisms will be on the next proposal, he or she sees the central negative as the one who will voice the criticism. The person who is constantly challenging the leader in the task and procedural areas is said to be the central negative. In fact, if the task leader were to leave the group for some reason, the group members would turn to the central negative for task leadership (Bormann 1975, 260–61).

The three leadership functions that a central negative will most frequently attempt to perform are evaluating ideas, agenda making, and instigating conflict. When a central negative is too strong in his or her challenge for leadership, he or she tends to engage frequently in two negative followership communication behaviors: dominating and blocking. When the central-negative role is properly played, whether knowingly or unknowingly by a group member, the impact is quite favorable. The central negative forces the group to carefully rethink its position and makes the task leader acutely aware of his or her responsibilities in terms of group productivity. It is often difficult to distinguish between the central-negative role, which is mainly positive in scope, and the self-centered follower, which is a negative role. But generally, the group members will know their central negative because the criticism that is emitted from this role tends to be strong.

6. *Questioner.* As we indicated in Chapter 1, the task leader, the social-emotional leader, the tension releaser, the information provider, and the central negative constitute the five major rules in a discussion group. The questioner is the first of five secondary roles frequently played.

The role of questioner is not played as often as it should be in small groups; only rarely does one person specialize in this role. Yet the role of questioner can significantly increase the quality of the group output. The person playing the role of questioner has the ability to incisively probe the ideas under discussion without threatening or alienating group members, and without challenging the task leader. The two task functions that the questioner performs are seeking ideas and seeking idea evaluation. The procedural function that the questioner most often performs is clarification.

7. *Silent observer.* A followership role in small group discussion which is not appreciated is that of the silent observer. During jury deliberations it has been found that the role of silent observer is an important part of the decision-making process. People playing this role tend to quietly observe and evaluate the discussion being carried on by more active members. However, it is their nonverbal approval or disapproval that ultimately resolves the debate (Forston 1968).

Discussion groups that exceed five members may have a person who silently observes much of the discussion, but when he or she does make clear—either verbally or nonverbally—what his or her conclusion is, it tends to be decisive. Prior to the formation of their opinion, people playing the role of silent observer will appear pleasant but evasive when asked for their opinion. A person playing the role of silent observer listens passively to all arguments and then forms an opinion.

8. *Active listener.* Predominantly nonverbal and supportive behaviors characterize the role of the active listener in group discussions. This role is frequently shared and played in good discussion groups. All members of a discussion group should feel an obligation to listen attentively and encourage other members to explain their positions. Occasionally a group member will specialize in the role of active listener by assisting in the performance of two leadership communication behaviors: summarizing and verbalizing consensus. The person playing this role tends to remain argumentatively neutral, while at the same time being actively supportive of any member attempting to contribute an idea or evaluate an idea under consideration.

9. *Recorder.* The role of recorder and the followership communication behavior of recording are isomorphic in small group discussions. This is the one role in which one communication behavior completely defines the role. At any meeting of importance, a group member will be designated as the official recorder of the meeting. Since low status is often attached to this role, and a person who continually plays it feels subservient to the rest of the group members, most discussion groups will rotate the role around the group. In formal organizations, a nonmember of the discussion group who has been specially trained in recording is brought in to do the recording.

10. *Self-centered follower.* While the above nine roles support the goals of the group, the role of self-centered follower works against the group's best interest. In fact, if this role is played by too many group members, the group will surely fail. The person playing a self-centered role is using the group for his or her own ends. The individual playing this role may engage in special-interest pleading, seeking help, or any of the other seven negative followership communication behaviors. While all group members will engage in some negative communication behaviors, a person is probably playing the role of a self-centered follower when he or she repeatedly engages in these negative behaviors.

FOLLOWERSHIP COMMUNICATION BEHAVIORS

Although Benne and Sheats and many other small group communication theorists regard many of the following communication behaviors as small group role types, we think it is more accurate to say that these behaviors are the utterances people occasionally use when they are playing the established, major roles. As we indicated above, an established small group role contains more than one type of communication behavior; the only exception to this is the role of recorder. Although any of the ten role types may exhibit any of the thirty communication behaviors included in leadership and followership, a given role tends to be identified by the expected frequency of certain communication behaviors. Thus, the task leader will frequently speak to the procedural leadership functions while the self-centered follower practices most of the seven negative followership communication behaviors. The seven positive followership communication behaviors are like the sixteen leadership communication behaviors in that they help move the group toward its group goals. However, their impact on moving the group is not as significant; thus, we have classified them as followership communication behaviors. Below are the most frequently occurring followership communication behaviors.

POSITIVE FOLLOWERSHIP COMMUNICATION BEHAVIORS

1. *Listening attentively.* Ideally, good listening habits should be present in all group members. In fact, one of the reliable signs of a mature discussion group is the degree to which group members listen attentively to the one who is speaking.

Attentive listening goes beyond social protocol. This followership communication behavior is central to a small group's success. If a discussion group develops a norm of attentive listening as expected behavior, each member will feel assured that his or her views will be heard and there will be less chance of conflict due to ambiguity or personality clashes. When ideational conflict does occur, there will be greater assurance that the differences of opinion are real and not the product of poor or indifferent listening.

2. *Assisting on procedure.* The efficient running of any discussion requires meaningful attention to the procedural details of the meeting. Chapter 5 contains advice to the designated leader about the procedural "nitty-gritty" of running a good meeting. In most group settings, the leader needs help with the procedural matters. Sometimes this is the performing of routine tasks such as distributing material or handling refreshments. During discussion it may be the subtle but important reassurances to the task leader that he or she is following the correct procedure.

Assisting on procedure is an important followership communication behavior because it shows support for the leader and helps build solidarity in the group. When several group members spontaneously pitch in on routine procedural matters, the group is demonstrating a sense of esprit de corps and cohesiveness which are obvious signs of a healthy group.

3. *Observing.* As we indicated above, when a person specializes in the role of silent observer, most of his or her communication behavior consists of the presentation of neutral statements and the affirmation of heated points in the discussion. Most small discussion groups do not have a person who specializes in this kind of communication behavior; but some of this followership communication behavior of observing must be performed.

It is important for every group member to occasionally sit back from the heat of argument and observe the interaction of other group members. These moments of objectivity allow for many important insights. Sometimes these insights relate to adjustments in our own behavior, when, for example, we realize we have been engaged in domineering and blocking behavior. Sometimes observing allows us to spot unnecessary tangents and put the group back on the right course.

4. *Energizing.* Some small groups seem to have a higher energy level than others, and some discussions crackle with electricity while others sort of drone along. Energizing communication behavior is mostly detected in the nonverbal dimension of the discussion. There is a lilt in discussants' voices, eyes sparkle, and members seem genuinely excited about the topic. In athletics we talk about members being "up for a game." As indicated in Chapter 5, the social-emotional leader will frequently use this communication behavior in an attempt to raise the level of the group's enthusiasm for its work. All members of discussion groups, while having their emotional "ups and downs," should feel some obligation to be enthusiastic and try to excite others about the work at hand.

5. *Compromising.* The very interdependent nature of a small group discussion requires that some compromising behavior must be done if group decisions are to be reached and group work satisfactorily accomplished. Regardless of what role a group member is playing, one part of that role is the compromising of one's vested interest. If a person appears to be playing the role of compromiser because he or she is forced to settle disputes among other group members, the group is probably not having a very good time of it and there is much dissension among the ranks. In mature discussion groups, members not only compromise some of their own opinions but they work to find common ground when conflicts occur among them. The social-emotional leader will tend to do this at the interpersonal level and the task leader at the procedural level; all group members engage in compromising behavior at the ideational level.

6. *Encouraging.* Within the context of group communication, there are many dyadic exchanges. These person-to-person communication exchanges have a positive effect on the group as a whole. Praising a group member's ideas or showing interest in a member's problems is a very necessary part of group discussion. When encouraging communication is performed by a high-status group member, it has an uplifting effect on the whole group. That is why experienced task leaders engage in a lot of encouraging communication behavior. Everybody needs to be praised and told he or she is doing a good job, even the leader.

7. *Recording.* As we indicated previously, the role of recorder and the followership communication behavior of recording are usually isomorphic in that most groups assign the task of recording in a meeting. However, on an informal basis most group members do some record keeping, and in good groups members will offer assistance to the recorder to insure that accurate records have been kept.

NEGATIVE FOLLOWERSHIP COMMUNICATION BEHAVIORS

1. *Dominating.* In one sense dominating communication behavior is not allowing other people to freely express their opinions on the topic. At times, a task leader may be domineering in insisting on strict adherence to some procedural matter, while at other times the person playing the central negative may tenaciously attempt to manipulate the group's opinion on a topic by browbeating them into submission. However, all group members occasionally engage in domineering behavior when a topic arises that is of particular importance to them. Groups will generally concede one special issue per member, but if a person continually engages a domineering behavior on a number of occasions, that member is perceived as a self-centered follower and is increasingly isolated by the group.

2. *Blocking.* This foot-dragging behavior is generally used to stop decisions from taking place. Delaying tactics are used by various group members in the course of a discussion. The repertoire of blocking behaviors is quite large. They include absenteeism, emotional tirades, filibustering, and incessant procedural objections. Oftentimes a person who is a self-centered follower continually engages in blocking behavior. The central negative also engages in blocking behavior by the very nature of his or her role.

3. *Self-confessing.* Sometimes a group member will show up for a task-group meeting and decide to turn the meeting into an encounter-group session—in effect, asking the group for its emotional support of his or her feelings. When these feelings are not related to the group, and the interpersonal disclosures seem to be unnecessarily intimate, we say the group member is engaging in a negative communication behavior inasmuch as the behavior causes the group to turn its attention away from the group goals. Once in a while a work group's productivity will go way down even though its cohesion and member satisfaction remains quite high. When this happens, a task discussion group has unknowingly transformed itself into a therapy group. Most experienced small discussion groups will restrict self-confessing behavior to either before or after the meeting.

4. *Seeking help.* While self-confessing behavior seeks help from the group at the interpersonal level on subjects not related to the group, help-seeking behavior is generally a request on the part of the group member that the group testify to his or her value to the group. Sometimes this communication is in the form of sulking, while at other times it takes the form of acts of self-mortification. All group members need "stroking," but if this behavior occurs too frequently in discussions, little work will be done since the group members will be too busy reassuring each other that they are capable of doing good work.

5. *Seeking recognition.* This is communication behavior that calls attention to itself by boasting. Kindergarten classes attempt to stop recognition seeking from interfering with daily work by restricting it to a given day. This day is generally called "show and tell." In adult groups this is sometimes called "bring and brag." At reunions it is called "stand and shout." In the course of a group's history, all group members will seek recognition; and in fact, good groups often formalize these occasions. But in the context of routine meetings, recognition seeking is a negative communication behavior.

6. *Special-interest pleading.* A group member is quickly labeled a self-centered follower if the member is engaged in special-interest pleading. One of the basic assumptions of a discussion group is that the members will come to the meeting with a "permissive and reflective" attitude and prepare to be persuaded by argument and evidence. When a member speaks on behalf of some outside group, and not as a member of "the" group, the group thinks the member is making a special-interest plea. If a discussion group contains five teachers and one student, there may be occasions when the student engages in special-interest pleading on behalf of students. If several members begin to engage in this behavior, it becomes extremely difficult for the group to reach consensus about its conclusions.

7. *Playing the clown.* Although the tension releaser uses humor for positive effects in the elimination of primary tension and the lessening of group conflict, horseplay at inappropriate times by the tension releaser or by other group members is a form of negative communication behavior. Groups can easily be tempted to digress from their work, and clowning around is one of the favorite ways. Sometimes, particularly after a hard work session, the whole group will get silly, and everything will seem hilarious; but most of the time, excessive "goofing off" will hurt group productivity.

AN INTEGRATED VIEW OF DISCUSSION

As we stated in Chapter 1, it is important to distinguish among group members, the roles they play in a discussion, and the communication behaviors that they perform. Figure 6.1 displays our integrated view of discussion. A discussion contains three to eleven people, with the ideal number being five to seven. The work group that generates an effective discussion has a potential range of ten roles, with five to six being the ideal number. The minimum number would be three: the task leader and two other roles. In Chapter 5, we

FIGURE 6.1

AN INTEGRATED VIEW OF DISCUSSION
PEOPLE, ROLES, COMMUNICATION BEHAVIORS, AND BREAK MOMENTS

People

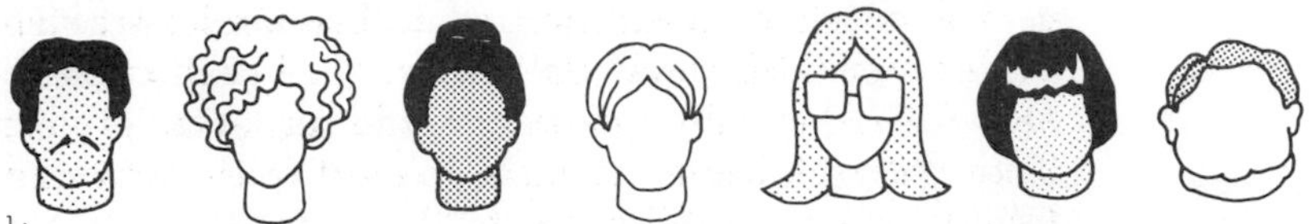

Minimum 3, maximum 11;
ideal size 5–7 people.   Tom   Mary   Pam   John   Sally   Kim   Joe

Roles

Minimum is 3; maximum 10;
ideal number is 5–6 roles.

Task leader	Central negative	Active listener
Social-emotional leader	Questioner	Self-centered follower
Tension releaser	Silent observer	Recorder
Information provider		

Communication Behaviors

Leadership: 16,
comprising 6 task,
5 procedural, and
5 interpersonal.

Contributing ideas		
Seeking ideas	Goal setting	Regulating participation
Evaluating ideas	Agenda making	Climate making
Seeking idea evaluation	Clarifying	Instigating group self-analysis
Visualizing abstract ideas	Summarizing	Resolving conflict
Generalizing from specific ideas	Verbalizing consensus	Instigating conflict

Followership: 14;
comprising 7 positive
and 7 negative.

Listening attentively	Dominating
Assisting on procedure	Blocking
Observing	Self-confessing
Energizing	Seeking help
Compromising	Special-interest pleading
Encouraging	Seeking recognition
Recording	Playing the clown

Break Moments:

CR talk
Encounter talk

Professional stories	Personal stories
"They" vilification	Self-disclosure
"We" identification	Empathetic listening
Group fantasies	

described sixteen leadership communication behaviors, and in this chapter we present fourteen followership behaviors. These thirty communication behaviors constitute the vast majority of role interactions, and certain clusters of communication behaviors serve to identify a given role, although a small group discussion with eleven people playing ten roles and performing thirty different communication behaviors probably never occurs. In addition, all small group discussions will contain some CR and encounter talk. A certain amount of discussion time will be taken up with the building of group pride and a personal agenda of group members. Figure 6.1 depicts the total repertoire that real groups draw from in discussions.

A MATURE DISCUSSION GROUP

Good discussions require that key roles be played and that important leadership and followership communication behaviors occur. Figure 6.2 contains a hypothetical layout of the proper mixture of people, roles, communication behaviors, and break moments that are needed for good group discussion. Notice that this well-developed group has formed the five basic roles of task leader, social-emotional leader, information provider, tension releaser, and central negative. In addition, a number of roles are shared by different people. For example, Mary and Sally share the information-provider role, while Pam and Sally share the questioner role. In terms of communication behaviors, Tom, the task leader, engages in most of the procedural and task leadership functions, but not all of them. For example, Kim, playing the roles of silent observer and recorder, still performs summarizing and visualizing abstract ideas. Even Pam, the central negative, performs important leadership behaviors such as instigating conflict and contributing ideas. By the same token, Tom and Mary perform many followership behaviors that are important to the group's success, particularly compromising and encouraging.

Figure 6.2 is a good group, not only for what they do, but also for what they do not do. Few negative followership behaviors occur in this group. Occasionally, John, the tension releaser, overplays his role and makes a fool of himself; and Pam in her role as central negative becomes too intense in producing conflict, begins to block the group's progress, and thus focuses attention on herself. Once in a while, Mary works too hard at the interpersonal level and

FIGURE 6.2
A MATURE DISCUSSION GROUP
PEOPLE, ROLES, COMMUNICATION BEHAVIORS, AND BREAK MOMENTS

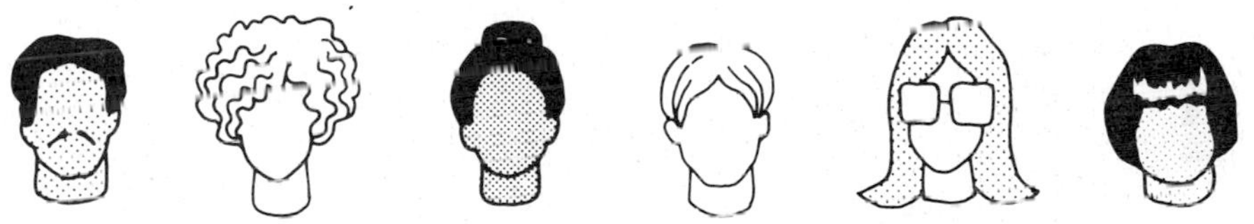

People	Tom	Mary	Pam	John	Sally	Kim
Roles	Task leader	Social-emotional leader Information provider	Central negative Questioner	Tension releaser	Information provider Questioner	Silent observer Recorder
Communication Behaviors Leadership:	Goal setting Agenda making Seeking idea evaluation Regulating participation Summarizing	Climate making Instigating group self-analysis Verbalizing consensus	Instigating conflict Clarifying Contributing ideas Evaluating ideas	Resolving conflict Climate making	Contributing ideas Generalizing from specific ideas Seeking ideas	Visualizing abstract ideas Summarizing
Followership:	Listening attentively Compromising	Encouraging Compromising Self-confessing	Compromising Blocking Seeking recognition	Energizing Playing the clown	Seeking help	Listening attentively Assisting on procedure Observing Recording
Break Moments	"We" identification	Listening empathetically Self-disclosure		Self-disclosure Group fantasies	"They" vilification	Professional stories

engages in self-confessing behavior. But overall, this is a mature discussion group. Tom makes certain that the procedural functions are performed and does a good job of regulating participation of group members. Mary creates a warm and nonthreatening climate for the group and continually verbalizes the group's consensus. Pam is continually challenging and questioning the majority viewpoint, which helps refine and clarify the group's efforts. John helps resolve conflict and keeps group members on their toes with his wit and charm. Sally is continually contributing ideas and important information to form the data base for the group's decisions. Kim records the group's proceedings and helps Tom run the meetings, while at the same time aiding the group to reach consensus.

Also, Tom is careful to spend some time in each meeting raising the group's consciousness through the retelling of past success stories. John also helps in consciousness raising through his vilification of completing work groups. Sally frequently points out that this is the best group she has been in by relating stories about a past work group which she considered to be terrible. In addition to making sure that the group's pride is sufficiently high, the group also is sensitive to each other's personal needs, and through this interpersonal talk has learned to empathize with and trust each other. Mary helps in this with her empathy and her willingness to make personal disclosures. The group in Figure 6.2 is clearly an experienced discussion group, in that there is clear role formation, and the communication behaviors move the group toward its goals.

AN AUTHORITATIVELY CONTROLLED DISCUSSION GROUP

Figure 6.3 depicts a group that is dominated by the task leader. It is probably not a very happy group to be part of, because the group's productivity is almost solely dependent on the abilities and energies of the task leader. Notice that Evelyn performs most of the leadership communication behaviors, but since she does so much work, there is a tendency for her to dominate the discussion. Since there is no social-emotional leader in this group, the resolution of conflict is difficult, and Ken has a hard time relieving tension. Bill is playing the negative role of self-centered follower. This makes Evelyn's job even more difficult, and since Bill is engaging in negative special-interest behavior, he obviously has some personal goals he is placing above the group goals. Finally, Sam is mostly recording what Evelyn does and helping her wherever he can to get through the meeting. It is possible to argue that the group in Figure 6.3 is not really a group, since crucial roles are not played and important leadership communication behaviors are not performed. In fact, when Evelyn is not present, Bill and Ken vilify her as an oppressive part of management. The shared group fantasy among Ken, Bill, and Sam is that Evelyn is the "Ice Queen." This fantasy relieves tension for the males in the group, but it does not work toward group cohesion and productivity.

AN UNCONTROLLED DISCUSSION GROUP

Sometimes discussion groups form that are fraught with conflict. Nothing comes easy. The productivity that takes place is always accompanied by a

FIGURE 6.3
AN AUTHORITATIVELY CONTROLLED DISCUSSION GROUP
PEOPLE, ROLES, COMMUNICATION BEHAVIORS, AND BREAK MOMENTS

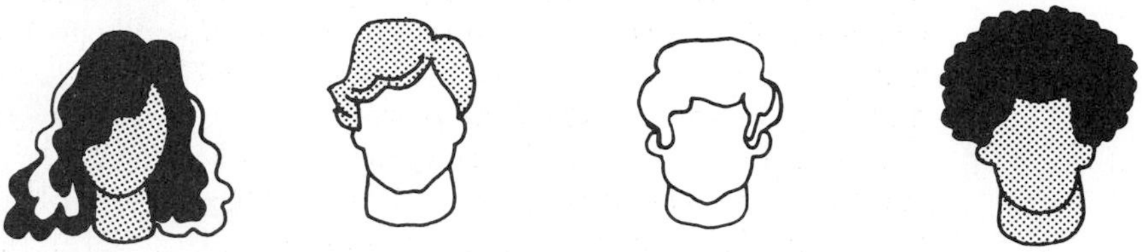

People				
	Evelyn	Bill	Ken	Sam
Roles	Task leader Information provider	Self-centered follower	Tension releaser Information provider	Recorder
Communication Behaviors Leadership:	Regulating participation Contributing ideas Agenda making Climate making Goal setting		Climate making Contributing ideas	Clarifying

Followership:	Dominating
	Energizing
		Blocking
		Special-interest
		  pleading
			Seeking recognition	Recording
				Assisting on
				  procedure

Break Moments:		"Upward they"
		  vilification
			"Upward they"
			  vilification
			Group fantasy	

great deal of "verbal fisticuffs." The discussion group displayed in Figure 6.4 fights and kicks its way to every decision it makes. Although the five basic roles are present, two people are playing negative self-centered follower roles. In addition, many of the leadership communication behaviors are not being performed, while the discussion is dominated by negative followership communication behaviors.

Lisa and Frank had supported Jane for group leader. When Jane lost out to Angelo, Jane, Lisa, and Frank began engaging in blocking communication behavior. It also became clear to the rest of the group that Jane, Lisa, and Frank only had their special interests at heart and not the group's. It has become extremely difficult for Ralph and Chin to play their roles successfully, given the distrust that exists within the group. It is only Ralph's energy, combined with Angelo's tenacity in sticking to the agenda, that allows productivity to take place.

In terms of communication break moments, there is very little encounter talk. The group members feel it is too risky to engage in personal disclosure. However, there is a great deal of CR talk. Jane, Lisa, and Frank have formed a "we" clique in the group. They often meet outside of group meetings and vilify the "they" (the other group members). Jane has started a fantasy about "Angelo the Angel" and portrays him as a company loyalist who is afraid to cross upper management. Angelo continually tries to create a common "we" identification, and Chin and Marty try to help, through the telling of professional stories that indicate their group is a good group. Yet, the group

FIGURE 6.4
AN UNCONTROLLED DISCUSSION GROUP
PEOPLE, ROLES, COMMUNICATION BEHAVIORS, AND BREAK MOMENTS

People							
	Angelo	Jane	Ralph	Lisa	Frank	Chin	Marty
Roles	Task leader	Central negative	Social-emotional leader Information provider	Self-centered follower	Self-centered follower	Active listener Tension releaser	Silent observer Recorder
Communication Behaviors Leadership:	Goal setting Agenda making	Instigating group conflict	Climate making Contributing ideas				Evaluating ideas Climate making
Followership:	Compromising Dominating	Special interest pleading Blocking	Energizing Encouraging	Special-interest pleading Blocking Seeking recognition	Special-interest pleading Blocking Playing the clown	Observing	Recording Assisting on procedure Compromising
Break Moments:	"We" identification	"They" vilification Fantasy		"They" vilification	"They" vilification	Professional stories	Professional stories

remains symbolically divided into a "we" and a "they"; and, as a consequence, member satisfaction is quite low.

THE SOCIAL DISCUSSION GROUP

Small work groups have a tendency to socialize too much. An intimate climate is easy to establish, and if there is no role conflict the group members may prefer to discuss themselves and not their work. Figure 6.5 depicts such a discussion group. This group is high on member satisfaction and consensus, but extremely low on group productivity. This group is really more an encounter group than a task group. Since they are in a discussion group, but are not getting much work done, they all are engaging in self-confessing followership communication. Bob is overplaying his role of tension releaser by clowning around too much, but Mike and Carol rarely engage in agenda setting leadership behavior, so Bob's excesses never get corrected. All three group members continually perform climate making leadership communication, not for the purpose of getting work done, but to ensure that everyone is happy with one another. If this were a social group, the communication patterns would be

FIGURE 6.5
A SOCIAL DISCUSSION GROUP
PEOPLE, ROLES, COMMUNICATION BEHAVIORS, AND BREAK MOMENTS

People	Carol	Mike	Bob
Roles	Task leader Information provider	Social-emotional leader Information provider	Tension releaser Information provider
Communication Behaviors Leadership:	Climate making Instigating group self-analysis Contributing ideas	Climate making Contributing ideas	Climate making Resolving conflict Contributing ideas
Followership:	Self-confessing Energizing	Self-confessing Seeking help	Playing the clown Self-confessing
Break Moments:	Self-disclosure Empathetic listening Personal stories	Self-disclosure Personal stories Group fantasy Empathetic listening	Self-disclosure Personal stories Empathetic listening

acceptable, but since it is a discussion group with work to accomplish, the work output is unacceptably low.

This group is very close to being labeled a pure encounter group. Encounter talk is no longer a break moment from the task discussion, but is the major agenda of the group. Person-to-person talk (personal stories, self-disclosure) takes up most of the group's time. The only CR talk that occurs relates to the group fantasy that they are the nicest people in the organization and that they enjoy working together. The problem, of course, is that they do very little work, even though their consensus seeking and member satisfaction are quite high.

The mature discussion group in Figure 6.2 is productive; the members are satisfied; and the group typically reaches consensus on major decisions. The authoritative group in Figure 6.3 is productive; however, there is low membership satisfaction; and "consensus" is often forced. The uncontrolled discussion group in Figure 6.4 never reaches consensus on major issues; its members are unhappy—even angry—although it maintains at least a low level of productivity. The social discussion group in Figure 6.5 usually reaches consensus; it has extremely high membership satisfaction; but it hardly ever gets anything done.

While we all strive to create mature discussion groups, we sometimes find ourselves members of the other three types. Next, we make suggestions on how a group can strive to be a mature discussion group. Thus far, it is clear that people must play certain key roles and a variety of leadership and followership communication behaviors must occur for a good discussion to take place.

SUGGESTIONS FOR EFFECTIVE PARTICIPATION IN DISCUSSIONS

● *Thoroughly prepare for discussion.* Occasionally, discussion groups will spontaneously create an idea that is truly remarkable. But most of the time productive results of group work stem from a lot of hard work by the individual members, most of which is done *before* the discussion convenes. If you want to have a good discussion, do your homework!

When you observe an experienced round table discussion on television, you do not see the hundreds of hours of research that go into its preparation. Few people, even those who are experts on a subject, can glibly recall the necessary evidence and arguments in the heat of a face-to-face discussion without sufficient advance planning. An hour-long discussion requires at least ten hours of preparation by each member, and probably even more on the part of the task leader. This ratio of ten to one is a good benchmark to follow in respect to routine business discussion; however, major policy decision-making discussions may require months of work in order to formulate an effective policy. Group discussions are only a waste of time when time is not taken to prepare for the meeting.

● *Stay within the ethical boundaries of group discussion.* In addition to your commitment to do your best to work for the group good, to deliberate rationally, and to be a fair player, you should work on your communication skills so that you can attack a person's ideas without attacking the person. In Chapter 8, we describe several group techniques for minimizing this problem, but in routine day-to-day discussions, each member must work at separating the person from the idea.

Experienced discussion groups have a high tolerance for verbal argument. They will interrogate and examine arguments in a vigorous fashion and at the same time avoid injuring the persons who formulated the arguments. Newly formed groups usually have to continually verbalize the fact that ideas, not people, are under examination. So when you are a member of a new discussion group, it is often helpful to say explicitly that you want to examine the argument with no intended offense against the person.

● *Contribute in the orientation stage of a group.* Everyone feels awkward or withdrawn during the first moments of a meeting. This is especially true if it is the first meeting of a newly formed work group. It is very easy for us to hold back and let someone else break the ice. It is also very easy to avoid asking clarification questions although just about everyone is anxious to know what the purpose of the meeting is. Experienced small group discussants resist these feelings of inhibition and assert themselves at the outset of the discussion— not only by asking questions, but also by suggesting ideas and evaluating ideas. These three kinds of communication (questions, idea suggestions, idea evaluations) are risk-taking behaviors. Nobody likes to appear foolish or ignorant, especially in the early stages of group formation; however, successful problem-solving discussions occur more frequently when the group members are willing to take communication risks.

• *Seek information and opinions.* As one can see in Table 2.1, Bales has identified the percentages that are allocated to the four major categories of his Interaction Process Analysis (IPA). One of the astounding comparisons is the large percentage of answers (56 percent) to the low percentage of questions (7 percent). This ratio of eight to one between the communication acts classified as answers and those classified as questions represents a significant imbalance in many group discussions. In fact, in a number of groups many more questions should be posed during the course of the group's development. By seeking information and opinions from discussants, one can improve the quality of the dialogue taking place. As a general rule, almost as many questions should be posed during the evaluation phase of a group as statements. This questioning provides a vehicle for the full exploration of necessary information and opinions regarding the discussion topic at hand.

• *Stress group productivity.* We have all been members of work groups that were made up of people we enjoyed being with, and we know that it makes the work go smoother if everyone likes each other. Yet we've also participated in group work with people we have not been particularly fond of but have sometimes found these unpleasant groups to be more productive than the happy ones. One sign of a worker's professional maturity is that person's ability to work efficiently and effectively with coworkers to whom he or she is not attracted. We rarely can choose who will be on our work teams, and members are never rewarded for how they get along with each other. On the other hand, they are sometimes reprimanded if interpersonal conflicts get in the way of their work. When all is said and done, the most important output is the group's productivity. Member satisfaction and consensus are two group outcomes that tend to enhance productivity, but even if there is little member satisfaction and even if the group rarely reaches consensus, it can still meet its most basic objective—productivity. Unhappy groups manage to be productive when enough of the group members are willing to overlook their individual differences and personality conflicts. Experienced small group discussants will reduce interpersonal conflict by pointing to the group's goals and the common need all members have for meeting them effectively.

• *Avoid "role ruts."* Research has shown that people play different roles in different groups because the tasks are different and the people forming the groups are different. We also know that members will change roles within a group when there is new membership. Thus, if you find yourself continually playing the same role in different groups, you are probably in a "role rut."

People get into "role ruts" not because the other members constantly force the same role on them, but because they "campaign" hard for a certain role. The easiest ruts to see are those in which the same people continually wind up being the task leader, the tension releaser, and the recorder in group discussions. If you find yourself continually emerging as leader of a work group, "try out" for another role in a group that you join. You may discover that in some groups you are better able to relieve tension than be the task leader. If you are always the first one to speak when the group grows silent and if you constantly try to make people laugh when they are uncomfortable with each other, you might try resisting your temptation to speak and wait to see if someone else can play the role. Ideally, groups try to fit the right people into each role. If you push too hard for a given role, it may reduce the optimum efficiency of the group at best, and cause unnecessary social conflict at worst.

● *Avoid the self-centered follower role.* Of the ten group roles, only one has a negative influence on the goals of the group. If a person plays this role in the group, the disruption that occurs is considerable. You should avoid playing the self-centered role, not only because it hurts the group but also because it hurts you. A person playing the self-centered role never experiences much membership satisfaction and runs the risk of being labeled an organizational deviant who is not a good team player. One of the most important items on a person's work record, in terms of professional advancement, is the perceived ability of that person to work smoothly and effectively within groups.

Even when a discussant is playing a positive group role, he or she should avoid the excesses of that role in terms of negative followership communication behaviors. Task leaders have a tendency to dominate, social-emotional leaders sometimes engage in self-confessing behavior, while tension releasers might err by playing the clown. If you monitor your behavior, you will be able to spot when you are having a negative influence on the group and be able to make the appropriate adjustment.

● *Help ease primary tension.* If somebody is trying to break the primary tension of the group with humor, that person should be encouraged through positive feedback and not socially ignored with looks of disinterest. We must remember that we all feel socially insecure in the first moments of a small group meeting and it is only through helping each other that we can get through primary tension. It is also important to remember to use humor that is funny to everyone in the group; thus, sex, racial, and ethnic humor are very dangerous. Generally, lighthearted humor directed at the "theys" who put the group in its problem-solving assignment can provide safe corporate chuckles.

● *Work to clarify role differentiation.* Shepherd (1964, 122–23) stated, "A successful group is one in which each member's role is clear and known to himself and to others in the group." Although role clarification is a well-understood goal in the development of a group, the means to that end are less clear. Newly formed work groups, and long-standing groups which have had changes in membership, must engage in a lot of experimentation in order to determine what roles a member can best play. Group development is retarded when experimentation is discouraged. Members should be encouraged to try different roles. For example, one member might become very comfortable in the role of information provider, but the group might suspect the person is better suited for a leadership role. It is also important to recognize that role formation is a dynamic, not a static, phenomenon in group development. Even established groups manifest some changes in role playing. So it is important to continually clarify in your mind what roles are being played by what members for the benefit of the group.

- *Support the task leader.* Secondary tension is the period in the group's life when members are searching for a task leader. When a person begins to emerge as leader, all members should encourage and support that member. The leader tends to do more work in a group and shoulder more responsibility; therefore, it is important that he or she have the full support of the group. This is especially important and difficult for the group if the task leader is not the appointed or designated supervisor of the work group. In Chapter 5 we discussed in depth the distinctions between designated and emergent leaders.

- *Perform leadership communication behaviors when needed.* There is a tendency to think that only the person playing the role of task leader is responsible for the performance of leadership functions in the group; however, members of mature discussion groups do not hesitate to perform the necessary leadership communication behaviors when needed. For example, most work groups can use an increase in the number of questions asked in the discussion. Seeking ideas and eliciting idea evaluation are leadership communication behaviors that should be performed by several group members. Similarly, both the summarizing and the verbalizing of consensus that need to be performed after periods of intense dialogue should be done by the group as a whole. Research on group discussions suggests that groups produce more ideas and solutions when they draw upon all the resources of the group members. It is the obligation of every member of a discussion group to maximize the group's productivity. This is most successfully done when all group members work at ensuring that the crucial leadership functions are performed.

- *Build group pride.* Consciousness-raising sessions have the effect of highlighting the positive characteristics of the group that can be the source of a group's pride. Unfortunately, this process is a comparative one and the group runs the risk of exaggerating its superiority over other groups. Therefore, it is important that the group build its pride upon a solid foundation of measurable productivity. Occasionally, it may be necessary for you to play the devil's advocate when consciousness raising is taking place and argue that the competing work groups have redeeming values. You may also want to tone down the vilification of the enemy. The upward "we-they" polarization between first-line work groups and upper management can sometimes become so exaggerated that it may hurt promotions within the work group. Furthermore, downward organizational communication may not be perceived as credible, thus injuring group productivity. This is not to say that you should not build the group's sense of pride, but the building of group pride can reach a point of diminishing returns, where it is no longer helpful to the group's productivity.

- *Create symbols and slogans.* Bormann and Bormann (1976, 70) observed: "Highly cohesive groups also always work out ways to identify their group; sometimes these are as obvious as insignia, or mascots, or the use of nicknames." After a group has established some ability to do work, the naming of the group can be formally discussed as an agenda item with very beneficial results. Thinking of a name, or a logo for a group helps the group discover what all the members take pride in.

Many of the discussion groups we have had in class could recall the nicknames of their discussion groups years later. These group names often capture the essence of the group. For example, some of our student groups named themselves "The Fantastics," "The Uncohesives," "The Six-Pack," and "The Best of the Rest." "The Fantastics" were *indeed* fantastic—they won all the classroom games, they wrote the best exams, and they presented the best classroom discussions. "The Uncohesives" had a difficult time in becoming a group. They finally began to take pride in the fact that they had nothing in common and worked together on that basis. "The Six-Pack" was a tremendous party group—they wrote the worst exams but they had a great time preparing for them. "The Best of the Rest" was not a better group than the "Fantastics," but better than all the rest.

American corporations that have adopted quality circle programs have rediscovered the importance of work groups' developing names and slogans for themselves, depicting their unique contributions to organizational productivity. Custom-designed T-shirts and caps are commonplace today, not only for college groups but also for corporate work teams. Although members will initially think that it is childish to name their group, develop a logo, and write a slogan, once these tasks have been accomplished they will have powerful rhetorical labels to help them become a group and maintain their group pride.

●   *Establish group traditions.* Tradition plays an important role in group life. We all have a member of our extended family who is the keeper of the family stories. At Thanksgiving or other traditional holidays, the family will gather, and soon Uncle John or Aunt Mary will begin to recall humorous anecdotes about family members. These stories help to maintain the family's sense of oneness and its sense of immortality. Many work groups within organizations behave in the same way. You may join a law firm that is a hundred years old and discover that there is a whole collection of stories about the firm's past accomplishments that compel you to do your best. All work groups should spend some time dwelling on their past accomplishments and retelling old stories as a means of both maintaining the group's maturity and assimilating new members into the group. New groups that are formed for short periods of time need to create a sense of tradition. Even in environments such as data-processing departments, where small work groups are constantly formed and reformed to perform tasks of short duration, it is important to celebrate traditions such as "We always have lunch at Charlie's when we finish writing a program in this department."

●   *Recognize individual differences.* As Carl Rogers (1970, 137) has indicated in his well-known book, *Carl Rogers on Encounter Groups,* one of the objectives that the National Training Laboratory has suggested as being important to organizations is to build trust among individuals and groups for the health of the organization as well as the welfare and development of the individual. In fact, Professor Rogers (1970, 114) has said of himself: ". . .I enjoy life very much more when I am not defensive, not hiding behind a facade, but just trying to be and express the real me." The encounter moments in the life of a work group allow the group to better understand the unique qualities of each member. Some of these individual differences everybody will like and celebrate; however, every member will have some personality traits and behaviors that are irritating to other group members. Learning to tolerate and accommodate some of the more unpleasant aspects of a group member is one of the surest ways to help a group develop and mature. People tend to do their best work when they feel they can be themselves in the group. A group environment that is tolerant of individual differences will work toward the elimination of what Carl Rogers has called a personal facade.

● *Keep self-disclosure within limits.* Every group needs a level of self-disclosure such that members know on whom they can depend. Some work groups require more self-disclosure than others. A team of firefighters who must often work cooperatively within a burning building will require a great deal of disclosure from one another so that they will know they can trust the other members to save their lives if need be. On the other hand, an accounting team that is conducting an audit of a corporation will need to know less about each other. A work group can err in either direction; the group can be either underdisclosed or overdisclosed. The goal is to find the level of self-disclosure that is fitting to get the job done.

Self-disclosures by a member are always interesting to a group but can often occur as a means to avoid the work at hand. The basic rule of thumb is that self-disclosure should only occur when personal conflicts have stopped work from taking place.

● *Manage interpersonal conflict.* Conflict is an important ingredient in the development of a group. It is healthy and necessary for some conflict to occur at the ideational level of a task group, during role formation, and between individual members. However, it is important to keep these conflicts within manageable boundaries. The more culturally and occupationally diverse your work group is, the more difficult it will be to set these boundaries. For example, when people disagree with one another on how to do a job, are they allowed to swear at each other? When members of a street gang are competing for roles, two members might literally fight over who should be leader, while in a corporation such behavior would be totally inappropriate. Most of the boundaries in which conflict can occur in a group will be spontaneously determined by the group as they discuss. Occasionally, it is necessary to talk privately with a group member if his or her rules of fair play are markedly different from those of the group. It is also important to take coffee breaks or digress into humorous stories when you think the group is genuinely close to crossing its boundary of acceptable conflict. When you feel this tension building out of control, act. Don't let it explode in front of you.

SUMMARY

Discussion participation was defined as positive or negative communication behavior that moves the group either toward or away from the group's goals. Communication leadership and followership behaviors are typically performed by people playing certain role types. The ten most frequently played roles in group discussions include: the task leader, the social-emotional leader, the tension releaser, the information provider, the central negative, the questioner, the silent observer, the active listener, the recorder, and the self-centered follower.

In addition to the sixteen leadership communication behaviors presented in Chapter 5, fourteen followership communication behaviors were identified, of which seven were positive and seven negative. The seven positive follower-ship communication behaviors discussed were: listening attentively, assisting on procedure, observing, energizing, compromising, encouraging, and record-ing. The seven negative followership communication behaviors—which are most often seen in people assuming a self-centered follower role—include: dominating, blocking, self-confessing, seeking help, seeking recognition, special-interest pleading, and playing the clown.

In mature discussion groups we find people performing numerous leader-ship and followership communication behaviors; and, in fact, certain clusters of these communication behaviors serve to identify given roles people play in groups. However, most people play more than one role in a group.

The chapter concluded with several suggestions for effective participation in discussions. These included avoiding "role ruts," avoiding the self-centered follower role, performing leadership communication behaviors when needed, staying within the ethical boundaries of group discussion, and thoroughly preparing for discussion.

REFERENCES

Benne, K. D., and Sheats, P., "Functional Roles of Group Members." *Journal of Social Issues* 4 (1948): 41–49.

Bormann, E. G. *Discussion and Group Methods.* 2nd edition. New York: Harper and Row, 1975.

Bormann, E. G., and Bormann, N. C. *Effective Small Group Communication.* 2nd edition. Minneapolis: Burgess, 1976.

Forston, R. "The Decision-Making Process in the American Civil Jury: A Comparative Methodological Investigation." Ph.D. dissertation, University of Minnesota, 1968.

McGrath, J. E., and Altman, J. *Small Group Research.* New York: Holt, Rinehart and Winston, 1966.

Poole, M. S. "Decision Development in Small Groups III: A Multiple Sequence Model of Group Decision Development." *Communication Monographs* 50 (1983): 321–41.

Rogers, C. R. *Carl Rogers on Encounter Groups.* New York: Harper and Row, 1970.

Shepherd, C. R. *Small Groups: Some Sociological Perspectives.* Scranton, Pa.: Chandler, 1964.

Wischmeier, R. R. "Group-Centered and Leader-Centered Leadership: An Experimental Study." *Speech Monographs* 22 (1955): 43–48.

CASE
STUDY

CASE BACKGROUND

The homecoming committee at State University has been meeting regularly since spring semester of the last academic year. The members of the committee are:

Tom Carleton, President, Dorm Council

Diane Wheaton, President, Greek Council

Carl Greene, President, Black Affairs Union

Toby Miller, President, Athletic Council

Maureen McNamara, Off-campus Representative, elected at large

Kirk Everitt, Fraternity Representative, elected at large

Gail Holmberg, President of Student Body at State University, ex officio member

Tom Carleton and Diane Wheaton, cochairpersons of the homecoming committee, are pleased with the progress that the committee has made thus far. There seems to be a revived interest in homecoming at State University, and the committee is genuinely interested in producing an exciting homecoming weekend. The committee has worked its way down to two decisions, namely determining the final criteria for building this year's floats, and finalizing the sequence of floats.

This one-hour meeting of the committee is to produce decisions on the above two issues.

CASE LOG

First Forty Minutes of the Meeting

Tom opens the meeting by having Maureen distribute the minutes from the last meeting. Receiving no corrections to the minutes, he distributes the agenda. The first item on the agenda is a presentation by Diane on the costs of floats last year compared to projected costs this year.

DIANE: As you remember, last year organizations were limited to $300 for float materials, all of it had to be purchased at Goldblatt's and K-Mart, and receipts had to be turned in to the homecoming committee. Cars and float wagons were donated. The receipts from last year show that all but three organizations spent all of the allotted money. I called the presidents of all the fraternities and sororities last week, and they all felt the allowable ceiling should definitely be raised by at least one hundred dollars. Considering inflation and the increased interest in Homecoming, I would recommend to the committee that we raise the ceiling to $400 per float.

KIRK: Why have any limit? Let's take the ceiling off and find out how really great homecoming floats can look. Dartmouth has gone to that procedure with their ice sculpturing during their ice festival, and they receive national attention. If we'd throw our energy into homecoming floats, we would make a name for ourselves and this university.

CARL: Let us all bow our heads in reverence of the wealthiest fraternity on campus. (Group laughter drowns Carl out.)

TOBY: Yeah, if old "moneybags Kilpatrick" hadn't died and left your fraternity all that money, you wouldn't be in favor of eliminating the financial ceiling.

KIRK: I'm serious, why do we always have to put mediocre equality ahead of excellence. It's not that we would spend that much more money than other groups; it's just that people would work harder. With the stuff you buy from Goldblatt's and K-Mart, it's just hard to get enthusiastic.

DIANE: My sorority is capable of spending a lot of money on a homecoming float too, but I think we must have a reasonable ceiling. First, because that is the only way you can have a contest for best float. My sorority has won the Greek "best float" award two out of the last three years, and we take a lot of pride in the work we did to win. If we won because we just spent more money it wouldn't be very meaningful. I like to win when competition is equal. The money ceiling makes it equal. The second reason we need a ceiling is to ensure a large number of floats. If ten wealthy fraternities and sororities build elaborate floats, a lot of other organizations will simply drop out of homecoming. Flaunting wealth is how Greeks got a bad name in the sixties.

MAUREEN: Personally, I don't care if the Greeks want to spend their money on floats. I don't think most students care one way or another.

CARL: I care, and the Black Affairs Union cares. Diane is right. What makes this homecoming parade a university-wide event, and not a Greek orgy, is that we keep a lid on the cost and promote good competition.

TOM: I think all the issues here are out on the table. I appreciate Kirk's concern for excellence, but it seems like there is some consensus to have some kind of cost ceiling on floats. I'm not sure we've arrived at the figure yet, however.

KIRK: I'd like to see a vote on whether we have a ceiling or not before we decide anything else. Better yet, let's not vote on this till our next meeting. It will give me time to poll the fraternities and sororities and see what their attitudes are. The fact that the Greeks spent their limit last year says to me that we should take the lid off and let costs find their own level.

TOM: I don't think we can postpone this decision past today. All organizations need to know the final decision of this committee so they can plan accordingly.

KIRK: I don't think it's fair that this committee should make a decision like this without first checking with the people we represent.

CARL: Now look at who's the champion of equality! (Tense group laughter)

TOBY: Kirk, why are you always throwing a monkey wrench into this committee's decisions? If you really felt that strongly about it, why didn't you bring it up earlier?

KIRK: Hey, look. You don't want to hear my opinion? Fine, I won't give it.

DIANE: Kirk, I understand what you're saying, and it is a reasonable position. In fact, some of the people in my house think the same way you do about homecoming floats. However, when I talked to the presidents of the various houses, they didn't seem to be upset about a ceiling per se but that $300 was too little!

GAIL: I think Diane's right. There is not a lot of sentiment for taking the ceiling off. And Tom is absolutely right, we must get a vote on this issue today. But Kirk does have a point. I like the idea of getting national publicity on our homecoming floats. I guess I support the idea of keeping things the way we are doing this year, but doing a study to see if we should do away with the ceiling next year. Would you like to head up that study, Kirk?

MAUREEN: I'm for that. Let's do a thorough study, then change the rule next year if we decide to.

TOM: I still need a vote for this year. What if we raise the ceiling to $400 like Diane suggested? All those in favor signify by saying "Aye." (Six "Ayes.") "Nays." (One "Nay.")

OK, let's go to the next item on the agenda: the route and sequencing of the parade.

Last Twenty Minutes of the Meeting

Carl Greene distributes a chart showing the order of last year's parade units and a map of the route the parade took.

CARL: Time's about up, so let's make this short and sweet. I move we adopt the same parade route sequence we used last year.

MAUREEN: I second that!

DIANE: Does that mean we draw lots again for what order the floats line up?

CARL: Right.

GAIL: The chancellor expressed an interest to me in riding in a car immediately behind the winning float. Can we make that accommodation?

TOBY: As long as we're passing out favors, we think the parade route should be extended two more blocks down College Avenue so it would go by the athletic dorm.

KIRK: Now look at who are *really* the privileged ones! Prime rib for dinner every night! (Group laughter)

CARL: Time's running out. O.K., we put the chancellor behind the winning float and we extend the parade route by two blocks. Can we all live with that?

DIANE: As I remember, the reason we never go by the athletic dorm is that the parade then has to turn left on Howard Street, and it's a narrow one-way street, especially with parked cars there.

TOBY: The cops can move the cars.

KIRK: I have got to get to class, let me know how the vote comes out.

MAUREEN: I have to go too!

TOM: I think we need more discussion on this issue, but we must have the decision by 8:00 A.M. tomorrow. Let's have a special meeting tonight at 7:30. If anybody has more suggestions or changes, bring them with you this evening.

CASE QUESTIONS

1.   How many different roles can you identify in this discussion?

2.   How many different leadership communication behaviors can you identify?

3.   What negative followership communication behaviors can you identify?

4.   Would you call Kirk a central negative or a self-centered follower? Why?

5.   Who besides Tom was engaging in procedural leadership communication behavior? Was it appropriate?

Self-disclosure by group members is necessary if stereotypes are to be broken down so that the group can function.

CHAPTER OBJECTIVES

In order to be a more effective discussant, when you read this chapter you should focus on the following interpersonal ideas and communication skills.

YOU NEED TO KNOW:

1. The interpersonal relationships in small groups.
2. The interpersonal process concepts.
3. The perceived individual differences in group members.
4. The different ways of defining words.
5. The nonverbal concepts of a small group.

INTERPERSONAL DIMENSIONS IN SMALL GROUPS

CHAPTER OUTLINE

This chapter is concerned with the individuals that make up a group. We know that the individual make-up of the people in a group has a lot to do with how well that group does in terms of productivity, consensus, and membership satisfaction. What we do not know is how individual differences affect group outcomes. We have not been able to establish many linkages among the myriad of individual variables such as personality, age, sex, and intelligence and what happens in a given group. However, there are a number of important factors in the interpersonal relationships among group members that need to be discussed if the dynamics of a discussion group are to be understood.

There are three key interpersonal relationships—inclusion, control, and affection—that seem to affect a group's overall ability to work together. There are also four reciprocal interpersonal behaviors that appear to help bind a group of people together into one cohesive work unit. They are mutual disclosure, trust, empathy, and understanding. There are also a number of individual variables, such as race, economic status, age, and sex, that are socially-culturally dependent, and that make it harder for heterogeneous groups to work together. Finally, the meaning that is carried via our verbal and nonverbal language system is fraught with ambiguity and is many times another source of interpersonal conflict in the group. An appreciation of these interpersonal variables helps us understand how small groups, particularly those engaged in the discussion process, must struggle incessantly for sufficient cohesion to achieve group goals.

KEY INTERPERSONAL RELATIONSHIPS IN SMALL GROUPS

In 1960, William C. Schutz reported that his work on the development of a new theory of interpersonal behavior would explain the interpersonal underworld of a small group. He called his theory FIRO, which stands for Fundamental Interpersonal Relations Orientation. This theory is based on the belief that when individuals join a group they have three interpersonal needs that they seek to satisfy. There is the need for *inclusion,* which deals with an individual's problem of being in or out of the group; there is the need for *control,* which deals with structuring people in some pecking order; and there is the need for *affection,* which relates emotionally to how close or distant people feel from the group. Schutz further classified each of the three interpersonal needs as deficient, excessive, or ideal (Schutz 1966).

INCLUSION

When we first join a group we are generally anxious about how we will fit in. We worry about being ignored; we worry about how committed we should be to the group; and we size up the other group members in terms of how much social interaction we should engage in. On one hand we want to be included in the activity, but on the other hand we don't want to get deeply involved with a group of people we don't know very well. In this situation, many of us tend to overreact or underreact. We may dominate the conversation with stories about ourselves and constantly fill every lull with any joke or cliché that comes to mind. When we underreact to social inclusion in a group we generally withdraw from the conversation, fidget with our coffee cup, or doodle on our notepads. We hesitate to submit any information about ourselves for group scrutiny. Thus, in any group encounter, we can plot ourselves on a continuum from undersocial, i.e., deficient; through social, i.e., ideal; to oversocial, i.e., excessive. Once we are an established member of a group, most of us seem to move along the continuum and learn to maintain the appropriate amount of social involvement (Schutz 1966, 24–28).

INCLUSION CONTINUUM

Undersocial	Social	Oversocial
(Deficient)	(Ideal)	(Excessive)

CONTROL

The division of labor that must take place for any task group to be productive gives rise to the need for control. Some people seem very competitive, assertive, and confident in structuring the various individual tasks. Schutz (1966, 28–30) calls individuals who have this tendency to dominate, *autocrats;* he says these people have a strong desire to create a power hierarchy with themselves at the top. At the other end of the continuum is the *abdicrat.* This is a person who abdicates all power and responsibility in his interpersonal behavior. This person goes along with the group and submits to being placed in a subordinate position. In the middle is the democrat who is comfortable with his or her own competency, is capable of assuming or not assuming group responsibilities, and seeks group decisions with regard to critical action of the group.

CONTROL CONTINUUM

Abdicrat	Democrat	Autocrat
(Deficient)	(Ideal)	(Excessive)

AFFECTION

The need for affection is the emotional dimension of the group. How well-liked are we by other group members? How intimate and affectionate should we be toward other group members? Are there cliques within our group? Do some people pair off and not share their intimate conversations with us in the group? These are the sorts of questions we ask in trying to satisfy our needs for affection in the small group. Schutz (1966, 30–32) states that some people are *underpersonal.* These people tend to keep everyone at a distance and seem to reject or not need personal contact in order to get work done. At the other extreme are the people who are *overpersonal* and can't seem to get anything done unless there is a strong love bond connecting them to the other group members. They have to feel very close to others before they can work with them. And of course we all strive to establish the proper distance between us and our other group members that allows us to do our work productively.

AFFECTION CONTINUUM

Underpersonal	Personal	Overpersonal
(Deficient)	(Ideal)	(Excessive)

Obviously, there are other interpersonal needs that are satisfied by group participation besides the three that Schutz identifies. Three additional needs that are worth mentioning, since they occasionally surface as a major reason for a person to become a group member, are *prestige, safety,* and the *need to do work.* Sometimes people join a group simply because it is a high status group in the community and they wish to say they are members. In a business setting, an employee might "hang out" with a certain clique for job security reasons because he or she believes being part of that group will make his or her position safer. Finally, an individual will have to join a group in order to fill certain work needs. For example, a cardiologist cannot perform open-heart surgery by him- or herself; it requires a team to do the job. Even these six needs do not explain everyone's reasons for joining a group, but they are certainly the important ones. Inclusion, control, and affection are interpersonal needs that can be monitored and managed for the good of the group.

FIRO-B

William Schutz developed a measuring instrument that contained six scales of nine-item questions that he called FIRO-B (B = Behavior). He developed this instrument to measure how an individual relates to other group members in terms of how he or she expresses his or her needs for inclusion, control, and affection; and how the individual wants others to express their needs of inclusion, control, and affection towards him or her. For example, if a person's need is for affection he or she might say, "I want to behave friendly toward people" (expressed behavior), and "I want other people to be friendly toward me" (wanted behavior). Another person might say, "I like to control people" (expressed behavior), "but I don't want people to control me" (wanted behavior). Yet another person would express the need to include other people in his or her social activities but not want other people to initiate the invitation for him or her to join them.

Ultimately Schutz's objective was to use the FIRO-B instrument to determine the interpersonal compatibility of group members, in the belief that the more compatible a group is, the greater its chances of achieving its task goal (Schutz 1966, 105). Schutz believed this to be true because a compatible group would not have to spend a great deal of its energy resolving its squabbles and thus could devote more time and energy to its task.

Figure 7.1 presents a schema of Schutz's interpersonal theory. By obtaining the scores for each group member in terms of his or her interpersonal needs of inclusion, control, and affection with regard to both expressed and wanted behaviors, Schutz could compile compatibility indexes for the group members and finally assess the compatibleness of one group versus another. The three compatibility indexes are originator, reciprocal, and interchange. Of the three, Schutz (1966, 10) believes that interchange compatibility has the most direct application to groups: *"Interchange* refers to the mutual expression of the 'commodity' of a given need area." For example, in terms of Figure 7.1, if everybody in a group circled 5 on inclusion, 4 on control, and 6 on affection for both expressed and wanted behavior, then the "interpersonal atmosphere" of the group should be very compatible. All the members want and receive agreement on deciding things democratically and they would all want to see that everyone was involved with the group's activity.

FIGURE 7.1
SCHEMA OF SCHUTZ'S INTERPERSONAL THEORY

Inclusion						
	High					Low
Expressed	6	5	4	3	2	1
Wanted	6	5	4	3	2	1
	Oversocial		Social		Undersocial	

Control						
	High					Low
Expressed	6	5	4	3	2	1
Wanted	1	2	3	4	5	6
	Autocrat		Democrat		Abdicrat	

Affection						
	High					Low
Expressed	6	5	4	3	2	1
Wanted	6	5	4	3	2	1
	Overpersonal		Personal		Underpersonal	

Adapted from William C. Schutz, *The Interpersonal Underworld* (Palo Alto, California: Science and Behavior Books, Inc., 1966), TABLE 4-2, p. 60. Reprinted by permission of the author and the publisher from William C. Schutz. *The Interpersonal Underworld.* Palo Alto, California: Science and Behavior Books, 1960

Application of FIRO-B to Group Discussion. Although we have serious reservations about the ability of Schutz's theory to predict quantitatively which groups will be most productive (Rosenfeld and Jessen 1972), we feel there is value in using Schutz's FIRO-B to explain qualitatively a work group's interchange compatibility in terms of inclusion, control, and affection—and for that matter any other interpersonal need a group would want to examine such as status or economic security. We think it is valuable for a group to systematically, but not empirically, assess their interpersonal compatibility. It would be valuable to know if most people like a high degree of group structure or not, or if most group members like to keep their emotional affections to people outside of the work group.

Figure 7.2 depicts an imaginary work group in terms of their interpersonal needs for inclusion, control, and affection as measured by Schutz's FIRO-B. As the group is formed, we would expect Alice and Tom to be somewhat withdrawn and disinterested, while Mary and Toni would relieve their nervousness by incessant chatter. We might expect that eventually Alice would clash with Henry or Mary on issues relating to the structuring of the task. However, if we push this analysis too far, we can become fatalistic about group development. After all, what we learn about group communication skills is designed to overcome obstacles such as the interpersonal make-up of the group membership.

The next section of this chapter deals with interpersonal process concepts that work towards building a livable, interpersonal environment for a small group.

FIGURE 7.2

HYPOTHETICAL GROUP IN TERMS OF SCHUTZ'S FIRO-B

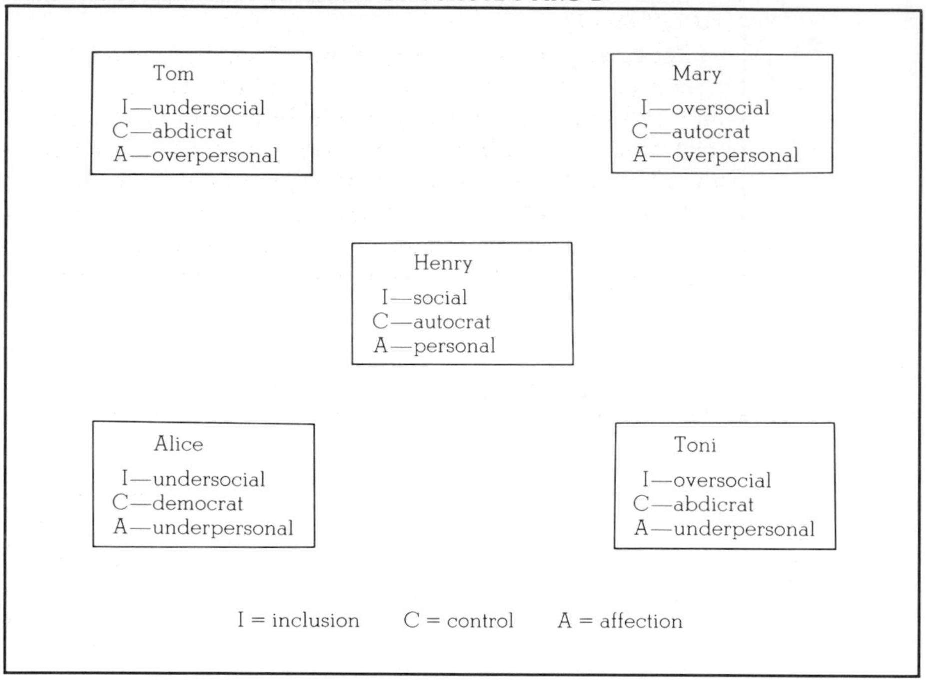

Tom
I—undersocial
C—abdicrat
A—overpersonal

Mary
I—oversocial
C—autocrat
A—overpersonal

Henry
I—social
C—autocrat
A—personal

Alice
I—undersocial
C—democrat
A—underpersonal

Toni
I—oversocial
C—abdicrat
A—underpersonal

I = inclusion   C = control   A = affection

IMPORTANT INTERPERSONAL PROCESS CONCEPTS

DISCLOSURE

Self-disclosure has long been regarded as a necessary process for an individual in maintaining a healthy personality (Jourard 1971, 28–33). Self-disclosure in groups is likewise necessary if a healthy work environment is to be maintained and if an open and candid discussion is to take place. The whole agenda of encounter groups is essentially self-disclosure. However, the amount of self-disclosure that occurs and is appropriate for a task group varies from group to group on the basis of the group task.

It is possible for an individual member of a group to be overdisclosed or underdisclosed depending on the nature of the group. A volunteer civic group which meets for monthly discussions on the efficiency of city government might not need to know that an individual member has a heart condition. However, if that same person is playing on that company's basketball team, that information should no doubt be disclosed to the group.

Finding the appropriate level of disclosure for a discussion group is never easy. In fact, just getting people to disclose anything personal is difficult. Newly formed groups will often require that each individual give his or her name and other pertinent information about him- or herself. Likewise, a new member of an established group may be required, many times in jest, to recite litanies about him- or herself. The new member can feel the group probing for new information. The group will keep prodding until they acquire an adequate amount of information about the new member.

One way to look at self-disclosure in a group is by means of the Johari window. Figure 7.3 portrays a five-person group from a Johari window lens (Luft 1970, 17).

For each group member Quadrant 1 signifies an area of self that is known to the group. When a group is first formed, this area may only include our name and other basic demographic information. Quadrant 2 is an area of ourselves that we are blind to but that is known to other members of the group. An individual's reputation may have preceded him or her in joining a group: for example, members of the new group may have been told that a member is bright and efficient, but he or she may not be aware that the group has been told. Quadrant 3 is a hidden area that is known to the individual but not to the

FIGURE 7.3
HYPOTHETICAL GROUP IN TERMS OF JOHARI WINDOW LENS

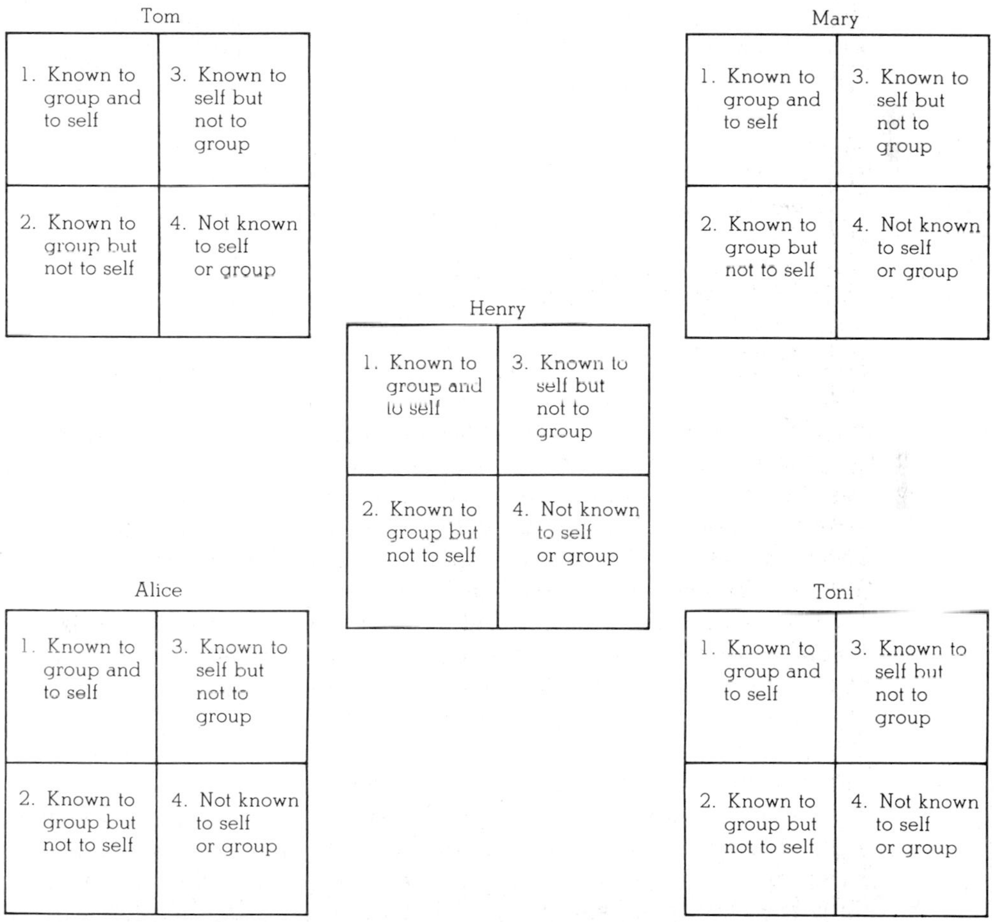

Adapted from *Group Processes: An Introduction to Group Dynamics* by Joseph Luft, by permission of Mayfield Publishing Company. Copyright © 1963, 1970, 1984 by Joseph Luft. See also *Of Human Interaction*.

group. For example, the individual may harbor a long-standing dislike of one of the group members, but may have never revealed that feeling to anyone. Quadrant 4 is the unknown area to both the self and the group. We know this area is there because we occasionally discover new knowledge about ourselves that neither we nor the group knew was there.

As self-disclosure takes place in a group, the size of Quadrant 1 will get larger, and the size of one or more of the remaining quadrants will get smaller. After a discussion group has developed a history, the group can readily list the information about individuals that used to be in Quadrant 3 and is now in Quadrant 1. In addition, an individual can also list some things that were in Quadrant 2 that have now moved to Quadrant 1.

The Johari window can also be used to help explain a group's level of group disclosure to outsiders. In this case, Quadrant 1 would contain information that nonmembers as well as members have about the group. Quadrant 2 would generally contain information that outsiders share with each other about the group, and of which the group is unaware. For example, a work group might be regarded as arrogant and "show-offy" by nonmembers. Quadrant 3 contains the group's secrets. A very efficient group may have a weak member, but they conceal this from outsiders because of their sense of group pride. Quadrant 4 is the unknown area that often contains hidden strengths or weaknesses of the group that surface during periods of stress or when a group is engaged in a consciousness-raising session.

TRUST

The establishment of interpersonal trust in a group is difficult to achieve and measure, although its presence or absence is readily recognized by its group members. Risk taking on the part of individual members is essential if trust is to be built in the group. The dangers of risk taking are greater in a group setting than in a dyad since there is more potential for a person to be "ripped off" by other group members.

The three major fears that form a barrier to establishing trust in task groups are: (1) the fear of not getting credit for the work we do; (2) the fear that the workload will not be equitably shared; and (3) the fear that individual self-disclosure will be used to the detriment of the individual, both in and outside of the group. Since most organizations reward individuals and not groups, group members always worry initially about their colleague's motives. If a supervisor or a coworker had developed a reputation for taking credit for other people's work, most people would not trust that individual in the group. We also worry that we'll be taken advantage of in terms of the amount of work we do for the group. Until a work group has produced some common effort, group members will constantly look for signs that the workload is not equally shared. As a work group engages in more and more face-to-face discussions, group members begin to disclose more personal kinds of communication. While this information helps the group to better understand the individual, that same information could be used against the individual if someone had malicious motives.

These fears are not unreasonable ones, and to some degree they will always be present in a work group. The best we can hope for is to keep these fears at a minimum and hope that, as the group develops a history of successful work together, trust will begin to be established. Research has shown that the best way to facilitate group trust is to maintain open lines of communication (Leathers 1970).

Trust is difficult to build in groups, but it is even harder to rebuild. Once group members have been betrayed or taken advantage of, the road back to a working relationship is very steep. Therefore, it is crucial that a group protect its trust as a precious commodity. When a member becomes suspicious, he or she should bring his or her fears out into the open for full discussion. Continual dialogue, combined with an honest effort by each group member, is the best way to maintain interpersonal trust in the group.

EMPATHY

DO NOT JUDGE TOO HARD

Pray do not find fault with the man that limps
Or stumbles along the road,
Unless you have worn the shoes he wears
Or struggled beneath his load.

There may be tacks in his shoes that hurt,
Though hidden away from view,
Or the burdens he bears placed on your back
Might cause you to stumble too.

Don't sneer at the man who is down today
Unless you have felt the blow
That caused his fall, or felt the pain
That only the fallen know.

You may be strong, but still the blows
That were his, if dealt to you
In the self same way at the self same time
Might cause you to stagger too.

From *An Act of Love,* by Florence McDonnell Cragan, R.N., 1959.

Empathy is not sympathy. Empathy is the ability to feel as another person feels, to emotionally be where another person is, even if you have not had exactly the same experience that triggered the emotion. Your father still might be living, but you are still able to empathize with a group member whose father has just died. Without empathetic understanding, judgments should not be formulated. Thus, the forming of opinions about fellow group members cannot be well founded unless there is empathy.

Empathy is hard to fake. All of us have caught ourselves saying, "I know how you feel," only to have the person respond, "Oh, no you don't." Maybe we did know intellectually, but we didn't take the time to feel it emotionally. Thus, empathetic understanding is as important as comprehending the ideas that are being transmitted in a group discussion. To listen empathetically takes time and effort. You can't just sit there listening for intellectual understanding. You have to pick up on the emotional tone of the discussant. The presentation may contain mostly a set of statistics, but the person's tone of voice may say, "This is extremely important to me, I have worked hard compiling this data, and I hope the group appreciates the work I have done."

Sometimes the group leader will be working hard getting the group through the agenda, and if you listen closely you may hear the person say, "I hope everybody can empathize with my job of being group leader; it takes a lot of effort to keep the group working on the same idea." When group members all work at empathetic listening, they generally learn to appreciate each other as individuals, and they better understand the roles people play in order to be more productive.

PERCEIVED INDIVIDUAL DIFFERENCES IN GROUP MEMBERS

What you see is often what you get in group member behavior. Societal stereotypes based on sex, age, race, education, socio economic background, and so on, are a very real part of the early formation stages of a small group. In fact, self-disclosure by group members is necessary if stereotypes are to be broken down so that the group can function.

The research based on these demographic and personality variables and how they affect group formation, productivity, and membership satisfaction is unreliable and incomplete. For example, Marvin E. Shaw (1976, 187), the eminent psychologist, has suggested the following hypothesis: "There is a tendency for the group leader to be older than the other group members." However, in McGrath and Altman's (1966, 62) thorough review of the leadership literature, they report quite the converse; that is, "Education, but not age or other biographical characteristics," are required for leadership. And even when researchers agree on their conclusions, there are so many exceptions that the findings are not very helpful in making judgments about group behavior.

Sometimes research findings that attempt to sort out different human behavior based upon demographic or personality differences produce great social controversy because such research attempts to prove causal links between, for example, the sex of a person and some predictable social behavior. We suspect that Marvin Shaw's (1976, 188) hypotheses dealing with the differences between men and women in groups are controversial for you; they certainly are for us. Shaw's hypotheses are: "Women are less self-assertive and less competitive in groups than are men; women use eye contact as a form of communication more frequently than men"; and, "females conform to majority opinion more than males." The indictment frequently given to Shaw's hypotheses is that the studies he reports are from the 1930s and 1940s and may not accurately depict the behavior of women as they participate in discussion groups today. However, we all know that the sexual composition of a group matters. If sexism exists in society, a natural expectation would be to see this manifestation in groups. The same would be true of racism and ageism. Ironically, many of the studies that have attempted to sort out the demographic influences on a group have in turn fueled the controversies surrounding the stereotyping that initially spawned the studies. Therefore, most of the advice that we provide in this section is based upon our own observation of student groups in classrooms, work groups in business, and recent communication studies conducted in the 1970s and 1980s.

SEX

Coed discussion groups appear to have different problems in the formation of group roles than groups made up of one sex. The biggest problem centers on who will be the task leader. The problem with female leadership is a cultural and unfortunate one. In the recent past—and we hope this will be less true in the future—it seemed that American women were forced to choose between being popular and being intellectual, and between being athletic and sexually attractive. Furthermore, even now she is provided with few role models of female leadership of male-female groups and is given little opportunity to play the role of task leader in her formative years. Few television programs, movies, or novels provide dramatic examples of a woman successfully leading male-female groups. In addition, segregated sports programs in high school do not provide opportunities for a young woman to try out the leadership role of a male-female group. Conversely, American males are conditioned to compete for the task-leader role and are made to believe that "losing" to a woman is twice as bad as losing to a man. The culture is also inundated with examples of male leadership and male dominated occupations. So we can expect that sex will be an issue in most coed groups and that this struggle will be particularly intense if the group has a tradition of being all male in the past. Thus, such items as the first female fire chief, the first female sheriff, and the first female naval admiral are news events.

Bormann, Pratt, and Putnam (1978, 150–153) simulated a corporate structure made up of small work groups at the University of Minnesota and tape-recorded the discussions of all the groups. This particular case study produced female dominance of the organization, a dominance that many males deeply resented. One group of males, the largest, withdrew from participation and became silent observers. Some males competed vigorously for leadership roles and, when they lost, felt "castrated." The smallest group of males remained active in supportive roles in their work groups. In essence, most males in this simulation had difficulty adapting to female leadership and power in the organization. In addition, Bradley (1980) discovered that women who demonstrated task competence in male-dominated problem-solving groups were treated more positively by the men than were women who did not demonstrate this competence; but Bradley also found that women who displayed this competency were not as well liked by group members. Yerby (1975) found that male group members experienced attitude difficulties with female leadership.

The two least disruptive roles that women play in groups appear to be (1) the social-emotional leader because of the stereotype that women are more nurturing than men, and (2) the recorder role because that is the traditional role women played in male-dominated work environments of the past. Gouran and Fisher (1984, 635) summarize sex-role research in small groups by pointing out that males are more likely to emerge as leaders and that females are more likely to engage in self-disclosure and be more aware of others' feelings in the group. Therefore, both females and males should be aware of the potential for people to be stereotyped into a particular role based on their sex. Also, one should look at conflict within the group to see if the disturbance is a result of disruptive or debilitating stereotypes.

RACE

Unfortunately, racial discrimination is a worldwide problem. It is particularly embarrassing to Americans because of our open commitment to justice and equality for all people. In racially mixed groups, race is an issue that pervades the group's formation. The first manifestation of race as an issue is majority versus minority. Most Americans have been raised in a majority environment of their race, so nobody is used to being stereotyped as the "minority." The fact that a group might think of itself in minority-majority terms complicates the evolvement of group roles. If a person of one race objects to a person of another race playing the role of task leader, he or she might be accused of being racist when in fact the person has nonracial reasons for objecting. On the other hand, the objections may be racially motivated, either consciously or subconsciously. Because of this, motives in racially mixed groups can be very difficult to determine.

Real and perceived cultural differences always cause problems in the socialization of a discussion group. This is most clearly manifested in the tension-releaser role. For example, if a long-standing work group has been using Polish jokes as a means of tension-release, the arrival of one of "those people" will cause the group a great deal of stress until it can find a new basis of humor. The problem is intensified if a group has been using racial humor and then becomes racially mixed. If a group is just starting out, members will feel tense until they can find a range of humor they can use to help in socializing the discussion group.

While it is more difficult to form a racially mixed group, there seems to be a rainbow at the end of the storm. Racially mixed groups that resolve their role problems tend to be very proud and productive. They have good reason for feeling proud because they probably had to work harder to become a group, each member having to invest more of his or her time and energy than members of other groups.

AGE

The return of older women to college campuses has produced classroom discussion groups that point up some of the problems that can occur when there are large differences in age among group members. The diaries from students in our small group discussion classes indicate that a woman in her late thirties working with six others in their late teens will initially be perceived as a "parent type" person, and not as a social equal. Sometimes the person labeled as a "parent type" does in fact feel and behave that way. A group will eventually process the perceived difference in ages and resolve it to the point where the "parent type" is a fully accepted member of the group.

In business and industry the age difference will generally occur in reverse. A young person will join a group which contains older and established members. In this situation, the young person is treated as a "kid" and does not receive equal social status in the group. The young person will tend to over-achieve and will constantly seek recognition for his or her contributions. The issue at stake is one of equality. On the issue of age, group members sometimes have a difficult time understanding the needs of the "parent type" or "kid" as they try to interact on an equal level with other members.

Another problem that age difference accentuates is the norming of the social conversation and social activities the group will engage in. A young person who finds that everyone else in the group is talking about purchasing retirement homes and the ins and outs of retirement annuities, may feel that he or she is on the outside looking in at the group. Likewise, an older person coexisting with younger group members may feel socially uncomfortable in conversations that deal with the latest dancing trends and night spots in the community. Groups that contain marked age differences must work harder to find social conversations that will serve as a common denominator by which group members can share their experiences.

EDUCATION

There is a general assumption that there is a connection between academic achievement and the ability to perform the necessary skills in day-to-day dis cussions. This assumption is based on the idea that people who go on to college are intellectually more capable than those who do not, and that the training the former receive in college enhances their ability to solve business and social problems.

In groups where there are marked differences in the educational levels of achievement, there is the expectation that people with more education should assume more responsibility in the discussion process. If the educated people in the group perform poorly or reluctantly, they can easily be held up to ridicule and scorn. If all members of a discussion group have college degrees, or at least some college experience, the socialization process is greatly facilitated. Despite sex, race, or age differences, the group can reliably draw upon a set of common experiences, even though the members may have gone to different colleges at different times. This is also a common tendency when people have shared similar experiences in the armed services or have lived in similar kinds of neighborhoods. The familiarity of education and experience serves as a common ground for discussion participants.

OCCUPATION

Occupations in our society are frequently ranked in national polls according to their status, and even if they were not, people seem to have a natural incli-nation to form some kind of "pecking order" based upon a person's occupa-tion. When a group contains marked differences in status as determined by occupation, a definite impact can be felt. This is particularly true if some of the members are in the professions—e.g., physicians, lawyers, professors, dentists —and the other members are not. The people in the professions may hold unfounded and stereotyped views of blue-collar workers' intellectual abilities. Likewise the blue-collar members may have some long-standing resentment against physicians and lawyers. These prejudices will generally surface in discussion groups that must agree upon a common decision.

Role playing in a mixed occupational group can be a very difficult process. The professional people might object to a blue-collar person emerging as task leader because they would feel loss in status, or the blue-collar members might distrust leadership from a person who is a member of one of the professions. Movies and TV dramas often exploit this conflict among occupations by producing surprising turnabouts in crisis situations. The scenario generally calls for a small group of people from mixed occupational backgrounds to be thrown into a common crisis. In the crisis it is discovered that one of the low-status persons has some special expertise that allows him or her to emerge as task leader of the group. However, most group discussions do not take place in a crisis context, nor do most group tasks require a specialized skill or knowledge data base that only one member possesses. Thus, most groups have to struggle through their differences in occupational status with no clear way to solve their problem. The tension is generally reduced by finding some basis of equality outside of their occupations.

INCOME

Money doesn't make a difference in groups, but a lot of money does! Major differences in the wealth of individual members affects the group, not only in terms of the status that members may attach to wealth, but in terms of their overall lifestyle differences. Even when group members find common topics to discuss, their perception of the same topic can be quite different. For example, if three students in a group are discussing where they are going to go over spring break, and two of the students indicate they are going home to work at a part-time job to help pay for their education, while the third student indicates she is flying to the Bahamas to go deep-sea diving, chances are the two working students will at least humorously chide the affluent one. The result of this conversation will have an impact on the affection and inclusion aspects of the group.

When socially concerned citizens form discussion groups to grapple with our country's problems, differences in wealth and consequently lifestyles in the group can produce conflict and alienation. If a group of midwestern grain farmers forms a discussion group to deal with low subsidy supports for their products, differences in income may matter. The wealthy farmers in the group may want to take one of their $80,000 tractors, drive it to Washington, D.C., and set it on fire. The small family farmer cannot afford the time or the tractor, and may feel left out of the group and frustrated because the lack of wealth did not allow for full participation. Conversely, a wealthy group member may be excluded from the group on the ground that he or she has not directly experienced the problems of the group; or the wealthy person may be made to feel guilty for not spending his or her wealth to reduce the problem the group is discussing.

PERSONALITY

Mann's (1959) article, "A Review of the Relationships between Personality and Performance in Small Groups," reveals that the bulk of research done on personality variables in small groups supports everyday experiences that we have as we work in groups. For example, as we indicated in Chapter 5, McGrath and Altman (1966) identified three personality characteristics—extroversion, self-assertiveness, and social maturity—that help one become an effective leader; also, more intelligent group members tend to be more popular, more active, less conforming, and more likely to emerge as group leaders. Group members who score high on empathy tests and who are generally socially well adjusted, contribute to the effectiveness of a group, while anxious and immature group members detract from the group's performance (Shaw, 1976). Furthermore, it appears that a person's tolerance for ambiguity (M. Burgoon 1971; Norton, 1976), a person's level of communication apprehension (J. K. Burgoon 1977; Sorenson and McCroskey 1977), and tendencies toward Machiavellianism (Bochner and Bochner 1972) are important personality variables that affect the performance and satisfaction of a work group. In general, then, the personality profile of members of an effective group shows that they are reasonably intelligent, are sensitive to an individual's personal needs, are competent communicators, and are somewhat extroverted and assertive without being overly dominant.

The proper personality mixture that makes for an effective group has not been determined. Should birds of a feather be flocked together? Do opposites attract and produce an electrical charge? Will too many dominants in the group spoil the group's productivity? Does the group need some drones as well as active workers? Experience tells us that extremes stand out in a group and are a source for group conflict. In the next chapter we discuss conflict caused by deviant personality types. If one group member is substantially brighter, or clearly slower than the group, criticism will be directed at him or her. Sometimes he or she will be rudely labeled with such names as "The Egghead," "The Computer," "The Dunce," and "The Neanderthal." The same seems to be true for the extroverted-introverted extremes.

HOMOGENEITY AND HETEROGENEITY

If you are in a very homogeneous group, no doubt group member values, abilities, and opinions are very much alike; thus, there should be less conflict in the social dimension of the group. However, task performance might not be as high when compared to a hetereogeneous group. Shaw's (1976, 235) synthesis of the research on homogeneity-heterogeneity produced the two following hypotheses: (1) "Other things being equal, groups composed of members having diverse, relevant abilities perform more effectively than groups composed of members having similar abilities"; and (2) "Groups whose members are heterogeneous with respect to personality profiles perform more effectively than groups whose members are homogeneous with respect to personality profiles."

Culturally we Americans are committed to the principle that heterogeneous groups are better than homogeneous groups. Fortunately, small group research appears to support the American ideal of pluralism. Although groups containing diverse memberships might encounter a number of problems in becoming a group, the rich and diverse backgrounds of their members make them potentially more capable of solving group problems than homogeneous groups. In short, it would be naive for you to ignore individual differences in group members, but it would be foolish, given his or her potential contribution, to exclude a person from membership because of demographic or personality differences.

VERBAL LANGUAGE CODE IN GROUPS

Two-person conversations are often marked by misunderstandings when the people cannot express themselves clearly enough. This problem is even more complex in a group discussion. The two basic problems that dyads have with verbal communication codes are the same in small groups. The first problem with our verbal code is the relationship between symbol and thought; the second is the group context in which it is used. It is a matter of semantics. What is the meaning of the words we use? Ogden and Richards (1923) said there is no necessary symbol between a word and a referent, while another well-known semanticist, S. I. Hayakawa (1964), made the same observation with his "the map is not the territory." The first problem which is central to the verbal language code really comes down to the difference between language and thought.

DIFFERENCES BETWEEN LANGUAGE AND THOUGHT

There are many ways in which we can quickly demonstrate to ourselves how inaccurately language symbols represent our thoughts. Even simple words when uttered to a group of people can produce a variety of different thoughts in the minds of a group. For example, if a group member said, "What is the block?" we can see in Figure 7.4 the possible resultant lack of common thought processes in the group.

FIGURE 7.4
DIFFERENCE BETWEEN LANGUAGE AND THOUGHT

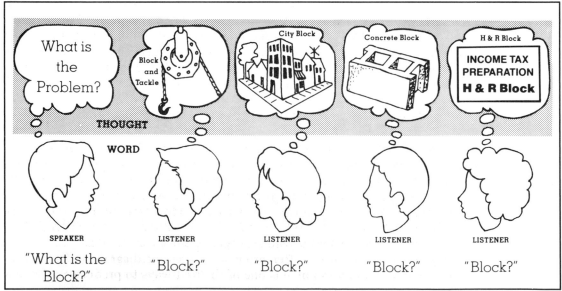

The person asking the question might have believed the symbol, "block," referred to the same object he was thinking about, but obviously it did not. Words often do not say what we mean, or at least they do not say enough of what we mean so that we can be certain that other members of the group understand our thoughts. Group discussants should continually promote more clarity and try to reduce the gap between language and thought. This can be helped by defining key words.

Many unfortunate and unnecessary conflicts take place in group discussions because the group failed to take the time to carefully define key recurring concepts in their discussions. However, even when group members attempt to define their key concepts, the group can continue to have difficulties because of the many ways a concept can be defined. It is therefore useful to examine the eight basic ways a word can be defined.

1. *Definition by origin.* If someone is called chauvinistic, one way to get at the meaning of chauvinism is to look at the etymology or origin of the word. It turns out that chauvinism, from the French word "chauvinisme," refers to Nicolas Chauvin who was an officer in the French Napoleonic army. This officer used to constantly get on his soapbox and boast how superior his country was to all others. People used to say, "There goes Chauvin again!" Anytime somebody bragged or flaunted himself, he was labeled chauvinistic. In today's society this term is used mainly to describe males who are chauvinistic in their attitude toward women. Established groups often create key words, and new members should seek the origin of them if they are thinking of becoming a member of that group. For example, a new member might be called "Ed, the Motormouth." The etymology of the expression in the group might refer to the last new member of the group whose name was Ed and who talked far too much for a new member. Thus, to be called "Ed, the Motormouth," would be a bad thing and an indication that the newest member should talk less.

2. *Definition by negation.* As strange as it sounds, we often define things in terms of what they are not. When we say that people are not immortal, we are defining human beings for what they are not, not what they are. When we say that a couple is childless, we are defining that couple in terms of what they do not have, not what they have. Small groups often develop definitions of what a good member of their group is by developing a list of things that a person does not do. For example, a good discussant is not rude, not dominating, and not ignorant.

3. *Definition by example.* One way of eliminating the ambiguity between a word and the thought it stands for is to provide a specific example of the thought. For example, in explaining what a dog is to a child, we often bring the dog over and show it to the child. In small group communication classes, instructors often play group games or create simulations so that the student can clearly see examples of group communication behavior that is difficult to comprehend in the abstract. The sixteen leadership communication behaviors can be quickly comprehended through the use of classroom demonstrations that create such behaviors as regulating participation or verbalizing consensus. In group discussions people often bring in pictures and diagrams of key objects because definition by example is one of the best ways to produce clarity in a discussion.

4. *Definition by description and classification.* We use description so automatically that we sometimes forget how basic this definitional process is to our understanding. If you open an encyclopedia, you might find a picture of an oak tree. Beneath the oak tree would be a list of characteristics that makes an oak tree an oak tree. Once described in terms of what is "oaky" about it, the tree is then classified in terms of what it has in common with other trees and how it differs from flowers. In group discussions incidents are often described and then classified in terms of the group's priority system. In small group communication research, we might describe certain communication behavior and classify that behavior as autocratic leadership behavior. The description and classification system in small group processes tends to frame what otherwise would appear to be a confusing set of events, thus giving the group a sense of procedural clarity and helping it proceed in an orderly manner.

5. *Definition by analogy.* The clarity that a definition by analogy can provide is based upon how closely alike two things are. If they are analogous and the group members have firsthand knowledge of one of them, they will have a simultaneous understanding of the second thing, even if they have not experienced it. There are two kinds of analogies: figurative and literal.

We have all experienced the process by which a hypodermic needle puts fluid into our body. Some mass communication theorists have drawn a figurative analogy between this process and the process by which television commercials put ideas into our heads. To the degree the television set is a hypodermic needle, a TV ad is a fluid and our intellectual comprehension is the arm into which the needle is plunged, we understand mass communication persuasion by the analogy of the hypodermic needle. The point we are making here is that while figurative analogies have the appearance of making us feel that we understand something that was previously unfamilar to us, when we push for a one-to-correspondence between the familiar and the unfamiliar we find that figurative analogies are absurd. However, despite our cautionary note about figurative analogies and their use, complex ideas tend to be best remembered when they are defined by a figurative analogy.

When a group has developed a history of solving problems, literal analogies become an important part of group discussions. If the group can conclude that the present problem is analogous to one they resolved last month, then they will probably proceed to look at the same solutions. Literal analogies are almost examples but not quite; that is why one should be cautious in their use because we tend to treat two analogous cases identically when in fact they are not examples of the same thing.

6. *Definition by function and purpose.* The function of an airplane is to provide transportation. We might also say that the purpose of an airplane is to fly. There is a close relationship between function and purpose, but they are not the same. The task leader's primary purpose may be to lead the group to the accomplishment of its group goals; in doing that, the leader and other group members perform a variety of communication leadership behaviors or functions. Purpose implies intent and function implies behavior. To simply define a group in terms of its function would beg the question—to what end or for what purpose? Thus, if a group can define its purpose it then can define the functions it needs to perform in order to accomplish group goals.

7. *Definition by operations performed.* In operational definitions, each word is defined in terms of some measurable behavior so that we can look across cases and quantitatively assess the similarity of like cases. However, in most face-to-face discussions small groups do not have the time or the resources to provide their own operational definitions of key concepts and perform their own experiments. Yet, when on rare occasions groups conduct their own research, they attain an unusually high rate of agreement about the meanings of words for which they have worked out operational definitions.

8. *Definition by context.* Because of the many denotative and connotative meanings that words acquire, we quite often do not know the meaning of a word until we hear it in context. For example, take the word "pitch." What is the meaning of this word? In the context of a baseball game we know what the word "pitch" means; in the context of a singing lesson, "pitch" means something quite different; and in the midst of a sales meeting, "pitch" has another meaning. Written transcriptions of group meetings are often misleading because they do not reveal nonverbal contexts in which the words were used. As we will see in the next section of this chapter, much of this meaning is carried by nonverbal cues.

Language theorists have pointed out that the meaning of a word is dependent upon not only the sentence and paragraph in which it is used, but also the nonverbal behaviors that accompany the verbal communication. Thus, understanding what is being said in a group discussion is a very complex affair.

GROUP-CREATED LANGUAGE AND THOUGHT

Small groups that work together daily, or even weekly, over time develop their own abbreviated language for discussing their work and for facilitating group decision making. A new member of a long-standing work group, or an outsider observing the communication of an established group, will be bewildered by an array of idioms and acronyms that only have meaning for group members.

Work groups that are parts of large organizations are notorious for their use of acronyms. We once attended a meeting in Washington that was called by the OEO to discuss funding of a project that would be supervised by MCHRD and occur at the ATTAC; but the whole project had to be approved by the OMB, assuming we had no problems with the EEOC. Needless to say, it was some time before these two midwestern university professors could decipher the language code of the federal employees. We later discovered that the meeting had been called by the Office of Economic Opportunity (OEO) to discuss funding of a project that would be supervised by the Mayor's Commission on Human Resources and Development (MCHRD) which would occur at an Area Technical Training and Assistance Center (ATTAC); but the whole project had to be approved by the Office of Management and Budget (OMB), assuming there were no problems with the Equal Employment Opportunity Commission (EEOC).

We sometimes mistakenly think that confusing acronyms are the special communication form of the federal bureaucracy, but as a new student on campus you may have encountered an array of acronyms without ever going to Washington. On our own campus, a student handbook designed to introduce students to campus organizations invites the students to "check out" the SOAP office. The handbook states the following: "SOAP is not the 'bar it sounds like,' rather, SOAP stands for all the 'zesty' experiences available to students on the ISU campus . . . for SOAP is the Student Organizations, Activities, and Programs Office" (Oldfield 1978, 6).

All work groups will develop acronyms and technical jargon that allow them to talk about their work efficiently. Sometimes it takes several months for a new member to master the group's language. Once this is accomplished, the member will feel a sense of inclusion in the group and may even enjoy watching another new member become bewildered as he or she confronts for the first time the group's "language." Sometimes group members mistakenly think that everybody speaks their language and proceed to release public communiqués that contain the group's ideas encased in the group's technical jargon. The public ridicule of federal publications or university research is often because the group's language appears to be, and may in fact be, a "foreign language" to them.

Long-standing groups will often provide a unique group label for certain behaviors that they wish to quickly praise or blame. For example, in an American culture if somebody were accused of being "a Benedict Arnold," most Americans would know the person was being labeled a traitor. Small groups develop similar labels, but since the group's history is not published a new member would not know what the label referred to. So if a new member were told to not be "a Greenwood," he or she might be bewildered. However, the established members of the group would know that Jack Greenwood was a former member of the group who always used to come late to meetings. They would know that whenever a member arrived late for a meeting, he or she was immediately labeled "a Greenwood" and called such for the remainder of the meeting. Over time, groups develop an elaborate array of idioms that are based upon the past history of the group. It may take a new member several months to uncover the important incidents in the group's past that give meaning to the verbal expressions that punctuate the group's daily discussions.

In sum, the language we use is not the same as our thoughts, just the best representation we have of them. Group language, then, is only a very rough representation of the individual and group thinking that has taken place in a discussion. Furthermore, the unique language developed by the group will only have meaning for its members.

NONVERBAL LANGUAGE CODE IN SMALL GROUPS

Numerous colleges and universities have adopted courses in nonverbal communication. Many of you may have been introduced to the nonverbal area in your introductory speech course or a course in interpersonal communication. The purpose of this section is to stress the importance of certain nonverbal variables in small group discussions. For convenience, we will discuss nonverbal communication in small groups according to two major dimensions: environmental and personal.

ENVIRONMENTAL DIMENSIONS

The three nonverbal environmental variables that affect communication in the small group are proxemics, objectics, and chronemics. The descriptions of each of these that follow are intended to enhance our understanding of how they influence group discussions.

1. *Proxemics.* The major concern of proxemics is the study of space. We are concerned not only with the personal bubble, or personal space, that we carry around with us, but with the territory, or fixed space, in which we find ourselves. Just as we mentioned in Chapter 2 when discussing the concept of "life-space" in Kurt Lewin's Field Theory, so it is with our notion of personal space in small group communication. Each person brings to the group his or her personal bubble or life-space. In a group in which a person is very influential, he or she might occupy more of the group's life-space than other less influential members. Conversely, a person who occupies a large amount of personal space may not give the time of day to other group members; this could lead to a bad discussion situation.

One should be able to recognize that personal space is dynamic, whereas territorial space is not. Territory, as a basic proxemic variable, is fixed space. When we consider territory, we often think of a protected area. Many of us protect fixed spaces that belong to us—in our home, work and play environments. Many of us have seen how a new infant has little fixed space he or she could call his or her own; however, it is amazing how quickly the child starts to stake his or her claim to new territory in a room and then a whole house! The difference between personal space and territory can be described as follows: if you claim a room as being yours, for example an office, that is territory; however, if you alter the amount of space you take up in a room when, for example, other employees come into your office, then you have changed the dynamic variable we identify as personal space.

The way in which personal space and territory relate to group discussions is through the study of small group ecology. By and large, small group ecology is concerned with such things as seating arrangement, who sits next to whom, the shape of meeting tables, and the like. Knapp (1978, 131–40) identifies numerous variables that are concerned with seating behavior and spatial arrangements in groups: leadership dominance, task, sex, acquaintance, motivation, and introversion-extroversion. These are all relevant topics that form a basis for the study of small group ecology.

In terms of seating arrangements, we typically see the task leader taking a prominent position at the head of the table. If the group is having a panel discussion, the moderator typically sits in the middle. The task leader's lieutenant, or social-emotional leader, usually sits next to the task leader or directly across from him or her. The task leader usually stakes a territorial claim in which he or she can assert his or her personal space bubble in a discussion group.

In terms of who sits next to whom, there are a number of factors involved. First of all, people who are dominant in asserting their personal space can sit anywhere they want to and next to whom they please. In many classrooms I am sure that you have noticed how certain instructors have asserted themselves in where they will sit and next to whom. Introverted persons simply do not get a great choice in selecting where they will sit or next to whom.

The shape of meeting tables also serves to govern the territory that is available to group members. In Chapter 3 we make no small point about "round table" and "square table" discussions. In fact, if group members insist on a square or rectangular table, persons will begin to see how their personal space bubbles are being minimized or enlarged in this given discussion territory. On the other hand, if the task leader and other group members encourage a round table discussion format, the likelihood of giving equalness to each individual's life-space in the group setting is noticeably enhanced.

2. *Objectics.* Just as the places in which group discussions are held have nonverbal nuances, so do the many artifacts and fixtures that accompany them. Think of the setting when you are called to the boss's conference room for the "big meeting." Name tags indicate the place you should sit at the long oak conference table. Glasses of ice water are set at each place. Pens and company stationery are placed by each discussant's name tag. Dignified landscape paintings line the walls of the conference room. This setting is much different from the informal meetings held around coworkers' desks on a daily basis! One of the basic differences between formal and informal discussion meetings occurs because of the influence of the nonverbal dimension of objectics.

The nonverbal variable of objectics is concerned with objects and artifacts. Objects in group discussions can include paper, pens, chalkboards, flip charts, and the like that are necessary for the group's functioning. Artifacts are typically things that "dress up" the discussion setting. For example, decorative items on conference-room walls dress up the formal discussion meeting. A general knowledge of objectics helps discussion planners assess the impact of various objects and artifacts on the formal-informal dimension of discussions.

3. *Chronemics.* A third environmental nonverbal variable is chronemics, or the study of time. Time has a tremendous impact on small group communication. First of all, one of the major differences between groups is their history—is the group a zero-history group or does it have a definite history? We know that the amount of time group members spend in a given group shapes, to no small extent, the historical tradition and acculturation processes of groups.

In addition to what constitutes time in small groups—history or no history—small group practitioners are concerned with the "when" aspects of chronemics. Staff meetings are typically held at the same time each week—"Monday morning meetings," "Friday lunch meetings," and so on. Whether or not the designated day and hour of the meeting is best for group members is largely immaterial; the important point for many organizations is to have regular meetings, in part for their own chronemic sense of normalcy.

One further apsect of chronemics on groups is *how long* the meeting lasts. Most people start to get uncomfortable if a two-hour meeting lasts longer than its assigned time period. Most formal discussion planners must insist that their discussants adhere to time limits. The what, when, and how long facets of chronemics represent the importance of considering environmental nonverbal variables in small group discussions.

PERSONAL DIMENSIONS

The three nonverbal personal variables that affect communication in the small group are vocalics, kinesics, and eye behavior. Each of these dimensions is related to how we perceive communication interaction and role behaviors in group discussions.

1. *Vocalics.* The sounds a person makes that accompany his or her verbal messages are called vocalics or paralanguage. Many speech practitioners have devoted their careers to enhancing the voice and diction skills of students. How sounds come out of a person's mouth influences a listener's perception of the person communicating a verbal message. Contrast a discussant who carefully enunciates each and every syllable and couches these syllables in golden pear-shaped tones with a group member who casually states his or her ideas with no such vocalic exaggeration. On the other end of the continuum, however, is the discussant who mutters his or her opinions in a low-pitched, gravelly voice.

In addition to the voice and diction aspects present in paralanguage, group members must be vigilant to identify emotional nuances that might accompany another member's contribution. The member might verbally say, "yes, yes!" but the sound of his or her voice says "no, no!" Just as with other elements of the nonverbal code, vocalics must be interpreted in light of both the individual involved and his or her interrelationship with the given group situation.

2. *Kinesics.* A second nonverbal personal variable that can affect communication in the small group is that of kinesics. In a broad sense, kinesics refers to body language. Various categories of body language that are of concern to speech communication scholars include posture, hand and arm gestures, facial expression, and total bodily movement. Many times a discussant's interest in the topic at hand will be indicated by his or her posture in a chair. If a member is sitting up straight in his or her seat, it probably shows that he or she is paying attention to the discussion topic. On the other hand, slouching, overrelaxed behavior might reflect a nonchalant attitude.

Hand and arm gestures very often represent not only how expressive a person is, but the enthusiasm he or she feels for a given topic. In fact, some kinds of gesticulation can even indicate the role an individual is playing in a group. Reporting results from a scientifically researched study, Baird (1977, 360) concluded that gesticulation of the shoulders and arms contributed significantly to members' perceptions of leadership behavior. In addition, other bodily actions such as crossing of legs, the folding of arms, and finger pointing may indicate, either intentionally or not, some aspect of a member's attitude toward the group. Facial expression, too, can reflect a member's feelings, although it is very difficult to be sure what many facial expressions mean in terms of possible emotions conveyed. Nonetheless, a careful analysis of kinesic behavior by group members will help in understanding the general feeling of the group using another lens of nonverbal communication.

3. *Eye behavior.* The third personal dimension of nonverbal communication in small group discussions is eye behavior. One of the standard axioms of small group leadership states: If you want to know who the real leader in the group is, closely observe to whom the other participants address their remarks. In most small groups, this method of identifying the leader holds true. Eye behavior of discussion participants can also display a number of personality and social dimensions. If the person does not look directly into the eyes of other group members, does he or she fear reprisals from the group and thus not look at them? Or, by not looking at someone, does he or she express lack of interest in a particular person or the ideas that person tries to present or both?

By considering the above personal dimensions, as well as the three environmental variables, one is able to make an assessment of how significant nonverbal communication is in small group discussions. Certainly the impact of particular nonverbal dimensions will be more significant in some groups than in others. For example, the personal dimensions of the nonverbal code are typical of one-time meeting groups; on the other hand, both personal and environmental nonverbal communication variables might combine to suggest subtle changes in the development of an unspoken language code in ongoing groups.

SUGGESTIONS FOR IMPROVING INTERPERSONAL RELATIONSHIPS IN GROUPS

1. *Providing emotional security for all members.* If the interpersonal climate of a group is safe enough for the most insecure member, then the group as a whole should be quite healthy. Therefore, you should attempt to determine which group member is most likely to feel excluded from the group, dominated by the group, or disliked by the group. If you make an effort to make that person feel comfortable, wanted, and included during the discussions, then the overall emotional security of the group should be strengthened.

2. *Risking self-disclosure.* When you feel comfortable with the task the group is performing, you should take the risk of self-disclosure. Generally, groups suffer from being underdisclosed and this is especially true if the members feel they are fundamentally different from one another. Disclosure by one member will usually lead to disclosure by other members. If you pick disclosures about yourself that are relevant to the group's task, and if they are disclosures you have made to other groups in the past without harmful effects, the risks to you should be minimal and you will contribute to the growth of the group's overall maturity. These self-disclosures are not necessarily weaknesses or insecurities on your part, but may in fact be revelations about your strength or expertise. A group needs to know the personal strengths of its individual members in order to maximize its productivity.

3. *Avoiding stereotyped judgments.* Small group research clearly indicates that the more pluralistic a group is, the more difficult time a group will have in forming. This is partly due to our tendency to stereotype people. If we notice only a person's sex, age, or race and cannot even remember his or her name, chances are we are stereotyping that person on the basis of demographic information rather than seeing him or her as a distinct individual. Another indication of the stereotyping that goes on in groups can be observed by listening to a new group trying to recall who the missing member is. A newly formed classroom group might say, "The missing member is that old, married woman with the hair piece who is trying to be a college student again." When group members are asked about this kind of stereotyping, they generally respond with a cliché such as, "We're good at remembering faces, but poor at remembering names!" What they are really saying is that it is easier to stereotype people on their demographics than it is to understand a distinct personality. So fight the tendency to categorize group members superficially and listen carefully to what each member has to say. This sort of extra effort will go a long way toward building trust and understanding in your group.

4. *Paraphrasing.* Paraphrasing should occur at both the emotional and ideational levels of a group discussion. Often group members will disclose common past experiences, but no one listens to anyone else. When one group member is talking about his or her successes as a high school athlete, another member might not be empathetically listening, but eagerly waiting to tell his or her athletic story. Paraphrasing a person's interpersonal disclosure is an excellent way to assure him or her that you were listening. If you say, "Oh, so you played three years of high-school basketball," the other person will probably elaborate on his or her story and feel more emotionally secure in the group. The payoff is an altogether improved perception of that individual by the group.

Paraphrasing is also a very important communication strategy for clarifying the ideas that a group is discussing. When a group is on an interesting topic there is a tendency for the members to throw in their ideas one after another without anyone attempting to paraphrase the ideas to check if everyone understands what is being said. The paraphrasing of another member's position not only aids in the clarification of the group's thought process, but it reassures that group member that his or her ideas are being listened to and appreciated.

5. *Heightening awareness of the nonverbal code.* If you could observe your group functioning from behind a one-way mirror but could not hear them, you would soon realize that the nonverbal group code was conveying a great deal of information. You would be able to assess the overall emotional state of the group and the general cohesion of the group as it worked on its task. However, if the nonverbal code were to be taken in context with the verbal code, you would be able to make a much more accurate assessment of the group's structure and potential for group operations and work. We emphasize the importance of nonverbal communication primarily because this dimension of communication has not received adequate attention and application until recent years. In the past we concentrated on the rational verbal aspects of group discussions. Blending the nonverbal code with the group's verbal language system provides us with a more accurate picture of what is taking place in the group. Of course, it would also be an error to overemphasize nonverbal communication and rely upon it as a primary means for inference about what is going on in the group.

SUMMARY

The interpersonal relationships that individuals develop and foster in small group communication were the focus of this chapter. These relationships include the dimensions of inclusion, control, and affection, which are measured to no small extent by the amount of disclosure, trust, and empathy that group members have for one another.

Our perception of individuals as group members is very often tempered by differences rather than similarities. Individual differences considered in the chapter included sex, race, age, education, occupation, income, and personality. How these differences are perceived by members often indicates the heterogeneity or homogeneity of the group's composition.

Crucial to our understanding of individual group members is a basic comprehension of how verbal and nonverbal codes function in groups. Eight different ways in which a word can be defined were included to illustrate differences between language and thought. Further, group-created language and thought were discussed in terms of the way the verbal code operated uniquely in a group. On the other hand, the nonverbal language code was found to be determined in part by both environmental and personal dimensions of nonverbal communication. Proxemics, objectics, and chronemics were the three environmental nonverbal concepts presented. The three personal nonverbal concepts considered were vocalics, kinesics, and eye behavior.

The chapter concluded with five suggestions for improving interpersonal relationships in small groups.

REFERENCES

Baird, J. E., Jr. "Sex Differences in Group Communication: A Review of Relevant Research." *Quarterly Journal of Speech* 62 (1976): 179–92.

_____ . "Some Nonverbal Elements of Leadership Emergence." *Southern Speech Communication Journal* 40 (1977): 352–61.

Bochner, A. P., and Bochner, B. "A Multivariate Investigation of Machiavellianism and Task Structure in Four-Man Groups." *Speech Monographs* 39 (1972): 277–85.

Bormann, E. G.; Pratt, J.; and Putnam, L. "Power, Authority, and Sex: Male Response to Female Leadership." *Communication Monographs* 45 (1978): 119–55.

Bradley, P. H. "Sex, Competence, and Opinion Deviation: An Expectation States Approach." *Communication Monographs* 47 (1980): 101–10.

_____ . "The Folk-Linguistics of Women's Speech: An Empirical Examination." *Communication Monographs* 48 (1981): 73–90.

Bunyi, J. M., and Andrews, P. H. "Gender and Leadership Emergence: An Experimental Study." *Southern Speech Communication Journal* 50 (1985): 246–60.

Burgoon, J. K. "Unwillingness to Communicate as a Predictor of Small Group Discussion Behavior and Evaluations," *Central States Speech Journal* 28 (1977): 122–33.

Burgoon, M. "Amount of Conflicting Information in a Group Discussion and Tolerance for Ambiguity as Predictors of Task Attractiveness." *Speech Monographs* 38 (1971): 121–24.

Gouran, D. S., and Fisher, B. A. "The Functions of Human Communication in the Formation, Maintenance, and Performance of Small Groups." In *Handbook of Rhetorical and Communication Theory,* edited by Arnold, C. C. and Bowers, J. W., 622–58. Boston: Allyn and Bacon, 1984.

Hayakawa, S. I. *Language in Thought and Action.* 2nd edition. New York: Harcourt, Brace and World, 1964.

Jourard, S. M. *The Transparent Self.* 2nd edition. New York: D. Van Nostrand Company, 1971.

Knapp, M. L. *Nonverbal Communication in Human Interaction.* 2nd edition. New York: Holt, Rinehart and Winston, 1978.

Leathers, D. G. "The Process Effects of Trust-Destroying Behavior in the Small Group." *Speech Monographs* 37 (1970): 180–87.

_____ . "The Informational Potential of the Nonverbal and Verbal Components of Feedback Responses." *Southern Speech Communication Journal* 44 (1979): 331–54.

Luft, J. *Group Processes: An Introduction to Group Dynamics.* 2nd edition. Palo Alto, Calif.: Mayfield, 1970.

Mann, R. D. "A Review of the Relationships between Personality and Performance in Small Groups." *Psychological Bulletin* 56 (1959): 241–70.

McGrath, J. E., and Altman, I. *Small Group Research.* New York: Holt, Rinehart and Winston, 1966.

Norton, R. "Manifestations of Ambiguity Tolerance through Verbal Behavior in Small Groups." *Communication Monographs* 43 (1976): 35–43.

Ogden, C. K., and Richards, I. A. *The Meaning of Meaning.* New York: Harcourt, Brace and World, 1923.

Oldfield, J. *The Check Book: ISU Student Organization Handbook.* Normal, Ill.: ISU Printing, 1978.

Rosenfeld, L. B., and Jessen, P. A. "Compatibility and Interaction in the Small Group: Validation of Schutz's FIRO-B Using a Modified Version of Lashbrook's PROANA 5." *Western Speech* 36 (1972): 31–40.

Schutz, W. C. *The Interpersonal Underworld.* 2nd edition. Palo Alto, Calif.: Science and Behavior Books, 1966.

Shaw, M. E. *Group Dynamics: The Psychology of Small Group Behavior.* 2nd edition. New York: McGraw-Hill, 1976.

Sorensen, G., and McCroskey, J. C. "The Prediction of Interaction Behavior in Small Groups: Zero History Versus Intact Groups." *Communication Monographs* 44 (1977): 73–80.

Yerby, J. "Attitude, Task, and Sex Composition as Variables Affecting Female Leadership in Small Problem-Solving Groups." *Speech Monographs* 42 (1975): 160–68.

CASE
STUDY

DIARY OF GEORGE CRAMER

CASE BACKGROUND

George Cramer is taking a small group course at Midwestern College. George is a transfer student from a junior college located in the northwestern United States. He transferred to Midwestern College because he heard that the school had a good accounting department and because he is interested in becoming a C.P.A. George is taking the small group communication class because he feels somewhat uneasy in group settings, and since he would like to move up the managerial ladder he wanted to learn how to lead work groups. George has felt like an outsider ever since he arrived on campus. He hasn't joined any social organizations and he feels his dorm floor is full of freshmen who are into first-year college social activities that do not appeal to him.

George has been assigned to a classroom work group whose task is to examine and report on a major small group communication dimension. The group will be required to give a class presentation for which they will receive a common grade. Each member must turn in an individually kept diary of the group.

George's group consists of the following members:

Pat Riley, junior, English literature major, 25, female, white, Catholic, divorced, no children, lives in off-campus apartment, raised in large industrial city.

Dale Dickson, freshman, physical education major, 18, male, white, Protestant, single, lives in dorm, from small, rural southern town.

Marlene Goldstein, junior, mass communication major, 20, female, white, Jewish, engaged, lives in sorority house, raised in a large eastern city.

Aaron Reed, sophomore, premed major, 19, male, black, Protestant, single, lives in off-campus apartment, from a medium-sized midwestern city.

Lusharon McDaniels, senior, criminal justice, 21, female, black, Protestant, single, lives off campus, from large, urban western city.

George Cramer, junior, accounting, 20, male, white, Protestant, single, lives in dorm, from small town in the northwestern United States.

CASE LOG

Entry, First Meeting

Today was our first meeting. Our group looks very interesting. It doesn't look like we have much in common, but that's what is interesting. The women dominated the meeting, particularly Marlene. She thinks that since she is a mass communication major that she knows all about our topic, which is "group norming." However, Lusharon feels her background in criminal justice makes her an expert. We didn't get much done and I didn't have much to say.

Entry, Second Meeting

The women were at it again. Talk! Talk! Talk! I don't think "us guys" got three words in edgewise. I hate to stereotype, but Marlene sure is pushy! She keeps trying to organize us, and nobody's appointed her leader. I think Dale objects to Marlene's bossiness, but he doesn't say much either. I don't understand Aaron at all. He seems bright, but he doesn't assert himself and attempt to shut Lusharon up. She's as bad as Marlene! We still have not "normed out" our opinions on what to do on the topic.

Entry, Third Meeting

Hooray for Aaron Reed! Today he tried to take charge of the meeting and give the group some direction. Lusharon sided with Marlene and attacked Aaron's knowledge of group communication since he spent most of his time with his nose in a book or a test tube studying chemistry. I really felt sorry for Aaron and wanted to say something to him, but I didn't. What really surprised me was that Dale seemed to take the women's side while Aaron was being picked on.

It looks like Marlene has firmly established herself as leader of the group and Lusharon is "the wicked witch from the west" who supports her. I can't understand why Lusharon would not support a fellow black as group leader. Oh well, we have our assignments for the next meeting. I'm assigned to compile a bibliography of articles from sociology on group norming. That's all right with me; I'll do what I'm told.

Entry, Fourth Meeting

Aaron was absent. I told the group that they had been too rough on him, especially Lusharon. It turned out that it was get George Cramer day! Pat Riley seems like the nicest woman of the three; she at least defended me when Lusharon accused me of being a "typical, mousy accounting major who doesn't speak up!" I told the group that they had gone too far on personal attacks on both Aaron and myself. Our group didn't need to engage in quasi-psychological analysis of our members to get this job done. I submitted my bibliography and left early. I'm not sure this is a very good classroom exercise.

Entry, Fifth Meeting

The night before the meeting Pat Riley called me at the dorm. She said she called up to apologize about the last meeting, and that I was right that the group overstepped its bounds. She tried to assure me that the group would stick to the job at hand. With those assurances, I agreed to continue to meet with the group.

The meeting was the best work session we had. I felt that Lusharon was still hostile toward me, but Marlene made several attempts to include me in the discussion, and Aaron and I had a friendly chat at the end of the meeting. The group agreed to meet at Pat's apartment for our last meeting before our presentation.

Entry, Sixth Meeting

Tonight our group became a group. We all felt we were a part of a common effort. The meeting was very friendly, and Pat was a great hostess! Marlene is still a little pushy, but she did a great deal of work on the topic, and if it wasn't for her we would still be trying to figure out our topic.

After our presentation was all planned out and ready to go, we ended up talking about our feelings toward each other in the group. Dale really surprised me. All along he had been very threatened being a member of a group; he said he did not have much ability to make a contribution given the topic of the group. Dale's statement caused Aaron to confess that his premed studies had prevented him from working for the group as hard as he should have, but he was pleased that Marlene had done so much work and thanked her for it.

I was also surprised that the group had got together without me knowing it and presented me with the "Research Award" for all the library work I had done. I was flattered.

I am certain that our presentation will go well tomorrow. I only feel bad that our group will break up just when we were starting to work well together.

CASE QUESTIONS

1.   How would you describe George's interpersonal relationships with other group members in terms of affection, inclusion, and control? Did his relationships change over the course of the meetings?

2.   What key disclosures occurred in the group that helped in the group's interpersonal development?

3.   What kind of stereotyping did George seem to do? In what ways were George's stereotypes wrong?

4.   Did the group in stereotypic fashion force Pat into playing a nurturing and motherly role?

Most people's initial reaction to the word conflict is apprehension, in that there is a certain inherent risk in conflict communication.

CHAPTER OBJECTIVES

In order to be a more effective discussant, when you read this chapter you should focus on managing conflict communication in groups.

YOU NEED TO KNOW:

1. How to avoid "groupthink."
2. The moral of the canary fable.
3. The negotiation bargaining styles.
4. Major ways to manage conflict in groups.

UNDERSTANDING AND MANAGING CONFLICT COMMUNICATION IN GROUPS

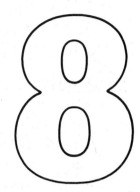

CHAPTER OUTLINE

CONFLICT COMMUNICATION: "RISKY SHIFT" AND "GROUPTHINK" PHENOMENA

"RISKY SHIFT"

"GROUPTHINK"

COMMUNICATION CONFLICT INHERENT IN THE ORGANIZATIONAL CONTEXT

COOPERATION AND COMPETITION IN AND AMONG WORK GROUPS

REWARD STRATEGIES

RESOURCE DISTRIBUTION PROCEDURES: THE CANARY FABLE

BARGAINING AND NEGOTIATION: A FORMAL PROCEDURE FOR RESOLVING CONFLICT IN ORGANIZATIONS

INDIVIDUAL TENDENCIES IN GROUP CONFLICT

NEGOTIATION/BARGAINING STYLES

THINKING PATTERNS

PROFESSIONAL-CONSCIOUSNESS STATES

CONFLICT-PRODUCING PERSONALITY TYPES

INTEGRATED MODEL OF GROUP CONFLICT

SUMMARY

REFERENCES

CASE STUDY: STATION HOUSE NUMBER SIX

As we indicated in Chapter 1, conflict communication is pervasive in group discussions. Also, it is such an important concept that we are devoting this chapter to understanding and managing conflict communication. Most people's initial reaction to the word conflict is apprehension, in that there is a certain inherent risk in becoming involved in conflict communication. Right after being fearful of conflict, there is a tendency to avoid it; we search for a way to manage it. We have already indicated in previous chapters that a great deal of conflict in groups is inevitable. In fact, conflict is necessary for groups to be successful. However, there can be too much conflict, thus deterring a group from its goals. Perhaps the best way to understand conflict communication is in terms of its focus (Putnam and Jones 1982). Conflict in groups can be found in three locations: the organizational context that the group is working within; individual variables such as personality, thinking patterns, and past group experiences; and the group problem-solving process.

Before considering specific loci of conflict in groups, it is important that you understand two macroissues of conflict communication, which have been popularly identified as the "risky shift" and "groupthink" phenomena. The "risky shift" phenomenon deals with the issue of whether individuals make riskier decisions in groups than when acting alone, thus enhancing intragroup conflict, while the "groupthink" phenomenon is a dangerous condition in which no conflict communication is occurring.

CONFLICT COMMUNICATION: "RISKY SHIFT" AND "GROUPTHINK" PHENOMENA

The book, *The Organization Man* by William H. Whyte (1957), was one of the more popular characterizations of life in organizations in the 1950s. Whyte's description of group decision making was consistent with the academic view of the time—that groups generally made more cautious and conservative decisions than managers acting alone. In this context, Stoner's (1961) research caused group scholars to reexamine group versus individual decision making. Stoner found that groups made riskier decisions than individuals. Wallach, et al., quickly replicated Stoner's research design getting the same result. These findings took on heightened importance in light of the nuclear confrontation that was occurring between the United States and the Soviet Union. While Wallach and others were finding a "risky shift" effect in their tightly controlled laboratory studies of groups, Irving Janis (1972, iii) was asking the question: "How could bright, shrewd men like John F. Kennedy and his advisors be taken in by the CIA's stupid, patchwork plan (Bay of Pigs)?" Janis (1972, 206) answered his question by proposing what he called the "groupthink" hypothesis: "The greater the threats to the self-esteem of the members of a cohesive decision-making body, the greater will be their inclination to resort to concurrence-seeking at the expense of critical thinking." Janis (1972, 9) called this tendency of some highly cohesive groups to avoid ideational conflict "groupthink," with the intention of aligning it with George Orwell's novel, *1984,* in which Big Brother develops "newspeak," "double think," and "crime think." Thus, "groupthink" alludes to the complete conformity of the group at the expense of engaging in conflict communication for the purpose of improving the quality of the group's decision. It's easy to see in the context of nuclear war why small group scholars would want to carefully examine the phenomena of "risky shift" and "groupthink." However, these two macroissues also have importance to you and us as we participate in ordinary problem-solving groups within our respective organizations.

"RISKY SHIFT"

Stoner's (1961) research produced unparalleled excitement, as measured by the number of studies that were conducted, probing the question: Do groups make riskier decisions than individuals? Cartwright (1973, 223) counted 196 studies completed from 1961 to 1971 alone. Early in the decade numerous scholars replicated Stoner's initial findings, while carefully using the original twelve-item Choice Dilemma Questionnaire (CDQ). Researchers varied age, sex, occupation, and nationality and still got robust findings that supported Stoner's original hypothesis that groups make riskier decisions than individuals (Shaw 1981, 70). As social scientists became convinced that there was a "risk-shift effect," they began to concentrate on developing theoretical explanations that account for groups making riskier decisions than individuals.

The initial explanation that was most widely accepted and had a common-sense base to it was the "diffusion of responsibility" hypothesis. The argument explained the results by simply saying that an individual is more willing to support a risky decision when he or she is a part of a group, rather than acting alone, because the responsibility is diffused among the group members. This explanation seemed credible until further research on the "risky shift" phenomenon started to produce results that showed groups making more cautious decisions than individuals. Researchers found that when they used different items to discuss other than the original twelve, they often got more cautious results from the group. Furthermore, a close examination of the twelve items in the original CDQ revealed that some of the twelve items produced more cautious reactions by the group than by the individuals. (Cartwright 1971; McGrath 1984.) These new findings shook our confidence in the original findings that groups make riskier decisions than individuals. Clearly the findings required more elaborate explanations. Three theories were forthcoming: social comparison theory, persuasive argument theory, and cultural value theory.

The cultural value theory suggested that risk is more valued in some cultures than others. For example, Hong (1978) found that Chinese made more cautious group decisions than Americans, and Americans seemed to make riskier decisions both acting alone and in groups. Thus, it was concluded that Americans place higher value on risk taking and make riskier decisions.

The persuasive argument explanation was clear-cut when all the studies showed groups making riskier decisions than individuals. This explanation merely asserted that the most risk-prone individuals in the group tend to be dominant communicators who influence other group members to their positions. Hamilton (1972) conducted research in an attempt to see if risk-prone discussants were more interested, verbose, and assertive, but he did not find any difference between low risk takers and high risk takers. Furthermore, when research began to show that some groups tended to make more cautious decisions than individuals, both Shaw and McGrath concluded that the exchange of information and arguments in a discussion tended to polarize or accentuate previously held positions. Thus, the group discussion itself had a significant and long-lasting impact on the participants' opinions, but that one could not predict a direction of the group's decision in terms of risk taking or cautiousness. Some studies suggested findings where discussion of a topic reinforced initial positions of cautiousness or risk taking.

The final explanation is the social comparison theory. This theory argues that we use decisions to compare ourselves to each other, and that we will adapt our position in the discussion to our previous self-image of how we compare to the norm. Thus, if we regard ourselves as above-average risk takers, and everyone in the discussion is conforming to our level of risk taking, we will "up the ante" and suggest even more risky decisions, thus producing the accentuation effect (McGrath 1984). Also involved in this explanation is a sense of conformity; i.e., if the majority of the group is in favor of greater risk taking, there is a tendency of deviants to conform. Conversely, if the majority position is cautious, there will be pressure to conform in this direction (Olmsted and Hare 1978). Twenty five years ago we seriously asked the question: Do groups make riskier decisions than individuals? For a decade or so we thought they did. As Cartwright (1973, 226) pointed out, "The accumulation of data demonstrates that groups are not invariably riskier than individuals." However, these hundreds of studies are not without practical value to the average group discussant, as these studies highlight key ideas about risk and conflict in groups.

Organizational culture probably influences risk-taking behavior in groups. Most of the studies done on "risky shift" have been lab studies in which college students have been put together for the first time for a short period to arrive at group decisions; thus, it is difficult to generalize about the ability of these studies to characterize work groups in organizations. However, some of the field studies on the "risky shift" phenomenon, and our own consultation experience in working with organizations, lead us to believe that organizations in general, and specific work groups within them, develop normal behavior with respect to the "riskiness" of their decisions.

The high-tech organizations that have grown so rapidly in the 1970s and 1980s have developed reputations as high risk takers. Peters and Waterman (1982), in their book, *In Search of Excellence,* celebrate this risk-taking behavior at Hewlett-Packard and other organizations. And, of course, there have been numerous articles about Apple Computer in regard to their risk-taking behavior in the development of their computers, especially the MacIntosh model. This is in contrast to the stereotyped cautious decision making of public utilities. Our point here is not to categorize corporations on a continuum of being risky or cautious, but rather to emphasize that it is important for you to assess your work group and your organization's risk-taking tendencies, and compare them to your own propensity to take risks.

The research on "risky shift" seem to say that if you join a work group that has a tradition of high risk taking, and you perceive yourself to be a cautious decision maker, you can anticipate a certain amount of conflict communication that can be attributed to this difference. Conversely, if you are a high risk taker serving on a committee of other high risk takers, group communication may intensify your own and others' risk taking tendencies, resulting in a riskier decision than you would have made yourself.

It appears that risk taking is more topic-bound than group-bound. While some groups may make riskier decisions than other groups, and others may make more cautious decisions, it appears that the topics groups discuss have more bearing on the riskiness of the decision, than does the fact of whether group members are high or low risk takers. For example, one of the twelve situations in the CDQ that tends to produce a risky decision is the problem that relates to an electrical engineer's decision on whether to switch jobs or not. In this problem the group is asked to estimate, on a scale of one to ten, the chances of a new company's surviving; and then the group must decide whether the engineer should leave a secure job and take a job with the new company that would provide a better salary and more career opportunities (Kogan and Wallach 1964; Hong 1978; McGrath 1984). Furthermore, when new situations were contrived, other than the original twelve—like gambling problems—groups consistently made more cautious decisions than they would have made acting alone. Indeed, our own experience of serving on various university committees lends credence to the topic-bound nature of "risky shift." For instance, committees are traditionally more cautious about personnel decisions than about the purchasing of additional equipment: awarding tenure to a faculty member who will be around for twenty-five years is a different kind of decision than purchasing a typewriter that might be replaced in a relatively short period of time. Here, again, you should examine your group's tendency to treat some topics in a "riskier" fashion than others. Even though you may stereotype yourself as a high risk taker, you may discover on some topics that you are very cautious. This is also true of groups. In some situations, groups may be high risk takers; in others, they are quite cautious.

Group discussions affect decision making. Although it has long been held in the field of communication that face-to-face discussion affects the opinions of its participants, the research on the "risky shift" phenomenon, which was primarily conducted by social psychologists, provides new indirect support on the potency of small group discussion. In almost all the studies done in the lab and field situations, there was a shift of opinion in the minds of the participants as a result of having a discussion. While it is difficult to predict whether a group or individual will make a more risky decision on the basis of having a discussion, in almost all cases the discussions intensify the individual member's tendency to be more risky or more cautious. One explanation for this shift of opinion is that the information and arguments presented in the discussion reduce a person's ignorance on a topic and thus allow the group members to move further in one direction or another. Thus, the sharing of information reduces uncertainty. Group members are now willing to take riskier decisions because they have more information, or a group makes a more cautious decision because the group arguments have convinced members to be more cautious. It seems clear that group decision making may produce different decisions than individuals acting alone. And, as we have indicated previously, on some topics groups definitely make better decisions than individuals (Collins and Guetzkow 1964). Unfortunately, we do not know after extensive research of the "risky shift" phenomenon, if groups make riskier decisions than individuals (Cartwright 1973).

"GROUPTHINK"

Irving Janis examined seven different decision-making situations of U.S. policy-making groups at the highest level of government, covering the 1940s to the 1970s: Pearl Harbor, Marshall Plan, North Korea, Bay of Pigs, Cuban Missile Crisis, Vietnam, and Watergate. In five of the seven situations, he found the phenomenon of "groupthink" to be operating. In summing up his analysis of these case studies, Janis generalized his findings as follows:

> The more amiability and esprit de corps among the members of a policy-making in-group, the greater is the danger that independent critical thinking will be replaced by groupthink, which is likely to result in irrational and dehumanizing actions directed against out-groups. (1982, 13)

Furthermore, Janis discovered that the absence of ideational conflict significantly lowered the quality of the decisions reached. Courtright (1978) conducted a laboratory experiment to assess the effect of the "groupthink" phenomenon in a controlled setting. He concluded "that the absence of disagreement is the most important manifestation of the groupthink syndrome" (Courtright 1978, 245). While Courtright's study did not show a statistically significant relationship between "groupthink" and poor group decisions, his data was in the direction of suggesting that such a relationship exists (Courtright 1978, 244). These findings seem to square with our everyday experience with decision-making groups. In fact, this data is consistent with the overall data base in small group communication for what makes a good group discussion.

While Janis has articulated eight symptoms that point to the presence of groupthink, he reasons that they start appearing when groups are overly cohesive. For purposes of this textbook, we would call a group having this high-cohesion condition an overly consciousness-raised group. The first symptom is the illusion of invulnerability. As the old adage goes, "pride goes before a fall." Sometimes groups become so full of themselves that they believe they are not capable of mistakes and thus are capable of making hasty decisions. Janis's description of the Bay of Pigs fiasco and the decisions of Nixon's Committee to Re-elect the President (CREEP) vividly depicts the dangers that face highly consciousness-raised groups. There is, indeed, the danger that proud, successful groups will skirt the difficult parts of decision making that require conflict because they do not want to cause dissension. After all, the group is too good to be wrong. It is important to remember that just because a group raises its consciousness into believing it is a good decision-making group does not mean that it is, or will be, with every decision it makes—especially if it puts satisfaction ahead of productivity.

Two more symptoms of "groupthink" that Janis found are the group's continuous stereotyping of enemy leaders as evil and stupid, and the group's unquestioned belief in its own morality. These two symptoms will appear when a group engages in too much Stage Two CR talk. If the group places too much emphasis on the "vilification of the they," it will eventually dehumanize its adversaries—as we have previously indicated in Chapter 2. Once this is done, it is easy to morally justify an inhuman treatment of the group's enemies. Certainly, Adolf Hitler's decision-making groups demonstrated this in their treatment of Jews, and Janis's research of CREEP demonstrated anew this phenomenon when he pointed out descriptions of the people the committee named on the "enemies list." The CREEP group eventually justified to itself the break-in to the Democratic headquarters in the Watergate building, plus a number of other break-ins and other illegal activities, because they were directed against the "enemy." Specialized crime teams, like SWAT and narcotic units, can easily generate these two symptoms because of the nature of their work and, in many cases, the true nature of the criminals they seek to catch. Every year newspapers report instances where police tactical units, in their overzealous pursuit of the "they" (criminals), have violated the civil rights of Americans. As we said in Chapter 2, it is important not to emphasize or encourage extended CR sessions that vilify the "they." Your group will stand a better chance of avoiding "groupthink" if it focuses on its own positive work behaviors and, in the case of decision-making groups, its ability to engage in ideational conflict, than if it dwells on the weaknesses of other groups.

Janis depicts three symptoms that move a group toward unrealistic uniformity, which in turn helps produce the "groupthink" syndrome. They are: a shared group illusion that consensus has been reached on an idea when in fact it has not; the corollary symptom that each member is the only one who feels he or she has doubts (self-censorship); and the recurring behavior of the group's attacking any member who dissents as being disloyal. These three symptoms taken collectively tend to produce a group culture that is very intolerant of ideational conflict. What is missing from a group suffering from "groupthink" is the role of central negative that we talked about in Chapters 2 and 6. Not only that, but the group celebrates the absence of conflict as a sign of a healthy group. As we have indicated before, we think the sign of a healthy group is an atmosphere in which the members of the group can tolerate large amounts of ideational criticism.

When the "groupthink" syndrome is present, not only do decision-making teams stifle dissent within the group—which we sometimes label "The Smokey the Bear Syndrome," meaning that the group stamps out a deviant idea before it has a chance to spread—but the group also develops insulation to protect itself from any ideas outside of the group that threaten the group's consensus. Janis says there are two symptoms relating to outside ideas. One is the emergence of self-appointed "mindguards," who feel it is their duty to protect the group from adverse information. During the Nixon years in the White House this was commonly called the "Palace Guard." The other symptom is the group's habit of rationalizing its rejection of new information on the basis of its being either inaccurate or irrelevant to a reexamination of the group's policies. The Westmoreland libel trial against CBS, which took place in 1984, brought to the surface information about General Westmoreland's decision-making group that indicates that his team may have been suffering from the "groupthink" syndrome. Information officers outside Westmoreland's immediate group kept reporting that the size of the enemy force in Vietnam in 1967 was twice as large as General Westmoreland and his group of advisors would accept. The Tet offensive of 1968 indicated that the larger figures of enemy troop strength were more nearly correct. This has left many to wonder how Westmoreland could have discounted information from otherwise reliable agents. CBS claimed conspiracy existed in which Westmoreland's group deliberately lied to President Johnson in order to make the war appear more winnable. A simpler explanation may be that General Westmoreland's team was suffering from "groupthink."

An examination of the "groupthink" syndrome leads us to make four recommendations to you that will help your groups avoid the debilitating effects of "groupthink." They are: (1) encourage ideational conflict; (2) assist in the development of the central negative role; (3) guard against leader domination of ideas; and (4) keep CR within limits, so that outside ideas contrary to the group's ideas will be more easily accepted.

COMMUNICATION CONFLICT INHERENT IN THE ORGANIZATIONAL CONTEXT

Work groups do not exist in isolation from one another but are necessarily parts of a larger organization. The informal and formal structures of an organization largely determine the degree of conflict that occurs within a work group and among the groups that constitute the organization. The reward system the organization uses for individuals and groups, and the procedures to disperse scarce resources, are two major touchstones for assessing the degree to which individuals and groups will cooperate with each other. Scholars in a number of academic disciplines have been studying what have come to be called "mixed motive games" to help determine under what conditions individuals will compete and cooperate with each other.

COOPERATION AND COMPETITION IN AND AMONG WORK GROUPS

The Prisoner's Dilemma Game has been frequently used by scholars to assess the degree of cooperation or competition that occurs in a group. This game provides a vivid simulation of how conflict can be increased in a group if communication is restricted. Figure 8.1 shows the basic matrix of a Prisoner's Dilemma Game.

FIGURE 8.1
BASIC MATRIX OF A PRISONER'S DILEMMA GAME

The game is called a Prisoner's Dilemma because the matrix simulates the choices two criminals would have if they were caught committing a crime by police. The police immediately separate the criminals and tell each one that he or she has but two choices: turn state's evidence against the other criminal, or remain silent and let the other criminal turn state's evidence. If both remain silent, they both win big (+ $10/+ $10); if one turns state's evidence and the other remains silent, one criminal wins big and the other loses (+ $15/− $5). When a group forms partnerships and plays this game among its membership, trust is quickly destroyed if no communication is allowed, while if full face-to-face communication takes place after each round of a ten-round game, more cooperative behavior occurs (Steinfatt, Seibold, and Frye 1974).

As we can see from Figure 8.1, Y is a cooperative choice and X is a competitive choice. If Bill and Sally both select Y (cooperation), they each win $10; however, if Sally chooses Y and Bill "rips her off" with a competitive X move, then Bill wins $15 while Sally loses $5. If Bill and Sally play several rounds of this game, the simple choice of X and Y can build into a rather involved game to determine if they can trust each other.

It is also quite easy to build a mixed motive game for a group so that there is a high incentive to cooperate or a high incentive to compete. Consider the rather popular game, "Win as Much as You Can," displayed in Figure 8.2.

This game can be played easily by either four or eight people. When eight people play the game, there are four partnerships. The game commences with the direction that each partnership, after two minutes or less of discussion, decides on either X or Y. This choice is concealed from the other three dyads in the group. At the end of the first round the dyad choices are revealed. If there are four Xs, all four partnerships lose a dollar. If there are four Ys, all four partnerships win a dollar. And, as can be seen in Figure 8.2 if three partnerships choose Y and one partnership selects X, the Ys lose a dollar each, and X wins three dollars. As you can see, X symbolizes a competitive move and Y indicates a cooperative move. It's apparent that if everybody in the group chooses Y, they can all win money. However, the organization of this game is such that there is an incentive for one partnership to be competitive if they can persuade the other partnerships to be cooperative. Whether people cooperate or compete depends a lot on how the reward system is set up and how much trusting communication is established and maintained among group members. The outcomes of this game will also vary considerably if we have three groups of four partnerships each playing the game simultaneously—especially if only one partnership out of the twelve is rewarded for having won the most. In this configuration, there is now a new incentive for cooperation within a group, while increasing competition among groups. These mixed motive games are more than just fun to play. They also simulate reward systems of organizations which either increase or decrease conflict within and among work groups.

REWARD STRATEGIES

All organizations have a tendency to structure work in groups but then reward individuals; i.e., individuals get promoted, not groups; and salary increases tend to occur in individuals as compared to clusters of individuals being rewarded for group productivity. Organizations run the continuum—from

FIGURE 8.2
WIN AS MUCH AS YOU CAN

Directions: For ten successive rounds you and your partner will choose either an "X" or "Y." The "Payoff" for each round is dependent upon the pattern of choices made in your group:

4 Xs:	Lose $1.00 each
3 Xs: 1 Y:	Win $1.00 each Lose $3.00
2 Xs: 2 Ys:	Win $2.00 each Lose $2.00 each
1 X: 3 Ys:	Win $3.00 Lose $1.00 each
4 Ys:	Win $1.00 each

Strategy: You are to confer with your partner on each round and make a *joint decision*. Before rounds 5, 8, and 10 you confer with the other dyads in your group.

ROUND	STRATEGY		CHOICE	$ WON	$ LOST	BALANCE	
	TIME ALLOWED	CONFER WITH					
1	2 min.	partner					
2	1 min.	partner					
3	1 min.	partner					
4	1 min.	partner					
5	3 min. + 1 min.	group and partner					Bonus round payoff is multiplied by 3.
6	1 min.	partner					
7	1 min.	partner					
8	3 min. + 1 min.	group and partner					Bonus round payoff is multiplied by 5.
9	1 min.	partner					
10	3 min.	group and partner					Bonus round payoff is multiplied by 10.

Adapted from group and partner. Pfeiffer, J. William, and Jones, John E., *A Handbook of Structured Experiences for Human Relations Training*, Vol. II (La Jolla, Calif.: University Associates, 1974), p. 67.

those that only reward the individual for performance to those that provide group rewards through profit centers and profit sharing. That is to say that if the product you are working on is a success, there may be bonuses and stock options tied directly to the group effort. Thus, there are a lot of incentives for X or Y in all organizations.

If you are part of a sales team, there might be tremendous incentive to compete with other sales people if most of the major rewards (like bonuses and vacation trips) are tied directly to your performing better than other sales people in your group. In fact, you may be reluctant to share your sales "secrets" with other sales people, even if requested by management. Groups may also become very competitive with one another if the reward system of the organization encourages it. For example, if a company has five product centers, we might find that four of the five product centers are producing and profiting 30% for every dollar invested, while the fifth product center is prospering but only getting a 15% return on dollars invested. This situation creates an incentive for the four most profitable groups to request that the fifth group be eliminated so that its resources can be distributed to the four remaining groups in order that they may expand. In American universities this "game" is sometimes played using student majors and credit hours generated as the means for keeping score. Growth in computer science departments in the 1980s can justify adding faculty on the basis of increasing student majors, oftentimes at the expense of less prosperous departments. In this situation there are incentives for departments to compete rather than cooperate with others. Consider your own case in a small group discussion class. If your class is divided into five discussion groups and the professor tells you that there will be one group that will receive an "A" and one group that will receive an "F," there will be a lot more conflict among the groups than if the instructor allowed the potential for all groups to receive an "A." Likewise, within your discussion group, conflict communication will be, in part, dependent upon the reward system. If everybody receives the same grade, there is a high incentive for cooperation; however, if the professor stipulates that one student will receive an "A," one student will receive an "F," and the remainder of the students will receive "Cs," the group conflict would probably become intolerable if the group were to present a panel discussion on a given topic.

The singling out of an individual in a group, or of one group from a number of groups, may also become a source of conflict. For example, a basketball team has to work interdependently to accomplish its goal of winning; but if one individual is continually recognized in the sports page for individual achievements, dissension may develop on the basketball team—especially if it appears that the star player is putting individual goals ahead of team goals. Recognition of an individual on a team is always a potential disrupter of group cohesion. In American fire departments, there is a well understood professional norm that an individual firefighter should avoid publicity that characterizes him or her as a hero. Almost all firefighting and rescue work requires members of work teams to work closely with one another in situations in which loss of life is always a possibility. Therefore, it has become very important for firefighters to put team goals ahead of individual goals. As a consequence, team recognition in the newspaper is acceptable, but individual recognition is shunned.

RESOURCE DISTRIBUTION PROCEDURES: THE CANARY FABLE

The whole process by which work groups are allocated limited, and sometimes scarce, resources (the budget process) is a major source of conflict within and among work groups in organizations. Imagine a huge canary cage, with 1,000 canaries flying around in it, but perches for only 500 canaries. If the canaries are the needs of the organization (equipment, personnel, supplies), and the perches are the money the organization has to spend, we realize the fundamental point about organizations: the legitimate request of work groups for new personnel, equipment, and supplies always exceeds the resources allocated by the organization for these purposes. Thus, the "Canary Game" is played each year as the new budget for the organization is approved. You can readily see that if you have a canary cage with 1,000 canaries and 500 perches it is very tempting for a manager of a canary cage to keep banging the side of the cage in order that the canaries keep flying. If the birds settle down, they will realize there are not perches for everyone, and some will be forced to settle on the newspaper at the bottom of the cage—which is a source of much humiliation and conflict! The banging on the canary cage is generally manifested by changes in budgetary forms, delays in processing, and periodic changes in the procedures for distributing resources. This "Canary Game" is so fundamental to conflict within and among groups in organizations that we think we can best explain it in terms of a fable—"The Canary Fable."

Chapter One: First-Line Supervisors Request Subordinates to Bring Canaries. Every year appointed leaders of work groups in organizations request from their members a list of what resources they need to do their work. At this level of the organization these are cute little three-ounce canaries. At this point in the budget process, a first-line supervisor might retrieve three or four dozen canaries. However, if it is an inexperienced manager, the supervisor may make public promises to the group members about how he or she is going to get a cage (funds) for each and every one of those canaries. In a university, the first-line work unit would be academic departments, and the canaries in a communication department might typically be faculty and clerical positions, computers, and teaching aids. (See Figure 8.3.)

Chapter Two: Middle Manager Slaughters Canaries. We have a dean whose favorite canary weapon is a hatchet. When chairpersons bring their boxes of canaries to her office, there is much screaming and yelling, with feathers and blood flying everywhere. Normally, our dean is a very calm, collected, and sensitive person, but not during the canary season! She is particularly violent with any canaries that have promissory notes tied around them—the ones that read: "Please save this canary. I promised one of my workers that it would survive. Signed, The Chairperson." After this middle-management slaughter, the first-line supervisors leave with only six or seven surviving canaries—and some of those are badly beaten (beaks missing, legs broken). Middle managers always end these slaughter sessions with the same request: "Go back to your department and rejustify why your remaining canaries should survive, and have them back to me by next week." Of course when the first-line supervisor returns to his or her work group, there is much conflict among group members

FIGURE 8.3
FIRST-LINE SUPERVISOR SAYS, "BRING ME YOUR CANARIES!"

when they realize that some members' canaries were killed outright and only a few wounded ones remain. The first-line supervisor generally resolves this conflict by raising the group's consciousness through the use of Stage Two upward and lateral "theys." In the case of the university, the department chairperson explains with great dramatization how the cold-hearted dean slaughtered the poor canaries, all of whom deserved to live! The department chairperson then explains to the work group that if they all don't pitch in and repair the remaining canaries, some other competing group (i.e., the psychology department) will get all the cages and none of our canaries will survive. (See Figure 8.4.)

Chapter Three: Central Administration Massacre.   After the first round of canary killing, first-line supervisors bring in their mended canaries to middle-line managers. These canaries are, of course, no longer three-ounce canaries. They are more into the twenty-five or thirty-pound class. They are even beginning to be a little assertive in their chirping! It is now the middle manager's turn to walk into the central administrator's office with a smile on

FIGURE 8.4
MIDDLE AND UPPER MANAGERS SLAUGHTER CANARIES

his or her face and a box of chirping twenty-five to thirty-pound canaries. It is now the central administrator's job to massacre canaries. We had a vice-president whom we used to call "Leon the Assassin." He never messed around with knives and hatchets; he was strictly a "gun man"! His favorite weapon was a double-barreled shotgun. He would tell the deans as they arrived to throw their canaries up in the air. Then he would tell the deans to dive to the floor. He would then fire at the canaries from behind his file cabinet. The dead birds would fall on the prostrate deans—it was a horrible sight! The deans would gather the remaining wounded canaries and scurry back to an emergency meeting of their first-line supervisors. This annual meeting always has the same agenda—"Help Save Our Canaries." In the College of Arts and Sciences, for example, you would find that the dean rallies the supervisors using the same CR process that the first-line supervisors used only a month before with their departments (Stage Two "we-they"). The dean describes the vice-president (provost) as some sort of a lunatic who feels he is on a mission from God to slaughter all of the college's canaries. And, of course, the heads of the departments in the Arts and Sciences College are asked to unite and help mend the wounded canaries, or else the College of Business will get all of the cages.

Chapter Four: President Chooses the Survivors. Each vice-president in an organization is responsible for bringing his or her surviving canaries to the president's office to determine their fate. By this time in the budgetary process, the surviving canaries are clearly in the hundred-pound class. These are budgetary needs that are so important that a bad decision could have a major impact on the health of the organization. If you've ever noticed, the top floor of any administration building of any organization is very quiet. Secretaries talk in low whispers. Nobody screams and yells at the canary-killing sessions here as they did at the first and second levels. It is important

FIGURE 8.5
THERE ARE SIX TWO-HUNDRED-POUND CANARIES
ON THE TWELFTH FLOOR BUT CAGES FOR ONLY FOUR OF THEM

that the rest of the organization not know what hundred-pound canaries are getting killed; besides, hundred-pound canaries can be dangerous and are thus prepared for a silent kill. The president at our university is generally known as "Uncle Lloyd" during most of the year, but during the canary season he is known as the "Gherka" (named after the famous silent killers of the Tibetan mountains). Leon, now "Leon the Meek and Mild," quietly herds the hundred-pound canaries into the president's office. The "Gherka" looks each canary in the eye, and if it blinks he cuts its jugular vein. Leon meekly smiles and dutifully catches each canary as it falls, so that the rest of the organization will not be disturbed. Leon returns to the council of deans with the surviving canaries and unites the five academic deans by explaining that the president is a cold-blooded canary killer. If they don't repair the surviving canaries, the computer center, student housing, and the campus police will get all of the cages. With the final canaries repaired and returned to the president's office, the scene is set for the final act of the fable. (See Figure 8.5.)

Final Chapter: There's a Two-Hundred-Pound Canary in the Quad, and I Think It's Ours!   CEOs in organizations experience the same fate at the end of the canary season. If you walk into their offices during this time you will find the president sitting at a desk with his or her eyebrows curled, with shoulders rounded as if the weight of the world were upon them. If you will then look at the top of the curtains, you will see why the president is so glum. There sit six two-hundred-pound canaries, and the president knows there are cages for only four. No matter how you figure it, needs exceed resources; and these are not trivial needs sitting in the president's office. After all, these six canaries survived three slaughters. One false move and one of these big birds could ruin a president's career. This is why the quietest office on campus is the office of the president.

The president of our university has been through over ten canary seasons. Let's say, for sake of argument, that he goes to the board of regents and, through administrative dexterity, he comes away with the fifth cage. (For a private corporation, the CEO would approach the board of directors.) When the media report that "Uncle Lloyd" has acquired a new cage (more funding), so that five out of six of our two-hundred-pound canaries are caged, do you think it is likely that the faculty and students of ISU will form a spontaneous rally on the quad with big banners saying "Yea, Yea, Uncle Lloyd; Thanks for the Extra Canary Cage!" Of course not. What do the faculty and students who got their canaries caged (i.e., received funding) say? They say, "It's about time! Anybody who knows anything about a university knows we've needed those resources for a long time." Some of the more cynical professors might remark that the canary cage is obsolete, or "it's too little, too late."

What about the groups in the university who had supported, and resupported, the importance of the remaining canary who does not have a cage? Well, once the budget is announced, the uncaged canary flies out of the window and rests on a tree in the quad. After all, the bird is too large to kill; in fact, it might sit there all year just chirping away. The group that didn't get its canary caged generally organizes impromptu CR sessions around the canary. They point up at this large bird in the tree and exclaim, "Don't you think a canary that big should be in a cage? Heck, it could destroy this whole campus!" Professors not familiar with the canary fable will say things like "Any idiot can see that that canary needs to be caged! If I were president, I would see that that canary was caged! We need a new president to cage that canary!" (Stage Four CR.) The more seasoned and cynical professors will say things like "This loose canary is clear evidence of campus politics! It's a known fact that the president likes 'business-type' canaries and hates multi-colored arts-and-sciences canaries!"

Thus, every year in every organization, there will be work groups CRing at the end of the canary season with the statement: "There is a two-hundred-pound canary loose, and it's ours." (See Figure 8.6.)

Moral of the Fable

1. First-line supervisors must kill canaries. Even though it is important for a supervisor to build group morale and be an active team player, it is important as part of the budgetary process that he or she reject some funding requests. However, some supervisors don't understand this, so they hatch many more canaries than they need and send them up to the middle managers in flocks, hoping that some will survive. This produces waste and inefficiency in organizations and will ultimately affect the productivity of every work group in the organization.

2. Canaries should be killed at the appropriate level of management. Some managers really hate to kill canaries and will try to pass on this responsibility to the managers above them. If this becomes a widespread practice in organizations, you can find the CEO being asked to kill a three-ounce canary. An even worse situation is when upper management actually seeks out the opportunity to kill three-ounce canaries instead of letting lower-level management take a whack at them. However, the worst of all situations is when a

FIGURE 8.6
THERE IS A TWO-HUNDRED-POUND CANARY
LOOSE IN THE ATRIUM AND I THINK IT'S MINE

first-line supervisor doesn't trust the middle manager's judgment about his or her department's canaries. In this situation the first-line supervisor goes over the head of the middle manager and makes a special plea to upper management for his or her canaries.

3. Employees should have empathy for canary killers. Since canary needs always exceed resources, employees should understand that it is a difficult job to choose what canary should live—especially when you get into the two-hundred pound class. When you find your two-hundred pound canary loose in your organization, remember it is probably not politics or ineptitude on the part of upper management—it is just organizational reality.

BARGAINING AND NEGOTIATION: A FORMAL PROCEDURE
FOR RESOLVING CONFLICT IN ORGANIZATIONS

Thus far in the book, we have been explaining small group communication as it occurs in a typical problem-solving discussion group or an everyday work group that has a common task that can be achieved only through intermember cooperation. There are, of course, other types of groups within organizations. One group that is unique is the bargaining, or negotiations, group. The typical decision-making group in an organization will certainly have conflict in reaching agreement on a decision, but we assume that most of that conflict is cognitive, ideational, role, or personal in nature. We assume that the group members share common goals and motives, and that they are all seeking to find the best solution. However, a bargaining or negotiation group has an added dose of conflict that makes the communication process different from that of ordinary decision-making groups in an organization.

Bargaining/negotiation groups tend to have members who are "representative" of other groups. Oftentimes, the group members come to the negotiation meeting with conflicting proposed outcomes, and the bargaining/negotiation group must somehow reach a compromise on an outcome (McGrath 1984).

We have studied the communication patterns of bargaining/negotiation and have found groups to be quite different from Fisher's explanation of the four-stage development of a task group. It appears that bargaining groups go through three communication stages in the process of reaching an agreement: (1) at the beginning of the bargaining session, the negotiators tend to engage in a lot of information gathering and some rather careful compiling of facts that relate to the case; (2) the second phase is characterized by a great deal of argumentative conflict in which the participants argue strongly for their pre-discussion preferred outcomes; and (3) if concessions are made and it appears that a compromise can be reached, the bargainers then begin to introduce interpersonal communication with more positive statements about each other (Putnam and Jones 1982; Douglas 1962). Sometimes groups simply become deadlocked in their negotiations. In 1960, Osgood (1962) developed a model for reducing the communication impasse; he called this GRIT (Gradual, Reciprocal, International Tension-reduction). Basically this model calls for one side in the dispute to make a small concession in hopes that the other side will reciprocate. Osgood argues that, building upon success, the combatants can incrementally move toward settlement through reciprocal concession. If this fails, bargaining negotiation groups generally turn to a third party and ask them to intervene either in arbitration or mediation. Frequently, federal mediators are asked to come solve labor-management disputes. In fact, the very threat of bringing in a third party can instill enough fear in the two sides to make them work towards an agreement.

Social psychologists have been studying the variables that tend to affect the outcome of bargaining or negotiation groups. They found that when the group members regard themselves as formal representatives of some outside group (e.g., a union) these group members will be more competitive, make fewer concessions, and be less likely to reach agreement than group members who do not regard themselves as representatives of a formal, outside group (McGrath 1984, 99). In addition, bargaining groups will have a harder time reaching a settlement if their members were elected by a constituency, if members of an outside group observed them negotiating, if the group member has made prior commitments to his or her group before the decision is reached, and if there has been a history of distrust among the negotiation members from past bargaining sessions (McGrath 1984).

As difficult as bargaining and negotiation appear to be, there are some communication behaviors that will increase the chances of a negotiation group reaching agreement. Semlak (1982) suggests seven communication strategies, of which we discuss four, that can help in conflict reduction in bargaining/ negotiation groups.

1. *Sincere communication.* "Good faith bargaining" has always been a touchstone for successful negotiators. Part of this involves being sincere in the proposals you are making and, if you do make concessions, being willing to back them up. Further, "good faith bargaining" is not just a tactic, but an effort grounded in trustworthiness. People you are negotiating with must believe you are really trying to "negotiate" a settlement. The United States is continually questioning whether the USSR is bargaining in "good faith" in arms talks, or whether they are merely utilizing the talks as a tactic as part of their overall nuclear strategy. Conversely, the Soviet Union makes the same charge against us.

2. *Nonpolarizing communication.* It is important for the bargainers in a negotiation to avoid dramatizing or, if you will, emphasizing, that one faction's gain is another faction's loss. For example, in labor-management negotiations, there may be a number of issues to be agreed upon. A worker's increase in salary could easily be perceived as labor's gain and management's loss. However, there might be a mutually acceptable solution on wages which increases workers' revenues without necessarily draining the management's treasury. The company may offer profit sharing, which would potentially increase workers' wages if productivity went up; therefore, both management and labor would win. Try to avoid, at the beginning of a negotiation, characterizing issues in win-loss terms. As a group you might find creative solutions that are win-win, or not as painful as win-loss.

3. *Signposting.* In the course of a negotiation it is important that the bargainers erect signposts that mark certain issues as non-negotiable. In the typical labor-management negotiation in which a strike has occurred, labor usually signposts the rehiring of strikers as a non-negotiable issue. You can frequently hear an example of signposting communication by listening to three students negotiating over the particulars of renting an off-campus apartment. One student might quickly indicate that she will not share her bedroom with another roommate, while another student insists she will not live in a basement apartment, and the third negotiator signposts being within walking distance of the campus. These three students may compromise on such things as price of the apartment, furnishings, and guests after midnight; but they have signposted early in the discussions that a private bedroom, no basement apartment, and walking distance to campus are not negotiable.

4. *Interpersonal communication.* Sometimes people stereotype negotiation as abrasive. While it is true that harsh words may occur during a negotiation, it is important that you do not personalize the discussion. You should attack ideas, not persons. Furthermore, many important negotiations are carried out in a very amiable environment in which wit and humor are important interpersonal communication skills. Even when issues of war and peace are negotiated by representatives of foreign states, the bargaining participants often describe each other in warm personal terms. In other words, one can be a tough negotiator without being verbally abrasive and hostile; indeed, it would appear that the best negotiators are, in fact, very likeable individuals who have developed their interpersonal communication skills as a means of facilitating successful negotiations.

INDIVIDUAL TENDENCIES IN GROUP CONFLICT

Individuals bring with them to work groups different approaches to problem solving. We think the four most important individual differences related to group conflict that need to be explained to you are differences in negotiation/ bargaining styles, thinking patterns, conflict-producing personality types, and professional-consciousness states. These tendencies have been regarded as an important part of self-awareness concerning how an individual behaves in a group conflict situation. In fact, training instruments have been developed which can precisely profile your tendencies in the above four areas of conflict in management settings. Most major American corporations run regular training courses in these areas. Our description of these various classification systems should allow you to gain a general understanding of how you have been behaving in group conflict situations.

NEGOTIATION/BARGAINING STYLES

Historically students were trained in problem-solving discussion to search cooperatively for the best answer. Yet, our observations of actual problem-solving groups indicates that all group members do not come to the discussion with the same degree of cooperativeness, nor are all group members as assertive about their opinions. Kilmann and Thomas (1975) developed a categorization of negotiation/bargaining styles based upon an individual's willingness to cooperate and his or her willingness to assert his or her position. They label these styles as follows: competing (forcing), collaborating (problem-solving), compromising (sharing), avoiding (withdrawal), and accommodating (smoothing).

1. *Competing.* If you use a competing style when you bargain or negotiate, you are very assertive about what you want from the group, and you are not willing to compromise your basic beliefs in order to reach a settlement. You view group discussion on a problem as basically a win-loss situation: either your viewpoint wins out or you lose. You will marshal evidence and argument to prove the correctness of your view, and you will use whatever legitimate or expert power you have in order to get the group to see things your way. Invariably you will be involved in a struggle of leadership in the group.

2. *Accommodating.* On the other hand, if you find yourself frequently using an accommodating style, you tend not to assert your own personal view; in fact, you may avoid taking positions in the discussion that would create controversy. You are willing to set aside your own views on how the problem should best be solved in order to reduce ideational and interpersonal tensions. You will quickly cooperate with people who have a legitimate power and expert knowledge. Using this style, it will be easy for you to play the social-emotional leader in the group.

3.   *Avoiding.* If you adopt this negotiation style in a group, you are adopting what firefighters call a "stay low and go" philosophy! Fire officers advise rookies that when they face more fire than they can handle, the only safe place where there is oxygen is on the floor; so they recommend that the firefighters stay low and get out of there! The avoiding style is unassertive and uncooperative. When you use this style, you gingerly duck or postpone any confrontation. People with little organizational power, or without firm beliefs in how the problem should be solved, often adopt this approach to conflict situations. This style blends most closely with the silent observer role.

4.   *Collaborating.* Collaborating is the opposite of avoiding. If you use this style, you are approaching a group discussion with the philosophy that everybody can win. You will be prepared to immerse yourself in the complexities of the issues, or the interpersonal conflicts as the case may be, with an eye toward a solution. You will not hesitate to bring all the issues to the surface and get them out on the table, because you have a basic belief in the group's ability to reach an agreement that maximizes the benefits for everyone.

5.   *Compromising.* When using a compromising style, you may be seeking a quick solution to the conflict. Your strategy is to explore what concessions need to be made by all parties in order to reach agreement. You believe not everyone can get everything they want, especially if consensus is to be reached. If you are using this style you may find yourself in a leadership struggle, especially if someone else is using a competing style, as you are trying to continually resolve conflict. Collaboration is marked by a creative solution; compromise is marked by an expedient solution. (Kilmann and Thomas 1975.)

THINKING PATTERNS

In formal negotiation groups, it is expected that members of the negotiation group think out in advance the positions they want to take, and then during the group meeting argue their respective cases as best as they can. However, in an ordinary decision-making group, it is not immediately apparent how people will prepare for the meeting. Some will view the meeting as an opportunity to advocate a solution that they have thought through in advance. Other group members will see the meeting as a process of inquiry in which the best solution will emerge; thus they will prepare for the meeting by becoming informed on the topic but will not form an opinion of what constitutes the best decision prior to the meeting. These two contrasting approaches to problem-solving discussions can produce a great deal of conflict and change the very nature of the communication process (Wright 1975). If two or more people take an advocacy approach, the meeting will resemble a debate or a formal negotiation session. But if everybody views the meeting as a reflective thinking process in which group inquiry will produce the best solution, the communication process of the group will resemble the integrated model we outlined in Chapter 2.

In addition to the potential ideational clash due to whether people view problem-solving from an inquiry or adversary perspective, there also exists the potential for conflict because of predispositions that people may have toward five different thought patterns:

- *Pragmatist.* A person who is predisposed to look for pragmatic solutions on a given task will stress solutions that are expedient and have high utilitarian values. This person will often want to cut through or bypass the complexity of reasoning, or of bureaucratic red tape, and push the solution that works.
- *Philosopher.* A group member who takes a philosophical look at problem solving will probe the issues in a search for the fundamental values that should govern or form the criteria for the given solution. This type of person is sensitive to any ethical ramifications of a group decision. The philosopher is the keeper of the group's conscience.
- *Conceptualizer.* A group participant who specializes in abstract formulation of the problem, and who constantly looks for ways to group similar-looking data and contrast it with extraneous data, is a conceptualizer. This person specializes in antithesis and synthesis types of argument.
- *Planner.* Team members who push for well-defined objectives and are constantly structuring all the facts of the problem are the engineers or planners of the group. They want a good, clear working model or blueprint of the problem, and they constantly tidy up the discussion by ordering the various arguments and information into the group's schemata. The planner is often the keeper of the group's agenda.
- *Energizer.* People who approach problem-solving meetings with a great deal of enthusiasm often view the solution to a problem as attainable if the group energetically pursues it. When the group becomes frustrated with the apparent insolubility of the problem, this person will call for more team effort. That is why the energizer is sometimes called the group's cheerleader.

PROFESSIONAL-CONSCIOUSNESS STATES

In Chapter 2 we explained that CR talk is a naturally occurring part of all group discussions, and that all groups do a certain amount of Stage Two "we-they" communication. CR talk produces group pride and identity, which can potentially conflict with upward, downward, and lateral "theys." However, not all members are at the same level of group consciousness. In fact, creating a group consciousness for new members, and raising and sustaining consciousness of old members, is a continual source of conflict. In American organizations, experienced professionals generally refer to five classic states of professional consciousness: burnout, young Turk, "old buffalo," company loyalist, and cynic.

- *Burnout.* A burnout has no professional consciousness—it has literally been "burned out" of him or her. In movies and novels this person is sometimes portrayed as an employee who had fought the good fight at one time, but is no longer capable of rallying any professional pride to do the job. He or she is just putting in his or her time until retirement. Certain professional work groups tend to produce a higher percentage of burnouts than others. Police, paramedics, high-school teachers, and computer programmers are occupations where burnout is a frequent occurrence. Also, if a person comes into a job highly consciousness-raised, it is difficult to maintain such professional intensity for a whole career. Thus, anybody in an occupation or any group is potentially susceptible to becoming a burnout. If you have burnouts in your group, you don't expect them to do much work. If they have paid their dues in the past, you tend to protect them.

- *Young Turk.* A young Turk is known not by his or her chronological age but by his or her consciousness. We personally know young Turk professors in their sixties and seventies. A young Turk is a highly consciousness-raised group member. If there is no fire in the eyes of a burnout, a young Turk's eyes are blazing. A young Turk is constantly seeking ways to improve the group and to raise its status in the organization. Young Turks are quick to act out Stage Four consciousness against the group's "theys," particularly if it means conflict wih the "theys." Also, young Turks have a tendency to be impatient and ostrasize group members who are not performing at high levels of productivity or at as high a level of exuberance as they do. Thus, young Turks tend to want to ostrasize burnouts, and they constantly challenge "old buffaloes" to be more assertive. Young Turks are valuable group members who can raise the level of group productivity and pride in the group; but if they are not tempered they can push the group into burnout or too much conflict with other groups in the organization.

- *"Old Buffalo."* "Old buffaloes" provide stability to the consciousness of the group. An "old buffalo" possesses a level of group pride that is sufficient to do acceptable work in the group for long periods of time. An "old buffalo" will put in a reliable eight hours of work and then leave his or her professional identity at the work place as contrasted with a young Turk, who will want to engage in professional talk after work each night, as well as intensely at every weekend party. An "old buffalo" will tell a young Turk that he or she is too intense and might become a burnout; on the other hand, a young Turk thinks an "old buffalo" is plodding along at too slow a pace. "Old buffaloes" tend to collect the sacred stories of the group and generally have a good long-range perspective of the group's role in the organization. "Old buffaloes," in addition to providing stability, are excellent at orientating new members to the group and minimizing conflict the work group might have with competing groups in the organization.

- *Company Loyalist.* You never hear of a company loyalist actively participating in Stage Two of a CR session. The company loyalists never ventilate about upward "theys" (supervisors), competing "theys" (competing work groups), or downward "theys" (people being served). They embrace an almost static state of group euphoria. Everything about their professional identity is OK every day they work. A company loyalist is the "milk and cookies" person of the organization: he or she has a Pollyanna view of company life. A person who is a company loyalist represents a kind of ideal state of professional contentment in a group. However, this level of consciousness oftentimes does not seem credible to other group members. People in other consciousness states often try to provoke the company loyalist into saying, in a fit of righteous indignation, something derogatory about the organization or a competing work group. The company loyalist is an important counterweight to the cynic.

- *Cynic.* A person who has a cynical state of consciousness in the group has a contemptuous distrust of the company: the group's CR and rally talk are seen as merely one more way to falsely motivate workers. A cynic does not want to be part of a symbolic "we" and would prefer to be independent of all group and organizational influence. As a consequence, a cynic will not only graphically attack the "theys" of a group; he or she will also attack the positive symbolic "we" of the group as hubris. The cynic can play a valuable role in the forming of a group's professional consciousness, in that he or she tends to keep the group humble. However, a cynic left unchecked can demoralize a group's pride and shake the confidence of new members.

CONFLICT-PRODUCING PERSONALITY TYPES

In Chapter 7 we pointed out that research on personality and group performance has isolated four personality variables as being salient to group performance: extroversion, self-assertiveness, social maturity, and intelligence (McGrath and Altman 1966; Levy 1970). While we don't know what the right combination of positive personality variables should be for the ideal group, we are painfully aware of some of the irritating personality types that are the source of much interpersonal conflict in groups. The five are the aggressor, the doormat, the egghead, the airhead, and the whiner. These five are unacceptable deviations from the four basic personality traits: the egghead and airhead are not normal in terms of intelligence; the whiner is socially immature; the doormat has no self-confidence; and the aggressor is off the scale in terms of self-assertiveness.

- *Aggressor.* An aggressor is an abrasive and overly dominant person in the group. People with this personality type put themselves up and put others' ideas down. They tend to overreact to criticism and tend to attack you personally for attacking their ideas. They are outspoken and bold to the point of recklessness. When the decision is made, they feel like they beat you out, and you generally feel humiliated and angry. Being assertive and being dominant can be good qualities in a group member, but in this case too much of a good thing is detrimental to the group.
- *Doormat.* These persons are too submissive for their and the group's own good. In Harris's *I'm OK, You're OK,* the doormat definitely thinks he or she is not OK. These members constantly irritate the group because they are always kicking themselves before the group has a chance to do it. The minute you challenge their ideas, they immediately give in and proceed to describe how inadequate they are. You have no respect for this person since they do not seem to respect themselves. The doormat is literally the doormat of the organization; everyone walks over him or her. Doormats always complain that life is falling in around them and that they are not in control of decisions. (Harris 1967) Consequently, the other group members feel frustrated that the doormat will not take responsibility for group decisions. Furthermore, the group does not like the doormat to act as if he or she can't affect group outcomes.
- *Egghead.* Although intelligence is a very important group personality variable, a person who portrays him- or herself as, or flaunts the fact that he or she is, much more knowledgeable than other group members, can become a royal pain in the group's psyche. Eggheads tend to parade their intelligence before the group and demand that deference be paid. Generally, the egghead will select a vocabulary that is beyond many group members. This negative personality type is an intellectual snob who quickly becomes insufferable in

group decision making. Sometimes group members wait cautiously for hours for an opportunity to pounce on any error the egghead might make in his or her thinking process. If defeating the intellectual becomes the center of group activity, the best possible solution can often be lost. On the other hand, domination of a group by an egghead can often eliminate the potential synergetic nature of group decision making.

● *Airhead.* The airhead goes under a variety of group names: dunce, dummy, Neanderthal, and group idiot. The airhead projects a group personality that would accurately be portrayed in a low double-digit I.Q. score. This person backs away from all ideational conflict with the claim, "I just don't understand what's happening." When group members chide the airhead with comments like "How could you have graduated from college?" the airhead seems to be mystified by the fact also. Group members always suspect the airhead of faking it—nobody can be that dumb. Airheads avoid doing a lot of the hard work for the group because they don't appear to be intellectually fit. As a consequence, other group members become angry and sometimes complain that they don't have any excuses for not working, compared to the airhead. The airhead has been personified in many movies as being the "dumb blond"; however, it has been our experience in studying groups that airheads are randomly distributed across sexes and hair-color types.

● *Whiner.* Crybabies, or whiners, exhibit extreme social immaturity. You ask them to come to a meeting and they whine. You ask them to do work in the group, they whine. You criticize them, they cry. Whiners avoid doing their fair share of the work simply because it's so irritating to hear them whine when they are assigned any. Ironically, whiners seem to complain that they are given too much work to do when, in fact, they are doing less than the average. Whiners tend to complain about minor things in group procedure, even down to the size of the meeting room, the comfortableness of the chairs, and the room temperature. Group members may have legitimate complaints, or they may have some individual idiosyncrasy that would require group adaptation. For example, a group member might be a diabetic and need to take frequent snack breaks during long work sessions, or a member might be allergic to smoke or animal hair. Most groups adapt to these individual needs; however, for the whiner, it is not possible for the group to make adequate compensation. No matter what the group does, the whiner still whines.

INTEGRATED MODEL OF GROUP CONFLICT

A general theory of group conflict does not exist. The integrated model of group conflict displayed in Figure 8.7 does indicate that conflict is pervasive in group life, and the model categories five primary sources of conflict that blend together to form the specific nature of any small group. The five primary sources of group conflict are ideational, role, CR, interpersonal and stylistic.

The possible permutations of these five sources that might be present in a given group are in the tens of thousands. For example, we might have a task leader who emphasizes a pragmatic thinking style, has a young Turk consciousness, and tends to be an aggressor, using a competing style for resolving conflict. On the other hand, we could have a person who frequently plays a

FIGURE 8.7
INTEGRATED MODEL OF GROUP CONFLICT

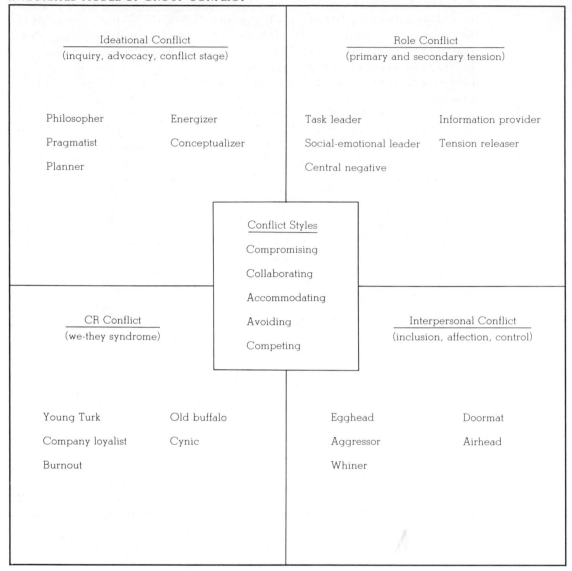

central negative, prefers a philosopher thinking pattern, is a cynic, and in weak moments might resemble a whiner who also uses a competing style. This combination would certainly provide other group members with an interesting spectacle at group meetings! In contrast, it is also possible, but not likely, that a long-range planning committee for an organization could be populated with burnouts and airheads who tend toward conceptualizing thought patterns and the avoiding style of conflict resolution. In this situation, it is highly unlikely that a task leader would emerge or that much work would be accomplished.

Without a theory of group conflict, it is not possible for us to predict what mixes of conflict will produce what results. Two things can be gained from the above description. First, you can use this typology as a reference for your own self-analysis that will allow you to better monitor your communication in a group. We think if you do that, the very process of self-analysis will allow you to become a more productive group member. Second, we believe that even in the absence of a conflict theory, there are some general pieces of advice about how to manage group conflict that we and our colleagues have gleaned from professional observation of small group interaction of work groups. The following suggestions should help you manage conflict in problem-solving groups.

Try to insure that the group has examined the problem from all five thought-pattern perspectives. It is apparent that if the group only looks at a problem pragmatically, they may become too expedient and overlook important long-range needs. Conversely, if the group unduly focuses on a philosopher pattern, they may come up with a great idea that may not work in practice. Thus, a specialization in any of the five is inherently wrong. The group must give some thought from all perspectives.

Move your group away from a mode of advocacy to a spirit of inquiry. The less a decision-making group resembles a formal negotiation group, the less the potential for harmful conflict. Also, it is possible to produce more ideational conflict in a context of reflective thinking. If your group persists in a mode of advocacy, you need to increase the amount of factual information (Marr 1974) and increase the amount of time the group is in face-to-face interaction (Putnam and Jones 1982). These two efforts will help to reduce unnecessary conflict, especially when a group has taken on a formal negotiation form.

Encourage the development of the central negative role in order to increase ideational conflict. High levels of ideational conflict are essential for good group decisions. It is important that group members feel comfortable when playing the role of central negative. Janis (1983, 267) believes that it is so important in the avoidance of "groupthink" that he would have groups formally assign a person to the role. We don't advocate formally assigning someone to a role, but we do recommend that all group members be alert that the central negative role is being played.

Work toward a compromising or collaborating negotiation style. Most decision-making groups in organizations do not long tolerate a competing style of leadership unless it happens to be a powerful appointed leader. On the other hand, groups tend to lose respect for members who constantly exhibit an accommodating or avoiding style. Thus, in most groups you should try to be assertive and cooperative.

Avoid extreme CR states in a group. The normative consciousness-raising state of a work group ideally should be a blend of Turk, "buffalo," loyalist, and cynic consciousness. If the group is all Turk, its decisions may be too radical. If it's all "buffalo," the decision may be too incremental. If the group is all loyalist, the group may only restate the status quo. And, if the group becomes too cynical, or burned out, the group won't arrive at a decision.

Manage your individual behavior so that you avoid being stereotyped. We all have our bad days in group life when we tend to act like an aggressor, egghead, airhead, doormat, or whiner. Yet, if you find your group is reacting negatively to you, it may be that you have established a pattern or habit of group communication that is causing group members to place you in one of the five negative personality stereotypes.

SUMMARY

This chapter has examined the pervasive concept of conflict as it is manifested in small groups. Two macrophenomena, "risky shift" and "groupthink," provide anchors on a general continuum of conflict. There are instances where groups are more willing to take risks than individuals. On the other hand, groups can become so agreeable and individuals can all start thinking so much alike that "groupthink" is the product, at the expense of the ideas-in-conflict process.

Our presentation of the "risky-shift" phenomenon led us to the following generalizations: (1) it appears that risk taking is more topic-bound than group-bound; (2) group decisions affect decision-making; and (3) organizational culture probably influences risk-taking behavior in groups. We made four recommendations to assist your small groups in avoiding the debilitating effects of "groupthink": (1) encourage ideational conflict; (2) assist in the development of the central negative role; (3) guard against leader domination of ideas; and (4) keep CR within limits, so that outside ideas contrary to the group's ideas will be more easily accepted.

Our discussion of communication conflict inherent in the organizational context focused on cooperation and competition in and among work groups. Reward strategies and resource distribution procedures, illustrated through the Canary Fable, were stressed. Bargaining and negotiation were discussed as a formal procedure for resolving conflict in organizations, placing emphasis on strategies of (1) sincere communication, (2) nonpolarizing communication, (3) signposting, and (4) interpersonal communication.

We examined various individual tendencies in group conflict, including negotiation/bargaining styles (competing, accommodating, avoiding, collaborative, and compromising), thinking-pattern predispositions (pragmatist, philosopher, conceptualizer, planner, and energizer), professional-consciousness states (burnout, young Turk, "old buffalo," company loyalist, and cynic), and conflict-producing personality types (aggressor, doormat, egghead, airhead, and whiner). These individual tendencies were all included, as well as the five major group roles, in our integrated model of group conflict. Suggestions for managing conflict derived from this model are: (1) try to insure that the group has examined the problem from all five thought-pattern perspectives; (2) move your group away from a mode of advocacy to a spirit of inquiry; (3) encourage the development of the central negative role in order to increase ideational conflict; (4) work toward a compromising or collaborating negotiation style; (5) avoid extreme CR states in the group; and (6) manage your individual behavior so that you avoid being stereotyped.

REFERENCES

Cartwright, D. "Risk Taking by Individuals and Groups: An Assessment of Research Employing Choice Dilemmas." *Journal of Personality and Social Psychology* 20 (1971): 361–78.

_____ . "Determinants of Scientific Progress: The Case of Research on the Risky Shift." *American Psychologist* (March 1973): 222–31.

Collins, B., and Guetzkow, H. *A Social Psychology of Group Processes for Decision-Making*. New York: John Wiley & Sons, 1964.

Courtright, J. A. "A Laboratory Investigation of Groupthink." *Communication Monographs* 45 (1978): 229-46.

Douglas, A. *Industrial Peacemaking*. New York: Columbia University Press, 1962.

Goldberg, A. A., and Larson, C. E. *Group Communication: Discussion Processes and Applications*. Englewood Cliffs, N.J.: Prentice-Hall, 1975.

Hamilton, P. R. "The Effect of Risk-Proneness on Small Group Interaction, Communication Apprehension, and Self-Disclosure." Unpublished master's thesis, Illinois State University, 1972.

Harris, T. *I'm O.K., You're O.K.* New York: Harper and Row, 1967.

Hong, L. K. "Risky Shift and Cautious Shift: Some Direct Evidence on the Culture-Value Theory." *Social Psychology* 41 (1978): 342-46.

Janis, I. L. *Groupthink: Psychological Studies of Policy Decisions and Fiascos*. 1972. 2nd edition. Boston: Houghton Mifflin, 1983.

Kilmann, R., and Thomas, K. "Interpersonal Conflict-Handling Behavior as Reflections of Jungian Personality Dimensions." *Psychological Reports* 37 (1975): 971-80.

Kogan, N., and Wallach, M. *Risk-Taking: Study in Cognition and Personality*. New York: Holt, Rinehart, and Winston, 1964.

Levy, L. H. *Conceptions of Personality: Theories and Research*. New York: Random House, 1970.

Marr, T. J. "Conciliation and Verbal Responses as Functions of Orientation and Threat in Group Interaction." *Speech Monographs* 41 (1974): 6-18.

Marston, W. M. *Emotions of Normal People*. New York: Harcourt, Brace and Company, 1928.

Mayer, M. E. "Explaining Choice Shift: An Effects Coded Model." *Communication Monographs* 52 (1985): 92-101.

McGrath, J. E. *Groups: Interaction and Performance*. Englewood Cliffs, N.J.: Prentice-Hall, 1984.

McGrath, J. E., and Altman, J. *Small Group Research: A Synthesis and Critique of the Field*. New York: Holt, Rinehart and Winston, 1966.

Olmsted, M. S., and Hare, A. P. *The Small Group*. Second Edition. New York: Random House, 1978.

Osgood, C. E. *An Alternative to War or Surrender*. Urbana, Ill.: University of Illinois Press, 1962.

Peters, T. J., and Waterman, R. H., Jr. *In Search of Excellence*. New York: Warner Books, 1982.

Pfeiffer, J. W., and Jones, J. E. *A Handbook of Structured Experiences for Human Relations Training.* Vol. II. La Jolla, California: University Associates, 1974.

Putnam, L. L., and Jones, T. S. "The Role of Communication in Bargaining." *Human Communication Research* 8 (1982): 262–80.

Semlak, W. D. *Conflict Resolving Communication: A Skill Development Approach.* Prospect Heights, Ill.: Waveland, 1982.

Semlak, W. D., and Jackson, T. R. *Conflict Resolving Communication.* Dubuque, Iowa: Kendall/Hunt, 1975.

Shaw, M. E. *Group Dynamics: The Psychology of Small Group Behavior.* 3rd edition. New York: McGraw-Hill, 1981.

Steinfatt, T. M.; Seibold, D. R.; and Frye, J. K. "Communication in Game Simulated Conflicts: Two Experiments." *Speech Monographs* 41 (1974): 24–25.

Stoner, J. A. F. "A Comparison of Individual and Group Decisions Involving Risk." Unpublished master's thesis, Massachusetts Institute of Technology, 1961. (Cited in Cartwright 1973.)

Whyte, W. H., Jr. *The Organization Man.* Garden City, N.Y.: Doubleday Anchor, 1957.

Wright, D. W. *Small Group Communication: An Introduction.* Dubuque, Iowa: Kendall/Hunt, 1975.

CASE
STUDY

CASE BACKGROUND

Captain William Foley has just returned from a meeting called by the battalion commander. At this meeting station captains were instructed to discuss major personnel and management problems. The captains identified three major problem areas:

1. A conflict between suppression firefighters and those assigned to rescue squads and ambulances. A special point of contention here was the division of labor regarding housekeeping chores.
2. Fire department standards have been changed to accommodate mandatory minority quotas. This has led to what captains think is unusually harsh treatment of probationary firefighters.
3. Excessive transfer of personnel across firehouses and from one shift to another. Many firefighters believe that this has led to a reduction in the effectiveness of the firefighting team on the fireground, at times even endangering lives unnecessarily.

Each captain was instructed to discuss these three problem areas with a select group at his or her respective station. The personnel at Station Number Six who were asked to participate in the discussion were the following:

Captain William Foley, 56, World War II veteran, high school graduate, 30 years service in the city fire department, captain of the firehouse.

Lieutenant Martin Vuttera, 35, Vietnam veteran, high-school graduate, EMT (emergency medical training) trained, 13 years service in city fire department.

Firefighter Dennis Arnold, 31, college graduate, EMT trained, 6 years service in the city fire department.

Driver Engineer Jim McCarthy, 46, Korean veteran, high-school graduate, 22 years service in the city fire department, part-time electrician.

Firefighter Ed O'Bradovitch, 55, World War II veteran, high-school graduate, 31 years service in the city fire department.

Firefighter Michael Murphy, 25, high-school graduate, attending junior college on a part-time basis, 4 years service in the city fire department, son of a retired firefighter.

Probationary Firefighter Zachery Washington, 21, 2 years active duty in the U.S. Army, high-school graduate, 6 months service in the city fire department.

CASE LOG

CAPTAIN FOLEY: The BC has instructed all the captains in his district to get feedback and suggestions from each house on these issues. The first issue is this constant fighting between the rescue squad and the rest of the house. I for one am tired of all the petty bickering that goes on. As far as I am concerned, a firefighter is a firefighter is a firefighter, regardless of their job function.

MCCARTHY: That's the point, Captain, we're all equal except that the rescue squad keeps asking for special privileges. For decades it has been the tradition of firefighters to share housekeeping chores equally. Now, suddenly, the rescue squad wants to change these traditions.

ARNOLD: What's wrong with change? Twenty years ago there weren't rescue squads. The record supports our case. We make three times as many runs as you do. We don't have time to be doing dishes. If you're going to be putting an IV into someone's arms, you don't want your hands full of grease three minutes before you do it.

MURPHY: Look, Arnold, the reason you and Vuttera don't have time to do dishes is because you always hang around the hospitals after you make a run trying to make time with the nurses! Sometimes I think you regard yourselves as being on the hospital staff!

LT. VUTTERA: No, wait a minute, Murph! Before you even come onto this department I did seven years on the back step of the engine company. So don't you tell me I am not a firefighter! What Arnold and I, and for that matter what the guys running rescue on other shifts believe, is that the amount of work we do in rescue demands a change in the traditional housekeeping rules.

CAPTAIN FOLEY: Vuttera, I want you and Arnold to present me a plan as to what kind of changes you would recommend. We'll discuss your plan the next time we're on shift. Right now, I want to get to this second issue. Evidently the BC has been receiving complaints from probationary firefighters about harassment.

O'BRADOVITCH: Hey, Washington? You been crybabying to the brass?!

WASHINGTON: I haven't but I probably should've! You make enough racial slurs in a day to have driven Martin Luther King to violence.

MCCARTHY: We call Murphy "Shanty," and Vuttera "Dago." So, if you can't take the heat, get out of the firehouse.

O'BRADOVITCH: You should have been around here when probationary firefighters really got initiated. You wouldn't have lasted a week!

CAPTAIN FOLEY: Outside of language, do you have any specific complaints, Washington? (Long silence)

WASHINGTON: No, sir.

CAPTAIN FOLEY: OK, let's get to the last item. The BC is hearing complaints about excessive transfer of personnel. Do you guys have any complaints?

O'BRADOVITCH: Bill, you and I have served a lot of years together. I'm telling you, it's just not the same as it used to be. In the old days we used to work with the same guys month in and month out, year after year. Everybody knew what everyone else was going to do on the fireground. Remember when I fell through two floors to the basement in that old warehouse on 43rd Street? I knew you would get me out of that fire! These young kids today! They move from one house to another so fast, I don't even know their names. How can you trust them?!

MCCARTHY: Foley, what are those ''clowns'' downtown trying to do? You go tell the battalion commander we want a moratorium on transferring for a year.

MURPHY: I agree with Jim. No more transfers. They can stick those transfers in their bugles!

LT. VUTTERA: Captain, I think the deputy chiefs are not in touch. They don't know what is going on! They don't know what's going on with rescue, and they don't know what's going on when they transfer people.

ARNOLD: They're so dumb that everytime we get some of the problems resolved in a house, they up and transfer half of us. What do you say let's start a petition for ''no more transfers,'' and everybody sign it! How about you, Captain? Why don't you draw it up?

CAPTAIN FOLEY: No petitions! We're not starting any of that stuff in this house! I got my time in, and I'll retire before I get involved with any of that ''radical'' stuff!

O'BRADOVITCH: I don't know, Bill. Whose side are you on? Maybe, you're buckin' for chief instead of retirement?

CAPTAIN FOLEY: I'm not afraid to criticize the chief when he deserves it, but there have to be some departmental transfers. A moratorium just won't work.

MCCARTHY: The point is, Captain, nothing ever works. There isn't a solution to this problem.

ARNOLD: I think there are changes that could make the transferring problem better. Despite our differences on rescue versus suppression, I think we are really a good work group. Captain, why don't you suggest to the chief that groups who can prove their excellence should be excluded from the policy?

CAPTAIN FOLEY: That's not a bad idea. Marty, are you keeping notes on what we're deciding?

LT. VUTTERA: Yeah, I've been keeping notes on everything that's been said.

CAPTAIN FOLEY: Good, then why don't Murphy and Washington draw up criteria for excluding our group transfers and have it ready for the next meeting.

CASE QUESTIONS

1. Critique Captain Foley's management of this meeting. What did he do well? What could he have done better?
2. What CR states are discernible in this meeting?
3. What was Captain Foley's conflict-resolution style?
4. What ideational thought patterns were present in this meeting?

THREE

APPLICATIONS
TO SETTINGS
AND SITUATIONS

Quality Circles are work groups comprised of company volunteers whose purpose is to achieve productivity and quality through participative decision-making.

CHAPTER OBJECTIVES

In order to be a more effective discussant, when you read this chapter you should focus on group discussion procedures as they apply to business and industry.

YOU NEED TO KNOW:

1. The basic principles used to determine when to call a meeting.
2. The unique features of each type of routine business meeting.
3. The differences among types of business work groups.
4. The basic characteristics of professional conferences.

TYPES OF BUSINESS
WORK GROUPS
AND MEETINGS

CHAPTER OUTLINE

WHEN AND HOW TO CALL A MEETING
1. Mastering time
   a. Advance notice of meeting agenda.
   b. Scheduling meetings at the best time.
   c. Starting and ending meetings on time.
   d. Regulating participation.
   e. Getting the job done.
   f. Meeting follow-up.
2. Understanding tradition
3. Being productive
4. Maintaining group satisfaction
5. Gaining group consensus

ROUTINE BUSINESS MEETINGS
1. Monday morning meetings
2. Monthly meetings

3. Decision-making meetings
4. Planning meetings

EVERYDAY WORK GROUPS
1. Long-standing work groups
2. Project work groups
3. Pre-fab work groups
4. Quality circles

PROFESSIONAL CONFERENCES
1. The one-day conference
2. The three-day conference
3. The convention

SUMMARY

REFERENCES

The first eight chapters of the book present most of what we regard as important in terms of theoretical principles and techniques of small group discussion. This chapter, as well as the next, takes group discussion out of the classroom and the research laboratory and places it in the natural settings of business and governmental organizations. We expect that upon graduation you will find yourself, within a very short period of time, in a supervisory position within a white collar environment. This chapter looks at small group discussion in terms of three distinct communication events within an organization. They are: the routine meeting, the ongoing work group, and the professional conference.

WHEN AND HOW TO CALL A MEETING

One of the first decisions you will make as a new supervisor is whether you should call a meeting. The temptation to call one is almost irresistible. A pet peeve of professionals working within an organization is that they are always going to too many meetings. A similar gripe is that even the necessary meetings they go to are often ill planned. Therefore it is important to consider certain criteria to determine whether a meeting should be called. We recommend enumerating in your own mind the following benchmarks before deciding to call a meeting.

1. *Mastering time.* If the almighty dollar governs an organization, then the almighty clock governs the work within it. Time becomes money, and thus, from the organization's perspective, wasting time is a major fault. Moreover, you will find that everyone guards his or her own time jealously. When you call a meeting of a dozen people, you are taking up the time of twelve people who may feel that you are wasting their time. So from both a personal and an organizational viewpoint, time is the overriding issue. In calling a meeting, you should be governed by the following six time constraints.

　　a.　Advance notice of meeting agenda. Important meeting time can always be saved by sending out agenda and any other helpful materials in advance of the meeting. This material should be as brief and succinct as possible and should be proportionate to the importance of the meeting. By that we mean participants should not be asked to read four hours of material in order to hold a fifty-minute meeting on a minor issue. In preparing for your meeting, always think of how much time participants will have to spend in preparing for it, and govern your material accordingly.

　　b.　Scheduling meetings at the best time. Routine business meetings are fixed, often on a yearly basis, so that people can schedule around them. If you are setting up a fixed meeting time for a weekly meeting, try not to schedule it an hour before or after lunch on a Friday. If you think about how you schedule your classes at college, you know how meetings are scheduled in business settings. However, if you are putting together an ad hoc meeting, you will want to schedule it when you can get everyone together, and this may cause some inconvenience. The best way to find the right time to hold an ad hoc meeting is to send out a work calendar for the week and have the members check the work periods they have free.

c.   Starting and ending meetings on time. Participants of a meeting sometimes feel they can arrive a few minutes late, but they expect to come out on time. As an appointed leader of a group discussion, you can delegate everything but control of the clock. People will forgive your interruptions if it appears that you are trying to get them out on time. Also, if you delay the starting of your meetings ten minutes to accommodate the stragglers, you will soon discover that everyone is a straggler and your meetings always start late!

d.   Regulating participation. As you recall, in Chapter 5 we discussed sixteen leadership communication behaviors of which the regulation of participation was one. In our work with government and business organizations, one of the recurring complaints we hear about meetings is that a few people tend to dominate the meeting and that consequently there is not enough time for others to speak. You also recall that in Chapter 3 we recommended the nominal group discussion technique as one means of eliminating this complaint. The leader should do everything in his or her power to see that sufficient time is allotted to all participants in a fair manner.

e.   Getting the job done. One of the common mistakes made in meetings is to have more on the agenda than there is time to cover. Leaving a meeting with an agenda half-done, when you had expected that the work would be accomplished, is a frustrating experience. Your group goals should be cast in time frames. Don't prepare an agenda that you know you can't finish. As soon as you discover that you can't get through the agenda, set a new goal—such as to accomplish three out of five items.

f.   Meeting follow-up. While there are many reasons for a follow-up memo, one of them is to confirm that the members did not waste their time. When group members have worked hard and productively for several hours, they like to know that their efforts were appreciated and that the outcomes were beneficial. Make certain that you cover these two points in a follow-up memo.

2.   *Understanding tradition.* When you are new to an organization, one of the more important things you need to understand is the tradition of meetings that has evolved and developed in the organization's history. You want to take note of what kind of day-to-day meetings are held, who calls the meetings, what problems get solved through the use of a group, what agendas are used, and what is the protocol for who gets invited to what meetings. A good starting point from which to gather this information is the memo correspondence that was left behind by your predecessor and the secretary's calendar of meetings attended during the past year. You may discover that you intentionally violate some of the norms established for group meetings, but you should at least be consciously aware that you are doing so and that you have good reason for making the change.

If you go to work as a marketing researcher in some large organization, you might discover that you are expected to call a meeting to present the results of your research regarding a new product. The tradition of the company might call for you to begin the meeting with a twenty-minute slide show that concisely and graphically displays your findings. Therefore, if, unaware of the tradition, you sent out a thirty-page report in advance of the meeting and then attempted to lead a round table discussion about the product, with the vice-president of marketing as one of the participants, you might discover that nobody had read the report and that the vice-president was mad at you for not only "not doing your homework" but for trying to usurp power. An examination of the tradition of the marketing division's meeting habits could have told you what is not written down in the company handbook, namely, that a new product's group meeting in this company is an initiation ritual for new researchers. The tradition is that you show off your hard work via the twenty-minute slide show and then stand for interrogation by more experienced researchers, with the vice-president standing by.

Every organization has its own tradition of group meetings. We cannot enumerate all their variations in this textbook; however, you can discover them if you will spend time carefully researching the habits of the groups in your organization.

3. *Being productive.* After reviewing the research in the social sciences on group versus individual productivity, Shaw (1976, 78) concluded: "Groups usually produce more and better solutions to problems than do individuals working alone." Shaw's conclusion is tempered by certain necessary conditions. For example, groups do better than individuals if the problem calls for the creation of ideas or the recalling of information, if the load can be divided among members, and if the group members have an opportunity to identify and correct each other's ideas. Shaw's conclusion (1976, 79) also depends on most members having essentially the same knowledge base.

As you can see, there are a lot of strings attached to the conclusion that groups are better at solving problems than individuals. That is why it is often difficult for a supervisor to decide whether a given task should be assigned to a group or an individual. For example, if the problem were how to develop architectural drawings for the new plant, it might be better to assign that task to the company's architectural engineer. An executive committee could provide input at the beginning and end of the project, but it would not be helpful to have persons unskilled at architectural drawing doing the detail work. However, if a supervisor were in charge of an advertising agency which needed to develop a new ad for a soft drink company, she might conclude, probably correctly, that a five-person work group of ad account supervisors would be better than one individual. She might even employ the ideational techniques we discussed in Chapter 3.

Unfortunately, most of the real-world decisions that a group faces in assigning work either to a group or an individual are not as clear-cut as the two extreme examples cited above. What usually happens is that a subgroup is formed with broad responsibilities to decide what the division of labor will be; that is, which tasks should be performed by the group and which by an individual. As a work group develops some history, members start to work out for themselves this fundamental problem. The basic rules of thumb for resolving this problem are the following: (1) If the group has a member who is much better than the rest, who is committed to the goals of the group, and who can solve some subaspect of the problem, he or she should be assigned the task. (2) Although groups are slower than individuals at completing tasks, there are some problems that the group must solve together. At a general level, the group members have to agree upon their goals and their ability to do the work; moreover, they must make sure that the group's work is sufficient and good enough for public scrutiny.

Generally, groups will produce more and better ideas than individuals and will reduce the chance of random error. Yet groups take more time to do their work. A supervisor must constantly weigh the tradeoffs of time versus quality, and may sometimes decide to settle for less quality in order to get a job done on time. Even when the best way to solve a problem qualitatively is by group effort, a supervisor may still decide that an individual should solve the problem given the quantity of time the group would have to spend on it.

4. *Maintaining group satisfaction.* Conscientious supervisors are always concerned with the morale of their subordinates. Meetings frequently serve as the focal point for boosting group morale and motivating workers to higher productivity levels. As we indicated in Chapter 2, corporations, particularly their sales divisions, hold consciousness-raising sessions for their workers. Sometimes outside speakers are brought into the meeting to give inspirational speeches designed to raise the consciousness of the group. First and last meetings for project groups are often CR sessions which induce in individual members the feeling that they are satisfied to be members of the company.

Quarterly meetings in which the profits for the quarter are presented also produce membership satisfaction. It would be sufficient for the supervisor to send out the quarterly productivity figures via memo, but what usually happens is that the work unit is brought together in a meeting, the data is flashed onto a wall, and the group shares in the general satisfaction with a job well done.

The membership satisfaction meeting is often overdone. In fact, we frequently see in movies and TV programs satires on the motivational meeting, in which the supervisor makes one more phony, incompetent plea for more productivity while the overworked group members sit disgruntled in the audience voicing snide remarks. Insincere or overdone motivational meetings are counterproductive; yet, when a properly designed membership-satisfaction meeting is planned, results for the organization and the individual can be beneficial.

In Chapter 6, we presented ways to help in the development of your group. Implicit in these suggestions is the notion that it is generally more rewarding for an individual to be praised for good work in the presence of fellow group workers than in private. Holding a group meeting in which rewards are presented may seem corny, and group members will always say they don't need the attention, but if the meeting is well planned and the rewards are meaningful and well chosen, the increase in membership satisfaction can be most dramatic. Also remember the importance of group rewards, especially if you can present them in the presence of other groups. The general point to remember here is that meetings are often held in which the major purpose is not productivity but increased member satisfaction.

5. *Gaining group consensus.* In the business world, people occasionally complain that a meeting was unnecessary because everybody had already agreed to the solution that was proposed at the meeting. However, consensus meetings are very important. A group's final face-to-face discussion of a plan of action is important in terms of gleaning commitment from members on the group effort. The group may take an hour kicking the same old reservations around the room and in the end reach the predicted conclusion; however, the ritual of thrashing out all the "ifs" and "buts" is necessary if the members are to feel truly committed to the decision.

Knowing that face-to-face consensus produces commitment has caused some unscrupulous supervisors to call consensus meetings prematurely thus restricting the time the group has to discuss alternate proposals. Forcing consensus on a group reduces membership satisfaction and ultimately productivity. Consensus is an important group output but it must flow naturally from the group. An experienced supervisor will delay the calling of a consensus meeting until it can be predicted that consensus is achievable; even then the supervisor will allow ample time for the group members to verbalize all the major issues before they commit themselves to the group decision.

ROUTINE BUSINESS MEETINGS

There are four basic types of business meetings: Monday morning meetings, monthly meetings, decision-making meetings, and planning meetings. Each of these four fundamental types of meetings in business organizations tends to be distinguished by its own unique leadership style, discussion format, and agenda system. In addition, each type can encounter unique, potential dangers during the course of routine meetings. These are discussed for each of the four types.

1. *Monday morning meetings.* A routine weekly meeting within a formal organization generally calls for a "tell" leadership style on the part of the supervisor. If it is a Monday morning meeting, the supervisory group may have met the Friday before to hear their boss conduct a "tell" meeting in which information was transmitted down the hierarchical structure. Therefore, on Monday the supervisor is acting as a communication conduit, transmitting directives from higher up in the organization. Most subordinates appreciate an efficient, task-oriented presentation of this information. You might ask, Why doesn't the supervisor just place this information in a memo or on a bulletin board? The answer is that most organizations have found that these are not reliable channels of information unless the content is reinforced by a face-to-face meeting between superiors and subordinates. Consequently, the Monday morning meeting was created.

City police and fire departments hold Monday morning types of meetings for each shift. The daily meeting is a microcosm of the weekly meeting in that the agenda is a random list of pertinent pieces of information that the work force must comprehend. Television programs frequently dramatize the tone and give-and-take of the typical Monday morning type of meeting, in which humorous one-liners often poke fun at the organization. The supervisor should not misunderstand the meaning of these jokes. The group still wants to receive organizational information firsthand, but it has become traditional in American organizations that the supervisor should bear the brunt of some humor.

The typical hodgepodge agenda of a Monday morning meeting (see Figure 9.1) might appear disjointed and incomprehensible to a person who is not a member of the work group!

FIGURE 9.1
TYPICAL AGENDA FOR A MONDAY MORNING MEETING

MONDAY MORNING AGENDA
(8:30–8:45 a.m.)

I.   Reminder of OSHA regulations that have been consistently ignored (also posted on bulletin board).

II.   Restatement of production goals and deadlines for unit (10 percent ahead of last year).

III.   Form C needs to be filled out by Wednesday in order to qualify for additional life insurance coverage.

IV.   Mary finally delivered her baby last Thursday (9 lbs., 10 oz.). Send cards to City Memorial Hospital, Room 540.

V.   Anyone wishing to bowl in the company bowling league needs to sign up by Friday (nonrefundable $5.00 entry fee required).

There are two pitfalls that a supervisor should avoid when conducting Monday morning meetings. The first danger is that the meeting may become a social event in which the work force spends the first hour drinking coffee, eating rolls, and talking about what they did over the weekend. The group members will naturally fall into this conversational pattern and will object, sometimes loudly, when the supervisor drags them away from the social hour to the first point on the agenda. However, the supervisor is responsible for seeing that the meeting starts and ends on time, and both the organization and the work group will eventually hold him or her responsible if the task of the Monday morning meeting is not accomplished. Thus, the supervisor must maintain a "tell" leadership style in running Monday morning types of meetings.

The second danger to the supervisor of Monday morning meetings lies in not strictly regulating participation during the meeting. Almost any point on the agenda can provide sufficient stimulus for an hour-long group discussion. OSHA regulations, production goals, and company social events can easily encourage the more verbal group members into heated discussion. If the supervisor allows these discussions to occur, the planned agenda will not get covered. Over time, the group members will become angry because they were not informed about issues that later proved to be important to them. So despite obstacles and temptations, the leader of a Monday morning meeting must tenaciously stick to the planned agenda and finish it within the brief time allotted.

2.   *Monthly meetings.* Many organizations bring their work groups together in a formal meeting once a month. Although a monthly meeting has some characteristics in common with a Monday morning meeting, it also has several distinguishing characteristics. Supervisors of monthly meetings tend to adopt a "sell" leadership style. The meeting contains some elements of a consciousness-raising session. Since the work group meets only twelve times a year, there is a need to spend some time celebrating the reasons for the group's existence and the fact that it is doing a good job.

With this goal in mind, monthly meeting agendas often contain guest speakers. If it is a monthly sales meeting, a vice-president might attend in order to thank the members for the job they have been doing; or an outside speaker may give an inspirational speech about the job they do. The agenda may also contain report presentations by several group members. The report presentation tradition is especially prevalent in civic and volunteer groups. Besides conveying information, the presentation of reports by different group members symbolizes the teamwork that the group is maintaining.

The leader of monthly meetings adopts a "sell" leadership style because he or she usually feels obliged to explain the group activities of the previous month and to sell the group on what must be done in the next. Unlike the Monday morning meeting, there will often be a period of general discussion on what the group feels it can reasonably accomplish over the next thirty days.

A typical agenda for a monthly meeting is presented in Figure 9.2.

When a group does not meet on a weekly basis, the danger of a monthly meeting is that it might be used as a vehicle for ventilating the members' complaints. In the course of thirty days, any active group can develop a shopping list of gripes that might lock the group into Stage Two of a CR session, the "they" (i.e., the "enemy") often being the formal leadership of the group and the larger organization to which the group belongs. The designated leader of the monthly meeting must deal with some of the complaints that come from the floor but cannot allow these issues to dominate the meeting. The best way to avoid this problem is for the leader to use one or both of the following methods: agree to meet afterwards with group members who have a complaint; or establish a policy that complaints must be brought to the leader a week in advance in order to become a formal part of the agenda. This will allow the group to formally discuss major problems without becoming immersed in minor and ephemeral gripes.

3. *Decision-making meetings.* Decision-making meetings require considerable leadership skills to run; they also involve distinct risks to the leader. The appointed leader of a group must deliberately decide if he or she is willing to give up some formal authority and live with the results of a group decision. Group decisions are often better than individually made decisions, and membership satisfaction is increased whenever everyone participates in the making of them. However, the decision the group reaches may be quite different from the one the leader would make on his or her own. Sometimes leaders try to straddle the fence by adopting a "sell" leadership style for a decision-making

FIGURE 9.2
TYPICAL AGENDA FOR A MONTHLY MEETING

PTA MONTHLY MEETING
(Thursday, 7:00–9:30 p.m.)

I.   Minutes of last meeting (Secretary)
II.   Reports by officers
       A. President
       B. Treasurer
       C. Historian
III.   Approval of Lincoln School Carnival budget (Marge Weston, Chairperson)
IV.   Principal's moment (Principal Edgar M. Norris)
V.   Presentation of School Board candidates (each allotted fifteen minutes of speaking time)
VI.   Question and answer period
VII.   Reception

meeting. Nothing infuriates a group more, however, than a leader who is trying to "engineer" a group's deliberations to some preordained conclusion.

In a decision-making meeting the leader needs to adopt a participatory leadership style and be willing to live with the results of the group process. For the group to work effectively, members must receive advance information in order to discuss the issue effectively, and they must be given sufficient time to reach their conclusion.

The previous history of the group's decision-making experience is an important consideration. If the group is holding its first decision-making meeting, the leader will probably first have to use the NGD and brainstorming techniques described in Chapter 3 as a means not only for generating ideas and solutions to a problem, but also for increasing the participants' willingness to discuss with each other. On the other hand, if the decision-making group has a history of making decisions, the members have probably adopted their own recognizable pattern for wading through the issues and reaching consensus. The leader would be well advised in these instances to stay with the established procedure. However, most decision-making meetings bring together a group of people who do not fall at either end of the continuum; that is, they are neither a zero-history group nor a well-seasoned, decision-making group. In this middle range a leader should develop a problem-solving agenda as a rough outline for conducting the meeting.

An adaptation of the Ross Four-Step Agenda (see Chapter 3) might be used by a decision-making group. (See Figure 9.3)

Groups hardly ever follow the planned agenda in a decision-making meeting. A leader should expect the group to digress into trivia and to jump around from causes to criteria to solutions. Experience will tell a group leader when a group's meandering is excessive and needs to be controlled. Decision-making groups need a guiding hand as they work their way toward a solution. Thus, the planned agenda is a benchmark to measure how far the group has

FIGURE 9.3
THE ROSS AGENDA FOR A DECISION-MAKING GROUP

THE ROSS AGENDA FOR A DECISION-MAKING GROUP

I. Definition of problem
   —15 percent drop in overall production
   —5 percent drop in quality
II. Analysis of problem
   —possible causes:
   1. recent adoption of flextime
   2. increased use of part-time help
   3. antiquated machinery
   4. union contract problems
III. Criteria
   —solution must be attainable within six months
   —solution must meet budget constraints
IV. Solutions: to provide a good solution is our primary task
   —some solutions
   1. ?
   2. ?
   3. ?

wandered from its major task and should be used as a reminder to the leader to get the group back on track.

If the chronology of the agenda system is rigidly enforced, the group will feel intimidated, and the quality of the decision will probably be poor. Also, if a leader forces consensus, many group members may later work against the "agreed-upon" solution since they did not agree to it at the meeting. It is very important that the leader take the time to reach genuine consensus or at least get a commitment from the people holding a minority view that they will work with the majority for the common good.

4. *Planning meetings.* Planning committees generally have a great deal of autonomy in structuring their activities and in reaching their final conclusions. The problem with being in charge of a planning committee is that the organization to which the committee belongs will probably react negatively or positively only after the plan has been submitted. This means that a planning committee may have put in hundreds of hours of work and become strongly committed to a plan that might ultimately be rejected by the larger organization. Another problem the leader of a planning committee has is lack of enthusiastic participation on the part of all the members. If a leader is not careful, the workload for planning can easily become a one-person job—his or hers!

Successful planning committees typically go through three phases. The first phase, which sometimes constitutes a whole meeting, calls for the leader to adopt a "tell and sell" leadership style in order to explain the planning project to the group members and convince them that each of them has an important role to play. A second phase requires the leader to change to a participatory leadership style in order to gather the information necessary for the group to plan properly. The third phase is the structuring of the activities that the planning committee will perform in order to reach its final goal. This phase demands that the leader adopt a delegating leadership style since members will be required to work independently on subparts of the plan.

The planning of a company picnic calls for the enactment of all three phases of a planning committee's life cycle. The leader must convince the members that a complaint-free picnic can really be produced if everyone works hard. Next, the leader must join the committee in listing all the important jobs that go into putting on a company picnic. Finally, the committee will need to draw up a modified PERT agenda (see Figure 9.4) to see that all their efforts are coordinated and that the picnic comes off successfully.

Since a planning committee requires a great deal of planning outside a formal meeting structure, it is necessary for the leader to contact the group members individually to ensure that the reports will be presented on time in meeting the PERT chart schedule. It is also important that influential members of the organization be approached for their reactions to the preliminary thinking of the planning committee. This will ensure that the committee's results do not come as a surprise to the organization, and, conversely, that the reaction of the organization to the plan does not come as a surprise to the committee. This need for communication between the planning committee and the organization it serves is sometimes formalized when an opinion questionnaire is distributed by the planning committee, seeking information and reaction from the organization. However, most of the time a planning committee tests its ideas informally in the organization.

FIGURE 9.4
A MODIFIED PERT AGENDA FOR A COMPANY PICNIC

```
  I.   The goal is the holding of the company picnic.
 II.   Events that must occur before picnic can occur:
        —reserving pavilion
        —determining games and programs
        —awards and prizes
        —securing entertainment
        —determining the kinds of food and beverage needed and purchasing them
        —determining who is eligible to come to the picnic
        —assessing company for funds for picnic
III.   Determining the order of events before the picnic is held
 IV.   PERT planning chart for picnic
  V.   Time needed
 VI.   Determine critical path
```

EVERYDAY WORK GROUPS

In Chapter 2, we presented four benchmarks for analyzing a work group. They are: (1) the amount of group understanding and agreement; (2) the formation of group roles; (3) the level of interpersonal trust and empathy; and (4) the degree of group identification and group pride.

In addition to what we have already said about work groups, it is valuable to recognize that there exist four different types of work groups within organizations. They are the long-standing work group, the project group, the loosely formed "prefab" group, and the quality circle. On a day-to-day basis, you will find yourself a part of one of these groups. Although you can process these four kinds of day-to-day groups in terms of the above benchmarks, the application is different for each work group and is treated separately in this chapter.

1. *Long-standing work groups.* Every successful organization has a number of famous, long-standing work groups that over the years have performed at such high levels of productivity that their group tradition and pride transcend the passage of time and numerous changes in personnel. These groups seem to develop a life of their own such that new members feel compelled to act out the traditional roles and maintain the legendary high levels of productivity. These long-standing work groups have a rich collection of symbols and slogans that have been handed down over the years from one worker to another. Even the communicative interaction among the group members and between the group and the rest of the organization often becomes stylized and predictable over the years.

Pledge classes of fraternities and sororities create over time, within their respective organizations, expectations that literally dictate the behavior of new inductees. The pledgemaster role is so classic that the role invariably plays the person who is asked to perform it; by that we mean a half-century of fraternity brothers in one chapter on one campus could get together at a reunion and discover that they all had essentially the same pledgemaster. Similarly, the roles and communication patterns among roles at Boys Town have become so well established over the years that boys who lived there in the 1940s describe a communication pattern that still occurs in the 1980s. Army veterans describe their military training similarly; and corporations such as General Motors, Firestone, and IBM have work groups with long-standing traditions that seem to demand each new member perform in predictable ways.

One of the more visible long-standing work groups in our society is the Supreme Court. Presidents and Congresses have tried to "pack" the Supreme Court to ensure that their version of American justice is maintained. However, again and again the Court has asserted its tradition of independence. The most dramatic example of modern times was the Court's decision that President Nixon should turn over his Watergate tapes to the special prosecutor. Even though Nixon had recently appointed a number of the justices, the group's tradition of independence from the executive branch was reflected in a unanimous decision, and the President had to capitulate.

The legends and stories of long-standing work groups within organizations portray them as "larger than life." New members of organizations soon hear the stories of these groups and are attracted to them. Competition to join famous work groups is always keen, and initiation to them is frequently formidable and sometimes dangerous. However, the status that goes with being a member of a long-standing work group is so enticing that the immortality of the group is assured, so long as the organization continues to live.

Although long-standing work groups have many strengths, they also have obvious weaknesses. It is very difficult to introduce change into the group even when it is desperately needed. Changing the communication behavior of such a group is particularly difficult. Group meetings tend to take ritualistic and almost religious forms in some groups. When a change in situation demands a change in group policy, tradition becomes an enemy rather than an ally of the group leader. Scottish units of the British army traditionally walked into battle with bagpipes skirling, but this traditional behavior became almost suicidal in the context of World War II. And, of course, the British tradition of wearing red coats into battle in the 1700s provided American squirrel hunters with a decided advantage.

In less dramatic but equally detrimental ways, long-standing work groups within organizations develop communication habits that are counterproductive. Because of its traditions, a work group may meet only once a month when in fact it should meet weekly. In general, our ever-industrializing nation, in which the organizational clocks have been speeded up, has not correspondingly streamlined its ceremonial traditions. Changes for the sake of efficiency are met with resistance, in part because valuable portions of the group's discussion tradition are dropped in the process. This loss of traditions has produced less colorful groups, and has reduced the rich variety of groups that used to exist. In our current stage of development, organizations seem to prefer good conforming work groups rather than the maverick groups of the past.

2. *Project work groups.* The complexity and interdependence of modern society manifests itself in organizations such as the project work group. Suppose a collection of highly trained and specialized individuals were brought together for a brief period of time—six months to a year—to complete a specified project. The individuals that formed the group probably would not have much history of working together, and the group itself would have no long-standing tradition dictating its expected level of productivity nor an established set of symbols or slogans. In short, the leader and the group participants would have to start from scratch and build on the basis of the suggestions for developing a work group we made in Chapter 6.

The United States space program to put a man on the moon by the end of the 1960s quickly recognized the problem of building a project from newly formed work groups. In the absence of any established criteria of what a good space work-group was, NASA created a comparative standard for judgment. The directors of the space program gave several project groups the same task and had them compete against each other in order to determine excellence in productivity. Professors in small-group-discussion classes often use this same technique when student groups are formed for short periods of time. Each group tends to determine its success on a comparative basis. For example, the success of each group can be determined by comparing its presentation of a problem-solving panel discussion with the performance of the other groups.

Unfortunately most project groups do not have parallel project groups to be compared with; therefore, the group must generate for itself levels of cohesion and group morale sufficient to meet the productivity goals that have been set by the organization or by the group itself. It is useful to look at a new project group in terms of the three generic types of groups we describe in detail in Chapter 2. The project group must clarify its goals, evolve its roles, and establish an acceptable level of productivity. In terms of consciousness-raising, pride in the group must be built, symbols and slogans need to be created, and the group must establish a tradition. Finally, from the perspective of encounter groups, the project group must engage in self-disclosure, develop interpersonal trust, and tolerate individual differences.

Contrasted to zero-history groups that are formed in classrooms in the university for research purposes, newly formed project groups in business organizations do not have the time to build the social dimension and the interpersonal aspects of the group before productivity demands must be met. A new project group must first set its goals and start generating a successful work record so that the group will raise consciousness on its ability to do work and not its capacity to socialize. This requirement will place a great deal of pressure on the project leader. Early meetings of project groups require more advanced planning and outside work on the part of the leader than other kinds of meetings in the business environment. The leader must also maintain a high degree of one-on-one contact with group members to ensure that the early work is completed on time and is of high quality.

Once the project group has established a history of good work, the leader can begin to have the group engage in consciousness-raising. This can be done in the early moments of a meeting by celebrating the competency of group members and bragging that the group is made up of "the cream of the crop." The group might also develop a symbol or slogan to put at the top of the memos they send to each other. If the group members habitually work late hours, for example, and start referring to themselves as "night owls," the leader might send each of them a stuffed owl to put on his or her desk. It is easier for group members to raise their consciousness if they have some territory they can call their own—ideally, a special room that is reserved for them, where they can keep special materials and which they can decorate with their slogans. When a regular room cannot be acquired, portable paraphernalia that can instantaneously decorate a room is the next best thing. Stylized name plates, a couple of placards, and a stuffed owl may be all that is needed.

As the group develops a history of work success, and as the members create a symbolic reality that they can take group pride in, individuals in the group will begin to engage in specific self-disclosures. At first, these disclosures tend to be comparative ones, such as "This project work group is the best one in the company," or "The people in this group are sure nicer than the ones in printing products." The project leader must remember to keep self-disclosure within limits. The project group is a temporary formation, and most of the members will be in and out of these kinds of groups. If self-disclosure is pushed beyond the boundaries of what it takes to get the job completed, individuals in the group may later feel resentful (when formed into new groups) if they think that people in the organization know too much about them.

The major advantage of project groups over long-standing groups is that the members are free to create their own group tradition. Yet, this is also the project group's leading drawback. The project members know their group is a very temporary thing and it is difficult to get them to commit sizable amounts of energy to building a group that will break up in the next eight months. Also, project group members tend to have a lot of "hidden agendas," which often produce a great deal of special-interest pleading. Many times, project group members are also representatives of long-standing work groups within the organization. Thus, it is difficult to establish loyalty and trust within the project group.

3. *Prefab work groups.* Some modern organizations have completely abandoned long-standing work groups, and find that project groups are inappropriate to the product or service of their organization. The loosely formed work group, or, if you will, the prefabricated group, has entered the mainstream of several American service industries. The job descriptions of this type of work group have been meticulously defined and rigidly structured so that a collection of people with no previous experience of working together can quickly form a work group that will produce a predictable level of productivity. Fast-food chains in the United States are the most obvious examples of industries that use prefab groups. These organizations use a highly fluid work force, yet, despite the high turnover, each neighborhood outlet reliably turns out the same product in about the same time. This has been accomplished by building human groups that resemble assembly lines. For example, a hamburger can be assembled by group interaction in much the same way as the serial construction of an automobile. Many large fire departments have gone to the prefab model for building groups because of the high turnover of firefighters from shift to shift through time swapping and the taking of vacation days. People who have been a part of long-standing and prefab groups generally report that there is more membership satisfaction in the long-standing work group than there is in the prefab. The potential for unusually high productivity is in the long-standing group; members reluctantly admit that the productivity of prefab groups is "reliably average," but to achieve "average" group work takes tremendous corporate effort. McDonald's Corporation has developed a training manual, more than 700 pages long, that spells out in no small detail how such things as lettuce, pickle, special sauce, cheese, and all-beef patties go together on a sesame seed bun to produce a Big Mac. Likewise, Walt Disney Productions has an elaborate training program that even scripts what an employee says when taking you on a jungle safari, so that every jungle safari in Disneyland and Disney World is exactly the same, time after time.

The weakness of the prefab group lies in its strength—namely its predictability. The group will perform the way it has been trained to work, but it rarely creates solutions to problems or adapts to new situations. Thus, a prefab group may work satisfactorily for the production of fast-food items, but it is inappropriate at a management level.

4. *Quality circles.* Edward Deming and Joseph Juran are two Americans who are generally credited with starting the "QC" movement in Japan in the 1950s. The movement has now spread to the United States and throughout the world as a means of participatory decision making. Juran (1976, 15) defines a quality circle (QC) as "a small group of departmental work leaders and line operators who have volunteered to spend time outside of their regular hours to help solve departmental quality problems."

The use of workers as an integral part of management problem-solving teams was probably started in 1890 by Ernst Abbé of Zeiss Company in Germany. He asked master and journey craftsmen to assist in the development of new optical machinery. By the 1920s, Bell Laboratories was using teams of people to assist in quality control, and by the late 1940s, IBM had discovered that they could develop better electronic computers by having the engineers consult with first-line supervisors and workers on the production of the product (Ingle 1982).

After World War II, General Douglas MacArthur invited Edward Deming, a statistician for the U.S. government, to Japan to lecture on quality control methods to Japanese management. In the 1950s, Joseph Juran went to Japan and lectured on the need for "total quality control" (TQC). Their efforts, which launched a national Japanese program to improve the images of Japanese products, produced amazing results. By 1960, the Japanese government declared November to be National Quality Month, replete with "Q" flags, seminars, posters, and weekly television programs. By 1973, six million Japanese workers were participating in over half a million quality circles. In 1977, the International Association of Quality Circles (IAQC) was created. Today thousands of American companies have adopted quality circle programs. (Baird 1982; Ingle 1982.)

The procedure for setting up a QC program has become standardized throughout the world. It seems to work best in industrial settings and with the participation of experienced, skilled workers. The typical structure contains the following elements: a plant steering committee of about fifteen people, which oversees the program; a program facilitator, who reports directly to the steering committee and is responsible for coordinating QC programs; circle leaders, who are generally line supervisors in a work area; and circle participants, who are nonmanagement employees who volunteer to participate. The circle will contain three to fifteen members, but often will divide into subcircles to solve specific problems. (Baird 1982.)

Typically, the first thing a quality circle does is engage in consciousness-raising and learn problem-solving techniques. The consciousness-raising

FIGURE 9.5
LOGO OF QC TEAM AT ABC COMPUTER

discussions invariably produce the name of the QC and the development of a logo. Illustrative of this process is the experience of a QC group at Sundstrand Hydro-Transmission at LaSalle, Illinois. There, the second-shift QC team, which contains maintenance, tool room, and tool grind employees called themselves "Skilled Crafts" and created a group logo (see Figure 9.5 for another QC logo). The QC program at Sundstrand, which was started by Ron Zindner, is called T.E.A.M.—"Together Employees Accomplish More."

Once the group consciousness has been created, the facilitator will train the members in group problem-solving procedures. The problem-solving agenda systems and discussion techniques that we presented in Chapter 3 constitute most of the training. As a historical footnote, the first problem-solving agenda system used by QCs was introduced by Deming and is now known as the Deming Wheel—a four-part schema: (1) plan, (2) do (collect data), (3) check (analyze), and (4) act (control). (Ingle 1982, 9.)

It's apparent from what we have said in the first eight chapters why quality circles have been so successful. First of all, they allow mature, experienced workers to participate in management decision-making. This does much to reduce the "we-they" syndrome dividing management and labor. It also allows the first-line supervisor (appointed leader) the opportunity to adapt to a participative or delegative style of leadership, which might have been against company policy prior to the development of QCs. Workers obviously take a great deal of pride in successful team effort that not only improves a product but also results in recognition going to the workers for their creative solutions.

However, QCs are not a panacea for management problems of quality control. First, in industries that are heavily unionized, volunteering for a quality circle may be viewed as being disloyal to the union, especially if the union distrusts management and believes that QCs are merely a "plot" to increase worker productivity without increasing compensation. Another problem is that after approximately a year's time, a QC can run out of important problems to solve. The first two or three problems might be fun to solve; however, it will become increasingly difficult for the QC to keep finding problems whose solutions will produce major results. So there is a danger that the QC will become a CR or pure encounter group. Finally, a QC decision-making group is subject to all of the problems that might beset any decision-making group. For example, the appointed leader may dominate and not allow role formation, or the group might become mired in secondary tension and never resolve its leadership problem. Yet, despite its weaknesses, the QC is a valuable and unique type of discussion group that will likely increase in popularity in the United States throughout the rest of this century.

PROFESSIONAL CONFERENCES

There is a special communication event that sooner or later most professionals attend. The conference is a well-defined concept in our society. Over time, certain expectations have developed as to what kinds of meetings and discussions will take place at conferences. A conference is really an umbrella term that refers to a number of different kinds of events that are in fact quite distinct. The three events we will discuss in this section are the one-day conference, the three-day conference, and the week-long convention. Every conference is really a series of meetings and small group discussions in which all the group types that we discussed in Chapter 2 and all the discussion formats, problem-solving agenda systems and techniques that were presented in Chapter 3 tend to occur in a short period of time for a large number of people. We call this event a conference. Organizations have many reasons for holding conferences. We get together to share information, to raise our professional consciousness, and to interact as professionals in a social setting. We also solve problems and improve our professional skills. Finally, we hold conferences for ritualistic reasons. It seems obligatory that any professional organization with self-respect should hold at least one conference a year, with many members attending, in order to show its vitality and strength of purpose.

1.   *The One-Day Conference.* A day is a very brief period for a large group of people to work together for some common purpose and expect to attain some kind of result. Thus, in one-day conferences, which are often called workshops, the organizers tend to focus the conferees' efforts on a few topics and try to keep the size of the group manageable—frequently no more than two or three hundred.

The conferees are brought together in a general assembly for brief welcoming speeches by the planners, followed by the presentation of the day's agenda. All members will have received a copy of the agenda in advance, but it is reviewed at the opening session. The social highlight is the conference luncheon at which an outside expert generally gives a speech that amplifies the theme of the conference. At the end of the day the conferees are usually brought together again so that the output of the conference can be celebrated by the conference planners.

The expectation of one-day conferees is that each of them will actively participate at the conference. This expectation is usually met by breaking the conference into small groups that work for specified periods of time. If the purpose of the conference is to solve a problem, conferees are assigned to small groups, each with an appointed leader and a special agenda. Well-run conferences will tend to use discussion techniques like brainstorming or the NGD technique in the meetings. Less experienced conference planners will break people into buzz groups without specifying a leader or a structure. If you are the appointed leader of a small group at a conference, you should remember your obligation to keep the group's agenda within the time frame and expect to handle the procedural communication behaviors by yourself.

If the purpose of the conference is the development of skills, the conferees tend to be divided into small groups, with each small group meeting designed to work on a given skill. Oftentimes, there is a workshop leader assigned to each group to facilitate the learning process. For example, at conferences for elementary education instructors, there might be workshops on storytelling, reading, and modern math. There are two keys to the success of this design. The first key is that the facilitators of the day-long workshop should help the members but refrain from dominating the group. Too often the leader of the workshop turns the discussion into a monologue. The second key is that planning should be done to determine the number of workshops that can be held in an hour and to estimate the probable number of attendees at each workshop. If two hundred teachers show up for the storytelling workshop and only five for the modern math session, obviously the conference has not been well planned.

If you are in charge of planning a one-day conference, in addition to the actual structuring of the conference you will be responsible for all the physical comforts of the attendees. This generally includes providing adequate meeting space for the small groups and an assembly hall to accommodate the whole group at one time. You should remember that you are the host or hostess and that the more you attend to the details involved in running a conference— name tags, parking, coffee and rolls, before-and-after correspondence with the attendees—the more effective your conference will be. Moreover, if each member who attended your one-day conference was able to take an active part in the day's events, and if no attendee was inconvenienced due to some planning error with facilities, your one-day conference will have been a success. To emphasize: the knowledge of small group discussion techniques can only aid in the achievement of a successful conference.

2.   *The Three-Day Conference.* A three-day conference is often held over a weekend and, in reality, usually runs two and a half days at the most. The three-day conference typically has the same purposes as the one-day conference; however, its structure is much more complex. Three-day conferences become necessary when attendees have to travel from out of state, in which case travel considerations are a major planning issue for the organizers. The conference will usually start on a Thursday or Friday evening and run through Sunday morning. This structure allows a half-day of travel time for people flying in from various parts of the country. While coffee and rolls in the morning provide socialization for the one-day conference, a cocktail party on the first evening of the three-day conference provides an opportunity for people to gather socially before the working meetings begin the following morning. It is not uncommon for small groups of people to engage in informal consciousness-raising sessions during this evening cocktail and registration period.

The evening socialization and registration period will have a positive influence on the conference only if all the physical needs of the attendees have been met. At a three-day conference this means that lodging, food, and transportation have been carefully coordinated so that the conferees do not have to spend their time solving logistical problems. Thus, three-day conferences tend to be held at a lodge, a large motor inn, or an adult education facility so that sleeping quarters, meeting rooms, and restaurants are all located in one spot.

The next morning the first order of business is usually a general session, a business meeting, or a combination of both. Typically, this general session has a keynote speaker who is from within the organization—for example, the president of the group. The advance agenda is handed out at registration, and it is assumed that after the general business meeting the attendees will go to their work meetings.

Modular scheduling of work sessions is a popular design for three-day conferences. For example, if a group of elementary education teachers were to hold its conference over three days instead of one, the conference directors might schedule storytelling, modern math, and remedial reading workshops in such a way that they were repeated over the course of a day. The whole structure of the workshops would be designed so that everybody could attend every workshop. An alternate structure for three-day conferences is to build three one-day conferences within the three-day conference. When this is done, the conference agenda clearly delineates the three major work areas and then outlines the workshop within each one. The advantage of this structure is that people can register for all or part of the three-day conference. For example, a conference might be scheduled to start on Wednesday evening and run through Saturday afternoon, with the option that people could register for Saturday only. This sort of scheduling allows for maximum attendance at the conference and gives the attendees the opportunity to decide how active they want to be in the conference.

Participant expectation for a three-day conference is very similar to a one-day conference. The people attending expect to be very active in each small group meeting, and they expect to have a designated leader with expert knowledge of the topic who will handle procedural communication. The round table format is popular for work sessions. Frequently a lecture-round-table format is used; i.e., the lecturer provides a brief stimulus statement, a demonstration, or both; and then he or she becomes an active participant in the following discussion. A variation on the modular workshop structure is to break the conference up into morning and afternoon units and have a stimulus speaker for each half-day session who speaks to the whole assembled conference. The attendees are then assigned to buzz groups to interact on the topic. A major error that frequently occurs in using this design is the failure of the conference planners to assign leaders for the buzz group discussions. In the absence of a designated leader the buzz groups frequently flounder around looking for structure, or digress into social conversation. In either case little productivity occurs, and the members feel their time has been wasted.

The keys to the success of the three-day conference are essentially the same as those for a one-day conference. The attendees need to participate actively in the meetings, their physical needs must be met, and their small group discussions must be well planned in order to maximize their productivity.

3. *The Convention.* A convention is generally a week-long conference, which is a wonder to behold. Major conventions take a year to plan properly. The planning is done by a number of committees that somehow manage to solve the logistical and structural problems of bringing thousands of people together under one roof and having literally hundreds of meetings come off on schedule. Conventions do not have cumulatively structured discussion meetings as shorter conferences do. Each two-hour period is designed to be independent from all other two-hour periods that occur over the course of a week, and yet there is a logic to the overall design. Professional conventions are structured to handle special-interest areas and subgroupings of the profession. The American Medical Association's convention recognized that cardiologists, gynecologists, and psychiatrists need to meet separately to discuss their common interests, and that each specialty needs to hold workshops unique to its professional interests. Thus, the organizational schema of a convention is best understood by examining the planning committees of each major interest area. In effect, a convention may have several mini-conventions for each area of interest running simultaneously. In this way, a pediatricians' business meeting could be held at the same time as the cardiologists'. However, despite the apparent fragmentation at a convention, there is an overall theme and a common professional identity that holds it together.

Conventions tend to be held in large metropolitan areas where it is easier to accommodate the needs of large numbers of people for a week. Large cities are easily accessible by air, train, or car and offer a variety of restaurants and entertainment. Many progressive cities have built convention centers which include or are next to hotels that can accommodate thousands of convention-goers. The professional convention, when properly run, is a consciousness-raising experience for those who attend. The convention is full of ritualistic meetings, symbols, and slogans that help renew one's professional identity. The many luncheons and evening socials provide ample opportunity for informal consciousness-raising sessions to occur.

The general session on the first full day of the convention is an important ritualistic meeting which serves to both unify the convention members and emphasize the common theme that will be carried through over the next several days. The occasion calls for a major keynote speaker of national or international prominence, one who will attract the mass media to cover the speech. Once the general session is over, most of the formal consciousness-raising will take place at the various business meetings of each of the divisions.

The small group meetings at a convention run the gamut of what was presented in Chapter 3 in regard to the variety of discussion formats, problem-solving agenda systems, and specific discussion techniques used; however, except for those meetings labeled workshops, the majority of the group discussions will use rather formal symposium formats or a modified panel discussion with a forum period following. The people who attend conventions do not expect to participate actively in all the meetings they attend. Many times they are content to listen attentively to a well-planned symposium, especially if they will receive a copy of the symposium's proceedings afterwards. This expectation has led some convention planners to publish their proceedings, tape the special-interest sessions, or do both.

In addition to attending the special-interest meetings, symposiums, and workshops, highly involved convention-goers serve on numerous long-standing committees and special task-force groups which not only plan the annual conventions, but provide major direction for the profession as a whole through the publication of professional journals and the support of professional research. These committees also formulate the organization's stance toward the public and wrestle with major controversial issues within the profession.

The key to a successful convention is to have a hierarchy of planning committees—from the steering committee, through the interest-area committees, to the local hospitality committee. These committees in turn plan the structure of small group discussion sessions that are under their jurisdiction. A successful director of a convention must delegate much of his or her work to small work groups and small planning committees. Planning and delegation of responsibilities are also keys to a successful convention.

SUMMARY

In this chapter, the discussion principles described in the first part of the book were applied to work groups, routine meetings, and business conferences. Each of these three kinds of real-life small group communication events was thoroughly examined.

Five basic principles a supervisor should use in determining whether or not to call a meeting were presented. They included: mastering time, understanding tradition, being productive, maintaining group satisfaction, and gaining group consensus.

Four basic types of routine business meetings were detailed: the Monday morning meeting, the monthly meeting, the decision-making meeting, and the planning meeting. Such particulars as agenda and supervisory leadership styles were highlighted.

In addition, four different types of everyday work groups were identified: the long-standing work group; the project group; the prefab group; and quality circles. Long-standing work groups feature a rich history of group traditions, replete with the telling of legends and stories. Project groups are asked to establish goals and start generating a successful work record on a given organizational project. Prefab groups are loosely formed work groups which follow strict procedures and policies to generate predictable group outcomes. Quality circles are work groups composed of company volunteers, whose purpose is to achieve higher productivity and quality through participative decision-making. The latter type of work group was discussed in terms of its phenomenal growth and impact during the past decade.

The chapter closed with a brief discussion of the major forms of professional conferences: one-day and three-day conferences, and the convention.

REFERENCES

Baird, J. E., Jr. *Quality Circles: Leader's Manual.* Prospect Heights, Ill.: Waveland Press, 1982.

Cuffe, M., and Cragan, J. F. "The Corporate Culture Profile." In *International Association of Quality Circles Annual Conference Transactions* Memphis: International Association of Quality Circles, 1983.

Gouran, D. S. "Variables Related to Consensus in Group Discussions of Questions of Policy." *Speech Monographs* 36 (1969): 387–91.

Ingle, S. *Quality Circles Master Guide: Increasing Productivity with People Power.* Englewood Cliffs, N.J.: Prentice-Hall, Spectrum, 1982.

Juran, J. M. "The QC Circle Phenomenon." In *QC Circles: Application, Tools, and Theory,* edited by Amsden, D. M., and Amsden, R. T. Milwaukee: ASQC, 1976.

Ouchi, W. G. *Theory Z.* Reading, Mass.: Addison-Wesley, 1981.

Shaw, M. E. *Group Dynamics: The Psychology of Small Group Behavior.* 2nd edition. New York: McGraw-Hill, 1976.

Steiner, I. D. *Group Process and Productivity.* New York: Academic Press, 1972.

Wright, D. W. *Small Group Communication: An Introduction.* Dubuque, Iowa: Kendall/Hunt, 1975.

This chapter will focus on the communication among groups in organizations. It is not our purpose to provide a comprehensive treatment of organizational communication but merely to suggest how the theory and practice of small group discussion might have application to business and governmental organizations. In this chapter we will deal with four major ideas. First, that information is the lifeblood of an organization and that the information flow among small groups is vital for understanding organizational behavior. The second idea is the socialization process of small groups within an organization. Third, we make a number of suggestions on how to improve communication among the various groups within the organization. The fourth idea is that it is useful to look at organizations in terms of the eight basic small group concepts. In short, the previous nine chapters have explained intragroup communication; this chapter is concerned with intergroup communication as it occurs within the framework of a formal organization.

INFORMATION: THE LIFEBLOOD OF AN ORGANIZATION

The circulatory system of the human body provides a crude analogy for comprehending the importance of information flow in an organization. If information in an organization is not being effectively pumped up from the production groups to the decision-making groups, the effect on the organization is the same as if oxygenated blood is cut off from the brain. If blood does not reach the hands and the feet of the body, the limbs soon cease to respond to directions from the brain. Likewise, if information is not accurately transmitted from decision-making groups down to the production groups, work does not get done. Just as the arteries carry the blood to different parts of the body, so do format channels such as interdepartmental memos and face-to-face meetings carry information which is the lifeblood of an organization.

Although blood is needed for life, too much of it in one place at one time in the body can produce a hemorrhage. So it is with organizations, in that information overload can occur if too much information gets pumped into a given group. The worst kind of hemorrhage is, of course, cerebral. Thus, most organizations attempt to be very efficient with respect to the amount of information that their key decision-making committees use. In order to understand the use of information in a small group, it is necessary to understand how groups fit into the organizational structure of companies.

1. *Formal Organizational Structure.* Ordinarily we think of information as flowing either up and down or laterally in an organization; and further, we think of this information as being transmitted in formal and informal channels. One starting point for analyzing information in small groups in organizations is to begin with the first-line supervisor and the work group he or she manages.

The first principle to understand about intergroup communication within an organization is that each group does not communicate all of its information to the rest of the organization, nor does the organization communicate all of its information upward. Thus, we find that a first-line supervisor does not transmit upward all that he or she knows about his or her group. There are group secrets that never leave production. For example, in a firefighter group there may be an older member who can no longer perform the job well; however, the rest of the group protects him or her, and the information remains a group secret. Sometimes a production group in a factory knows the most time-saving way to manufacture a product, but the information is kept secret for fear that production quotas will be raised if the information gets out. When the first-line supervisor goes to meetings with other first-line supervisors, in effect another group is formed. In this group, the first-line supervisors will have privileged information that the group will not want to go up or down the organization. Thus, we can see that information is filtered, and there is never one place in an organization where all information is stored.

The second principle is that all managers in an organization are formally members of at least two groups and thus must keep some information from each of the groups of which they are a member. This principle causes most managers to experience the "rock and the hard spot" syndrome. The first-line supervisor's work group wants its manager to disclose all of his or her information to them; yet if the first-line supervisor does so, the organization will begin to distrust the supervisor, and dismissal will follow. Also, if the first-line supervisor will not disclose any organizational secrets to his or her work group, the workers will not trust their supervisor, and he or she will soon have no information to pass upward. Thus all managers between the basic production group and the president of the organization must maintain a communication balancing act because of their multigroup membership within the organization. And the more formal groups a supervisor belongs to, the more difficult it will become to juggle information so as to maintain the loyalty of the respective group members. For example, if a university professor is chairing an academic department and serving on a university budget committee, that individual is a member of three formal organizational groups: the academic department, the college council of department chairs, and the university budget committee. The budget committee will have information that it would not want directly communicated to the department; e.g., tentative allocations of monies for summer school. The department has information it does not want communicated to the dean's college council of chairs; e.g., the frequent classroom absences of an older professor. The college council of chairs has information that it does not want to go down to the department or up to the university budget committee; e.g., tentative plans for adoption of flextime for civil service employees in the college. Maintaining loyal membership in each of these three groups is difficult for the professor because all groups in an organization have an insatiable appetite for information. In fact, the *third principle of intergroup communication in organizational settings is that groups constantly crave more information, because information is power.* Thus, span of control —that is, the statement of how much horizontal power a manager has—is an important organizational concept. However, since there are limits to the number of groups in which a person can maintain membership and from which he or she can receive reliable information, organizations constantly adjust the number of groups an individual is responsible for.

Presumably, the higher up one is in an organization, the more power one has. But this power is in fact information, and information is filtered at each level as it goes up or down. Thus, an organization could be stacked so high that the executives become powerless because they do not have access to enough reliable information. This problem of executive powerlessness is also a problem of the chain of command through which information flows vertically.

Within the formal structure of organizations, information flows both horizontally and vertically, but not effortlessly or accurately. Each group maintains proprietary rights over some information, and each manager has to try to maintain multiple-group loyalty through the disclosure or nondisclosure of information. Finally, power in any organization, whether it be through span of control horizontally or chain of command vertically, is tempered by the amount and quality of information that flows from group to group within the organization. The limits of formal intergroup communication within organizations have long been recognized, and informal channels of communication have been developed as a means of supplementing and verifying the information that flows through the formal channels.

2.   *Informal Communication Channels.* Informal communication systems exist in all organizations. In fact, Keith Davis (1978, 116) argues that "informal communication is the other half of a complete communication system, and thus is an important part of organizational communication." In order to relate successfully to each other, groups are often dependent on the grapevine. The informal channel of communication serves three purposes in intergroup communication: (a) as a supplementary channel of communication, (b) as a check and balance on information received in the formal structure, and (c) as a means of acquiring other groups' "secret" information.

a.   A supplementary channel of communication. Since everybody recognizes the existence and importance of an organizational grapevine, many managers of groups will intentionally send their messages both formally via memo and informally through the grapevine. The grapevine is accessible through a number of social settings in which members of different groups interact, such as car pools, morning coffee in the cafeteria, and weekend recreational events. Occasionally one or two members in an organization become notorious carriers of grapevine information. In one organization, it might be a switchboard operator; in another, a person who delivers the departmental mail; and in yet another, a social butterfly who moves from department to department giving out and receiving information. These members are generally ridiculed behind their backs; nevertheless, people in the organization tend to rely on them as one source of information.

Several of our graduate students have studied intergroup communication within organizations in order to understand the grapevine and determine the importance of it to the organization (Sandifer 1976; Sabaini 1979). Their research supports the notion that managers are aware of the grapevine and use it intentionally to ensure that important information gets to all groups. In one study the researcher found that of five groups reporting to one supervisor, one particular group continually received partial and fragmented information. It was determined that the reason this group was receiving more fragmented information than the others was that its members were housed in a different building and did not eat lunch with the other work groups. This social isolation prevented the grapevine from reaching them (Sandifer 1976).

b.   *A check and balance on information received in the formal structure.* In large organizations which have a long chain of command, the grapevine is used by receivers of downward-flowing information as a check on the accuracy and the intent of the messages. Official organizational communiqués tend to be very "machine sounding" and hardly ever give the reasons for organizational policies. The grapevine is used to discover the emotion behind the message and the degree to which the organization is committed to carrying out the policy.

For example, the telephone company in any city in any given year will probably send out a memo to all line crews, stating that the company does not want several crews to congregate at the same restaurant for morning coffee. Immediately upon receiving this directive, the telephone work groups will ask through the grapevine what happened that caused this memo to be sent and, further, what does it mean? The grapevine may soon contain the information that the memo was prompted by several citizen complaints about six trucks parked at Kesley's Restaurant. The grapevine message might also indicate that top management is not really mad, but that the line crews had better change to other restaurants and go to them in smaller groups so that the citizens will quit complaining. Similar memos are probably sent each year in police, postal, and all public utility organizations. The point is that all organizations use the grapevine as a means to determine the "real meaning" of official intergroup communication, particularly the information that flows downward in the organization.

c.   *Acquiring other groups' "secret" information.* Since information is power, and all groups within an organization have information they want kept confidential, some groups—particularly highly cohesive ones existing in highly competitive organizations—will systematically gather "secret" information from various groups within the organization so that their group will have an advantage over competing ones. In this situation each member of a group will check out information through his or her own social contacts and share it later with the others.

Rumors of a pending layoff of personnel will generally trigger a work group's efforts to gather another group's secret information about which work groups will be laid off and when. In these crises, work groups are amazingly successful at discovering the best-kept secrets. Hollywood war movies repeatedly dramatized the well-known ability of army platoons to discover where they were being sent to fight, despite the best efforts of command groups to keep the information secret. Sometimes competing organizations do this to each other. In this situation, the small groups of each organization work cooperatively against the groups of another organization. We see this behavior when the news media compete against the executive branch of government, or when executive groups compete against legislative committees. The Watergate scandal is probably the most famous example of this. When all work groups are trying to acquire the secrets of other work groups, an organization can rapidly become an unpleasant environment in which to work. As a general rule, work groups should not actively probe for the secret information of fellow work groups unless there is some crisis that makes it necessary. Groups are just like people; they demand and deserve some privacy.

3.   *Common Problems in Intergroup Communication.* In earlier chapters we have repeatedly argued that competition among work groups is healthy and makes for more cohesive groups that are in turn more productive. Yet we have also commented that competition reaches a point of diminishing returns. One of the best measures to use in determining whether too much competition exists in an organization is to examine the information flow and determine what kind of errors are occurring. These can be ones of omission, substitution, distortion, or filtering, or a combination of these kinds of errors.

  a.   *Omission.* As competition increases among groups, more group information will be kept secret. This is clearly manifested by examining intergroup memos. The frequency of the memos and the length of them will decrease. For example, when a quality control department in an organization is trying to pinpoint the reasons for badly manufactured merchandise, the groups responsible for making the product may start omitting key information that would be needed to trace the manufacturing of the item, thus thwarting quality control's attempts to fix blame.

  b.   *Substitution.* Organizations that are highly competitive often have exacting deadlines for the production of work. Furthermore, production of work tends to be serial in that it passes from one group to another. For example, engineering may have to make drawings before the foundry can make the castings, and the castings have to be heat-treated before assembly work groups can start putting together a car. In this environment each work group wants the maximum amount of time to do its step in the manufacturing process. This situation sets up the classic case of deadline substitution so that the grapevine becomes very active as each work group tries to identify the "real deadlines."

  c.   *Distortion.* Insecure first-line supervisors occasionally threaten their work groups unnecessarily by distorting information that comes from decision-making groups further up the chain of command. A first-line supervisor may say to his or her subordinates that if production falls off "heads are going to roll!" The original information that come from upper management groups may have simply been a statement that urged increased work group productivity. When distortion occurs in information it is generally in the intent of the message. Work groups will change the intent of the message in order to enlarge their power base.

  d.   *Filtering.* As we have already indicated in this chapter, information overload can occur with intergroup communication. Filtering is a process that helps reduce the amount of incoming information to a new group. A ten-page handout that comes to a supervisor may be reduced to a one-page handout at the Monday morning meeting. In addition to being filtered, the intent and the tone of the message is often altered. This occurs most often when angry phone calls come in to the supervisor of a work group. The secretary receiving the incoming call will frequently filter out anger and frustration and merely report the information to the supervisor. Although there are obvious advantages to reducing the amount of information, the filtering process can also be disadvantageous when important information is left out and when work groups do not know that other groups are upset with them.

ASSIMILATION OF GROUPS INTO THE ORGANIZATIONAL CULTURE

The goal of any organization is the same as that of any living species—immortality. Organizations are living entities that have a cultural and symbolic past and a basic impulse to survive. Researchers have found that one of the important ways in which organizations stay alive is by the nourishment and development of "sacred" organizational stories. If a member of a successful organization is asked why the organization grew and became successful, he or she will proceed to tell a story that takes on mythical qualities. If a foreigner asks an American to account for the success of the United States, a similar myth would unfold. Similarly, every organization has a "sacred" story on how the company grew. One company on *Fortune's* 500 told how its humble but talented scientists repeatedly created new products and thus opened up new markets. The competitive edge of the company was that they always led the field with innovative products, leaving their competitors in a position of playing catch-up. As you might suspect, the most revered part of the company was the research and development division. The high-status work group within the division was the research chemist unit. Placards attesting to the chemists' successes hung on their walls, and pictures of their mythical predecessors were displayed outside the lab. Any chemist who worked for the company knew all the traditional hero stories of the successful group. These kinds of stories form an important part of any company's identification (along with myths, rituals, and corporate sagas), and you can measure an individual's involvement in an organization by the number of sacred stories he or she knows (Cragan 1971; Sykes 1970; Bormann 1983; Pacanowsky and O'Donnell-Trujillo 1983).

Sacred stories are the means by which individuals attain an understanding of, and loyalty to, their work groups. As the new worker begins to interact with members of other work groups, he or she has to adjust to the other stereotypes created by the sacred stories of competing groups. Finally, the new worker will be assimilated into the whole organization by learning corporate stories that are transmitted during companywide social events (Cheney, 1983b; Jablin, 1984).

1. *Group Loyalty.* The assimilation of a new member into a work group takes place in terms of territory, dress, language, and storytelling. A new member soon learns the territorial boundaries of his or her work group, the unwritten dress code, and the unique idiomatic language of the group. If, say, a man were to go to work as a production electrician in a factory, he would soon discover that all electricians dress similarly, complete to their electrician's pouches, and that their dress is different from that of machinists and painters. Furthermore, the new electrician would soon be immersed in "14 wire versus 12 wire" and what size "lugs" to use on transfers; and while he learned where to eat, where to shower, what to wear, and how to sound like an electrician, he would also learn the sacred stories about electricians that would further intensify his recognition of himself as an electrician in the work group.

If the new worker in question had joined the sales force of the company instead of the production electrician work group, the process would have been the same, only he would have learned how to walk and talk like a salesman, and the sacred stories would have related to the success of the sales division. For example, the stories might have explained that the division had the best insurance sales per year, the lowest turnover rate, and the best record of people being promoted to corporate headquarters.

In most companies the new worker soon identifies with his or her new work group and feels pride in it; however, contact with competing groups within the organization will soon test the loyalty of the group member.

2. *X, Y, and Z Management Cultures.* Organizations are hybrids of X, Y, and Z management cultures. We discussed these three different management styles in Chapter 5. An X culture has managers who exercise authority and closely supervise subordinates. In an X environment, innovation, quality control, and policy decision making are almost solely the responsibility of management. A Y culture is a humanized analog of X, in which supervisors are sensitive to the needs of their workers, and the workers are allowed input into company decisions. The Z culture is team-oriented participatory management, in which the lines between supervisor and worker are blurred, and all members of the organization feel responsibility to one another and to the production of quality products and services.

In American organizations today, there are wide-ranging discussions and experiments in an attempt to find the right hybrid management culture that will provide the highest productivity and membership satisfaction for a company. William Ouchi (1981) believes that the Japanese have been successful because they have adopted a Theory Z culture. Peters and Waterman (1982), after studying a number of successful American corporations, concluded that openness in communication and informality in and among work groups was one key to success. Kilmann (1985), in explaining corporate culture, highlighted workers' sense of confinement and restraint in a Theory X culture as a major cause for productivity problems in some American corporations. Cragan et al. (1985) discovered that subordinates who worked in a ZY hybrid management culture were three times more satisfied with their work group than subordinates who were working in an XZ culture.

A worker's ability to be assimilated into an organization in part relates to his or her understanding of the management culture of the organization. Table 10.1 presents twelve salient issues that can be examined in order to determine the management culture of an organization and describes the way in which each of the three cultures (X, Y, and Z) handles each issue.

3. *Intermingling of Groups.* The new electrician or salesperson who attends a first meeting in which representatives of other work groups are present will discover that he or she has been stereotyped as a member of a particular work group. The comment might be "Oh, you're the new electrician!" or "So you're our region IV salesperson!" or "And you're our new accountant!"

At subsequent intergroup contacts, however, the new worker will begin to hear some negative stories about his or her work group. For example, at our

TABLE 10.1
ANATOMY OF MANAGEMENT CULTURES: X, Y, AND Z

Organizational Issue	Theory X	Theory Y	Theory Z
Corporate Hero	Manager is assertive and task oriented (has task skills)	Manager is friendly, compassionate and understanding (has people skills)	Manager is open minded and committed to participatory management (has group skills)
Corporate Villain	Manager is task incompetent; does not know work he or she supervises	Manager is insensitive, aloof, and uncaring; has no concern for workers	Manager is not a team player, does not allow workers to participate in decision making
Innovation	Creation of new ideas is management's responsibility	Workers make some suggestions for new ideas	Managers and workers feel joint responsibility for creating new ideas
Quality Control	Management is solely responsible for seeing that work is done correctly	Management encourages workers to take responsibility for quality of their work	The organization is quality-control conscious through the use of QC groups
Decision Making	Decisions are made by those in charge	Managers seek the advice of subordinates before making decisions	Workers participate with managers in group decision making
Personal Problems	Personal problems are left at home and not brought to work	Supervisors will empathize and counsel workers about personal problems	Organization has formal structures for handling all personal problems of workers: the organization is a "family"
Time Management	Workers' time is closely monitored (e.g., time-cards); managers set deadlines for task completion	Work has some time flexibility to complete task	Time is unstructured; workers are encouraged to set own timetables for completing task
Group Meetings	Meetings are held primarily for telling subordinates about management decisions and expectations	Meetings are sometimes held to solicit information from workers for management decision making	Participatory decision-making meetings are held including managers and workers
Trust	Little trust exists between management and workers	Managers are selective in what workers they trust and confide in	Trust is pervasive among managers and workers
Motivation	Major reason for working is to earn income	Employees have developed good working relationships	Employees have strong personal attachment to the organization's goals and identity
Promotion	Hard work gets most people to the top; workers are promoted on the basis of task accomplishments	Hard work, plus knowing the right people, is the way to get promoted	Dedication and persistence to organizational goals is the long-term key to promotion
Job Security	Job security depends on how well a worker does work and how much that work is needed	Job security is dependent upon a good relationship with management	Company makes lifelong commitment to employees

Derived from Cuffe, M., and Cragan, J. F. "The Corporate Culture Profile." *International Association of Quality Circles Annual Conference Transactions*. Memphis: International Association of Quality Circles, 1983.

university our work group is responsible for teaching the basic communication course to most freshmen. There are numerous sacred stories about the basic course—most of which are good, some of which are bad. One of the bad stories has been around for nearly a decade and refuses to die. The gist of the story is that a nonverbal communication assignment was made that called for the "simulation of a murder" in order to study the communication reactions of passersby to this kind of incident. Two of the spectators turned out to be carrying real guns while another was the fiancée of the "murdered" student. The experimenters had failed to alert security about the classroom simulation, and the "shot" student had failed to tell his fiancée. Needless to say, the simulation created quite a furor both on campus and off, although, fortunately, no one was hurt. The meaning of the story as it is told year after year by competing work groups identifies the course as a "wild and crazy" one and not the "meat and potatoes" curriculum offering it should be. New workers who come into our department are told this story in order to insulate them from the shock of hearing it from an outside worker. They are also told some good sacred stories so that they can respond to any criticism. This insulating process is done by most work groups so that the new workers' pride will be maintained when they encounter outside competing work groups.

As a new worker gains the trust of a work group, sacred stories that tell "where the bodies are buried" will be told. These are secret group stories and are not to be told to outsiders. One of the important tests of a new member's loyalty will be his or her ability to preserve the confidentiality of a work group's secret stories, especially ones that reflect badly on the group.

4. *Socialization into the Whole Organization.* Many organizations promote a number of social activities such as bowling and baseball leagues, and some even have their own recreational parks for their employees. When a new employee begins joining company-sponsored social and recreational activities, he or she hears corporatewide stories that all members of the organization know regardless of the work group they are in. These stories produce an arsenal of material that a new worker can use to explain to outside people why the organization is outstanding and why he or she is proud to be a member of it. Because knowing a number of mythic corporation stories helps in the rapid assimilation of a worker, he or she soon feels like an old-timer. A new worker can look as though he or she has worked for the company for years, if he or she can tell a number of organizational stories.

Although organization-sponsored activities help to assimilate a new worker, there are some potential dangers. The first is the problem of never being able to get out of a stereotyped role. Just as people are stereotyped within groups by their race or sex, they are also stereotyped according to their work group. Law enforcement officers frequently get trapped into an organizational "ghetto." There is a tendency in most cities for police officers to work and play together to the exclusion of other people; consequently, they never stop being a "cop." Physicians, dentists, and lawyers also tend to fall into the same trap. Fairly soon, members of these groups start to think of themselves exclusively as desk sergeants or urologists and fail to have an existence separate from their job. In short, they no longer play the role of desk sergeant or urologist, but the role plays them.

The effect of this organizational lifestyle can be measured in part by high divorce rates. A marriage partner may find it is easy to love John or Mary, but not a cop or a dentist. In fact, a psychologist friend of ours recommends that everyone should pound a nail into a tree outside of their home, and before they go inside their home at night, they should take off their invisible role and hang it on a tree.

We have long recognized the importance of separating our professional roles from our personal lives; however, many organizational structures create pressures which tend to fuse the two together. When this happens we usually talk about a person being married to his or her job. When you leave college and join some organization, survey the company-sponsored social activities, and select one that appeals to you. This is important because participation in a company organization will expose you to organizational stories; however, remember that you also need to seek outside social contracts so that people will relate to you as a person and not as a member of a work group.

If you want to test the importance of separating role from person, try dropping the stereotyped role you have as a college student when you are at home at social gatherings. When college students are home socializing at their neighborhood hangout, the first few minutes of conversation tend to be filled with asking and answering two questions: what university are you attending and what is your major? If you want to have a different kind of evening, don't raise these subjects. Instead, simply describe yourself in terms of the role of your summer job; e.g., short-order cook, street cleaner, salesclerk, tree trimmer, or lifeguard. You will discover that a lot of people will not talk to you very long. Furthermore, their nonverbal cues will indicate that you haven't much status. But learning to maintain a conversation with another person without "credentialing" yourself through your role description will help you understand the difference between your professional role and yourself, and will permit you to develop more meaningful relationships.

EFFECTIVE COMMUNICATION AMONG GROUPS WITHIN THE ORGANIZATIONAL CULTURE

1. *The role of the CEO.* Bormann's (1983) research has led him to conclude that a major role of the CEO (chief executive officer) of an organization is to disseminate the organizational saga to as many members of the company as possible. The organizational saga contains the complete professional consciousness of the company. It includes sacred stories that explain what kind of people work at the company, how the company came to be successful, and why the company is immortal. Sometimes these sagas are written up in book form and distributed to new employees. For years, new employees at State Farm Insurance Company were given a book, *The Farmer From Merna,* that detailed in dramatic form how this large insurance company had grown from a small farmer-oriented insurance company to nationwide prominence through the retention of certain basic, time-honored principles. Even though a company may have formal documents detailing its saga, the organization is a living entity and is continuing to change, so the CEO must continually retell the old stories and update the saga with new ones.

2. *The role of the house organ.* A new employee should always take time to read the back issues of the organization's regularly published in-house newspaper. Some organizations come out with a daily report, but most have a weekly or monthly publication. This publication will be rich in group stories and will give a new employee a vivid picture of the successful work groups in the organization. The company newspaper will also carry in detail any campaign that the company may have waged in the name of higher productivity. Occasionally a few of the company's sacred stories will be retold, especially in anniversary issues. If a new employee carefully reads the back two years of the house organ, he or she should be able to communicate with members of other work groups without the worry of making professional blunders. Merely complimenting members of a work group on one of their past successes should provide a healthy basis for communicating with members of that group.

If you are a new supervisor of a work group, you should attempt to get your group some publicity in the company newspaper. Of course, the article should contain some mention of the group's productivity if it is to have a beneficial effect. You should also get to know the people in public relations who write the stories and can help you recognize the type of stories they are looking for. Sometimes you can get publicity for your group when the members are involved in planning some recreational function for members of the organization. You may feel that it is unethical to intentionally seek publicity for your group, but we do not agree. In fact, we believe you have a professional obligation to make visible the positive aspects of your group, not only for the benefit of the group members but for the health of the organization. The vitality of an organization is in part maintained by the various groups being aware of the positive qualities of other work groups in the organization. The house organ is a major vehicle in facilitating this end.

3.   *The role of interpersonal communication channels.* The editor of the house organ is the objective third party who reports the stories about your work group. The same communication principle applies to the use of interpersonal communication channels. A supervisor of a work group cannot brag about the accomplishments of his or her work group very often without creating negative reactions from other work groups. The successful way for groups to brag is through a third party. The supervisor of marketing will brag to the accounting work group about how good the salespeople are. When the salespeople find out that marketing is bragging about them, they might then feel inspired to brag to the purchasing department about how good a work group the marketing people are. Once this chain reaction gets started, groups will start telling positive stories about other work groups, and the total effect will be beneficial to the organization's productivity and its members' satisfaction.

Negative stories about work groups can spread in an organization in the same way positive stories do—only with terrible consequences. It can be a very punishing experience to be part of an organization that is constantly telling bad stories about itself. As a general rule, you should remember that there are no advantages to you or your work group in spreading bad stories about your fellow work groups.

4.   *The role of key sacred stories.* Ill-advised work groups sometimes use the mushroom philosophy in orienting a new employee to his or her work group in the organization. The basis of this philosophy is to keep new members in the dark as much as possible. However, enlightened supervisors initiate conversations with new employees and inform them, through the company's stories, about what is considered to be correct behavior within the organization. For example, if padding expenses by the sales staff is a long-standing pet peeve among the organization's managers, then the new employee needs to hear the stories about unfortunate Albert and Alice who were fired from the company for billing the company for a dinner they didn't eat.

Sacred stories are "sacred" because they are stories that reveal beliefs with respect to productivity, social behavior, and company policy that long-standing members of the organization understand and generally follow. The basis of any practical joke on a new employee usually revolves around getting the employee to go against the principles embedded in a sacred story. In one organization we have studied, a plush elevator is reserved for top management and is only supposed to be used by them and the people who work on the top two floors of the home office building. The marketing work group in this company enjoys instructing a new employee that he or she is required to ride the executive elevator. About the second time the new employee gets on with a group of executives and stops on the third floor, the new employee is told sternly that he or she should not ride on the executive elevator. The vice-presidents of the company are aware of the marketing division's standing joke and always play their roles to the hilt! Thus, the real sacred story is not that one elevator is reserved for executives, but that the VPs know about marketing's practical joke and enjoy participating in it.

5. *The role of humaneness.* Supervisors should attempt to reduce new employees' anxieties on how they will be treated by the company. This can be done most effectively by relating stories in which past new employees have made "beginner's mistakes" and still were given a chance to improve, or about employees' illnesses and how their jobs were protected while they were away from work.

It is also a good idea to spend some time describing the social diversity that exists within the organization so that a new employee's fears of social compatibility will be eased. There is always the question: "How will I fit in?" Most people have exaggerated fears about how much conformity it will take to be successfully assimilated into a work group.

6. *Work groups are territorial.* In Chapter 7 we identified proxemics as being an important nonverbal variable in small group communication. If you want to understand how really important space and territorial rights are in an organization, you should serve on a planning committee that is designing a new building. The majority of the planning committee's time will be spent arguing which work group should occupy which space in the new building. If the presidential and vice-presidential offices are on the top floor, then how high up in the building a group is indicates its status in the organization. Who gets the corner offices? Can a work group occupy a whole floor? These kinds of matters are very hard for a planning committee to deal with. Some organizations have attempted to minimize the fights over territory and the status attached to space in a building by taking large open rooms and dividing them into modules that form no particular pattern. However, we have heard continual complaints from work groups that this design does not give them a defined territory and they feel frustrated because of it. The work groups feel fragmented and sense a loss of group cohesiveness. Groups seem to need a clear boundary and want to know when someone has entered their work space.

Aside from power and status, the territorial rights of a group also affect formal intergroup meetings. When members of several groups are going to meet, there is always the issue of whose turf they will meet on. Since there is always a "home-team advantage," most major organizations provide "neutral" meeting rooms. Sometimes the issue of neutrality is solved by agreeing to meet for lunch at some "neutral" restaurant. However, experienced work groups know it is important that competing work groups know they can hold meetings in each other's territory. It is just like visiting someone's house—the first time you visit, you feel awkward and uncomfortable; the second time you and the host or hostess both feel more at ease. Intergroup meetings share the same principles as a home visit. The host or hostess should provide genuine hospitality and do everything to make the group feel at home.

One of the major reasons organizations try to break down the formal barriers of work groups is that sometimes groups build such psychological barriers that outside groups are afraid to enter their work space. The reduction of intergroup communication generally spawns negative stories about work groups and in the long run hurts the productivity of the organization. When territorial walls begin to build up between two work groups, supervisors often schedule a social event for them, such as a softball game or picnic. The effect of the social gathering will be that the two groups will feel more comfortable in crossing territorial boundaries at work.

New employees are well advised to form a mental picture of the territorial boundaries that separate work groups in the organization. Without being rude, new employees should cross these boundaries and engage in conversation with members of other work groups. Over time, this type of action on the part of the new employee will pay dividends as he or she begins to work with outside groups.

7. *Group goals and organizational objectives.* Powerful work groups can sometimes be so successful in meeting and exceeding their goals that the organization is harmed. Competition among university departments over student majors and general studies requirements of certain basic courses can harm the university, thus emphasizing the principle that group goals must be consistent with organizational objectives. It is reasonable that an academic department should want to increase its number of majors and ensure that most students are exposed to the basics of its discipline. However, some departments can work so aggressively and successfully that their gains become somebody else's losses. Philosophy and history departments might acquire so few majors that the integrity of their programs is jeopardized. It would certainly be against the goals of the university to allow departments of history and philosophy to be ruined. Most people would argue that students should be exposed to some history and philosophy.

All organizations are similarly limited by the number of people, time, and money available. Work groups within organizations find themselves continually competing for these limited resources. For example, in business organizations, product work groups compete for limited advertising resources. If one product group becomes too successful at monopolizing the advertising department's people, time, and money, the sale of other products may suffer. In governmental agencies the same problem will occur if one department becomes too effective at acquiring tax money. In other words, work groups in the organization should not succeed at the expense of others. Just as an individual's goals must be in concert with the purposes of a group, so too must group goals be in harmony with organizational objectives.

8. *The organizational rally.* In the 1930s Adolf Hitler demonstrated his ability to synchronize small group CR sessions of Nazis with large political extravaganzas, the most famous of which were the Nuremberg rallies. As it turns out, all human rallies appear to contain the same communication elements, whether they are political, religious, or corporate rallies (Cragan and Shields 1981, 189–91). In the 1980s many American, and certainly most large Japanese, corporations have placed renewed emphasis on the corporate rally as a means of raising the corporate consciousness and building organizational pride. We define a corporate rally as *a large group communication process which synchronizes with the stages of small group CR sessions to reinforce the "oneness" of the corporate culture.* The process, which we are sure you have participated in or observed numerous times (or participated in and observed), has five steps when done correctly. If you have not worked in a corporation and been to a corporation rally, you have certainly observed graduations, which are a university rally, or seen on television the religious rallies of a Billy Graham crusade, or watched a national political convention.

Step One. *Appropriate use of proxemics.* Put another way, the room must be small, but not too small. For rallies to have their maximum effect, it appears that the participants need to be crowded together in one space—be it a room, an auditorium, an athletic stadium, or a shopping-mall atrium. This is also important if the event is being televised. People seeing the rally on television judge its success or failure, in part, on whether the room is crowded or not. People who are responsible for picking the hotel or corporate convention center for rallies have high on their list of priorities the availability of a large space that they can fill with company employees, but not overfill. For example, if the corporation is holding its annual sales meeting, and the planners anticipate 2,000 attendees, they do not want to hold their rally in a convention center that holds 8,000, because the presence of thousands of empty seats will have a dampening effect on the company's ability to CR. On the other hand, if they select a room that seats only 1,500, and the ventilation is bad, it will also be difficult to "rally" the employees.

Step Two. *Appropriate use of music and banners.* Established organizations have already created over the years, through the process of small group CR and large group rallies, a common identity that is well understood by organizational members (Bormann 1983). Along with this organizational tradition, it has been the human custom to use music and banners to help reinforce the *we-ness.* Hitler's Nuremberg rallies were replete with German marching music and Nazi flags and banners (Bosmajian 1971). Over time organizations have what they regard as "appropriate" music and banners for their rallies. University graduations contain music, banners, and robes that relate to the pomp and circumstance of long-term learning.

Step Three. *Appropriate use of preliminary speakers.* The political religious, or corporate rally builds toward the major speaker. In addition to proxemics and music and banners, warm-up speakers are used to "warm up" the audience for the ideas the featured speaker will provide. We call this the John-the-Baptist role, in that John was loved but not the beloved. He helped prepare the way for Jesus Christ. In the same way, preliminary speakers must be linked by the audience, but their speech-making powers should not overshadow the main speaker. We tend to remember the times when the "baptizing speaker" is better than the main speaker. Every time Ed McMahon gets more laughs than Johnny Carson, Johnny threatens to fire him. At musical concerts if the warm-up group is better than the superstar you came to hear, the audience feels let down when the main group is performing. The same is true of speech making at rallies. National political conventions allow us all to see this phenomenon at work every four years. The John-the-Baptist error occurs frequently. In 1972 at the National Democratic Convention, the keynote speech of Barbara Jordan outshone George McGovern's acceptance speech. Other examples include Ted Kennedy's preliminary speech prior to President Carter's acceptance speech in 1980, and Governor Mario Cuomo's keynote before Mondale's speech in 1984. What these three preliminary speakers did was to vividly portray the consciousness of Democrats in a more skillful and persuasive way than the superstars who followed them. When corporations are holding their annual sales meeting, it's important that the warm-up speeches only prepare the way for the featured speaker and not take the limelight away, in order for the rally to have its maximum effect.

Step Four. *Appropriate use of the featured speaker.* The major speaker should need no introduction at a rally. Everyone is waiting for the featured speaker. At a religious crusade, Billy Graham would be instantly recognizable. President Reagan's persona would precede him at a Republican gathering. What is true of religious and political rallies is true of a corporate rally. At the Mary Kay Cosmetics annual rally, the rally participants would be eagerly awaiting Mary Kay's speech. The same would be true of a speech given by Ed Rust at a State Farm rally or Lee Iacocca at a Chrysler stockholders meeting.

The mere face-to-face presence of a major superstar has a major consciousness-raising effect in and of itself. However, for the communication process of the rally to have its maximum impact, the featured speaker's message should contain three elements that draw their persuasive strength from Stages Two, Three, and Four of the small group CR process in which the audience would have participated numerous times preceding this rally. In a Lee Iacocca speech, we would expect references to the Japanese competition, low productivity, and government regulations (Stage Two) that had been standing in the way of Chrysler's growth. He would then go on to describe the new identity of the Chrysler worker (Stage Three) and how he or she had overcome the economic and production barriers. Finally, he might fashion some dramatic statements that might be the theme for this year's new sales program which had previously been discussed in smaller sessions of Chrysler management (e.g., "We're Back!" at Chrysler, or State Farm's "Join the Apple Core"). In a religious crusade, a featured speaker like Billy Graham would focus on sin (Stage Two), the good Christian (Stage Three), and proselytizing (Stage Four) with new Christian behavior.

Step Five. *Appropriate use of collective action.* The last stage of a rally is the same as the last stage of a small group CR session, which is to reinforce the oneness of the consciousness through collective behavior. At a Billy Graham rally, participants are asked to literally get out of their seats and go forth and accept Christ. At a university graduation, students come forth and receive their diplomas. At political rallies and corporate sales rallies, music is played, slogans are shouted, balloons are released, and people march from the hall with the clear purpose of electing their candidate or increasing sales.

Organizations that tend to survive for a long time have developed a balance between small group CR sessions and organizational rallies. If an organization continually holds small group CR sessions and numerous rallies through the year, it will be able to induce a high intensity among its workers. However, there will be a tendency for workers to "burn out" (Bormann 1983). Organizations like Century 21 in real estate, Amway in home products, and Mary Kay in cosmetics create highly motivated sales forces through intense CR sessions and organizational rallies; but they also have high turnover, as it is difficult for most people to maintain a highly raised consciousness over a long period of time. On the other hand, corporations like Upjohn, 3M, and State Farm have created identities for their sales forces that are founded on lifelong commitment, with significantly fewer doses of CR sessions and rallies. These organizations seem to have a larger proportion of lifelong sales personnel. The same is true of political and religious organizations. Traditional political organizations such as the Republic and Democratic national parties tend to maintain a corps of political operatives as compared to third parties that burn brightly but for a short period of time. These are indicative of groups that cannot sustain consciousness raising over time.

Although many organizations (business, political, religious) have created formal CR groups and have carefully designed mass rallies to interface with them, most groups spontaneously create CR episodes in their day-to-day group meetings, and organizational rallies may have evolved over time on a "hit-and-miss" basis without much planning on the part of management—they merely adopted practices that worked. We hope that you will be able to recognize when your everyday work group, whether it is a classroom group or a planning group in a company, slips into CR discussion. All people who participate in groups need a sense of group identification and pride; and CR talk is the communication process by which this is achieved.

SMALL GROUP CONCEPTS AS APPLIED TO INTERGROUP COMMUNICATION

The eight group concepts we presented in Chapter 1 have a research base to support their viability as an explanatory model of intragroup communication. We use these eight concepts in this chapter to explain intergroup communication within an organization, but we use them very loosely and analogously since there is no firm research data to support these concepts as a way of explaining organizational communication. Despite our reservations, we believe that the eight intergroup concepts can provide a useful outline for showing what happens as groups interact with one another within an organization.

1. *Interaction among groups.* In Chapter 1 we described communication interaction as an intragroup concept that focused on the frequency, distribution, and meaning of messages occurring among group members. When this concept is applied to organizational communication, we see that it can be used to explain a great deal of intergroup communication. Speech communication researchers often conduct communication audits of organizations (Goldhaber 1979). An important part of a communication audit is the study of messages as they flow from group to group within organizations. The audit may show that just as some individuals are not talked to within a group, some groups are isolated and do not frequently communicate with other groups. Sometimes the audit will demonstrate that too much communication is taking place in a downward direction and that the production groups are overloaded with information.

Studying the communication interaction among groups will also reveal the omissions, substitutions, distortions, and filtering of messages that can occur. A systematic study of both the formal channels and the grapevine of the organization provides a clear schema of the group-to-group communication within the organization. This descriptive information will usually provide insights into how to improve the organization, both in terms of member satisfaction and productivity.

2. *Group roles.* Just as you need to know what role you are playing in your work group, you must know what role your group is playing in the organization. If one took a PERT organizational chart that depicted work groups in the organization, one would find that the groups play different roles in the development, marketing, and sales of a company's product. Using this pattern of visualization, a worker in an organization can see that groups have roles at different phases of the organizational process. A product must be researched and developed before it is produced, marketed and sold. Each work group must realize its group role responsibilities as they relate to the larger whole.

In addition, we can see how groups take on different roles as they change purposes. In one organization that we are familiar with, the officers of the company make up the basic management team. Once a month these company officials become the board of directors of the company. In fact, the members of the board of directors hold different titles than their day-to-day management labels. The role of the board of directors is quite often different from the role of the executives running the company, and yet the people who make up these two groups are exactly the same. Just as the roles of individuals change in groups, so do roles of groups change in the make-up of an organization.

3. *Organizational norms.* There is a base line of behavior that is expected of all members regardless of what work group they are in. Sometimes corporations prescribe dress codes in order to dramatize the fact that thousands of people are all working for one organization. The costumes that employees of fast-food chains wear, and the uniforms that airline personnel wear, are clear examples. However, normed behavior of any organization goes beyond clothes and is not dependent upon the wearing of a uniform.

State Farm Insurance Company releases many national television commercials that portray their field agents discussing their sense of professionalism. When State Farm first started producing these commercials, it hired people to play the role of a State Farm agent. However, State Farm employees could distinguish an impostor from the real thing. After receiving many employee complaints, State Farm is now using its own agents in the company's commercials.

Like groups, organizations demand some conformity. If you plan to go to work for an organization, you should expect to feel pressure to assume the "normal behavior" of employees within the organization.

4. *Conflict among groups.* Competition among groups is a natural phenomenon in organizations. In private profit-making organizations, there are traditional conflicts that occur among traditional work groups. Production groups clash with quality control groups, and marketing and sales divisions easily find themselves in disagreement. For example, the goals of the quality control groups could have an adverse effect on those of the production unit; therefore, it is necessary to keep the competition within bounds in order to produce a well-made product. When quality control becomes too intense, production will find ways to subvert it, eventually making it impossible to effectively inspect for quality. Marketing and sales often clash over who knows the customer better. The sales force's claim to knowledge is firsthand experience with the customer, but marketing will often argue that sales cannot see "the forest for the trees." Marketing's claim to superior knowledge is based on its quantitative, comprehensive examination of the product and the market. If sales overwhelms marketing, a company product is "rolled out" without any overall marketing plan. However, if the product is not selling well, the sales force will soon ask the marketing group for advice on where and how to sell it. If marketing completely dominates sales, the home office may soon lose all feedback from the sales force in the field, and marketing will be at a loss to see how to reposition the product once the initial sales have tailed off. Again, the key to success is balanced conflict between marketing and sales. While there is bound to be conflict between such groups as quality control and marketing, and sales and marketing, each group must respect the other. If during the "we-they" stage of CR sessions opposing groups vilify one another, it can have a detrimental effect on intergroup respect. Keeping intergroup conflict at a tolerable level is one of the more difficult jobs of a supervisor.

5. *Organizational cohesiveness.* During World War II many of the private heavy-industry organizations that were responsible for building planes and tanks became extremely cohesive organizations. Every work group felt an overwhelming need to cooperate with other work groups in order to maximize the productivity of the organization. However, in environments in which an all-out war effort is not being maintained, organizational cohesiveness is a lot harder to achieve.

In peacetime, organizations generally create campaigns, complete with posters and slogans, that often resemble the war propaganda of World War II. The object of the campaign is not winning a war but achieving a production goal. Volunteer organizations like the American Cancer Society will decide on an annual contribution goal and then develop slogans and strategies for urging each member group to attain it. The sales divisions of private organizations hold similar production-oriented campaigns in which they set some goal with a time deadline and attempt to get the whole organization to work toward it.

In the early 1970s, 3M Corporation embarked on a campaign to turn the recession around by being the first major corporation to show a substantial increase in sales and profit. All the work groups in the corporation held monthly meetings designed to get them to achieve their individual production goals. When the campaign proved to be successful, the president of 3M went on national television during prime-time hours and thanked the 3M employees for their hard work. The result of this year-long campaign was a marked increase in the cohesiveness of the 3M Corporation. Periodically, all organizations dramatize some common cause in order to get competing work groups to work cooperatively and productively.

6. *Membership satisfaction in the organization.* In addition to an employee's membership satisfaction in a work group, it is important that he or she have overall satisfaction with the organization. For example, a data processor may be quite happy in the DP department but dissatisfied with the larger organization. It is difficult to measure the variables that go into determining member satisfaction with a company. We know that money, a sense of accomplishment, good work groups, and job security are important; but we also know that there is that "something extra" that some organizations seem to have that makes their employees especially satisfied.

Some organizations have what might be called a personality that the employees respect. Happy members of such an organization will have a wealth of stories about the company's positive social impact on the community and about how the organization cares for employees who have experienced misfortune of one kind or another. On the other hand, if an organization is perceived as being callous and insensitive toward its employees, stories to this effect will abound. Some organizations seem to go overboard in trying to provide for the membership satisfaction of their employees. Some companies have built recreational facilities for the families, complete with racquetball courts and swimming pools, in order that both insiders and outsiders will see what is being done to provide for the employees' happiness.

7. *Consensus in the organization.* When an organization's work groups consensually agree upon the goals of the organization and the means of attaining those goals, membership satisfaction and productivity are enhanced. Sometimes an organization will be fragmented because its work groups are divided about what the goals of the company should be. For example, in the automobile industry, groups constantly try to reach agreement on the kinds of cars their firm should manufacture. They ask: Should the company build small cars that are more economical to operate? Should the company build more luxurious automobiles that cater to the ever-increasing whims and desires of the driving public? Should the company build both kinds? If so, how many of each? And so it goes. The point is that groups within organizations must arrive at consensus just as individuals do in their respective groups. And if there is a major difference of opinion in the organization about its goals, these differences will manifest themselves as conflict within every group in the organization. In small companies, and in divisions within large organizations, annual retreats are sometimes held in an effort to achieve consensual agreement on the organization's goals and the means to achieve them.

8. *Organizational productivity.* The most important measurement of any organization is productivity. The ultimate goal of any organization is immortality. Productivity is the best measure of organizational life. In the short term, organizations will sacrifice membership satisfaction in order to achieve productivity, but in the long run organizations that survive are ones that maintain cohesive work groups who consensually work towards common production goals and who are reasonably proud and satisfied with their achievements.

SUMMARY

The chapter focused on major principles of intergroup communication in organizations. Attention was paid to four specific areas: information flow among and within organizational groups; the socialization process of small groups in the organization; the extension of the eight basic small group concepts to the communication behaviors of an organization; and suggestions on how to improve intergroup communication.

The first section, on information flow in the organization, considered such concepts as the formal organizational structure, informal communication channels, and common problems in intergroup communication. This latter area included traditional information-flow problems such as omission, substitution, distortion, and filtering.

The socialization process means the assimilation of groups into organizational life. Basic notions such as group loyalty, the natural intermingling of groups, management styles (X, Y, and Z) and socialization into the total organization were mentioned.

The chapter presented eight principles to aid you in enhancing effective communication among groups within the organization. As we have suggested throughout the book, discussion is complex within the small group. It is just as difficult sometimes to recognize that groups do not work in isolation. The information presented in this and the previous chapter should aid you in applying discussion principles to everyday work situations in organizations.

The eight small group concepts presented in Chapter 1 were applied to intergroup communication. Although these concepts are based primarily on small group research, they provide an additional way to view communication as it occurs in organizations.

REFERENCES

Bormann, E. G. "Symbolic Convergence: Organizational Communication and Culture." In *Communication and Organizations: An Interpretive Approach,* edited by Putnam, L. L., and Pacanowsky, M. E. Beverly Hills, Calif.: Sage, 1983.

_____ . "Symbolic Convergence Theory of Communication: Applications and Implications for Teachers and Consultants." *Journal of Applied Communication Research* 10 (1982): 50–61.

Bosmajian, H. *Silent Messages: Readings in Nonverbal Communication.* Glenview, Ill.: Scott, Foresman and Company, 1971.

Botan, C. H., and Frey, L. R. "Do Workers Trust Labor Unions and Their Messages?" *Communication Monographs* 50 (1983): 233–44.

Cheney, G. "On the Various and Changing Meanings of Organizational Membership: A Field Study of Organizational Identification." *Communication Monographs* 50 (1983a): 342–62.

———. "The Rhetoric of Identification and the Study of Organizational Communication." *Quarterly Journal of Speech* 69 (1983b): 143–58.

Cragan, J. F. "Organizational Myths: A Possible Methodology." Unpublished paper, University of Minnesota, 1971.

Cragan, J. F., and Shields, D. C. *Applied Communication Research: A Dramatistic Approach.* Prospect Heights, Ill.: Waveland, 1981.

Cragan, J. F.; Cuffe, M.; Jackson, L. H.; and Pairitz, L. "What Management Style Suits You?" *Fire Chief* 29 (March 1985): 25–30.

Cuffe, M., and Cragan, J. F. "The Corporate Culture Profile." *International Association of Quality Circles Annual Conference Transactions.* Memphis: International Association of Quality Circles, 1983.

Davis, K. "Methods for Studying Informal Communication." *Journal of Communication* 28 (1978): 112–16.

Goldhaber, G. M. *Organizational Communication.* 2nd edition. Dubuque Iowa: Wm. C. Brown, 1979.

Jablin, F. M. "Assimilating New Members into an Organization." In *Communication Yearbook 8,* edited by Bostrom, R. N., 594–626. Beverly Hills, Calif.: Sage, 1984.

Kilmann, R. H. "Corporate Culture." *Psychology Today* 19 (April 1985): 62–68.

Ouchi, W. G. *Theory Z.* Reading, Mass.: Addison-Wesley, 1981.

Pacanowsky, M. E., and O'Donnell-Trujillo, N. "Organizational Communication as Cultural Performance." *Communication Monographs* 50 (1983): 126–47.

Peters, T. J., and Waterman, R. H., Jr. *In Search of Excellence.* Reprint. New York: Warner Books, 1982.

Sabaini, D. D. "An ECCO Analysis of the Informal Communication Patterns at the Illinois State University Union-Auditorium." Unpublished master's thesis, Illinois State University, 1979.

Sandifer, N. G. "Communication Patterns in a System: A Field Study." Unpublished master's thesis, Illinois State University, 1976.

Sykes, A. J. "Myth in Communication." *Journal of Communication* 20 (1970): 17–31.

Tompkins, P. K. "The Functions of Human Communication in Organization." In *Handbook of Rhetorical and Communication Theory,* edited by Arnold, C. C., and Bowers, J. W., 659–719. Boston: Allyn and Bacon, 1984.

Trujillo, N. "Organizational Communication as Organizational Performance: Some Managerial Considerations." *Southern Speech Communication Journal* 50 (1985): 201–24.

Whyte, W. J., Jr. *The Organization Man.* Garden City, N.Y.: Doubleday Anchor, 1957.

Small group process theories are like different camera lenses in that they produce different pictures of group member communication.

CHAPTER OBJECTIVES

In order to be a more effective discussant, when you read this chapter you should focus on small group research skills.

YOU NEED TO KNOW:

1. The theory-making machine.
2. The small group analogs.
3. The small group research issues.
4. How to evaluate small group communication.

STUDYING AND EVALUATING SMALL GROUP COMMUNICATION

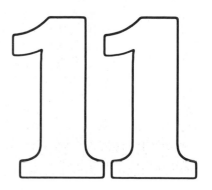

CHAPTER OUTLINE

You are an automatic theory-making machine. Human beings just can't keep from theorizing. We have to theorize or we would not survive. You have already formed many theories about small group discussions automatically, simply because you have been an active member of many discussion groups. Stop and think about the answers you would give to the following questions: What makes for a good discussion? Why do groups waste time? What causes conflict among group members? What kind of leadership makes groups work effectively? Why do you get along well in some groups and not so well in others? After reading the first ten chapters, you should be able to formulate answers to these questions because of the small group communication theories we have presented.

A CONCEPTUAL MODEL OF A THEORY-MAKING MACHINE

Small group process theories are like different camera lenses in that they produce different pictures of group member communication. We are attracted aesthetically to some theories because of their pleasing quality. We are also attracted to some theories because they conform to our sense of reality about small group discussion, just as we reject others that do not. It would be possible to take all the small group theories we have and "take a picture" of one small group discussion using all the different theoretical lenses. Afterwards we would have many different looking "pictures" of the discussion, all of which might be valid explanations of what took place. Initially we would accept the picture that conformed to our personal notion of reality, but eventually we might accept the theory that predicted how people might behave in future discussions, since in the final analysis we want productive discussion.

The three photographs shown below are pictures of the same college student taken with two different lenses. It is apparent which two photographs were taken with the "fish eye" lens. That lens sees Debbie quite differently from how she appears in the picture produced by a standard lens. Which picture is the most valid or correct image of Debbie? If you say the one taken with the standard lens, it is probably because your eye lens sees reality the same way as that lens; thus, photograph 3 captures your sense of reality. However, if you are a fish, or have chemically altered your reality, photographs 1 and 2 may represent your sense of reality. What you will accept as a correct picture of Debbie is as much dependent upon your perception as it is on the lens.

We have described a number of process group theories in this book. Your acceptance of them is predicated on three things: (1) *Aesthetics:* Whether or not you like the metaphor that forms the theory's base, that is, whether or not it is aesthetically pleasing for you to view groups from a given theoretical lens—for example, dramatistically or mechanically. (2) *Realism:* Whether or not the theory looks at reality in the same way you do. If you tend to look for underlying rules that govern behavior, you will probably like rule-governed theories; and if a theory emphasizes the same kinds of communication behaviors of groups that your personal lens sees, you will probably accept the theory as valid. (3) *Utility:* Whether or not you think the theory will be useful

FIGURE 11.1

PHOTO 1

PHOTO 2

PHOTO 3

to you in future group meetings. Ultimately, process theories are treated like method theories in that we wish to predict the consequences of behavior. If we can, we will then follow behavior that will produce expected outcomes. In our culture, the usefulness of a theory tends to be the most important measure of its acceptance. Throughout this book we have presented useful recommendations that various small group discussion theories have suggested. In this chapter, we try to explain how these theories are formulated.

Once a theory has been "manufactured," we often attempt to model it in order to explain and describe its important parts. We also might build a physical model to stimulate the theory. The conceptual model is probably the most common type of model in small group discussion. In Table 11.1 we show Leonard Hawes's (1975) definition of the key concepts you will need to know in order to compare and contrast various small group theories. You may want to refer to this table as we discuss these important notions about theorizing.

Figure 11.2 contains a conceptual model of our theory of how theories are produced, so in a sense it is a model of a theory of theory-making. We hope that you will build conceptual models of your theories of discussion which will represent in some different form or substance, or both, your verbal statements and the relationships contained in them. We have argued, as we show in the model, that the starting point for a theory is a metaphor. This ignites your brain to form concepts into logical statements that in turn produce a description. Next, or sometimes simultaneously, you begin to test out your formulation. This is done first by converting your concepts into variables via operational definitions, of which, as the model indicates, there are three types. Afterwards, you run the appropriate test, followed by an evaluation of the theory according to a threefold criteria system: aesthetics, realism, and utility. Finally, one either accepts or rejects the theory.

Most organizations are intensely interested in what makes a good group leader. They might, for example, want to know what kind of communication style a leader should adopt to manage an inexperienced discussion group. In

TABLE 11.1
BASIC PARTS OF A THEORY

PARTS	DEFINITIONS AND DESCRIPTIONS
Theory	A theory is designed to explain the hows and whys and not just the whats. It describes, and one hopes predicts, but certainly accounts for, the causal relationships among its component parts. Theories are made up of statements consisting of concepts and logical terms, and it is a relationship among these statements that constitutes a theoretical explanation of a phenomenon.
Concepts	Concepts are descriptive terms either for things that we can directly observe, such as people or tables; or for things that are not directly observable, such as emotions and beliefs. Concepts are useful, clear, ambiguous, or well defined, but they are not true or false.
Operational Definitions	Well-defined concepts are ones that have been operationally defined; i.e., the procedures that will be done in measuring a concept are clear enough for other scholars to repeat them and get the same measurements. ''Stage fright'' is a concept; it may have the same meaning as ''speech anxiety,'' but a given piece of research would have a specified operational definition. While speech anxiety and stage fright may be ambiguous at the semantic level, operational definitions of these concepts would be the same or not the same.
Variable	A variable is an operationalized concept. Once we have sufficiently defined in operational terms a concept so that we can start to measure it in our research, we call it a variable. Thus, a variable is a symbol to which numbers are assigned.
Statements	Theories are made up of statements. Statements contain concepts in some logical form. Statements relate concepts to each other in one of three ways: (1) disjunctive (either A or B); (2) conjunctive (both A and B); or (3) conditional (if A, then B).
Hypothesis	A hypothesis is a statement that is proposed to be true if the statements from which it is derived are true. All the concepts in the hypothesis must have operational definitions. A hypothesis is a statement that specifies the necessary conditions of a prediction. For example, the more orientation statements that occur in a discussion, the greater the likelihood of the group reaching a consensus.
Metaphor	Metaphors create new concepts and help frame our new theories. Metaphor produces an interaction between two ideas that are seemingly unrelated but show certain similarities, thus resulting in new ideas.
Analogy	Metaphors suggest analogies. Analogies demonstrate in detail the correspondence between otherwise dissimilar things. They generally do it either structurally or functionally.
Model	A model represents a theory or part of a theory using new materials. A plastic-tubing-and-Styrofoam splice might be used to represent part of an atomic theory. See our model in Figure 11.2 as another example. Models are not theories, but theories are often represented in the form of a model.

Derived primarily from Hawes 1975.

Chapter 5 we provide a number of answers to this question; however, one answer or theory is that a novice group would need a "telling" style of leadership (Hersey and Blanchard 1977). Hersey and Blanchard believe that when an organization has a very immature work group, the leader needs to adopt a no-nonsense, highly task-oriented leadership style that clearly explains to group members how they should do their work. The ignition metaphor for this theory could well be the pumping up of a flat tire so it will

FIGURE 11.2
CONCEPTUAL MODEL OF A THEORY OF THE THEORY-MAKING MACHINE

	Formulation	*Testing*	*Evaluation*	
Ignition (Metaphor or Analog)	Concepts are formed Logical relationships of concepts Statements (e.g., if-then)	Operational definitions Variables determined Types of operational definitions: 1. Questioning 2. Observing 3. Direct measurement	Aesthetics Realism Utility	*Outcomes* (Acceptance or Rejection)

roll smoothly down the road. The leader has an inexperienced work group that needs to be told how to do their job so they may be productive. The important concepts in this theory are a telling-style leader, an immature work group, a task, and the group's productivity. If we put these concepts in logical relationships to each other, the research statement we form would read as follows: If the leader tells the group how to do the task, the group will be productive. If speech communication scholars were to test this theory, they might compare a telling with a delegating style of leadership and directly measure which approach caused an immature group to do more work. On the basis of utility we would accept or reject the theory.

Throughout this book we have presented conceptual models of small group communication theories in an attempt to be clear about what a given theory is and how it works. Our judgment about what theory to use has been basically a utilitarian one. Thus, the test of our theory of the theory-making machine is whether or not the model contained in Figure 11.2 makes it easier for you to understand how theories of small group discussion are created.

MAJOR ANALOGS FOR STUDYING SMALL GROUP COMMUNICATION

No general theory of small group communication exists. We have subtitled this book, *An Integrated Approach,* because we literally have combined, or stitched together, numerous low-level theories of small group communication in order to provide you with one coherent overview. This section contains the eight basic camera lenses that scholars have used over the last fifty years for their starting point in building small group theories. Figure 11.3 depicts these eight analogs, or ignition metaphors.

The *individual-group mind* approach assumes that what is true for an individual is true for a group; thus a group will think rationally and have a unique personality. The *historical-analytical* approach reconstructs past group experience and, with analytical skills, creates an explanation of the present. A *dramatistic* approach assumes that group behavior resembles

FIGURE 11.3
ANALOGS FOR STUDYING SMALL GROUP COMMUNICATION

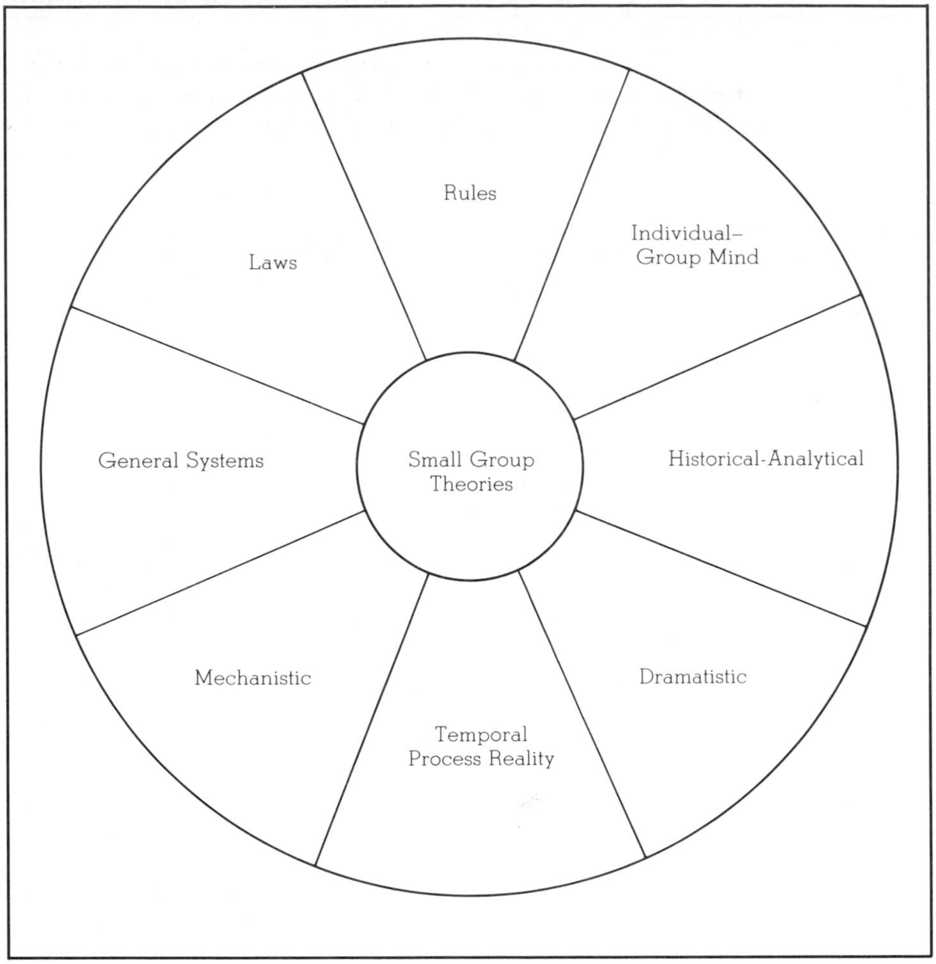

dramatic life, complete with roles, heroes, and fantasies, and that the primary focus of study is meaning, emotion, and motive, which are contained in the communication of group members. A *temporal process reality* lens looks at group communication over time with an eye for change, the purpose of this approach being to provide a rich description of the phasic development of groups. The *mechanistic* model assesses input-output variables of the group and attempts to determine relationships among them. *General systems* theory conceives of groups as unique entities that interact with the environment and whose parts are interdependent on each other; the purpose of this theory is to explain the group as a system and how this system interfaces with others. The *laws* analog assumes that small groups are governed by the same types of laws that govern all objects in the universe—just as there is a law of gravity, there are laws of small group behavior—thus, the purpose of this approach is to discover the laws of small group behavior in order to assess causes and make predictions. The *rules* approach assumes that small groups develop conventions or norms of behavior that occur with enough regularity so that it is possible to explain the general rules of small group communication, but that these rules can change over time from group to group, so they don't constitute laws; the purpose of this approach is to discover "rules of thumb" for anticipating small group behavior.

Table 11.2 displays examples of communication concepts and specific research that are illustrative of the eight current analogs for studying small group communication. Our purpose here is not to provide an exhaustive

TABLE 11.2

AN ANALOG CATEGORIZATION OF SMALL GROUP COMMUNICATION CONCEPTS

Analog	Representative Group Communication Concepts	Research Exemplars
Individual-Group Mind	Problem Solving	Dewey (1910)
	Synergy	McBurney and Hance (1939)
	Agenda Systems	Larson (1969)
	"Risky Shift"	Stoner (1961)
Historical-Analytical	"Groupthink"	Janis (1983)
	Gender and Power	Geist and Chandler (1984)
		Bormann, Pratt, and Putnam (1978)
Dramatistic	Roles	Bales (1970)
	Group Fantasies	Bormann (1975)
	CR Talk	Bormann (1983)
	Sagas	Chesebro, Cragan, and McCullough (1973)
Temporal Process (Reality)	Task Stage Development	Fisher (1970)
	Role Stage Development	Bormann (1975)
	Encounter Stage Development	Bennis and Shepherd (1956)
	CR Stage Development	Chesebro, Cragan, and McCullough (1973)
		Poole (1983)
Mechanistic	Output Variables: Productivity, Consensus, Member Satisfaction, Quality of Work	Gouran (1969)
		Gouran and Fisher (1984)
	Numerous Input Variables: (e.g., Orientation, Gender)	Leathers (1972)
General Systems	Internal-External Systems	Homans (1950)
	Interacts	Fisher and Hawes (1971)
	Information Flow in Organizations	Monge (1977)
Laws	Law-like Generalizations about Small Group Communication (e.g., Group Size, Cohesion, and Leadership)	Hall (1953)
		McGrath and Altman (1966)
		Collins and Guetzkow (1964)
		Shaw (1981)
		Berger (1977)
Rules	Ethical Commitments	Cushman (1977)
	Group Norms	Donohue, Cushman, and Nofsinger (1980)
		Bormann (1980)
		Cushman and Pearce (1977)

classification system of small group communication concepts, but merely to demonstrate the usefulness of recognizing the metastructure behind our knowledge of small group communication theories. As we go through an explanation of Table 11.2, try to remember the theories as we presented them in greater detail in previous chapters. We hope you will see the theoretical structure that we have used for writing this book.

1.   *Individual-Group Mind.* One of the first analogs used by communication scholars to develop small group communication theories was the inference that what is true about the individual mind may be true of the group mind. Chapter 3 contains numerous examples of useful agenda systems that are a product of this analog. The idea that John Dewey's five-step reflective thinking process of the individual mind would work for the "group mind" in problem-solving has been demonstrated in research and application. The most contemporary use is in quality circles, which we described in Chapter 9. The general probing of this analog has allowed us to structure similarities and differences between the individual and group mind. The synergistic effect of group thinking is a good example. Researchers found in solving certain problems through a process of open communication that groups could produce a better answer than their best individual working alone. We continue to probe for situations in which groups are better or worse than an individual in problem solving. The whole line of research on "risky shift" contained in Chapter 8 demonstrates the continued utility of the individual group mind analog.

Thus, if we were filming a decision-making group and had the *individual/ group mind* lens on, we would tend to highlight the rational arguments that were occurring, with an eye for their sequence, clarity, and persuasiveness.

2.   *Historical-Analytical.* Small groups are viewed as a historical object of study in which ethnographic research is appropriate. A small group scholar can almost view him- or herself as an archaeologist-anthropologist of small group communication when using this camera lens. The research material that this lens focuses on would be the minutes of group meetings, departmental memos, and other group artifacts that would be used for reconstructing the historical past of a group in order to make some cogent observations about small group communication. Irving Janis's work on "groupthink" that we described in Chapter 8 is a good example of theorizing from the historical/analytical analog. Janis looked at a number of policy decision-making groups, and after producing a historical reproduction of the communication of groups, he posited his "groupthink" hypothesis. The case studies we provide in this book are also examples of historical reconstructions of group life. Sometimes the findings from the historical/analytical analog are used as a basis for research from other analogs. For example, Cartwright's lab research on "groupthink" flows from the mechanistic analog but was made possible only by Janis's research.

When group researchers have the *historical/analytical* lens on, they are looking at trace materials and artifacts of small group communication so that they can reconstruct and explain past group behavior.

3.   *Dramatistic.* For over forty years this analog has provided useful insights into small group behavior. Obviously, the ten roles we describe for you in Chapter 6 come from this analog. Twenty years of research at Harvard by Robert Bales and at Minnesota by Ernest Bormann have demonstrated that group fantasies play an important part in group development. Furthermore, Bormann's (1983) general communication theory of symbolic convergence conceives of group life as a symbolic reality in which a group identity is created, raised, and sustained through consciousness-raising talk. Clearly Stage Two and Stage Three consciousness-raising talk is highly dramatic in that the "theys" are villains and the "wes" are heroes engaged in some struggle. The spontaneous activity of many groups to name themselves and create logos certainly seems highly explainable from a *dramatistic* perspective. Many small groups tend to be caught up in their unique group identities.

When you have a *dramatistic* camera lens on, you will not be focusing on the rational discussions of the group members but rather on the hidden agenda of role formation, the break moments when groups engage in consciousness-raising talk, and the fantasy chains that may spontaneously occur during group discussion.

4. *Temporal Process Reality.* The notion that communication patterns in groups change over time has played a major role in the development of small group communication theories. The explanatory power of our integrated model which we present in Chapter 2 is derived from the *temporal process reality* analog. All four types of talk (problem-solving, role, encounter, and CR) have stages or phases to their communication development, i.e., the talk that occurs at time one is different from the talk occurring at times two, three, or four. Thus, Fisher found four stages of problem-solving talk; Bormann found two stages of role talk; Bennis and Shepherd found two stages of encounter talk; and Chesebro, Cragan, and McCullough found four stages of consciousness-raising talk. Attempting to determine the distributional and sequential patterns of communication has been a major line of research for communication scholars.

When you have this lens on, you study groups over time and examine the changes in communication patterns with an eye for how these patterns affect group development and goal achievement.

5. *Mechanistic.* Scholars have focused for a long time on four basic outcomes of groups: productivity, consensus, membership satisfaction, and quality of work. The mechanistic analog encourages one to look for what variables might affect or be responsible for or influence the four major group output variables. At a microlevel, such input variables as gender, intelligence, and power are studied, while at a macrolevel the recipe we offer in Chapter 1 represents a mechanistic view in that it has interaction, roles, norms, and conflict cohesively blending to generate the outcomes of productivity, membership satisfaction, consensus, and quality of work.

When one views small group communication from a *mechanistic* lens, one tends to look for critical variables that might affect group outcomes. For example, Gouran has found that orientation communication behavior positively affects a group's attempt to reach consensus. The previous ten chapters are sprinkled with findings that come from this mechanistic analog.

6. *General Systems.* General systems theory describes reality as an assembly of interdependent objects or components that engage in regular interaction, the system possessing both structure and a set of processes. One example of a system is the solar system. Its components, such as the planets and the sun, engage in regular interaction; for example, the flow of energy from the sun to the planets. If this interdependence is interrupted through the loss of the sun's energy, or the removal of Mars from its orbit, it would have a catastrophic effect on other planets in the system. In addition to its observable structure and processes, it is apparent that the solar system has a boundary. Systems theorists like to talk about systems being open or closed. Like the solar system, systems that have closed boundaries tend to run down and die for lack of new input; open systems, such as our bodies, tend to grow and change because we take in outside things like oxygen and food. George Homans (1950) set forth a sociological theory of groups based on systems in much the same way we have described the solar system.

If we examine Homans's systems theory, we find that the basic components are the people who make up the group. The interdependence of the group members is expressed in three ways: statements of activities, statements of sentiments, and statements of interaction. These kinds of statements are further delineated by specific boundary-setting behaviors: elaboration, differentiation, and standardization. These boundary-setting stages we call norming behaviors in small group systems. Further, these three modes of norming behavior occur overtly in what Homans identifies as the *internal* system; that is, the face-to-face group within which members interact. Homans distinguishes this internal system from an external system. In essence, many of the rules that are developed and that eventually govern the behavior of individuals in the group—internal system—are initiated, influenced, and even dictated by group members' outside sources of norming behavior; i.e., external systems.

If we look at how a typical discussion group interacts, we can understand better how Homans's system theory explains the way in which a group develops. Imagine, if you will, a group composed of four members discussing a controversial topic such as birth control. The four individuals are the basic components of the internal system of this face-to-face group. Some members may be conservative on the issue of birth control while others may be liberal. The results of the discussion would be dictated by previously held beliefs, as might happen, say, if one member were a strong Catholic. This would be an example of an external system; that is, the group to which you continue to belong regardless of your other day-to-day group memberships.

Communication is the basic interaction that creates Homans's group system and maintains it. For the last thirty years, speech communication scholars have tried to specify which communication acts and interactions work toward the development of healthy, productive discussion groups. In 1971, Fisher and Hawes described an Interact System Model that could serve as a basis for building a systemic explanation of small group communication. At present, we have not conducted enough successful research to categorize the various communication transactions that go into a systemic description of a discussion group.

With the *general systems* lens on, this book has attempted to provide numerous useful descriptions of the communication process of groups which have been influenced by a systemic approach.

7.   *Laws.* The natural sciences have developed some very powerful theories by discovering laws of nature; e.g., the law of gravity, the laws of thermodynamics, and laws of gases. We seem quite convinced that these laws existed before we discovered them and that they will still exist after we've found them.

Social scientists have long hoped to emulate the natural sciences by developing covering laws for human behavior. However, the results to date have been mixed. Yet, small group scholars have uncovered what some would call law-like behaviors in small groups. For example, Hall (1953) created the law-like generalization: Cohesion is the force that tends to result in members' remaining in the group; i.e., one will remain a member of a group if the forces pull him or her more toward group goals than away from them. McGrath and Altman (1966) in reviewing the leadership literature concluded that the key characteristics to becoming a leader are personality variables including social maturity, extroversion, self-assertiveness, high group status, education, intelligence, and training in leader techniques. If one could generate law-like statements about a person's inability to be a leader, one would conclude that they were missing one or more of the characteristics. Shaw and Collins and Guetzkow have reviewed small group research for the purpose of developing law-like generalizations about groups. Two generalizations that Shaw (1981, 77–78) makes, comparing the effectiveness of individuals with that of groups, are typical of scholars using a *laws* analog for developing small group theories:

a. Group judgments are superior to individual judgments on tasks that involve random error.

b. Groups usually produce more and better solutions to problems that do individuals working alone.

When using a *laws* camera lens, you should focus on causal explanations of communication interaction among group members.

8. *Rules.* Small group researchers "who are using the rules perspective are searching for an account that incorporates gaming behavior and normative regularities that are not described by some iron law of nature but are in conformity with conventional, breakable rules" (Bormann 1980, 46–47). These rules theorists believe that in the area of human action a degree of choice exists; and since humans monitor their own behavior, it makes more sense to think of small group communication in terms of rules and normative behavior than in terms of covering laws (Cushman and Pearce 1977).

The five ethical commitments of a good discussant that we discussed in Chapter 4 are examples of normative rules. Also, our discussion in Chapter 1 of group norms and how they develop is consistent with the rules theorists' perspective. At present, there is little research in small group communication that identifies a set of rules that are typically created by a small problem-solving group.

When you have a *rules* camera lens on, you focus on recurring behavior that becomes expected of group members, and you try to determine how these norms or rules help the group achieve its goals.

An integrated approach requires that the small group researcher not be prejudiced against any lens, but be open to new insights. However, as Gerald Miller (1983, 35) has observed: "Despite the lip service paid to the value of theoretical pluralism or 'multiple perspectives' many communication researchers 'itch' to discover the universal paradigm of communication behavior." We occasionally get "itchy," but we have never broken out into a complete rash. We think it is important that you remain a theoretical agnostic when it comes to the study of small group communication. We hope that you would try out these eight different research analogs because each one has something to teach you about small group communication. If you get the "itch" after looking through one of the lenses, and feel the urge to conduct your own original research in small group communication, we would encourage you to help build communication theory; but we would hope that you would not feel the need to denigrate and purge the alternative explanations from your mind.

SYSTEMATICALLY STUDYING SMALL GROUP COMMUNICATION

We hope that by now you are ready to get started on your own research project. How to ignite your ignition metaphor is always a puzzling first question. In the end, no scholar is ever quite certain of the exact origin of his or her research idea. Usually you can remember where you were sitting when you got the idea but not how the notion came into your head. Yet you can't think of something by thinking of nothing. You need to look at some "stuff." We would suggest three reservoirs that may stimulate your creativity. They are the eight small group analogs, previous research in groups, and your own previous experience as a group member.

GETTING STARTED

The eight analogs that we just described in the previous section are a good source for beginning your research. For example, one of our students came to class one morning after seeing a movie entitled *The Breakfast Club* and was excited about the prospect of doing a historical-critical analysis of the movie, as he believed there were many insights about small group communication included in the film. In 1973, Shields and Kidd had their ignition metaphor ignited: after seeing the movie, *The Poseidon Adventure,* they wrote up their analysis of the film and published it in a scholarly journal. Aesthetically you will probably find some analogs more pleasing than others. A "rules" perspective might strike you as a pleasing and even realistic way to look at small group communication and you may try to find yourself identifying communication irregularities that would constitute the "rules" of a social or work group you belong to. Our point here is to encourage you to let these eight analogs cross through your mind and see if one of them serves as an ignition metaphor— either because it is aesthetically pleasing to think of a group through a given analog, or because you realistically think that is the way small group communication is, or because you see some usefulness in viewing small groups through one of the eight analogs.

Another starting point, and certainly the most common one, is to read research on small group communication, on the assumption that something will attract you and lead you to create a new research idea. There are basically two strategies you can take in conducting this review of the literature. The first is to read secondary sources that summarize research findings for you, and the second is to read the original research reports that normally are contained in scholarly journals.

Two representative reviews of small group research outside the communication discipline are McGrath's *Groups: Interaction and Performance* (1984) and Shaw's *Group Dynamics: The Psychology of Small Group Behavior* (1981). McGrath organizes his review of social-psychological group research by classifying task groups into four categories in terms of their interaction patterns and the types of work they do. One type is a planning or creativity group, which specializes in generating new ideas; a second type is a problem-solving or decision-making group, which focuses on getting the right answer, such as a jury; the third type includes groups that deal with conflict resolution, in which there is a great deal of bargaining and negotiations; and the fourth type contains groups that are performing to meet a standard of excellence or competing with groups in a contest or battle, such as competitive team sports. Using a "laws" analog, Shaw reviews psychological and social-psychological group literature in an attempt to generate plausible hypotheses about group behavior. His major topics include: personal characteristics of members, composition and structure of groups, how groups form and develop, the physical environment of groups, leadership of groups, and how groups perform tasks, especially as they relate to individual peformance.

Within the communication discipline, two representative reviews of the literature are Gouran and Fisher's "The Functions of Human Communication in the Formation, Maintenance, and Performance of Small Groups" (1984) and Cragan and Wright's "Small Group Communication Research of the 1970s: A Synthesis and Critique" (1980). Gouran and Fisher use a mechanistic analog to describe communication research in small groups. They summarize the research on categories of variables such as characteristics of members and groups, group environment, communicative relationships occurring in groups, types of performance characteristics (e.g., problem-solving and creativity), and other responses such as consensus and member satisfaction. Cragan and Wright summarize research of the 1970s under six lines of research, three continuing and three new. The three continuing lines of research are studies on discussion, leadership, and the teaching of small groups. The three new are communication variables affecting group outcomes, process of communication in groups, and communication variables studied in small group settings. When you read these reviews, you should look for a topic that might attract your attention. For example, is it harder for a woman to emerge as a leader than a man? Does brainstorming increase the quality of the ideas a group can generate? What effect does trust-disrupting communication behavior have on membership satisfaction? If you find a topic area that interests you, you can then look up the original studies (primary sources) that are cited in the review so that you can see how these studies were conducted.

All professions have their scholarly journals in which they report their research. In the field of communication, the two professional organizations that sponsor journals are the Speech Communication Association and the International Communication Association. Three representative journals in which you will find original small group communication research reported are *Communication Monographs, Human Communication Research,* and *Central States Speech Journal.*

A final source of stimulation for a research idea is your own personal experience in groups. If you think back to some of the questions that you thought would be answered by taking a course in small group communication, you might find that one of those questions remains unanswered and that you are going to answer it by conducting your own original research. Typical questions that students ask us are:

- What makes a good leader?
- How do I become a leader?
- What communication skills will make me more successful in groups?
- How do you make groups more productive?
- How do you resolve conflict in groups?
- How do you handle members who won't work?
- How do you build group identity and pride?
- How do gender, race, and age of group members affect group outcomes?

Remember that you are a natural-born theory-making machine. You should not shy away from systematically seeking your own answers to small group communication questions.

RESEARCH DESIGN CONSIDERATIONS

In the late 1960s and early 1970s, a number of communication scholars became concerned with the nature of research that was being done in small group communication. Some believed that too much of our knowledge was derived from lab studies in which concocted groups were put together for a short period of time in order to manipulate a couple of communication variables and that too little attention was being given to communication theories that explained small group behavior (Bormann 1970; Fisher 1971; Mortenson 1970). Since that time, efforts have been made to study groups in more natural settings and to see that communication variables are central to the study and properly operationalized. However, it is impossible to construct the perfect study. There are always tradeoffs. Ideally your research should try to maximize three things: (1) the generalizability of the group or groups that you study to the whole population of groups; (2) the precision of control you have over your variables (i.e., how well they are operationalized); and (3) the realism of your research context (McGrath 1984). If you conduct a field study of natural decision-making groups in an organization, you will have great realism, but your control over the group and the concepts you are studying may be weak, and your ability to generalize will be low. On the other hand, if you create groups in the lab, you may have much precision but lack realism. In other words, no matter what kind of research design you develop, it will always have some methodological weakness in it. Your decision on what type of study to conduct should therefore depend on the type of research question you wish to pose, not on any *a priori* notions of design or data manipulation procedures. Once you've settled on a research question there are generally about ten major concerns or checkpoints you need to consider in designing your research. Table 11.3 outlines these issues and sample questions you need to be asking about each one.

TABLE 11.3
SMALL GROUP COMMUNICATION RESEARCH CONSIDERATIONS

Issue	*Questions*
Size of Group	Same size?
	Minimum size?
	Maximum number of members?
Unit of Group Communication	Communication act?
	Group interaction?
	Selected segments?
	Entire discussion?
Duration of Discussion	Thirty-minute discussion?
	Sixty-minute discussion?
	Day-long discussion?
	Year-long discussion?
Characteristics of Group Members	Gender?
	Race?
	Age?
	Trained?
Setting	Concocted (lab)?
	Natural (field study)?
	Historical-fictional?
Group Goal or Task	Information sharing?
	Problem solving?
	Idea generation?
	Consensus achieving?
Operational Definitions	Self-report?
	Trained observers?
	Direct measurement?
Researcher Intervention	Little control?
	Tightly controlled?
	Use confederates?
Data Analysis	Descriptive?
	Critical-analytical?
	Content analysis?
	Numerical manipulation of data?
Size of Research Sample	One group?
	Six groups?
	Thirty groups?
	1,000 members of groups surveyed?

Size of Group.   Some researchers in social psychology regard dyads (two persons) as a group (Shaw 1981). We do not. As we indicated in Chapter 1, we regard three as the minimum number of members for a group to exist. A more difficult question is to determine the outer limits of a group for your study. Certainly any number over nine would be risky, unless of course you are studying when cliques form in groups. Most researchers who concoct groups for lab studies choose sizes ranging from four to seven, with the most common group size being five members. In lab studies most researchers will try to control the variable of size by having each group have the same number of members. However, in field studies (conducted in natural settings) you often cannot control group size. It is important to remember that your study will always have to defend that you are studying "small groups."

Unit of Group Communication.   Obviously, communication scholars have a keen interest in how communication is treated in a small group study. Trying to figure out your operational definition of communication is deceptively difficult. Conceptions of the unit of communication range from single thoughts, individual statements, interacts, themes, and even whole-length discussions. (Cragan and Wright 1980, 204.) For example, Robert Bales set forth the idea that there were twelve communication "acts" that needed to be observed and counted in order to understand the development of a decision-making group. We provide Bales's (1950) operational definition in the form of his IPA instrument in Chapter 2. McCroskey and Wright (1971) believe it is important to study not only the communication act but the reaction to that act, so they created a different operational definition of communication interaction groups. Gouran (1969) concluded, after a lengthy review of communication literature, that eight communication acts appeared to affect group outcomes; they are clarity, opinionatedness, interest, amount of information, provocativeness, orientation, objectivity, and length. In Chapter 2 we explain the communication stages that Fisher found in task groups, Mabry found in encounter groups, and Chesebro, Cragan, and McCullough found in CR groups. Table 11.4 displays the lists of communication acts that were measured in these studies. We present these examples of operational definitions of communication to underscore that an operational definition of the unit of group communication is essential in explaining the communication you

TABLE 11.4
COMMUNICATION ACTS PRESENT IN THREE SMALL GROUP STUDIES

Author	Fisher (1970)	Chesebro, Cragan, and McCullough (1973)	Mabry (1975)
Unit of Communication	Verbal Interaction	Themes (Rhetorical Characteristics)	BSs System

Communication Variables	Asserted
	Seeking
	Interpretation
	Substantiation
	Clarification
	Modification
	Summary
	Agreement
	Favorable Toward
	  Proposal
	Unfavorable Toward
	  Proposal
	Ambiguous Toward
	  Proposal
		"I - you - us - we - they"
		Noncombative vs.
		  Combative
		Climate: Somber, Warm,
		  Hostile
		Temporal Aspects: Present,
		  Past, Future
		Fantasy
			Neutral System
			Neutral Assertions
			Dominant Assertions
			Antagonism
			Withdrawal Supportive Acts
			Assertive-Supportive Acts
			Group Laughter
			Group Tension
			Task-Determining Acts
			Group-Maintaining Acts
			Tension Displays

studied and why that communication is important in answering your research question.

Duration of Discussion.   Oftentimes group scholars refer to "zero-history" groups, which generally means a group was concocted for purposes of research; i.e., the members had never worked together before. Occasionally, ongoing groups are used for field experiments in which they are given a new topic to discuss for purposes of research, but the members have worked together in the past. The reason this issue is important relates to the argument over how long it takes for a group to develop its "groupness." For example, if five college freshmen are brought together for the first time to discuss an issue of common concern for fifteen minutes, would we think of them as "really" being a group? Is thirty minutes enough time? What about an hour? As you can see, this is a difficult issue to resolve; but as we said earlier in this section, there are tradeoffs in each research design. A zero-history group talking for thirty minutes might give you great control over your variables, but you would sacrifice much in the way of contextual realism. Again, the type of research question you are asking would determine whether a thirty-minute discussion would be adequate.

Characteristics of Group Members.   Group composition is another sticky issue. In Chapters 7 and 8 we indicated that a number of group member characteristics may affect group development and outcomes. These included demographics such as age, race, and gender, and psychographics such as thought patterns, personalities, and professional-consciousness states. These characteristics will be treated differently by you depending on your research question. If you are wondering what effect these characteristics would have on the group, then you would manipulate a given characteristic or characteristics to see what would happen. On the other hand, you may have a research question that might be difficult to answer unless you make sure membership characteristics don't affect it. Occasionally, in historical-fictional studies and field studies, an after-the-fact analysis is done in which group composition is used to explain what happened in the group. For example, in our case study at the end of Chapter 5, we asked you to assess the group's failure in light of the gender issue. All small group communication studies can be analyzed to see if membership characteristics can explain what is happening in the group.

Setting.   What would be the ideal group for providing the best answer to your research question? When you attempt to answer this question, there are three general types of groups you can use. You can use a natural setting in which you would have generally a pre-existing work group that would exist whether you conducted research or not. This might be a strategic type of planning group for a corporation, a jury, or a paramedic team. You also can create a group in the lab, and since you are the creator, you can concoct any type of group you wish. Finally, you can study the historical record of past small groups or examine fictitious groups created by novelists, screenwriters and playwrights.

Group Goal or Task.   A group goal or task is controlled or uncontrolled, and it may be important or unimportant to answering your research question; but certainly you have to be aware of what it is. Many times the dependent variable of small group communication is the outcome of the group task. For example, studies that attempt to determine how many ideas are generated by brainstorming or nominal groups would regard the task as central to their study. This would also be true if a researcher were trying to assess what group communication variables affect consensus. On the other hand, if you are studying the communication stages of a problem-solving group, you might only want to insure that the group has a good problem to work on and not really care what the actual conclusion is for each group in the study. For example, if the group is discussing the parking problem on campus, you might be concerned only with the interaction the group has and not the actual solution. In field studies you often cannot control the topic but still may be interested in the task outcomes. For example, a survey of quality circles might want to report the impact or quality of the solutions developed and implemented by QCs. In this case, this researcher might want to analyze the process of the QC and make inferences about its impact on group outcome, even though the research had no control over the task topic. Sometimes lab studies use group tasks that maximize precision of control but lack any real-world context. Once again, the nature of your research question will determine how important group goal or task is to your study.

Operational Definitions.   Operational definitions are procedures you follow in assessing each concept in your study that are clear enough so that other scholars could repeat your procedures and get the same results. Oftentimes operational definitions are referred to as instruments, and we discuss their reliability and validity. In other words, does the test measure what it is supposed to measure, and does it measure it the same time after time? For example, if you were trying to determine whether there was an inverse relationship between communication apprehension and leadership emergence, you would need an operational definition for leadership and apprehension. One strategy for a beginning researcher might be to search small group communication literature for a communication anxiety instrument which had already been found to be reliable and valid by previous researchers, and likewise an instrument to measure leadership. The three general classes of operational definitions that we include in our theory-making machine are self-report (questioning), observing, and direct measurement. Self-reports are generally paper-and-pencil tests that operationalize important concepts, but occasionally they are simple open-ended questions like "Who do you think is the leader of this group?" Bales's IPA is probably the most frequently used instrument in which trained observers record communication acts as they see them occurring in small group discussions. Direct measurement can include biofeedback, content analysis of group transcripts or minutes, and examination of group outputs such as productivity. Some researchers prefer to operationalize the same concept by all three means in order to insure that they really have what they think they have.

Researcher Intervention.   If you are analyzing the decision-making process of President Nixon's Committee to Re-Elect the President in an attempt to see if the committee was beset by "groupthink," you obviously are not intervening in the group process. On the other hand, if you are trying to determine what effect trust-disrupting communication has on a group, you might actually "plant" a confederate in your lab group and have that person operationalize your trust-destroying behavior. In this case you, the researcher, are exerting significant control over the communication process that is occurring in the group. How much direct manipulation of group processes is needed to answer your research question should be tempered by the tradeoff between your desire for precision and your need for realism.

Data Analysis.   By the time you have resolved the above eight concerns in research design, it should be apparent to you what kind of data analysis is appropriate for answering your research question. Many times a qualitative analysis of your data is most appropriate. If you are doing a descriptive analysis of a historical group, you may simply want to analyze and reason critically from the small group communication evidence you have assembled. Other times, your research question may require that you count and sum up different types of group communication and outputs. For example, how many procedural leadership behaviors do appointed leaders use in routine business meetings? This count might then be correlated to the number of topics covered in a forty-minute period. Here we would not only count and sum things up; we would also correlate them with other things we had counted. Thus, correlation statistics are often used in communication studies. If your research question requires complex statistical manipulation, you can generally look these statistical procedures up in standard textbooks on statistics. However, the advent of high-speed computers and PCs have popularized the development of statistical packages which have taken much of the drudgery out of quantification. One package to start with is the Statistical Package for the Social Sciences (SPSS-X), which is available at every university computer center and is also available for home computers (PCs). It is important that you understand the strengths and weaknesses of each statistical procedure in light of the research question you are asking; however, the best way to learn these statistics is on a need-to-know basis. If you need to know how to run a chi-square in order to answer your research problem, you will learn chi-square much more thoroughly and intimately than if you just study chi-square in the abstract. So your in-depth knowledge of statistical procedures will accumulate in direct relationship to the number of research studies you undertake.

Size of Research Sample.   Should you study one group? Six groups? Thirty groups? Or should you survey 1,000 members of different groups? Once again our tradeoff problem raises its head. An in-depth case analysis of a small group in a field setting might produce rich data that maximizes our realism goal. The 1,000-member survey might maximize our generalizability-to-the-population goal, but lack in precision and realism. If you are conducting a lab study, how many lab groups should you have? We don't have a very good answer for you. If we went by custom, lots of small group studies report sample sizes from six to thirty. On the other hand, many of these thirty-group studies only had thirty-minute discussions. Rest assured that no matter how many groups form the basis of your study, you will have some discomfort in answering the question: "Is my sample size large enough?"

The preceding ten issues are not necessarily all the issues you might consider when conducting a small group communication study, but they are the essential ones. We hope that this book will stimulate you to go forth and conduct your own research in group communication. The chances are, most of you have other plans! In any event, the preceding ten issues, combined with the eight analogs, can provide you with criteria for evaluating small group communication research. They will allow you to formulate your own judgments about the research you read and, as a consequence, the small group communication theories you accept.

SYSTEMATICALLY ASSESSING SMALL GROUP COMMUNICATION

Research instruments are essentially operational definitions of some theoretical concept. It is quite natural, and in fact necessary, that the communication literature contains numerous articles in which some instrument was used to systematically study small group communication. As you begin reading these studies, you'll discover that the same small group concept may be operationalized through the use of a number of different instruments. When you use an instrument that measures leadership, for example, the items contained in the instrument are by definition the key components that the researcher thinks constitute leadership. Thus, scholarly debates frequently occur over which instrument is the most valid measure of a given concept. Even apparently clear-cut and simple concepts like group consensus have been operationalized in different ways. In some studies, consensus meant that all group members had agreed to a specific policy, while in others, consensus was operationalized in the form of an instrument which measured how close a group was to reaching consensus (Cragan and Wright 1980). As we have indicated in Chapter 8 in our discussion of "risky shift," the operationalization of the same concept using different instruments can produce very different findings. When the CDQ was used to operationalize the concept of risk taking, a "risky shift" was found to occur; however, when group risk taking was operationalized differently, the group effect was not found (Cartwright 1973). It is important that you carefully assess the items that make up an operational definition of a key concept, because if you don't accept these items as being a valid measure of a concept, then by definition you would have to reject the findings of the study.

In this section we will not attempt to produce a compendium of all the instruments that have been used to study and evaluate small group discussions. Instead we present several examples in order to demonstrate how you can systematically go about assessing group communication. Of course, research instruments will fall under the three-part category system of self-report, observation, and direct measurement that we have described to you earlier in the chapter.

Self-Report.   When you ask group members to report information, you can have them describe or evaluate themselves, other group members, or themselves and other group members. You can ask for information from a group member before, during, and after a discussion. Prediscussion items of information are often demographic items that constitute an operational definition of a group member. Sometimes the prediscussion instruments measure some psychological concept or the discussant's predisposition toward a group communication concept or discussion topic. It is difficult for group members to do lengthy self-report instruments during their actual discussion, so research designs will sometimes require that the group members stop their discussion, fill out a paper-and-pencil test, and then resume talking. Probably the most frequent type of self-report is the post-measure. Another frequent type of instrument is one that calls for group members to evaluate the discussion in terms of some important group concept like membership satisfaction or group effectiveness. Tables 11.5 and 11.6 are examples of this.

The Wright Group Satisfaction Index contained in Table 11.5 lists twelve components that Wright believes constitute a measure of the concept of "group satisfaction." As you look at these twelve items, you need to ask several questions: Are there important attributes of group satisfaction that are *not* contained in this instrument? Are there unimportant items that don't appear to be attributes of group satisfaction? If the answer is "yes" to either one of these questions, you might want to argue that this instrument is not a valid operationalization of group satisfaction. Another question you need to ask is how this instrument was created. Did Wright just jot down these twelve items off the top of his head, or on the basis of his observing groups did he conclude these were the right items? If the latter were the case, this instrument would have what we call face validity; i.e., just looking at the instrument, one would conclude that it seems to contain the important components of group satisfaction. Oftentimes, instruments are used in research that have only face validity; that is to say, experts in group communication say that, based on their knowledge of group satisfaction, these twelve items are a good operationalization of it. However, frequently scholars go to a lot more trouble to see if their instruments are valid. Sometimes they compare their instruments to other instruments that are known to be valid. Other times, as is the case with the Wright Group Satisfaction Index, a factor-analysis procedure is used to "boil out" key discrete items from a much larger list of potential factors. The Wright Group Satisfaction Index was derived from a list of over one hundred items. Other instruments we have referred to in this book that have been created in a similar manner are Bales's IPA, McCroskey and Wright's IBM, Leathers's Feedback Rating Instrument, and McCroskey's Personal Report of Communication Anxiety.

An instrument like the Wright Group Satisfaction Index might be used in a study in which you are trying to determine if highly productive groups tend to be more satisfied than unproductive groups. Or you might use it in a study in which you are manipulating group membership characteristics and then assessing whether all-female groups are happier than mixed-gender groups. Yet, you may simply want to use this instrument as a way to systematically assess your group's satisfaction.

Table 11.6 contains a rather typical example of a group evaluation form. It asks the group members to rate the group's performance on items that most group discussion scholars would say are important for producing an effective symposium or panel discussion. The assumption is that if the group was

TABLE 11.5
THE WRIGHT GROUP SATISFACTION INDEX

Group Numbers_____

Group Name_____

Group Size_____

Directions: At the conclusion of your group's discussion, please mark each scale according to *how you think* the group *feels* about itself. None of the scales are necessarily "good" or "bad," "high" or "low." Please mark the space on each scale which you think identifies how the group *feels*. Make certain to answer all scales.
Thank you.

1. Relaxed	:___:___:___:___:___:___:___:	Pressured
2. Tension Inducing	:___:___:___:___:___:___:___:	Tension Releasing
3. Conformity	:___:___:___:___:___:___:___:	Nonconformity
4. Dissimilar	:___:___:___:___:___:___:___:	Similar
5. Unsatisfied	:___:___:___:___:___:___:___:	Satisfied
6. Constrained Feeling	:___:___:___:___:___:___:___:	Casual Feeling
7. Coordinating	:___:___:___:___:___:___:___:	Noncoordinating
8. Incompatible	:___:___:___:___:___:___:___:	Compatible
9. Gratifying	:___:___:___:___:___:___:___:	Nongratifying
10. Withdrawing	:___:___:___:___:___:___:___:	Contributing
11. Accord	:___:___:___:___:___:___:___:	Discord
12. Contention	:___:___:___:___:___:___:___:	Harmony

"excellent" on these items, an effective discussion should have occurred. If you were going to do a research project using the panel-discussion items as a measure of group effectiveness, you might want to include other measures of group effectiveness to insure that you are studying what you thought you were studying. For example, you might examine the audience's reaction to the discussion to see if they thought it was excellent. You might ask observers to rate the effectiveness of the discussion. In each case you might use a different operationalization of group effectiveness. If this triangular strategy produced results in which the audience, observers, and discussants rated the discussion "excellent," you would have confidence in your conclusion. The two group-evaluation measures (for the symposium and the panel discussion) contained in Table 11.6 ask the group member to make a rather global evaluation on a number of items. These sorts of instruments are frequently used as an in-class teaching aid in small group communication classes. If they were used in a research project, you might want to ask whether all group members are likely to have the same understanding of what is meant by group leadership or group cohesion. You might ask if there are other group concepts that should have been included in order to have a more "complete" evaluation form. Finally, you would probably want to provide operational definitions for such concepts as leadership and productivity in order to check the reliability of the members' rating ability.

Observation.   You can't see cohesion. You can't see membership satisfaction. In fact, most of the communication concepts you would systematically want to observe in small groups, you can't see. What you can look at are communica-

TABLE 11.6
GROUP EVALUATION FORM

Group Identification_____

Directions: Check the evaluative term which best describes the group's performance on each of the following aspects of the symposium or the panel discussion. Turn this form in to your instructor at the conclusion of the group presentation.

Symposium	Excellent	Good	Average	Fair	Poor
Definition of Problem					
Limitation of Problem					
Analysis of Problem					
Information-Sharing in Ques. & Ans. Period					

Panel Discussion	Excellent	Good	Average	Fair	Poor
Summary of Def. & Anal. of Problem					
Establishment of Criteria					
Evaluation of Solution					
Group Productivity					
Group Cohesion					
Group Leadership					

Directions: Circle the evaluative term which best describes the group's effectiveness on the symposium or the panel discussion.

Excellent   Good   Average   Fair   Poor

tion behaviors, and you can assign meaning to them. The first step, then, to systematically observing small group communication involves two procedures. One is to train observers to recognize different types of interaction. For example, in Table 11.7, we list a leadership behavior called "clarifying." What is "clarifying" communication and how is it different from "summarizing?" In order to reduce this ambiguity, observers are generally trained by showing them behavior that the researcher thinks is "clarifying" behavior and distinguishing it from "summarizing" behavior. The second procedure is to allow observers to practice coding behavior in order to become skilled at observing the communication behavior you want them to see, or to become adept at using the observational instrument.

The second step is creating inter-coder reliability. Assume that you chose to conduct a study, and part of your research design called for trained observers to determine which group members most frequently played which group roles. Or you might want observers to code leadership behavior as

TABLE 11.7
GROUP LEADERSHIP OBSERVATION FORM

Communication Behaviors	Group Member A	Group Member B	Group Member C	Group Member D	Group Member E
Task Leadership					
Contributing ideas					
Seeking ideas					
Evaluating ideas					
Seeking idea evaluation					
Visualizing abstract ideas					
Generalizing from specific ideas					
Procedural Leadership					
Goal setting					
Agenda making					
Clarifying					
Summarizing					
Verbalizing Consensus					
Interpersonal Leadership					
Regulating participation					
Climate making					
Instigating group self-analysis					
Resolving conflict					
Instigating conflict					

operationalized in Table 11.7. In this situation you might want to develop a frequency count of which group member performed the largest number of procedural leadership behaviors. A typical strategy in social-science research is to train three observers and have them simultaneously observe the same group discussion. If all three observers essentially saw the same thing, you have a strong case that the event actually happened. In the case of observing leadership communication, some simple correlation statistics could be computed to see how much alike the three coders' observations were of the same discussion. If they agreed 75% of the time or better, you would feel that they were accurately recording what you wanted them to record.

If the sixteen leadership communication behaviors contained in Table 11.7 are viewed as an operational definition of leadership, we raise a question of validity just as we did in our discussion of self-reporting instruments. Just because you can train three people to see and accurately record what you trained them to see, does not mean that you have necessarily found what you were trying to observe. To put it another way, instruments used by observers are operational definitions of concepts and you may disagree that the operational definition really captures the essence of the concept. If you were conducting a leadership study and you were trying to determine who the task leader was in a discussion, you might use the instrument in Table 11.7 and, with the help of trained observers, assess which group member engaged in the largest number of procedural leadership behaviors. Additionally, you might use a self-report instrument and ask the group members who they thought the group leader was. This strategy would give you an additional argument for concluding that you had identified the task leader. In using observational instruments, you need to make certain that your observers can see the behavior they are supposed to observe and that they have had the opportunity to practice in order to become skilled in using the instrument. But remember that even when you achieve inter-coder reliability you must still ask: Is the instrument a valid operational definition of the small group communication report you are studying?

Direct Measurement.   The advent of quality circles in American industry has created a lot of natural field settings in which the quality and quantity of a group's productivity can be directly measured. Heavy industry has, for a long time, had some rather exacting standards that had to be met or a part would be thrown off the assembly line. These direct measurements became easy dependent measures for assessing what types of groups produce better results. Also, groups' logos, memos, and communication patterns are things that can be directly observed and counted. In designing a small group communication study, including some direct measurement in the design is generally a good idea.

A rather typical lab study in which direct measurement instrumentation would be used is one in which nominal grouping, brainstorming, and unstructured discussion techniques are pitted against each other in order to see which technique produces more and better ideas. If the groups in the study were asked to suggest ways to improve parking on campus, some rather simple direct measurement should be used. First of all, the researcher could simply count the number of ideas generated by each group. Secondly, a committee of parking experts could rate the quality of each idea. While counting the ideas is clearly a direct measurement, rating the quality of ideas brings us back to our same old question: What is the operational definition of quality the judges use, and is it valid? In the case of quality control of manufactured parts, there are generally some rather exacting standards that have to be met. In the case of our parking judge experts, ambiguity is more obvious.

Our point here is that regardless of whether you use self-report, observation, or direct measurements, the reliability and validity of your instrumentation are constant. Whether you are creating your own instruments or using someone else's, recognize that it takes a great deal of thought and effort to systematically study small group communication.

SUMMARY

This chapter introduced you to some fundamental notions about studying and evaluating small group communication. The chapter began by identifying each individual as an automatic theory-making machine. Moving from an individual's natural curiosity to engage in theory making, we presented a conceptual model of a theory-making machine. Key distinctions among concepts, operational definitions, and variables were highlighted as they relate to statements and predictions we make about group communication.

As no general theory of small group communication exists, we combined eight analogs to illustrate the integrated approach to small group communication we have explained in this book. The *individual-group mind* analog assumes that what is true for an individual is true for a group. The *historical-analytical* approach reconstructs past group experience and, with analytical skills, creates an explanation of the present. A *dramatistic* approach assumes that group behavior resembles dramatic life, whereas the *temporal process reality* approach looks at group communication over time and tries to provide a rich description of the phasic development of groups. The *mechanistic* model assesses input-output variables of the group; while *general systems* theory conceives of groups as unique entities that interact with the environment and whose parts are interdependent on each other. The *laws* analog assumes that small groups are governed by covering laws, the same types of laws that govern all objects in the universe. The *rules* approach assumes that small groups develop conventions or norms of behavior that occur with some regularity. These eight analogs were discussed in depth and represent our metalevel integrated approach to small group communication.

Next, we looked at ways of systematically studying small group communication. You can begin doing small group research by being stimulated by one of the eight analogs, by doing literature review, or by personal experiences you have had in groups. When doing research or, for that matter, reading the published results of previous research, one finds that there are numerous design considerations that must be taken into account. What is the size of the group? What is the unit of group communication? What about data analysis? These questions were discussed along with seven other research design considerations. The chapter closed by looking at three specific ways (self-report, observation, and direct measurement) that are used to systematically assess small group communication. It was found that the reliability and validity of your instrumentation are most important when systematically studying groups.

REFERENCES

Bales, R. F. *Interaction Process Analysis.* Reading, Mass.: Addison-Wesley, 1950. Reprint. Chicago: The University of Chicago Press, 1976.

————. *Personality and Interpersonal Behavior.* New York: Holt, Rinehart and Winston, 1970.

Bennis, W. G., and Shepherd, H. A. "A Theory of Group Development." *Human Relations* 9 (1956): 415–37.

Berger, C. R. "The Covering Law Perspective as a Theoretical Basis for the Study of Human Communication." *Communication Quarterly* 25 (1977): 7–18.

Bormann, E. G. "Symbolic Convergence: Organizational Communication and Culture." In *Communication and Organizations: An Interpretive Approach,* edited by Putnam, L. L., and Pacanowsky, M. E. Beverly Hills, Calif.: Sage, 1983.

_____ . *Communication Theory.* New York: Holt, Rinehart and Winston, 1980.

_____ . *Discussion and Group Methods: Theory and Practice.* 2nd edition. New York: Harper and Row, 1975.

_____ . "The Paradox and Promise of Small Group Research." *Speech Monographs* 37 (1970): 211–17.

Bormann, E. G.; Pratt, J.; and Putnam, L. "Power, Authority and Sex: Male Response to Female Leadership." *Communication Monographs* 45 (1978): 119–55.

Cartwright, D. "Determinants of Scientific Progress: The Case of Research on Risky Shift." *American Psychologist* (March 1973): 222–31.

Chesebro, J. W.; Cragan, J. F.; and McCullough, P. "The Small Group Technique of the Radical Revolutionary: A Synthetic Study of Consciousness-Raising," *Speech Monographs* 40 (1973): 136–46.

Collins, B., and Guetzkow, H. *A Social Psychology of Group Processes for Decision-Making.* New York: John Wiley and Sons, 1964.

Cragan, J. F., and Wright, D. W. "Small Group Communication Research of the 1970s: A Synthesis and Critique." *Central States Speech Journal* 31 (1980): 197–213.

Cushman, D. P. "The Rules Perspective as a Theoretical Basis for the Study of Human Communication." *Communication Quarterly* 25 (1977): 30–45.

Cushman, D. P., and Pearce, W. B. "Generality and Necessity in Three Types of Human Communication Theory: Special Attention to Rules Theory." In *Communication Yearbook I,* edited by Ruben, B. D., 173–82. New Brunswick, N.J.: Transaction Books, 1977.

Dewey, J. *How We Think.* Boston: D.C. Heath, 1910.

Donohue, W. A.; Cushman, D. P.; and Nofsinger, R. E., Jr. "Creating and Confronting Social Order: A Comparison of Rules Perspectives." *Western Journal of Speech Communication* 44 (1980): 5–19.

Fisher, B. A. "Decision Emergence: Phases in Group Decision-Making." *Speech Monographs* 37 (1970): 53–66.

_____ . "Communication Research and the Task-Oriented Group." *Journal of Communication* 21 (1971): 136–49.

Fisher, B. A., and Hawes, L. C. "An Interact System Model: Generating a Grounded Theory of Small Groups." *Quarterly Journal of Speech* 57 (1971): 444–53.

Geist, P., and Chandler, T. "Account Analysis of Influence in Group Decision-Making." *Communication Monographs* 51 (1984): 67–78.

Gouran, D. S. "Variables Related to Consensus in Group Discussions of Questions of Policy." *Speech Monographs* 36 (1969): 387–91.

Gouran, D. S., and Fisher, B. A. "The Functions of Human Communication in the Formation, Maintenance, and Performance of Small Groups." In *Handbook of Rhetorical and Communication Theory,* edited by Arnold, C. C., and Bowers, J. W. Boston: Allyn and Bacon, 1984.

Hall, R. L. "Social Influence on the Role Behavior of a Designated Leader: A Study of Aircraft Commanders and Bomber Crews." *Dissertation Abstracts* 13 (1953): 1285.

Hawes, L. C. *Pragmatics of Analoguing: Theory and Model Construction in Communication.* Reading, Mass.: Addison-Wesley, 1975.

Hersey, P., and Blanchard, K. H. *Management of Organizational Behavior.* 3rd edition. Englewood Cliffs, N.J.: Prentice-Hall, 1977.

Homans, G. C. *The Human Group.* New York: Harcourt, Brace and World, 1950.

Janis, J. L. *Groupthink.* Boston: Houghton Mifflin, 1983.

Larson, C. E. "Forms of Analysis and Small Group Problem-Solving." *Speech Monographs* 36 (1969): 452–55.

Leathers, D. G. "Quality of Group Communication as a Determinant of Group Product." *Speech Monographs* 39 (1972): 166–73.

Mabry, E. A. "Sequential Structure of Interaction in Encounter Groups." *Human Communication Research* 1 (1975): 302–07.

McBurney, J. H., and Hance, K. G. *The Principles and Methods of Discussion.* New York: Harper and Brothers, 1939.

McCroskey, J. C., and Wright, D. W. "The Development of an Instrument for Measuring Interaction Behavior in Small Group Communication." *Speech Monographs* 38 (1971): 335–40.

McGrath, J. E. *Groups: Interaction and Performance.* Englewood Cliffs, N.J.: Prentice-Hall, 1984.

McGrath, J. E., and Altman, J. *Small Group Research: A Synthesis and Critique of the Field.* New York: Holt, Rinehart and Winston, 1966.

Miller, G. R. "Taking Stock of a Discipline." *Journal of Communication* 33 (1983): 31–41.

Monge, P. R. "The Systems Perspective as a Theoretical Basis for the Study of Human Communication." *Communication Quarterly* 25 (1977): 19–29.

Mortensen, C. D. "The Status of Small Group Research." *Quarterly Journal of Speech* 56 (1970): 304–9.

Poole, M. S. "Decision Development in Small Groups III: A Multiple Sequence Model of Group Decision Development." *Communication Monographs* 50 (1983): 321–41.

Shaw, M. E. *Group Dynamics: The Psychology of Small Group Behavior.* New York: McGraw-Hill, 1981.

Shields, D. C. and Kidd, V. "Teaching Through Popular Film: A Small Group Analysis of the Poseidon Adventure." *The Speech Teacher* 22 (1973): 201–7.

Stoner, J. A. F. "A Comparison of Individual and Group Decisions Involving Risk." Unpublished master's thesis, Massachusetts Institute of Technology, 1961. (Cited in Shaw 1981.)

AUTHOR INDEX

SUBJECT INDEX